Center Stage:
Operatic Culture and Nation Building in Nineteenth-Century Central Europe

Philipp Ther

Central European Studies

Charles W. Ingrao, senior editor
Gary B. Cohen, editor
Franz A. J. Szabo, editor
Daniel L. Unowsky, editor

Center Stage:
Operatic Culture and Nation Building in Nineteenth-Century Central Europe

Philipp Ther

Translated from the German by
Charlotte Hughes-Kreutzmuller

Purdue University Press
West Lafayette, Indiana

To the memory of Manolo Alarcon Ramirez, the true opera buff in our family

Copyright 2014 by Purdue University. All rights reserved.

Library of Congress Cataloging-in-Publication Data

Ther, Philipp, author.
 [In der Mitte der Gesellschaft. English]
 Center Stage: Operatic Culture and Nation Building in Nineteenth-Century Central Europe / Philipp Ther; translated by Charlotte Hughes-Kreutzmuller.
   pages cm. -- (Central European Studies)
 Includes bibliographical references and index.
  ISBN 978-1-55753-675-4 (pbk.) -- ISBN (invalid) 978-1-61249-329-9 (epdf) -- ISBN 978-1-61249-330-5 (epub) 1. Opera--Social aspects--Germany--Dresden--19th century. 2. Opera--Social aspects--Germany--Dresden--20th century. 3. Opera--Social aspects--Ukraine--L'viv--19th century. 4. Opera--Social aspects--Ukraine--L'viv--20th century. 5. Opera--Social aspects--Czech Republic--Prague--19th century. 6. Opera--Social aspects--Czech Republic--Prague--20th century. 7. Nationalism in music. I. Hughes-Kreutzmuller, Charlotte, translator. II. Title.
  ML3918.O64T5413 2014
  782.10943--dc23
                              2013042264

Contents

Abbreviations	viii
List of Illustrations	ix
Foreword	xi

Part One
Introduction	1

Part Two
The Royal Theater in Dresden
1. Organization and Control of the Royal Theater	31
2. Constructing National Culture	47
3. Europeanization and Musical Modernism	67

Part Three
The Polish Theater in Lemberg
4. Social Foundations	89
5. Provincial Opera	111

Part Four
The Czech National Theater in Prague
6. Launching the National Theater Project	133
7. A Theater for all Classes	149
8. The Opera Nation	159

Part Five
Comparison, Cultural Transfers, and Networks
9. Opera and Society	195
10. Nationalizing Opera	205
11. Cultural Exchanges and Europeanization	237

Bibliography	255
Acknowledgments	285
Index	287

Abbreviations

AND	Archive of the National Theater (Archiv Národního Divadla)
DALO	State Regional Archive L'viv (Derzhavnyi arkhiv L'vivs'koyi oblasti)
DJ	*Dresdner Journal*
EMTA	Echo Muzyczne, Teatralne i Artystyczne
SHAD	Saxonian State Archive, Dresden (Sächsisches Hauptstaatsarchiv Dresden)
MdKH	Ministry of the Royal House (Ministerium des Königlichen Hauses)
MMC	Minutes of the Managing Council (správný výbor)
NA	National Archive Prague (Národní archiv)
ND	National Theater (Národní divadlo)
PM	Presidency of the Gouvernement (Präsidium der Statthalterei)
PVS	Protocoll of the Great Assembly (valné schůze) of the National Theater Association
r.	year (rok)
SSD	Complete essays and poetry by Richard Wagner (*Sämtliche Schriften und Dichtungen Richard Wagners*)
t.	volume (tom)
TsDIAU	Central Historical State Archive of the Ukraine, L'viv

List of Illustrations

Figure 1. Star singer Emma Turolla. 21
Figure 2. Interior of the Semper Theater. 34
Figure 3. The Second Semper Theater in 1878. 36
Figure 4. The royal box in Dresden. 38
Figure 5. Realistic stage sets for *Tannhäuser* in 1866. 55
Figure 6. Caricature of Richard Strauss' orchestration of *Elektra*. 78
Figure 7. Count Skarbek, founder of the Skarbek Theater. 92
Figure 8. The Skarbek Theater, built in 1842. 93
Figure 9. Auditorium of the Skarbek Theater. 94
Figure 10. The new Lemberg Theater, opened in 1900. 105
Figure 11. A share certificate issued by the National Theater Association. 141
Figure 12. The Czech National Theater in Prague. 144
Figure 13. Original program of the Czech National Theater's guest performance in Vienna. 171
Figure 14. Positivist costumes for *The Bartered Bride* in 1892. 172
Figure 15. Symbolist stage sets for *Libuše*. 187
Figure 16. European landscape by the studio Brioschi, Burghart, and Kautsky. 240

Music example 1. *Die Folkunger* by E. Kretschmer. 59
Music example 2. The dance of the seven veils in *Salome*. 77
Music example 3. The clock symbolizing the ticking life of the Polish nation in Moniuszko's *Straszny Dwór*. 113
Music example 4. Dramatic scene from the fourth act of *Konrad Wallenrod*. 116
Music example 5. Folkloristic dance in J. I. Paderewski's *Manru*. 123
Music example 6. Opening scene from the musical melodrama *Hippodamie*. 167
Music example 7. Aria to the moon in *Rusalka*. 182
Music example 8. *Pohádka o Honzovi*. 183
Music example 9. Scene from *Lohengrin* accenting *deutsch* (German). 208

Music example 10. Nationally encoded Marsh from
    The Mastersingers of Nuremberg.   210
Music example 11. National mobilization in
    The Brandenburgers in Bohemia.   212
Music example 12. Construction of Polish national music
    in *A Life for the Czar.*   213
Music example 13. Final scene from *Halka.*   215

Foreword

Philipp Ther's *Center Stage: Operatic Culture and Nation Building in Nineteenth-Century Central Europe* is a most welcome addition to the series, Central European Studies. In 2006 Oldenbourg/Böhlau Verlag in Vienna published a book in German as Ther's *Habilitation* thesis that was based on the same initial body of research. He then revised the study for publication in Czech by Dokořán in Prague in 2008. Both these versions drew much praise in scholarly reviews. Now with this newly revised and expanded English version, a broader English-reading public will gain access to Ther's work, which adds important new dimensions to our understanding of middle-class public life in nineteenth-century Central Europe and the development of modern opera theaters during a critical phase.

Ther's thoroughly researched and perceptively argued study examines the evolution of opera theaters as major cultural institutions in three important regional capitals during the late nineteenth century: the Royal Theater (Semper Opera) in Dresden, the Czech National Theater in Prague, and the Polish Theater in Lemberg/Lwów/Lviv. He describes in vivid terms how the rise of modern social structures, particularly those of the urban middle classes, and of nationalist cultures and public life altered the character, repertoire, and public functions of these theaters. In the process Central European opera houses were transformed from institutions where aristocrats and the wealthiest of the middle classes went to be entertained by mostly imported Italian or French works to typically larger and technically more sophisticated theaters with more diverse although still stratified audiences and with mixed repertoires which included elements of native national opera and theater.

Ther's study demonstrates tellingly the centrality of the opera theaters to cultural, social, and political life in their cities and the surrounding territories during the late nineteenth century. In a carefully nuanced account he argues convincingly that none of the three cases saw a simple linear development from royal or aristocratic sponsorship to bourgeois domination. Moreover, no matter how strong and assertive nationalist political and cultural activists may have become in each community, they did not succeed in the long run in making native or "national" pieces dominate the opera and theater repertoire in these houses. Theater managers, artists, and audiences proved to be more committed to diverse repertoires that would include, they hoped, the best of both the national and the cosmopolitan. Ther also looks beyond the three culturally significant regional capitals to take into account the cultural life in imperial capitals such as Berlin and Vienna and offers stimulating insights about the development of the broader social, economic, and cultural circumstances of European and transatlantic opera theaters. One gains from this study a deeper understanding of the dynamics of changing sponsorship and the changing mix of international and national repertoires.

Scholars and students who are interested in modern Central European cultural and social history or in music history and members of the broader reading public who are interested in the development of the modern performing arts and the great Central European opera theaters will surely welcome this book as a volume in the series, Central European Studies.

Gary B. Cohen
Series editor

Part One

Introduction

Opera was *the* cultural institution of the nineteenth century. It functioned as a magnet to the masses, yet at the same time represented a quest for high culture. Opera was a marker of prestige by which its patrons demonstrated their wealth and power, and hence was a very political institution. Also as an art form, opera was at the heart of society.[1] As grand palaces of culture, opera theaters marked the center of European cities like the cathedrals of the Middle Ages. As opera cast its spell, almost every European city and society aspired to have its own opera house and many new theaters were constructed in the course of the long nineteenth century. At the time of the French Revolution, only a few dozen, mostly royal, opera theaters existed in Europe. But in the span of a hundred years, the continent's cultural landscape had been profoundly changed. By the end of the nineteenth century, nearly every large town possessed a theater in which operas were performed. This is especially true for Central Europe, upon which this book concentrates. The question of whether there were sufficient means or a public to maintain an opera house was secondary to the goal of being one of the cultured cities and refined peoples of Europe, of being a part of "European civilization."

For the most part this building boom—in terms of both culture and architecture—took place irrespective of social grounding or the existence of a middle class in the western European sense. Urban societies that saw themselves as peripheral, backward, or oppressed tended mostly to build large theaters. From Barcelona in the west to Odessa in the east and Helsinki in the north, Europe became equipped with a network of opera theaters which could accommodate far more spectators than today's theaters, thanks to large standing-room areas. This network was particularly dense in Central Europe. The opera theaters were opulently decorated, both inside and out, and provided spectacular entertainment night after night. While in the eighteenth century it was mainly princes who had new, luxurious opera theaters built, in the nineteenth century, they were commissioned by the nobility and an ascending middle class. Active involvement in opera had particular cachet in countries and cities with no royal court or independent sovereignty. As regional social elites strove for emancipation from the imperial centers, opera became a sign of prestige for culturally ascendant cities and aspiring national movements. This book investigates and describes this institutional and cultural dynamic which eventually even reached across the Atlantic.

From a financial point of view, the institution and the art form of opera was always a luxury. But it was a luxury that many people were willing and able to pay for. Not just the bourgeoisie, with whom opera is often associated, but people from all walks of life flocked to the theater. Contemporary reports tell us that servant girls, craftsmen, and even manual laborers filled the cheaper areas in the gallery and at the rear of the orchestra level. Thus the opera catered to a far broader public than it does today.[2] Audience members in the more expensive areas were there to see and be seen and to demonstrate their distinction.[3] This social function of a visit to the opera was so important that it did not become customary to extinguish all the lights during performances until the end of the century. Spectators' white evening garments shone in the semi-gloom of the auditorium and many eyes remained fixed on the visitors' boxes rather than on the stage.

What took place on the stage, however, could match any of today's Hollywood blockbusters. Live horses galloped past, rain literally came down in buckets, and Bengal light created fantastic color effects. While these performances can no longer be experienced firsthand, contemporary arts journalism conveyed a good impression of how Lohengrin entered the stage with his shining sword, the pyramids of Aida were revealed, and Orpheus slipped down into the underworld to the amazement of the audience. Opera invited people into a world of illusions. Daily newspapers advertised forthcoming performances and documented the public's responses to previous shows. Performance schedules had more in common with today's cinema programs than a sophisticated opera repertoire, aiming above all to fulfill the demand for novelty. The concept of cultivating "classic" pieces did not gain wide currency until the late nineteenth century.[4] A standard repertoire of the kind familiar today became established around 1900, at first in Europe and then in the rest of the world. The twenty-first century continues in cultural history terms, then, where the nineteenth century ended—another reason to look more closely at the great age of opera.

Opera was also a matter of politics, especially at times of civilian unrest and increased state repression. Both the institution of the opera and the art form gained an added political dimension and provided more than mere diversion and entertainment. Opera and the arts in general not only reflected the times but actually stimulated change. This can be best appreciated by considering opera from three different perspectives. First, analyzing the opera as an institution provides insight into the political and social conflicts and power relations within the respective societies. A second perspective comes to light on considering the opera theater and its auditorium filled with people from different social backgrounds and with different loyalties. The view of the opera from inside offers a vivid picture of the social barriers and divides that affected the societies and the ideals and utopias they cherished. A third aspect presents itself behind the curtain: repertoires, performance practice, and the music itself communicate much about the changing aesthetic tastes and values of European cultures.

Opera's relevance to political and social developments is illustrated by the introduction of mass scenes, which became a popular feature after the emergence of the French *Grand Opéra* in the *Vormärz* era between 1815 and 1848. In these scenes, choruses function as people's representatives on the stage and determine the course of the narrative action. Some operas, such as Rossini's *William Tell*, forced any ruling-class members of the audience to witness how common characters positively stole—and sang—the show from them.[5] This occurred at a time when modern mass society did not exist beyond centers such as Paris and Vienna and when national movements were just emerging. The notorious censorship of the nineteenth century, which was particularly rife in the period before 1848, is a clear indication that the dramatic arts were felt to hold explosive potential. Reactionary rulers feared that opera might politically mobilize their subjects by showing members of their own class or nation singing, fighting, and suffering on stage. The content and meaning of opera works are therefore of just as much historical interest as the social history of opera.

One should nevertheless resist drawing hasty conclusions about an opera's effect on the basis of its content. How operas were received depended on a variety of factors, including audience expectations, composition, and the success of each individual performance. Interpreting operas as historical sources therefore requires particular care. As any regular operagoer knows, a successful performance is not easily guaranteed. It may take just one soloist to drop out for audiences to reject a show. For this reason, only a few performances had a verifiable and direct influence on political and social events. Nevertheless, nineteenth-century intellectuals, from Hegel to Max Weber, believed in the far-reaching effects of opera thanks to its exulted status as a synthesis of the arts, as a *Gesamtkunstwerk*. Opera, they believed, could edify, emotionally educate, and mobilize audiences, particularly for the cause of the nation. This belief informed the work of central European composers including Richard Wagner (1813–1883), Stanisław Moniuszko (1819–1872) and Bedřich Smetana (1824–1884). Social elites also placed high hopes in the opera as an institution where audiences could be unified in their enjoyment of art, regardless of their social standing. Consequently, opera became associated with utopias of artistic and social unity.

Such utopias were a main ingredient of modern nationalism. This partially explains why opera was so closely linked to national movements in many European countries. Especially in Central Europe, and subsequently in other parts of continental Europe, opera came under "the spell of nations" and their respective nationalisms. Opera was increasingly regarded as an expression of the nation or, as Richard Wagner put it, of the "spirit of the people," the *Volksgeist*. The people that Wagner had in mind (*Volk* in German, *narod* in Slavic languages) was a nation connected by cultural bonds and a common history, and not defined by the boundaries and political organization of the state it inhabited.[6]

In the German lands and other parts of Central Europe, and later in Western Europe, opera became endowed with a national identity. This nationalist appropriation of opera had a deep impact on cultural practices. In the opera, it affected repertoire, plots, singing language, and stage production. The process by which opera was made national can be regarded as a form of cultural nationalization. The key agents of this process were not nation-states, but music publishers, members of the audience, and composers of Wagner's generation from various countries. When this book refers to the nationalization of opera, then, not the establishment of state control over opera is implied, but the process of making it more German, Czech, Polish, Russian, or French.

The widespread nationalization of opera may seem paradoxical at first. After all, music theater was an international cultural practice and almost synonymous with Italian opera until well into the nineteenth century. Yet, especially after the 1848 revolution, national traditions, singing languages, and even a new opera genre—the national opera—became established in Central Europe. Accordingly, some of the central questions this book addresses are why this process of cultural nationalization occurred, how far it went, and who supported it.

In keeping with the Andersonian approach to nationalism studies, the nation is understood here as a construct and not as a given.[7] This book explores the creative, artistic dimension of nation building in which composers played a key role. Especially in Central Europe, the arts, including the opera, were crucial for defining and demarcating the nation. This cultural nation-building was characteristic of the German lands, Bohemia, Poland, and other areas of Central Europe.[8] The term cultural or musical nationalism is used to denote the ideology of a national movement communicated via cultural or artistic media or more specifically via music. To analyze how masses were mobilized by these cultural means involves inquiry in the field of social history. Nationalism was of course not the only political issue that was negotiated in opera. Class awareness and an aristocratic, civic, or urban consciousness were also conveyed.

With these different levels of history—institutions, society, aesthetics, and music—this book interweaves strands of social and cultural history. In view of the range and inconsistency of literature available, this is not the place to attempt a binding definition of the concept of culture. Through the lens of "new cultural history," opera in the nineteenth century may be regarded as a cultural phenomenon in the anthropological sense; as a system of symbols and interpretations via which basic human needs and forms of expression can be deciphered.[9] This book is, however, also concerned with cultural history in a more narrow sense, in examining music as an art form and opera as a historical source. When considering opera as a historian and music lover, one must bear in mind an important difference between opera in history and today. At the beginning of the nineteenth century there were only a few theaters that exclusively staged opera. On the whole, opera houses performed a range of social and cultural functions and hosted a number of different events. Music theater and spoken drama played variously on different evenings along with occasional galas, wunderkind performances, and other forms of entertainment. During the Carnival holiday and to mark events such as trade fairs, theaters were converted into ballrooms. For the purposes of this book, an opera theater will therefore be defined as a venue that staged major operas and that had a permanent orchestra and an ensemble of singers. This broad definition is supported by the fact that opera was crucial for the financial survival of most theaters.[10] Although productions were costly, ticket sales were more lucrative than those for spoken drama.

The various perspectives described above mark out a field of issues and points of interest that German opera buffs would probably declare *unspielbar*: not performable, not feasible, too much for one work. Certainly, the field of inquiry must be delimited. The opening comments on opera in the nineteenth century were made without distinguishing between Western, Central, and Eastern Europe. This was quite intentional. The rise of opera was a phenomenon that spread across continental Europe and eventually beyond. The social history of opera is, however, primarily determined by local and regional contexts. The focus here, then, is placed on Central Europe, which in the nineteenth century consisted mainly of the German Confederation and the Habsburg Empire. For the purposes of this book, the Russian part of Poland is also included. Especially in the first two-thirds of the nineteenth century, the countries of Central Europe were linked by common social and political structures which gave rise to similar tensions in all of them. The Congress of Vienna led to the confirmation of the anciens regimes which in turn stimulated their societies' and nations' ambitions toward emancipation. While absolutist rule persisted and the royal courts and royal seats remained cultural leaders, the professional artists of the nineteenth century were not afraid to challenge royal authority over their domain. The nobility in Central Europe, too, played an important role in political and cultural spheres for a relatively long time. Also characteristic of this region was the linguistic and religious heterogeneity that led to the formation of "parallel societies."

Despite the focus on Central Europe, other parts of Europe will not be ignored. Paris, in particular—the "capital of the nineteenth century," as Walter Benjamin called it[11]—influenced cultural developments across the entire continent. This is particularly true for opera in Paris until the 1860s. The second European opera center was Vienna, which for many years was by far the most populous German-speaking city and a hub of Italian opera as well as the capital of an empire which stretched as far as to what are now parts of Romania and the Ukraine.

A great deal of literature exists on these two key cities, covering everything from operatic institutions to audience listening habits.[12]

Yet notable developments in European opera history also took place outside these imperial centers. Milan, with *La Scala*, is the most famous example of a city that is a politically minor, but culturally major force.[13] Prague and Dresden played similar roles throughout the nineteenth century. Politically their influence was limited but they were among the most productive opera cities on the continent. Especially in Central Europe, the imperial capitals provided less impetus for opera's development than the regional capitals, the cultural and musical lives of which have hitherto been largely ignored. In cities such as Dresden and Prague, artists often had more scope for creativity than in Vienna or Berlin, where opera was more likely to be subject to the requirements of the royal courts or the state.

Methods and Sources

In view of the wealth of literature on the cultural and music history of the imperial capitals, the case studies in this book will concentrate on the aforementioned regional capitals (*Landeshauptstädte*), and specifically on Dresden, Prague, and Lemberg (or Lwów, and since 1945, L'viv). There are sound historical reasons for analyzing the significance of these cities for European opera history. In the period explored here, Dresden hosted the most major world opera premiers of all German-speaking cities. With both Semper theaters, the first built in 1841 (and destroyed by fire in 1869) and the second built in 1878, the Saxon royal seat possessed an opera house of architectural as well as artistic renown and was instrumental in popularizing a national type of opera in the German-speaking lands.

Since the founding of the Estates Theater (formerly Nostitz Theater) and its legendary premiere of Mozart's *Don Giovanni*, Prague also played a key role in European opera history. An independent Czech theater established in 1862 lent the city on the banks of the Vltava additional cultural weight. While Lwów did not hold the same significance for Polish history as Prague did for Czech history, it became the de facto cultural capital of Poland in the last third of the nineteenth century. While Prussia and Russia repressed the Polish populations in their Partitions, opera in Lemberg flourished as a medium of free expression.[14]

To engage more deeply with the history of these cultural centers, this book makes historical comparisons based on a social history typology of opera.[15] Dresden, like Vienna, Berlin, St. Petersburg, and many other European cities, had a royal opera. This was the predominant form of opera house in Europe from the eighteenth century. By the example of Dresden, this book will consider how this type of institution adapted to the challenges of the nineteenth century, in which theater rapidly became more professional and opera began to attract a mass audience. The second ideal type of opera, in the Weberian sense, was the aristocratic theater, which is illustrated here by the Polish Theater in the Galician capital of Lemberg. A third type, which gained increasing significance over the course of the nineteenth century, was the civic theater; the main example discussed here is the Czech national theater in Prague along with occasional comparisons with the Leipzig municipal theater. These sociohistorical types are defined by the nature of the authority governing them, their inner hierarchies, audience composition, repertoires, and contemporary discourse on them. In the final section, however, the book will question the usefulness of social history typologies for analyzing the history of cultural institutions and genres. Is it really accurate to speak of a specifically royal, aristocratic or civic, that is, *bürgerliches* music theater in the long period between 1815 and 1914? In this respect, there is a fundamental linguistic challenge to overcome in English: in central European languages, the synonyms *bürgerlich*, *občanský*, and *mieszczański* are common in public and academic discourse. But the English equivalents are more problematic. Using the label *bourgeois* might distractingly suggest history seen through a traditional Marxist lens. Bürgerliches theater, in fact, had civic origins and was often criticized for being too bourgeois. William Weber used the term "middle class" in his study on musical tastes,[16] yet the existence of this specific class is a characteristic of western societies. In many parts of Central Europe, especially Poland and Hungary, there was no middle class in the English sense of the word. The members of the *inteligencija* who became a driving force in opera were often both impoverished and of noble origins. Bearing all these factors in mind, this book opts for distinguishing between royal, aristocratic, and middle-class theater. The question then arises of whether and how these social distinctions influenced repertoires and stage productions.

As is customary in historical comparisons, this book explores the differences and similarities between the compared objects. During the course of the research, it emerged that the similarities between royal, aristocratic, and middle-class theaters increased toward the end of the nineteenth century. What were the reasons for this convergence? Why did opera houses which were so differently orientated, organized, and financed grow increasingly similar in terms of repertoire and performance practice? How did a standard repertoire become established toward the end of the nineteenth century which was basically definitive for the opera world throughout Europe and even across the Atlantic?

Another important set of issues emerges from the complex relationship between nationalism and opera. Why and how was opera made national in terms of repertoire, singing language, plots, and, to a certain extent, stage production? Last but not least, what limits were there to nationalizing opera? Why and how were invented national opera traditions internationalized and interpreted for local purposes in a central European, European, or global opera market? Were there any countries or cities that did not follow the trend to make opera national? These questions can only be answered by considering the exponential increase in cultural exchange between the various cities with opera houses. Indeed, contact between them was so frequent and lively in the late nineteenth century that it can be regarded as a preliminary to present-day processes of European integration and globalization. But even at this earlier stage, such cultural mingling could provoke regional resistance.

In view of the connectivity of modern Europe, not only the case studies will be contrasted, as in conventional sociohistorical comparisons, but also the intensity of cultural exchange will be considered. For this reason, following the model of transfer history,[17] developed by Parisian historians, this book examines cultural flows between different opera centers. In concrete terms, it will consider the processes by which individual operas, styles, and genres were adapted to suit different theaters and publics as well as the concurrent conflicts and processes of demarcation. The convergence in repertoires and performance practice will be traced in the final section in terms of a process of "Europeanization." This view may seem irritatingly Euro-constructivist at first glance, but it explains the increasing convergence in opera (which tailed off after 1914) on two levels: structural, that is, the increasing similarity in opera practice, and discursive. Especially on the fringes of Europe, in the Russian Empire, in the Levant, and above all on the East Coast of the US, opera was perceived as a specifically European form of culture to be imported and adapted. This is where New York and the Metropolitan Opera come in.

But to return to the central European case studies: the cities Dresden, L'viv, and Prague were selected for comparison partly on account of their similar functions and sizes. At the beginning of the nineteenth century the capitals of Saxony, Galicia, and Bohemia, respectively, all had populations of between 50,000 and 70,000 and similar administrative functions. They were all centers of regional government and university towns with a well developed education system, press, and publishing. In terms of population composition, however, they differed significantly. While Dresden had a predominantly German-speaking population, Lemberg and Prague were multinational. While competing national opera cultures consequently emerged in the latter two cities, even in Dresden minorities played a more significant role than is commonly recognized in the historiography on Germany. The theater ensemble, at the very least, was a multinational composite. These cities also grew at differing rates. By the eve of the First World War, Lemberg had a population of 200,000—only half that of Dresden or Prague (due primarily to less industrialization)—but this did not prevent the cultural life of the city and opera in particular from flourishing.

Comparing cultural and music histories poses special challenges different from social history or sociological comparisons. While social historians can use data and other "hard" facts, comparing cultural history is more complex and requires special sensitivity. Can a given composer or work be compared to another? Which categories would apply if this were possible? This book will distinguish between four areas when comparing operas: the work's aesthetics, the intentions of its creator, the practice of its performance, and its reception by audiences and critics. In this way operas can be used as historical sources providing more information than just the libretto and its textual component.

This book does not claim to analyze the entire spectrum of music theater but will instead concentrate largely on opera. No evaluation is intended by this merely pragmatic consideration.[18] An equal analysis of operetta would simply go beyond the scope of this book. Opera's lighter cousin was, though, quite a prominent feature of repertoires as well as discourses on music theater. Operetta is therefore considered insofar as it influenced developments in opera.

Finally, the book covers a clearly limited time span. It opens at the time of the Congress of Vienna, which shaped the political and social events in Central Europe in the ensuing century. It closes with the First World War, the point at which the long nineteenth century ultimately ended. In terms of music history, a crucial break occurred in the years immediately preceding 1914, when musical modernism began to emerge and the aesthetic consensus within society disintegrated.[19]

In view of their political, social, and national importance, it is surprising that opera theaters have been neglected by historiography.[20] This is particularly remarkable considering how strongly nineteenth-century Germans and Czechs, in particular, identified with their country's music. In the past, musicology has focused on analyzing scores and largely disregarded music's institutions and reception. This esentially ahistorical approach is based on an understanding of music as a timeless value. In the last twenty-five years, however, much has changed internationally. Prominent musicologists have begun to demand more inquiry into the interpretation and reception of music.[21] As music, unlike literature and the visual arts, relies on its performance to be experienced, this is surely to be supported. Before the advent of recording technology, music could only be disseminated by repeated production, each time in a specific location with its attendant circumstances. Much can be gained, therefore, from analyzing music in view of its performance in changing political and social contexts. For historical inquiry, it is significant that music is generally performed by an ensemble in the context of an institution. The cultural practice of music engenders processes of socialization during performance and via audience reception. In this respect, there is a large area of convergence between musicology and the study of history.

While there is a considerable fund of literature on the opera houses in Dresden, Lemberg and Prague, most of it is more descriptive than analytical and somewhat superannuated.[22] The state of archival sources available is excellent. Nearly all the files on the royal theater survived the bombing of Dresden in

February 1945, making it possible to reconstruct in close detail how the royal theater of 1815, then still very much under the sway of absolutism, was transformed into a professionally run institution over which the royal family had very limited influence. In western Ukraine, the archive remained largely undisturbed by Soviet rule. The theater files from the Austrian era in the Central State Historical Archive of the Ukraine in L'viv (*Tsentralnyi derzhavnyi istorychnyi arkhiv Ukrayiny u Lvovi*, or *TsDIAU*) were merely relabeled in Russian (until 1956), then in Ukrainian. A national theater fund in the Czech national archive (*Národní archiv*) contains a wealth of information and a number of documents are also held by the theater department and archive of the national museum.

Press sources are particularly abundant on account of the strong public interest in opera in the nineteenth century. For the purposes of this book, only the major newspapers and specialist journals were analyzed, focusing on key productions. Another interesting source is memoirs written by singers and musicians, which provide particularly intimate insights into the opera world of the nineteenth century. All these different sources are drawn upon at different points in the book. The first chapter deals with the major trends in opera history in the nineteenth century, including the emergence of social and national differentiation. Three distinct narratives subsequently examine the opera histories of Dresden, Lemberg and Prague and their major theaters. I hope to have achieved a more readable quality here than is usual in scholarly comparisons. The concluding chapter, elucidating aspects of social history, considers the most important differences and similarities in the opera life of Central Europe while simultaneously looking beyond this part of Europe.

In order to ensure consistent comparisons, all case studies follow a similar storyline. First, they deal with institutional and social changes within the respective opera theaters, drawing on records from the theaters' administrative and supervisory boards. Space is also allotted to audience behavior and the many conflicts surrounding the various theaters, which is where press reports are key. Finally, the case studies explore the most significant changes in repertoire and performance practice and hence a key aspect of cultural and music history. This involves dealing with music scores, production on stage and opera's reception by its audience as well as by the general public. The final section of the book reflects on the social appeal of music theater, major aesthetic changes in the composition, performance practice and reception of operas and, in conclusion, cultural transfers and networks with special emphasis on Central Europe.

The book does not, however, have to be read in this order. Someone who is more interested in Prague than Dresden could jump straight to the case study of Prague. Those concerned mainly with aesthetic developments in German, Polish, and Czech opera might prefer to read the last chapter of each case study and the conclusion first. Points of interest for social history are dealt with in the first chapters of each case study and in the conclusion. Perhaps the whole book will cast a spell over some readers. Each case study follows its own dramaturgy and has its own leitmotif; the last section was written more in the vein of a closing act than the usual summarizing conclusion. Hence it is an operatic book that hopefully conveys some of the magic of opera.

Leitmotifs in Opera History in the Nineteenth Century

From its emergence as an art form and an institution, opera was closely connected to the princely courts. In the eighteenth century, only a few theaters were owned by aristocrats or burghers, among them Count Sporck's Theater in Prague and Emanuel Schikaneder's *Theater an der Wieden*. But these two theaters, like other nonroyal theaters, had limited life spans. Ultimately, only kings and the wealthiest aristocrats could afford to maintain opera theaters all year round. Initially, then, opera remained unknown by most people in Europe and its social relevance was limited.

At the end of the nineteenth century, however, the situation was quite different. By that time, a dense network of opera theaters had been built across the continent. Nearly every large European city with a modicum of municipal pride made sure it had an impressive opera house or at least a multipurpose theater in which operas could be shown. How did this once exclusive art form become so universally popular? By way of an overture, the following chapter discusses the political and social trends that propelled the development of opera in the long nineteenth century. Throwing light on these will provide the background to the three comparative case studies of Dresden, Lemberg, and Prague.

Toward a Synthesis of the Arts

To analyze the rise of opera in the nineteenth century, it is useful to examine its two major components, music and drama, individually. The poets and philosophers of the Enlightenment regarded music with considerable skepticism. In his *Critique of Judgement*, Immanuel Kant deemed the "art of music" (*Tonkunst*) the lowest among the arts since in his view it failed to convey content or values. Kant criticized the fact that music "speaks by means of mere sensations without concepts, and so does not, like poetry, leave anything over for reflection."[23] He could not reconcile music's emotionality with his concept of rationality. The poet and dramatist Friedrich Schiller wrote in a similarly disapproving manner about concert audiences: "However great the noise in the concert hall might be, the people are suddenly all ears when a melting passage is played. An expression of sensuality verging on the animalistic then tends to appear on all faces, drunken eyes swimming, open mouths all desire, an ecstatic trembling seizes their entire body, breathing is rapid and shallow, in short all the symptoms of intoxication appear: clear proof that the senses are reveling but the spirit or the principle of human freedom has fallen prey to the force of sensual expression."[24]

The Romantics, by contrast, took a very different view of music. For them, it was precisely music's ineffability that was captivating. Writers including Novalis, E. T. A. Hoffmann, and Wilhelm Heinrich Wackenroder commended and reflected on the emotional power of music. From the late eighteenth century, intellectuals such as these contrasted the real world, scarred by the Napoleonic Wars, the beginnings of industrialization and mass poverty, with the exulted world of music. Wackenroder wrote: "Oh, so I close my eyes to all the wars of the world—and quietly retreat to the world of music, as to the world of faith, where all our doubts and our suffering are lost in a sea of sound, where . . . all the fear in our hearts is at once healed by mere contact."[25] Elevating music to a universe of its own might have been a way to gain respite from the world but it did not imply retreating from reality. Music was in fact perceived as a matrix of and key to the material world. This idea was given philosophical endorsement by Arthur Schopenhauer. In his major work, *The World as Will and Representation*, published in 1819, he wrote: "The inexhaustible potential for melodies corresponds with nature's inexhaustible possibilities for creating different individuals, physiognomies and life paths." Schopenhauer identified human moods and modes of behavior in the different times and keys in music. Thus, an adagio spoke to him "of the suffering of a great and noble struggle which spurns all petty contentment," and the minor third conveyed "a sense of terrible apprehension." [26]

In Schopenhauer's view, music not only mirrored man's subjective experience of the world, as architecture, fine art, and painting did, but actually expressed the purest "essence of the Will." He therefore accorded it a higher status than other art genres. Schopenhauer's ideas contributed to the birth of the notion of opera as a synthesis of the arts, a *Gesamtkunstwerk* uniting all the arts under one banner, and turned Kant's classification of the arts on its head with permanent effect until well into the twentieth century. Music came to be so highly valued that Nietzsche, in his early writings, even argued in favor of "founding the state on music" and Max Weber proposed using music to build a new, better society in his sociology of music, published in 1921.[27]

Schopenhauer was one of the first writers to idealize composers as mediators between the physical world and the beyond: "The composer reveals the innermost nature of the world and articulates the deepest wisdom, in a language that his reason does not understand; like a magnetic somnambulist giving information about things of which he has no knowledge."[28] Later, Nietzsche and Max Weber glorified the composer as genius in their writings, as did the Czech public in its reception of Smetana. Schopenhauer's greatest opponent, Hegel—an opera enthusiast like many of his contemporaries—valued the linguistic component of opera. Hegel believed that opera could educate its audience by imparting concrete information. Richard Wagner took this idea up in his 1849 proposal for a German national theater: "Music is able, to a barely lesser degree than drama, to affect tastes and, yes, even morals."[29]

Hopes were projected not only on to the art form but also on to the institution of the music theater. In the nineteenth century, it was widely felt, especially among the bourgeoisie, that social divisions could be overcome in the opera house and all audience members be united in their enjoyment of art.[30] "The art of music," a Viennese commentator observed in 1808, "performs daily the miracle that was otherwise ascribed only to love: It makes all classes equal. Nobility and bourgeoisie, princes and their vassals, superiors and their subordinates sit together at one bar and, surrounded by sonic harmony, forget the disharmony of their rank."[31]

Opera, then, became the object of not just one but of two utopias of unity: first, an artistic utopia—the notion of a *Gesamtkunstwerk*—and second, a social utopia of all classes unified in the theater. Of course, history shows that these ideals remained elusive. Nevertheless, many thinkers held that music and especially opera could exert an important influence on art and society. This belief forms an initial leitmotif running through the history of opera in the nineteenth century and hence this book.

Opera and Nation

Opera was not only a mainly royal pastime in the eighteenth century; it was to all intents and purposes international. Repertoires, singing language, libretti, and ensembles were all imported from Italy, until the latter half of the eighteenth century, when French music theater began to set trends. Why, then, did opera come to be used as a mouthpiece of nations by the late nineteenth century in Central Europe and beyond? How was opera so profoundly "nationalized" in the course of a century in terms of singing language, narratives, and performance practice? These questions will be addressed in depth in the three case studies analyzing the central role that Dresden, Lemberg, and Prague played in the creation of German, Polish, and Czech opera. First, the context in which this transformation took place will be elucidated by considering three major factors: the institution of the opera theater, the most influential figures in music theater, and finally the operatic works themselves.

The idea to make opera national was rooted in the concept of the national theater. The *Théâtre Français* in Paris was the first example of a playhouse dedicated exclusively to national drama and established with the express intention of raising dramatic standards. Friedrich Schiller reflected German hopes for an equivalent national theater in his groundbreaking essay *Was kann eine gute ste-*

hende Schaubühne eigentlich wirken? ("What can be achieved by a good permanent playhouse?"). He, too, saw the theater as a place to educate and unify the people: "I can not possibly ignore the great influence that a good permanent theater would have on the spirit of the nation . . . in a word, if we could experience having a national theater, we would become a nation."[32] Constituting an early form of mass entertainment, before cinema, radio, or other media, theater had a far broader appeal than it does today. At a time when illiteracy was rife, many Enlightenment-inspired writers and bureaucrats hoped theater could be used as an educational medium.

Schiller's theories were much discussed not only in the German lands but also in Bohemia and Poland. In Prague, the composer Prokop Šedivý, borrowing from Schiller, wrote a "short treatise on the usefulness of an institutionally permanent and well structured theater." In it, he described theater as a "school of wisdom" with an "uppermost rank in the sphere of intellectual education and health."[33] Furthermore, Šedivý saw the theater as a place to promote and cultivate the Czech language, which was just beginning to be revived after years of German-language domination. In Poland, Wojciech Bogusławski, the long-standing director of the Warsaw National Theater and director of the Polish Theater in Lemberg, put forward similar ideas.[34] He, too, believed that a national identity could be conveyed on the stage and that drama could be used as a unifying device.

Inspired by Enlightenment philosophy, the Austrian Emperor Josef II founded the Viennese "Royal and National Theater" in 1776. Taking its direction into his own hands rather than entrusting it to an impresario or private entrepreneur, he freed it from considerations of budget and market forces and dedicated it primarily to educating the public. In this way, Josef II established a German form of lyrical drama (*Singspiel*) to rival Italian opera. Following this example, several royal theaters in the German lands were declared "national theaters" toward the end of the century, and their repertoires adapted to feature more patriotic pieces and German-language lyrical drama.[35]

At most of these theaters, however, the drive to provide educational national drama soon began to flag. Embroiled in the wars against revolutionary France, the royal courts tightened up their domestic policies and any trouble in the form of patriotic pieces, writers, or directors was not tolerated. In Prague, by contrast, the idea prevailed not only in name—the city was home to Count Nostitz's National Theater (*Gräflich Nostitzsches Nationaltheater*, or from 1798, *Royal Altstädter National Theater*)—but also in objectives and repertoire. The difference here, as in Warsaw, was that there was no royal court to seek hegemony over the theater.

Schiller remained an icon long after his early death and well after the Congress of Vienna. From 1829, groups of enthusiasts calling themselves "Schiller societies" went about rallying the public in the German lands to causes the poet had championed. Revered as one of the proponents of German unity, his name was invoked with even greater urgency after the failed revolution of 1848. The cult surrounding Schiller reached a climax on the 100th anniversary of his birth in 1859, which was marked with a gala performance at the royal theater in Dresden. In the characteristically nationalist tones of the time, the prologue declared: "Your call, 'Be united!' sounds from land to land; under your name a people will unite, the German people, proud to call themselves your people."[36] In Prague, Schiller was venerated not only as a "national poet" and in Schiller's centenary year, but Czech and German admirers competed to lay the largest wreath at his memorial.[37]

Schiller's stylization as the symbolic father of national theater may have been simplifying but it was a powerful vehicle for promoting the cause. In the run-up to the 1848 revolution, a series of treatises on national theater was published in Dresden, a center of German discourse on the subject. Influential personalities linked to the royal theater such as Eduard Devrient and Karl Gutzkow and chief conductor Richard Wagner all published essays on national theater.[38] They saw it as an instrument for improving standards without the interference of the ruling monarchs and princely families. The idea and different aspects of national theater were also debated in Vienna. In Budapest, the Hungarian National Theater began putting on regular performances in 1840. The National Theater in Poland was an essential organ of the nation after the country's partition, and even more so after the failed uprisings of 1830–31 and 1863. The Galician newspaper *Dziennik Literacki* wrote: "Now that our only treasure is our language, the theater is our most important national institution. . . . Its task is to teach our society the sacred virtues of our ancestors and to instruct the masses in our national sense of civic belonging; its task is very much a national one."[39] Surrounded by developments and discourses such as these, it is not surprising that Prague—on the road from Berlin and Dresden to Vienna—was also host to lively discussions about national theater. Since 1848, the main goal was national emancipation and the recognition of the Czechs as a European cultural nation.[40]

These ideas on national theater and the national function of culture were not merely discussed but actually embraced and put into practice by growing sections of the population. In the German lands, a choral movement grew parallel with the Schiller societies. Choral associations became so popular that they formed the second mainstay of the national movement, alongside the new gymnastics movement.[41] Choral festivals were significant gatherings, attracting participants from all over the German Confederation and even from Hungary and the Russian Empire. The choral movement's popularity was not dampened by the failed attempt to unify the nation in 1848 but continued to mobilize masses, climaxing in the German choral festival in Dresden (*Deutsches Sängerbundfest*) of 1865, which brought together a total of 200,000 participants.[42]

In Bohemia, too, choral and music societies played an important role in rallying people to the national cause. The *Hlahol* ("hall") choral society, founded in

1861, mobilized several tens of thousands to sing at the ceremony to lay the foundation stone for the Czech National Theater in 1868. The experience of singing together on such an occasion would, it was hoped, transmit a feeling of national belonging and social equality and forge emotional bonds between countrymen. Inspired by the Romanticism of the era, nationalists believed that the essence of the nation—the "spirit of the people"—could be divined through their song.[43] It was in this mood that the myth began to spread in Bohemia of the inherently musical Czech, and music became a matter of national pride. In neighboring Galicia, choral and music societies also gained popularity in the latter nineteenth century despite widespread poverty. Here and in other multi-ethnic regions, the existence of various rival national movements promoted the growth of local music scenes as they all vied to be heard.[44]

These societies were involved in a process of "cultural nation-building," which developed in the peculiar context of an imperial order. In the Habsburg Empire, eastern parts of Prussia and on the fringes of the Russian Empire, national movements did not emerge from geographically outlined nation-states but based the location and identification of their nations on largely cultural criteria.

Scholars and composers played a key role in this process of cultural nation-building. In Germany, for example, as early as 1802, reflections on the national characteristics of music were published by music historian Nikolaus Forkel, who declared the work of Bach to be emphatically German.[45] In this early Romantic period, cultural nationalism could still go hand in hand with a cosmopolitan attitude. This is illustrated by the work of Carl Maria von Weber, both at Prague's Estates Theater and as director of the German opera department at the Dresden Royal Theater from 1813 to 1826. Weber set to music a repertoire of mostly translated French works, some of which he regarded as stylistic paradigms. Just two decades later, views had become noticeably more rigid. Conservatory professor Adolf Bernhard Marx, whose *General Theory of Music* (*Allgemeine Musiklehre*) became one of the standard text books of the nineteenth century, divided the world of opera into three nationally defined schools of music. According to him, the Italians stood for melodiousness, the French for the best drama and musical effects and the Germans for truth, earnestness, and a "thoroughly cerebral force."[46] The editor-in-chief of the *Neue Zeitschrift für Musik*, Franz Brendel, developed this theory even further, identifying specifically German aims and objectives for opera. In a polemic, he demanded the rejection of the number opera and called for dramatic unity and for German opera to be raised "to the summit of national material." From there it was only a short step to the xenophobic writings of Richard Wagner in Zurich, where he distanced himself from Italian and French opera and wrote his notorious article on Jewishness in music.[47]

As Meyerbeer was to discover at his own cost as director of music at the Berlin Royal Opera, works were now only considered German if they were written by an ethnic German. In Central Europe, bloodlines dictated whether an opera was considered an *Originalstück* or *puvodní produkce*. Music lovers in Paris and Italy responded to Wagner's nationalism with indignance, especially after France's defeat by Prussia. But rather than rejecting Wagner's nationalist classification of music, they adopted it to defend their slighted nations and continue the debate on stylistic superiority. Similarly, in Prague, Wagnerians and anti-Wagnerians argued over national characteristics in music.[48] The history of opera, then, reflects changes in the way nations were defined and demarcated. These national codes became entrenched in music theater.

As nationalism built higher boundaries, the role of the national theater changed. While Schiller and his contemporaries had been concerned with general theater reforms, in 1853 the German Brockhaus encyclopedia defined "national theater" as a place where "only native pieces of essentially national character are to be performed."[49] By this time, then, the main goal was no longer to bring enlightenment to the people but to cultivate a specifically native repertoire and promote the nation. The concept of national theater took on similarly radical dimensions in the minds of Czech and Polish intellectuals. Having experienced the suppression of their own cultures in the wake of the quashed 1848 revolution, they rejected German theater as an instrument of neo-absolutist domination and cultural discrimination. In Galicia and Bohemia, after 1848, German was more than ever regarded as the language of oppressors and incriminators.

In contrast with Dresden and Vienna, where hopes for a national theater were abandoned after the failed revolution, in Bohemia, Hungary, and Poland the idea remained politically relevant. Although the insurgents of 1848-49 were pursued and punished, the national theater in Hungary stayed open and Polish culture in Lemberg continued to be fostered. In 1850, the government in Prague finally authorized a Corporation for the Erection of a Czech National Theater (*Sbor pro zřízení českého Národního divadla v Praze*), believing this would provide a safe outlet for general dissatisfaction and that the arts bore little relevance to politics. But as soon as the first public appeal to donate toward the national theater was issued in 1851, it became clear that this national theater was to be a monument to the aspiring Czech nation.[50] It was, then, an extremely political matter, and the government soon began trying to obstruct fundraising campaigns, prohibiting charity appeals and outlawing door-to-door collecting in private houses and inns. Consequently, these attempts at fundraising, which are examined in greater detail in the chapter on the Czech national theater, were eventually abandoned in the mid-1850s. But by then enough money had been raised to buy the plot for the future national theater, overlooking the river Vltava, and the project had taken root in Czech society.

Following liberalization in Austria in 1860-61, public fundraising went ahead with renewed zeal and by 1862 enough funds were available to construct a provisional theater. Like the Hungarian National Theater two decades earlier, the fledgling project struggled at first to collect a body of native works, especially in the field of music theater. But this shortfall was soon made up by Bedřich Smetana and other, today lesser known, Czech composers. A Czech repertoire was thus created even before the national theater was opened, and lovingly cultivated by Smetana as director of music. Under his auspices, a Czech ensemble was put together and imported operas were translated. Thus, in comparison with Hungary and Poland, opera in Prague was made national at a relatively early stage. Germany had provided the model: in nearby Dresden, Richard Wagner had begun translating imported operas and having ensembles sing in German, which had a direct influence on Prague's Estate's Theater.[51] The obstacles and opposition to this process of nationalization are explored in the individual case studies.

The choral movement, the drive for a national theater, and the success of Czech musical works sparked a new enthusiasm for opera in Bohemia on a par with that in Germany. The myth of the "musical nation," which had been popularized by the Czech national movement before the 1848 revolution, became an integral part of the country's national identity. Czech composers naturally benefited from this heightened appreciation of music. The saying *Kdo Čech, ten musikant* ("If you're Czech, you're a musician") soon spread beyond the borders of Bohemia. In 1879–80, the Leipzig music periodical *Musikalisches Wochenblatt* published a long article on the special musicality of the Czechs and their contemporary composers,[52] demonstrating the effectiveness of powers of suggestion: by the end of the nineteenth century, Germans and Czechs were indeed associated with what they had originally identified as their national music.

Music was less significant for the Polish concept of nation. While Polish intellectuals placed greater emphasis on native literature, the Russian and Prussian authorities played their part in suppressing drama and opera in the wake of the uprisings in 1830–31 and 1863. For many years, moreover, the nobility dominated Polish society. Without a culturally active, urban middle class, there was only a relatively small opera audience. Yet despite these institutional and social obstacles, around 1848, Polish opera was at least one generation ahead of Czech opera. This was due not least to the productivity of Silesian born composer Josef Elsner, who composed dozens of operas in the first third of the nineteenth century which were performed at the *Teatr Narodowy* in Warsaw and in Lemberg.[53]

In Stanisław Moniuszko, Poland also had a "national composer" whose work was regarded as the paradigm of a national style in opera and who enjoyed the same level of popularity in Warsaw and Lemberg as Smetana did in Prague. Public perceptions of these composers, in the nineteenth century and well into the twentieth century, were strikingly characterized by nationally defined concepts and standards. Was this connection between opera and nation a mere construct or invention? Or was there really something like a national style in music and if so, which harmonies or rhythms marked it out? Or did the process of making opera national and the creation of the national opera genre take place mainly in the minds of the audience? Carl Dahlhaus argues for the latter, which brings us to the social aspect of opera.

Opera and Society

The opera theaters of the nineteenth century not only performed important political and national functions but also a significant social one. Prague theater director Josef Šmaha noted wryly in his memoirs: "Today, do not many mothers with their daughters, prospective brides, go to the theater for the sole reason that they have the opportunity to approach potential bridegrooms? Thus the theater also has its social tasks. It is a meeting place for the young and the old world. It is a great social salon. The number of betrothals that have been prepared in the foyer of the theater!"[54]

Matchmaking was not the only social activity that took place at the opera. The opera provided society's elites and those who aspired to be like them an opportunity to parade their evening wear and jewelry and demonstrate their superior status and wealth by their appearance and choice of seats. Opportunities for self-presentation were not limited, as today, to intervals and a few minutes before the curtain is raised. Until the invention of electric light, auditoria were permanently bathed in the dim glow of candles and gaslights, setting off the diamonds and white evening gowns of elegant viewers to perfect advantage. The French sociologist Pierre Bourdieu has identified this aspect of a visit to the opera, concert house, or theater as the culture industry's "social distinction" function, allowing the various classes to demonstrate their social status.[55] Audience members' different reactions to the music, the depth of musical knowledge they displayed and judgement of the quality of performances reinforced this. But social distinction was not the only form of interaction among the audiences in Dresden, Lemberg, and Prague. In these theaters, members of the various classes mingled in the foyers and on the staircases as, unlike in London, for example, there were no separate entrances for different seating areas. Central European opera theaters were therefore simultaneously sites of social integration. The maids in the orchestra level and the private box owners above them all came to "see and be seen." Costing the equivalent of about three hours' pay for skilled work or the price of a large loaf of bread,[56] tickets would have been expensive for craftsmen or young school teachers, but not prohibitively so.

The presence of the beautiful, rich, and powerful acted as a magnet to the public and especially those with social aspirations. If an emperor, prince, or other personality was said to be attending, crowds flocked to the theater. These would, however, quickly dissipate when His Excellency or His Majesty made his departure.

Theaters fulfilled the role of a town's finest meeting place and were decorated accordingly. With every new theater, foyers and staircases took on more magnificent dimensions and ornamentation and society's elites basked in the glory of the institution that they had—directly or indirectly—financed.

Private salons sprung up in theater circles, creating opportunities for closer contact with singers, actors, and musicians. Theaters also held regular balls, which were popular social events and excellent sources of revenue. They were often themed around popular operas and visitors would come in costume. Following the huge success of Tchaikovsky's *Eugene Onegin*, for example, it became all the rage among the youth of Prague to attend balls dressed as Lenski or Onegin.

Theater's position at the center of urban society was reflected in the print media, which provided far more extensive coverage of events on stage and behind the scenes than today. Reports on the theater world ran several times a week on the first page of leading daily newspapers. Major premieres were previewed well in advance and reviewed afterwards, and composers, works, and productions championed or condemned in a print battle of polemics. Even such minor news items as roles being recast, a prima donna coming down with a chill, or a well-known tenor traveling through the area were deemed worthy of printing. Meanwhile, a specialist press sector was also emerging.

This extensive media coverage embraced a star cult which is still familiar to us today. The stars of the opera earned nearly tens times as much as orchestra musicians and more than twice as much as theater directors. Between 1870 and 1890 the fees for solo singers more than doubled as a result of the increasing number of opera theaters and the growing competition. Some singers were consequently able to amass incredible amounts of wealth during their lifetimes. The French baritone Jean Lassalle, a frequent guest performer in Prague and Dresden, grew so rich that he was able to buy a palace near the Champs Elysées.[57]

Lassalle and other star performers were admired not only for their voices but also for their appearances. In 1886, the periodical *Dalibor* described Lassalle in these glowing terms: "Nature gave him everything that an opera star can wish for: He is tall, magnificent, has a full-sounding organ with a steely timbre, a handsome, imposing figure and a noble looking face."[58] With his drooping eyelids, plump cheeks, and long straggly beard, he would not be considered typically good-looking by today's standards, but the ladies of the day adored him. Despite tickets double the usual price, each one of Lassalle's performances at the National Theater was sold out.

The public's fascination with female stars was even greater. When the Italian singer Emma Turolla came to stay in Prague in 1883, following visits to Vienna and Budapest, a group of excited fans was waiting at the station to greet her and escorted her joyfully through the city streets. Once in the theater, she was showered with flowers and presented with bouquets, some so large that two people were needed to carry them. When she left again in January 1884, the scene at the station was extraordinary. Crowds of admirers blocked the platform and screaming students waved their handkerchiefs, threw flowers at the half-opened carriage window, and ran alongside the train as it moved away. Some even jumped on and accompanied "Miss Turolla"—she was not yet spoken for—to the next express train station. Josef Kuffner, author of Prague's leading arts page in the 1880s and 1890s, quipped that *La Turolla* would have been awarded the sacred crown of King Wenceslas had she not had the audacity to leave.

Figure 1. Star singer Emma Turolla.

Emma Turolla was not only a cult figure among the Czech population in Prague. Germans also flocked to her performances in the National Theater. The *Národní listy* mockingly noted that the words *köstlich*, *superb*, and *göttlich* could be heard from all sides.[59] In Budapest, where Turolla stayed for a six-week guest performance in late 1883 and where she was eventually taken under contract, both the cost of the tickets and the commotion were even greater.

Compared with other singers of the time, however, Emma Turolla was small fry. The most famous prima donna of the latter nineteenth century was Adelina Patti. National Theater tickets for her performances during an extensive tour of Europe in fall 1885 cost five times as much as usual. Even the cheapest standing room ticket now cost one florin—as much as a well-paid craftsman earned in a day in Prague. Remarkably, Adelina Patti, who was already over forty by that time, drew such wide audiences entirely on the strength of her singing voice, which even Hector Berlioz had admired.[60] The arrival at the station of world-famous stars such as Patti became public events in Prague, Dresden, and Lemberg alike. Dozens or even hundreds of people lined the streets as the celebrity proceeded to the hotel, theater or café, calling and waving and trying to catch a glimpse of society's current favorite.

Guest performances by stars such as these were an important source of income for theaters. While Emma Turolla, for example, was paid a fixed fee of 500 florins for each performance in January and March 1884, the National Theater took twice or three times as much as usual in entrance fees. In January 1884 alone, the box office made a profit of more than 5,000 florins on her performances, about half the amount required to make up the deficit of the slow summer months.[61]

Paid such immense fees, top soloists often led rather dissipated lives. Tenors, in particular, who by the end of the century were earning more money and attention than sopranos, showed little consideration for convention. Karel Burian, an internationally acclaimed Wagner tenor, is a prime example. Although married, Burian had a reputation in Prague, where his career began, as a philanderer. The advances of this Tristan/Dalibor/Don José/Florestan, with his dark hair and light blue eyes, were apparently hard to resist. One evening, a cuckolded husband smuggled a stinking carp contained in a bodice soaked in sewage into Burian's dressing room.[62] When a disturbed Burian subsequently broke his contract with the National Theater and announced his departure to Budapest, the incident was splashed all over the press. In Dresden, where he was next engaged and rose to such fame that he eventually sang alongside Caruso in New York, a similar chain of events unfolded. Death threats were even delivered to the incorrigible tenor's dressing room and he was pursued in the streets by jealous husbands.[63] Toward the end of Burian's career, an unknown person dropped a caustic substance into his glass of water, rendering him unable to sing for two years. He died shortly after recovering his voice.

While celebrity misbehavior was condemned especially by the bourgeoisie, the public was also fascinated by both the on stage and real-life dramas surrounding the opera theater. Such gossip provided a diversion from humdrum daily life and considerably increased newspaper circulation. In 1888, a features section of *Národní listy* tellingly commented: "In all Prague, not one scandal—that is a scandal!"[64] With their lives of financial and sexual excess, theater stars tested and redefined society's moral framework. Divorce, for example, was still anathema to most in the mid-nineteenth century but was rapidly becoming common among ensemble members. By the turn of the century, many singers had survived a broken marriage, setting a precedent for the world outside the theater.

But opera was able to rise above the scandal. Even Karel Burian—as soon as his crystal clear tenor rang out—was respected as an artist. It was in relation to operetta that opera gained prestige and was increasingly perceived as a high art. From the 1860s, especially in Central Europe, a tendency to distinguish between serious and light music emerged, in tandem with criticism of operetta as a foreign and inferior genre.[65] In the eighteenth century, there was no concept of highbrow or popular culture. The exclusively royal and noble audiences distinguished only between *opera seria* and *opera buffa*, which were performed on different occasions. For this reason, the next section will look at the first important type of opera theater, the royal opera.

Notes

1. Hence the title of the German edition of this book: Philipp Ther, *In der Mitte der Gesellschaft. Operntheater in Zentraleuropa 1815–1914* (Vienna: Böhlau and Oldenbourg publishers, 2006). I am grateful to Böhlau Verlag for allowing me to reuse and extend three major parts of this earlier book.
2. Storey, "The Social Life," 8–13.
3. On this concept, especially in connection with perceptions of art, see Bourdieu, *Distinction*.
4. A strict distinction should be made here between the popular and the scientific use of the term "classic" or "classical music." In music history, the music of Haydn, Mozart, and Beethoven was first described as "Viennese Classic" and thereby sanctified in 1836. On the concept of classicism, see also *Ästhetische Grundbegriffe*, vol. 3, 289–304, and specifically in music, 293–304. See also Dahlhaus, *Musik des 19. Jahrhunderts*, 205.
5. On the epoch-making aesthetic significance and political content of the opera *Guillaume Tell*, see Döhring, *Oper und Musikdrama*, 127–30.
6. "Volksgeist," Wagner, *Die Nibelungen. Weltgeschichte aus der Sage*, in Wagner, *Sämtliche Schriften und Dichtungen* (hereafter *SSD*), vol. 2, 123.
7. See especially Anderson, *Imagined Communities*; Gellner, *Nations and Nationalism*.
8. On this concept, *kulturelle Nationbildung*, see Langewiesche, *Nation*, 82
9. On the changing concept of culture see Conrad and Kessel, *Blickwechsel*, 10–20; Ute Daniel, *Kompendium Kulturgeschichte*, 443–66. On New Cultural History see the anthology of that name by Lynn Hunt.
10. Walter, *Die Oper*, 7, 39, and especially on Germany, 71.

11. Benjamin, *Gesammelte Schriften*, vol. 5, 1, 45.
12. On the history of opera in Paris see also Johnson, *Listening in Paris*; Charles, *Paris fin de siècle*; Patureau, *Le Palais Garnier*; Fulcher, *French Cultural Politics*; Fulcher, *The Nation's Image*. For an overview of the history of opera in nineteenth-century Vienna see Hadamowsky, *Wien*, 400–40; for more detail see Hadamowsky, *Die Wiener Hofoper*; Jahn, *Die Wiener Hofoper*; Beetz, *Das Wiener Opernhaus* 1869–1955.
13. On the history of La Scala and Milan as a European city of opera, see Jutta Toelle, *Bühne der Stadt. Mailand und das Teatro alla Scala zwischen Risorgimento und Fin de Siècle*. This book is actually the fourth volume of the series, *Die Gesellschaft der Oper. Musikkulturen europäischer Metropolen im 19. und 20. Jahrhundert*, begun in 2006. Volume 1 is the aforementioned book on opera theaters in central Europe, volume 2 deals with opera and politics; volume 3 with opera as an approach toward European cultural history. So far ten volumes have been published on operatic cities such as Paris, Milan, Berlin, Prague, Budapest, and L'viv, For further information see the publishers' website www.boehlau-verlag.com/.
14. See also Wypych-Gawrońska, *Lwowski teatr operowy*.
15. On the fundamental theoretical principles of the comparison, see Haupt and Kocka, eds., *Geschichte und Vergleich*; also Hartmut Kaelble and Jürgen Schriewer, eds., *Vergleich und Transfer*; and Lorenz, *Konstruktion der Vergangenheit*, 231–84.
16. Weber, *Music and the Middle Class*.
17. Among the essential theoretical publications in this field are Espagne, *Les transferts culturels franco-allemands*; Espagne and Werner, *Transfert: Relations interculturelles*. German publications on the subject include Espagne and Middell, *Von der Elbe bis an die Seine*; Osterhammel, *Geschichtswissenschaft*; Paulmann, *Internationaler Vergleich*. On the special relevance of this approach for the history of east-central Europe, see Ther, *Deutsche Geschichte*, 173–78.
18. One of the operetta's biggest critics, Theodor Adorno, is himself criticized in Csàky, *Ideologie der Operette*, 17.
19. On the divides in music history that mark the beginning and end of the nineteenth century in music, see Dahlhaus, *Die Musik des 19. Jahrhunderts*, 1–42 and 319–32.
20. Among the few exceptions is the literature on Paris and France. Here, the books by Jane Fulcher and James Johnson are of particular interest, since they innovatively combine social and cultural history approaches and references to music examples.
21. On aims and objectives, see Hinrichsen. See also the *Cambridge Opera Journal*, published since 1989, and a central article therein by John Rosselli; see also Rosselli's other works on Italian opera and the journal *Musica e Storia*. See also the 2006 issue of the *Journal of Interdisciplinary History*, which contains more than a dozen articles on history and music.Other essential works of music theory referred to for this book include Dahlhaus, *Die Musik im 19. Jahrhundert*; Döring, *Oper und Musikdrama*; Eggebrecht, *Musik im Abendland*, and for the historical analysis of individual operas, *Pipers Enzyklopädie des Musiktheaters*.
22. On Dresden, the most important publication post 1989 is the anthology by Heinemann and John, *Die Dresdner Oper im 19. Jahrhundert*. In the GDR, the Hochschule für Musik published its own series of articles, many of which are very interesting. The most important book of the nineteenth century is Prölls, *Geschichte des Hoftheaters*.

    In L'viv, the situation is more complicated, as the Polish city fell to the Soviet Union in 1945. Nevertheless Polish authors have published much on the L'viv Theater since 1945. See especially Lasocka, *Teatr lwowski w latach 1800–1842*; Sivert, ed., *Teatr polski od 1863 roku*; Sivert, ed., *Teatr polski w latach 1890–1918*. A comprehensive publication is Got, *Das österreichische Theater in Lemberg*. On specifically opera his-

tory in L'viv, see Wypych-Gawrońska, *Lwowski teatr operowy*. The most important monograph published in the Soviet Republic of Ukraine is Palmarčuk and Pylypiuk, *L'vovskij gosudarstvenyi akademičeskij teatr*. On Prague's theater history and the National Theater, see Černy et al., eds., *Dějiny českého divadla*, vols. 2 and 3; Šejna, *Divadlo v české kultuře 19. století*; Němeček, *Opera Národního divadla*. The six-volume series, *Dějiny Národního Divadla*, was published in the interwar period (Prague, 1933–1936) and takes a very negative attitude toward the conservative founders of the national theater. The most important publication of the Habsburg period is Šubert, *Dějiny Národního divadla*. See also the three-volume monograph by Oscar Teuber on the German theater in Prague, which is also dealt with in two more recent publications, Jakubcová et al., eds., *Deutschsprachiges Theater in Prag*; and Ludvová et al., eds., *Hudební divadlo*, an encyclopedia on German-language theater in Bohemia.
23. Quoted in Eggebrecht, *Musik*, 668.
24. Quoted in Sponheuer, *Der Gott der Harmonien*, 181.
25. Quoted in Eggebrecht, *Musik*, 595.
26. All quoted in Schopenhauer, *Sämtliche Werke*, vol. 1, 364.
27. Nietzsche, *Richard Wagner*, 32; See also Nietzsche, *Die Geburt*, 13, 96; Braun, *Max Webers*, 45.
28. Schopenhauer, *Sämtliche Werke*, vol. 1, 363.
29. Richard Wagner, *Entwurf zur Organisation eines deutschen National-Theaters*, in Wagner, *SSD*, vol. 2, 269.
30. On the situation in France, see Johnson, *Listening*, 270–80. On the utopia of unity in Germany see Gall, *Bürgertum*, 201, 213; Trilse, *Eduard Devrient*, 435.
31. Quoted in Antonicek, *Biedermeierzeit*, 217.
32. Friedrich Schiller, *Was kann eine gute stehende Schaubühne*, 99. For a detailed account of the idea of the national theater in the German Enlightenment see also the monograph by Roland Krebs.
33. Quoted in Vodák, *Idea národního divadla*, 26.
34. On his life and work, see the in-depth biography by Raszewski, *Bogusławski*, 125.
35. On the idea of the national theater see Krebs, *L'idée*, and for a closer look at the same in central Europe, see Černý, *Idea*, 19.
36. *Kalenderblätter 1859*, 65. See also accounts of the Schiller celebrations in *Dresdner Nachrichten*, November 9–12 and November 14, 1859.
37. See also Teuber, *Geschichte, Dritter Theil*, 502.
38. On the discourse on national theater in the *Vormärz* period, see also Ther, *Teatro e nation-building*, 275 onward.
39. Quoted in Got, *Das österreichische Theater*, vol. 2, 720. The issues of December 20 and 27, 1867, and January 1, 1868, of the journal *Nowiny* ran a three-part essay on Polish theater along similar lines.
40. On the discourse on national movements expressed through theater, see also Macura, *Znamení*, 197. On the significance of amateur theater for nation-building see Hroch, *Na prahu*, 213–16.
41. On the history of this movement see Langewiesche, *Nation*, 132–71.
42. The part on Dresden discusses this celebration in more detail.
43. On this and the concept of folk song see Dahlhaus, *Die Musik des 19. Jahrhunderts*, 87–92.
44. On Bohemia see Storck, *Kulturnation*, 266. According to Storck, by 1870, 287 choral societies existed in Bohemia and 59 in Moravia. On Galicia, see Tokarz, *Kultura muzyczna Galicji*, 158–59.

45. On Forkel and early appreciation of Bach, see Hinrichsen, *Forkel*, 240.
46. Quoted in Hinrichsen, *Forkel*, 241. Marx's "Theory of Musical Composition" was published between 1837 and 1847. On the definition of German music in the period before the 1848 revolution and especially on the continuity of these ideas into the twentieth century, see Sponheuer, *Reconstructing Ideal Types*, 40. On Marx see also Applegate, *The Internationalism of Nationalism*.
47. Wagner originally published this text in Brendel's *Neuer Zeitschrift für Musik*. See also Gregor-Dellin, *Wagner*, 310.
48. On the conflict surrounding Smetana, Ottlová and Pospíšil, *K motivům*.
49. "Nationaltheater," *Allgemeine deutsche Real-Enzyklopädie für die gebildeten Stände. Conversationslexikon*. 10th ed., vol. 11 (Leipzig, 1853), 66.
50. See also the Czech text in NA (National Archive, formerly Central State Archive), PM 9, 858. The German version speaks of a "Bohemian nation" and a "Bohemian national theater."
51. In Vienna on the other hand, in the era of neo-absolutism, Italian opera gained renewed significance. See also Jahn, *Die Wiener Hofoper*.
52. For a translation and commentary, see Beckerman, *Dvořák*, 211–29.
53. On contemporary reactions to his operas, which were supported by national enthusiasm, see E. T. A. Hoffmann, *Joseph Elsner*, 191.
54. Šmaha, *Dělali jsme*, 119. On national theater as a "marriage market," see also *Divadelní Kalendář 1900*, 57–58.
55. For more on this concept, see Bourdieu, *Distinction*.
56. Entrance fees in Prague at the time of the provisional theater were 20 kreuzers (from 1900, 40 hellers) and remained constant until the turn of the century. On ticket prices see also Kadlec, *Družstva*, 49; NA, ND fund, Společnost ND, Shelf 16; *Divadelní Kalendář 1906*, 179 onward. In Lemberg the cheapest tickets cost 15 kreuzers (for more on prices, see also Sivert, *Teatr polski w latach*, 255), and at the Dresden Royal Theater they were hardly more expensive at 50 pfennigs. On prices, see Sächsisches Hauptstaatsarchiv Dresden (hereafter SHAD), Ministerium des Königlichen Hauses (hereafter MdKH), loc. 41, no. 13, 4. On the conversion of Saxon talers and German marks to Austrian florins and crowns, see Schneider, *Währungen*, part 2, 95–99 and Part 3, 406.
57. Thus reported Prague newspapers. See also Šubert, *Dějiny*, 159. On Lassalle's vocal qualities see Kesting, *Die großen Sänger*, vol. 1, 210.
58. *Dalibor*, March 7, 1886, 87.
59. "Magnificent," "superb," "divine." See also reports on Turolla's guest peformances in Prague in *Národní listy* of January 22, 1884; January 29, 1884; March 20, 1884; and July 6, 1884 in the sections *Feuilleton* ("Features") and *Dramatické umění a hudba* ("Dramatic Arts and Music"). On the cult surrounding opera stars in the German Empire, see Daniel, *Hoftheater*, 367.
60. See reviews of her performances in Vienna and Prague in *Národní listy*, December 21, 1885. From her earnings, Adelina Patti (1843–1919) bought herself a Victorian castle in Wales to which she had two new wings added. She was *the* world famous female star of the late nineteenth century and performed in all major European cities and beyond.
61. The exact amounts taken are listed in Šubert, *Dějiny*, appendix, XXIII. Šubert's list of daily takings between 1883 and 1900 is a unique source, the equivalent of which is unfortunately lacking for other theaters.
62. See also *Národní listy*, December 23, 1901, 3.
63. One deceived and irate husband from Saxony even followed Burian to Prague, where the tenor was placed under police protection. See *Národní listy*, April 1, 1911, 3.

64. *Národní listy*, January 8, 1888, 1.
65. The Austrian cultural historian Moritz Csáky has written a convincing assessment and defence of operetta. See Csáky, *Ideologie der Operette*, especially 17–24. On the conflicts surrounding operetta, see also the case studies in this book and part 5.

Part Two

The Royal Theater in Dresden

CHAPTER ONE

Organization and Control of the Royal Theater

The Tradition and Re-inception of the Royal Theater

Even in appearance, the royal theaters of the eighteenth century were unlike the grand opera theaters to come. Often integrated into the royal residence or, as in Vienna, Berlin, and Dresden, situated conveniently close by, they were by no means public institutions. Their primary function was to entertain the court and its guests and to provide a platform for the royal families. Each major European court vied with the next to host events with the best musicians and star singers.

The royal seat of Dresden became renowned for its theater in the eighteenth century. The Saxon princes, until 1763 also rulers of Poland, had a passion for lavish baroque display. Under August the Strong and his successors, opera performances featuring the best Italian singers could turn into celebrations lasting several days. The director of the royal theater was a *directeur des plaisirs*: his duty was to entertain the court, whatever it took.[1] Theater interiors were tailored to suit the court and its rulers. Seating was arranged in a classic horseshoe shape so that the centrally positioned royal box could be seen at least as well as the stage from most seats.

Even the stage was used for purposes of royal display. As Matthew Wikander describes in his book *Princes to Act*, kings and their families frequently took to the stage themselves. These episodes served to relax the strict court protocol and test moral and political boundaries. In the aftermath of the French Revolution, royalty abandoned such dilletantist pastimes but resumed them again in the Restoration period after 1815. The Saxon Wettin dynasty stood out as particularly active lovers of music theater. King Anton, who reigned 1829–1836, was a prolific composer, contributing dozens of volumes to the royal music collection. His successor, Friedrich August II, was formally trained in music and an excellent bass who sang at minor theater performances until his accession to the throne in 1836.[2] Princess Amalie, who received her musical training from Carl Maria von Weber, wrote cantatas and short operas from a young age. One of her compositions, the "Flag of Victory" (*Siegesfahne*) was performed at the royal theater in 1834.

Like the Habsburgs, the Wettins were closely involved in the running of the theater. Right up until the mid-nineteenth century, Kings Friedrich August II and Johann I appointed and dismissed conductors, soloists, and musicians, awarded pay rises and influenced performance schedules. The convenience of the royal family could play a decisive role in the fate of a work, as Richard Wagner was to find out. He conducted his first major opera, the over four-hour long work *Rienzi*, shortly after his appointment as Principal Conductor in Dresden. As the aging princesses Amalie and Augusta were not willing to remain seated for so long, the opera was divided into two parts. The first two acts were coupled under the heading "Rienzi's Greatness" (*Rienzis Größe*) and the remaining three acts[3], for which Wagner was obliged to compose an additional overture, were performed the following evening. This incident illustrates the imbalance of power at the royal theater. But while Wagner complied in this instance, he resisted the many sacred duties the orchestra and opera choir were expected to perform in the royal chapel. The increasing confidence of nineteenth-century artists, and their conviction that art should be autonomous, was beginning to clash with the traditional royal theater and its power hierarchy.

Artists and intellectuals in prerevolutionary Dresden asserted their creative prerogative much more than those in Vienna or Berlin. The process of change that this triggered—toward professionalism in the theater—is discussed in the following chapter. How was a royal theater, established with the sole aim of pleasing the monarch and the royal court, transformed into a professionally run, public institution from the 1860s? What factors contributed to Dresden becoming a center of German opera, first under Richard Wagner in the 1840s, then in the early days of the German Empire and again after 1900 at the dawn of musical modernism? These questions can only be answered in the light of the social and political contexts of the time. In other words, one must look at the history of Saxony to understand the development of German opera.

Ironically, the triumphant rise of Dresden's royal theater in the nineteenth century began with Saxony's catastrophic defeat in the Napoleonic Wars. After the Battle of Nations at Leipzig in 1813, Prussia and Russia made Saxony a *gouvernement* under the Russian prince Repnin-Wolkonski. A foretaste of the occupation rule of the twentieth century, this arrangement enabled the authorities to exploit the region's manpower and material resources at the same time as establishing order in a land that was ravaged by war.[4] At the Congress of Vienna two years later, Saxony lost half its territory and was reduced to a medium-sized state (*Mittelstaat*).

With the support of Saxon advocates of the Enlightenment, Repnin-Wolkonski initiated a number of reforms during his tenure as governor, which he and other members of the Russian nobility had previously championed in Tsarist Russia. He believed the monarchy should fundamentally alter its relationship to its subjects, and gained enduring popularity in Dresden by opening the main royal garden to the general public. Inspired by recent theater reforms in Russia, he also ensured that the court retained control of the theater and the royal orchestra, rather than leasing them to an impresario.

On his return to Dresden in 1815, King Friedrich August overturned some of Repnin-Wolkonski's administrative reforms but approved the changes at the royal theater—his most renowned cultural institution—and continued to invest in it. Count Vitzthum von Eckstädt was appointed General Director of the royal theater and orchestra. He promptly wooed Carl Maria von Weber away from Prague's Estates Theater to run a new German opera ensemble, which was established in 1817, supplementing the Italian opera. Vitzthum's actions were motivated by political as well as artistic considerations. A year previously, he had urged the king that "Saxony should now more than ever use the means at its disposal to distinguish itself by promoting the arts and sciences, as every other manner of gaining fame and standing is lost to us."[5] To him, an active cultural policy was the only way to compensate for Saxony's political relegation.

The vision of Saxony as a cultural prime mover motivated the Saxon government to also invest in other institutions including the art academy, picture gallery and academic colleges.[6] The newspaper *Dresdner Abend Zeitung*, edited by Friedrich Kind and Theodor Winkler, became a leading German-language journal for literature. Ludwig Tieck's salon drew Hegel and other illustrious visitors to the city on the Elbe. Ernst Rietschel, a prominent sculptor of the day, Ludwig Richter, a renowned painter, and the still young architect Gottfried Semper occupied important positions in the city's various royal and state cultural institutions.[7] As a major center of art and learning in the German lands, Dresden was able to maintain some of its historical influence on Poland stemming from the Polish-Saxon union, 1697–1763, and it attracted many Polish refugees fleeing punishment after the quashed uprisings of 1830–31 and 1863.[8] Richard Wagner noted with respect that the Polish "theater aristocracy" could clinch the success of an opera performance.[9] Dresden also cultivated close links with Prague and Vienna, and these rapidly intensified after completion of the railroad to Bohemia.

Two years after his accession to the throne, King Friedrich August II (1836–1854) commissioned academy professor Gottfried Semper with the construction of a new royal theater. Semper had previously distinguished himself by designing a number of smaller buildings and an expansive public forum linking the ward (*Zwinger*), the palace, the Brühl Terraces and the Elbe, thereby creating a symbolic bond between the old monarchy and the rising middle class. A convinced liberal, Semper designed one of the most sociopolitically significant theaters of his day.[10] While keeping the formal requirements of a royal theater, such as a separate entrance for the monarch and a generously sized royal box, he added amphitheater-like stalls which dominated the auditorium and allowed visitors of any rank to sit shoulder to shoulder—as at the Leipzig municipal theater. In this way, Semper created the prototype public theater, with the stage forming the focal point and a good view guaranteed from nearly all seats. The architecture's symbolic representation of a more egalitarian social order was especially striking in contrast to Berlin's Linden Opera, which had been rebuilt after a fire in 1843 as a faithful copy of the mid-eighteenth-century original, with boxes predominating, as if society had not changed at all.[11] Furthermore, Semper's theater was to some extent able to absorb the vibrations of the music, endowing it with remarkably good acoustics. In this respect too, then, Semper's "ringing instrument" eclipsed the Berlin Opera and most other contemporary theaters.[12]

Figure 2. Interior of the Semper Theater.

Despite the theater's progressive character, it brought the Saxon parliament (*Landtag*) into opposition to the king. In 1838, Friedrich August II had ordered the theater to be built at his own cost without consulting the representatives of the estates. But the following year he decreed that the *Landtag* should pay, in breach of its budgetary rights. This provoked vehement protests from liberal diet members from Leipzig and other cities. In the heated debates that followed, however, most were eventually convinced by the argument of Saxony's mission to be a center of culture. The king invoked the educational function of the theater and declared it the "glory of the crown" before appealing more directly to Saxon pride: "In all the more highly civilized nations the dramatic arts have played an important role . . . It is surely not in the interest and intentions of the nation to fall behind other nations, whose financial circumstances are less favorable, in this respect."[13]

The total cost of construction rose to 386,000 talers—considerably more than the projected 260,000 talers—and devoured nearly 10 percent of the state budget for the year 1841 combined with personnel costs. In terms of economic policy, this was akin to a return to absolutism. In the end, in a grand gesture of artistic patronage, Friedrich August and two of his sisters covered much of the cost. Thus the monarchy gained a resounding victory over the liberals in a struggle which illustrates the political significance of the opera.

In the long term, the new, attractive theater with a two thousand-seat capacity was expected to be more economical to run than the old opera. For some months after the grand opening, at which Goethe's *Tasso* and Weber's *Euryanthe* were performed, the king's investment seemed sound. The royal theater's deficit shrank to 9,200 talers in 1841—about a quarter of the subsidies required in previous years. This was largely thanks to increased ticket sales, up by more than half compared to 1840. After a while, however, it proved difficult to attract consistently large audiences. About ten percent of Dresden's total population, plus the court, could be classified as theater-goers. With less than 100,000 inhabitants, the audience potential in the Saxon capital amounted to no more than 10,000. In these circumstances, the same guests would have to be enticed to the theater several times a week. As the theater attempted to provide ever more thrilling innovations, costs rose but takings fell. By 1844, the theater's deficit had increased again to 40,000 talers—a record for the new theater—with the orchestra consuming an additional 45,000 talers annually.[14] To legitimize this burden on the civil list, the Wettins stressed the theater's educational qualities, thus adopting an originally middle-class, Enlightenment conception of theater and, like the Habsburgs, using the arts to support the monarchy.

When the first Semper Theater was destroyed by fire in 1869, it became clear how firmly the vision of Saxony as a cultural center and pride in the royal theater had taken root in the minds of the population. Dresdeners urged the government to rebuild the theater without delay, since it was "a credit to the nation, a national characteristic," as a conservative member of parliament put it, sparking heckles from the liberals that Saxony was not actually a nation. No objections were made, however, to a further conservative comment describing the Saxons as the "most cultured people in the world."[15] The *Landtag* continued to approve ever increasing expenditure until the second Semper Theater was finally completed at a cost of 1,184,000 talers. Following the founding of the German Empire in 1871, subsidies of almost half a million marks were invested in the theater annually.[16] Despite the king's occasional admonitions to economize, the deficit continued to grow—mainly due to the rapidly rising fees for soloists and cost of lavish stage sets and costumes. The royal theater came to resemble a bottomless pit into which more and more civil list money was thrown.

Figure 3. The Second Semper Theater in 1878.

Was the royal theater worth such tremendous sums? From an artistic point of view, the answer is a definite yes. The Dresden Opera presented a number of sensational artistic successes in the nineteenth century and in the years preceding the First World War, establishing Dresden's reputation throughout Germany and Europe as a center for the arts and culture. The Wettins exploited the widespread opinion that theater could educate and enlighten to their own ends and used the Semper Theater to show themselves as a dynasty of art lovers and patrons. Emphasizing Saxony's role as a cultural center implicitly contrasted it with the hated Prussian military state.[17] The rich cultural life of the royal seat provided a welcome diversion from the political problems arising in the wake of the failed 1848 revolution. The Semper Opera was one of the few places where the growing gulf between the monarchy and society could be bridged, both physically and mentally, by the universal appeal of the arts.

A Platform for the Royal Family

Since the emergence of the German national movement, the Wettins had an acute problem proving their legitimacy. They represented the ancien régime which had brought about Saxony's ruin in 1763 and in 1813. They ruled one of the medium-sized states on which the German Confederation was based and which precluded the formation of a German nation-state. Not only that, they were a Catholic dynasty in a Protestant land. The constitution they introduced in 1831 helped to consolidate their position for a time. Many contemporaries now saw a beacon of hope in liberal Saxony, in contrast to the military powers Prussia and Austria. In the 1840s, however, unrest grew as further reforms were rejected and Saxony became one of the hotspots of the 1848 revolution.

With the revolution crushed, the monarchy resumed control but its political dilemma remained. A return to the ancien régime was impossible, but so was obvious compromise with the liberals. King Friedrich August II, and later his successor Johann I, therefore tried to engage somewhat with the people and guide their disoriented souls, seduced by demagogues, as they saw it, back to righteousness. The royal theater provided an ideal setting for the Wettins to meet the public. Here they could show themselves to society's elites within a controllable public space.[18]

The curtain was raised on the royal theater's very own monarchy in April 1850, almost a year after Dresden's May Uprising of 1849. On April 23, 1850, a "contest of the gods" (*Götterwettstreit*) was mounted in honor of the marriage of Princess Maria Elisabeth to a Savoy prince. Featuring excerpts of the works of German and Italian writers, the program was an amalgam of various allegories on art, glorifying the two dynasties and highlighting the Wettins attachment to their people.[19] The entire performance, set to compositions by principal conductor Carl Gottlieb Reissiger, was repeated the next evening. It was not, then, a unique celebration but a reproducible art work. In this way, it could contribute to filling a repertoire diminished by censorship and purged of works by liberal authors and composers. More gala performances followed to mark various occasions in the ensuing years. The largest celebration of the nineteenth century in Dresden's royal theater was held on three successive days to mark the golden wedding anniversary of Johann I and his wife Amalie Augusta. The theater was festively illuminated and decorated and the ensemble played special jubilee overtures and prologues, with operas forming the climax of each evening.

Where the Wettins had previously sought entertainment in a courtly setting, they now basked publicly in the glory of opera. Theater-goers could witness the entire royal family in the royal box, enjoying the scene, the atmosphere, and the rousing music. An evening's amusement began with the monarchy arriving in decorated coaches, clad in fine gowns and jewels and waving graciously to the people. Although these were not spontaneous but staged displays of majesty, they conveyed to the public a sense of participation in royal life. The realities of everyday hardship and political oppression were momentarily forgotten in the glow of alliance with the monarchy. The Wettins, for their part, showed that they were willing to adapt to the demands of the ascending middle class.[20] But in this way they also imposed their cultural habits and preferences on their subjects. Royal mourning was brought into the public domain as well as celebration. When King Friedrich August II passed away in 1854, the theater was closed for several weeks, denying the public its usual diversion and underlining the solemnity of the situation. When King Albert I died in 1902, the curtain was dropped mid-performance as a mark of respect, leaving the audience no other option but to go home in dejection.

Figure 4. The royal box in Dresden.

At the start of the new century, the Wettins' attachment to the royal theater faded along with the family's fortunes. Friedrich August III endured a scandalous divorce a year before his accession and subsequently avoided public appearances in the theater. Thus the tradition of art-loving sovereigns died out with the last king of Saxony. Friedrich August III lived for the countryside and outdoor pursuits, shooting 600 deer, 1,200 stags and 23,000 pheasants over the course of his life. This left little time for the arts. Richard Strauss joked that considering "his Catholic Majesty's understanding of music," the lighting technician or cashier could take the conductor's place without the king noticing.[21] Now the seats in the royal boxes often remained vacant. Although the era of active royal theater patronage was over, its role in stabilizing the monarchy at critical times—after the revolution and Saxony's defeat by Prussia in 1866—should not be underestimated. The Wettins' cultural policy was one of the few issues on which they were able to achieve a broad social and political consensus.

Emancipation from the Court

In order to secure the success of the new theater, in both artistic and educative terms, King Friedrich August II enlisted the help of notable academics and artists. Richard Wagner, Eduard Devrient, Karl Gutzkow, and many other distinguished and influential figures of the prerevolution era came to work in Dresden in the 1830s and 1840s, definitively raising levels of achievement at the royal theater and opera. Wagner was an innovative conductor whose interpretations of works by Mozart and Beethoven were groundbreaking. Gutzkow set new standards as the theater's dramaturge and Devrient was one of the best-known actors of the day and an insightful theater reformer.

The Wettins soon found, however, that they could not keep these progressives under control.[22] Wagner caused a stir with his essay "On the Royal Orchestra," in which he called for limiting the amount of church services and intermission music to be performed by the orchestra.[23] Devrient and Gutzkow also published proposals for theater reform, demanding that authority be removed from court officials. These were no doubt inspired by General Director von Lüttichau, who had held his position at the royal theater since 1824, thanks to his connections at court more than his expertise. Indeed, Lüttichau, a former hunting page and chamberlain of the king, had not applied for the position on account of his special interest in theater but because he could no longer endure "the physical strain that my current profession involves . . . and especially service on horseback."[24] While his bid to exchange the saddle for the director's chair was successful, his subsequent path as director of the royal theater was strewn with conflicts.

With their open criticisms, the creative minds at the theater demonstrated unprecedented levels of confidence and self-awareness. They asserted themselves as the experts with the necessary qualifications to run a theater with an educational mission. Wagner, Director of Music August Röckel, Gottfried Semper, and many other intellectuals and artists employed by the royal court actively participated in the revolution in 1848–49. In Dresden, the theater was the epicenter of the unrest.

Once the revolution had been suppressed, the royal theater remained closed for several weeks. It was rumored that King Friedrich August was so angered at the theater staff's disloyalty that he was going to dismiss the entire ensemble.[25] In the event, Röckel was imprisoned for many years, Wilhelmine Schröder-Devrient, the leading female German singer of the prerevolution period, was charged with high treason, and a warrant was issued for Wagner's arrest. Lüttichau, however, returned to his post and proceeded to ban all politically suspect works from the repertoire, including the operas of Richard Wagner. The situation in many ways paralleled the concurrent state of affairs in Vienna, where all critical pieces were taken off the program and the Kaiser revived the tradition of Italian *stagione*.

In Dresden, as in Vienna, the postrevolution period proved to be Meyerbeer's big moment. *The Prophet* was premiered in January 1850 and went on to be staged an incredible 87 times by 1862.[26] It was an opera that suited the reactionary mood of the time, showing political activism in an extremely negative light. It told the story of the Anabaptist leader John of Leyden, an antihero who put personal convictions before the welfare of society and even that of his own followers. The opera contains much bloodshed, not in the course of social or religious strife but as the outcome of lies, betrayal, and jealousy. Insurgent peasants are portrayed as an easily manipulated mass, best restrained. In essence, the opera denounced the revolution and especially the revolutionaries. Contemporary critics praised the opera's "historical accuracy" and were impressed by its mass scenes and opulent historical costumes and set.[27] The antipolitical programming at the Dresden Opera lasted until the mid-1860s. Wagner's works were mostly avoided or dropped after a couple of reprises. As in Vienna, this was a time of artistic stagnation and relatively few world premieres. The newspaper *Allgemeine Musikalische Zeitung* put it in a nutshell when it reported a mood of "cozy contentment" at the royal theater.[28]

Artistic momentum was resumed after Lüttichau's retirement in 1862. Following the death of his immediate successor a few years later, no suitable replacement could be found within the royal court, and attentions turned to Baron (*Freiherr*) Julius von Platen-Hallermund (1816–1889). The former director of Hanover's royal theater had been made suddenly redundant when Hanover was annexed by Prussia and the royal court dissolved in 1866. In view of his excellent credentials and experience, the Wettins appointed him General Director in Dresden, thus entrusting a professional with the task, rather than someone at court, for the first time.

Platen maintained his distance from the court, despite being elevated to the "senior courtly ranks" (*Ober-Hof-Chargen*) in 1873, only ever communicating with King Albert via the Ministers of the Royal House. The new king, proud victor of several battles in the Franco-German War, was much less interested in the theater than the two monarchs before him had been. While Friedrich August I had taken part in devising programs, casting roles and even producing the occasional performance, Albert, whose primary interest was the military, was content to be a passive audience member. The mood within the theater changed. Comparing the new general director to Lüttichau, one observer wrote: "He never looks down on one as a Baron, Chamberlain, or His Excellency, despite being distinguished by very dignified behavior."[29] Under Platen, the theater staff enjoyed far greater artistic freedom. The young director of music, Ernst Schuch, in particular, seized the opportunity to improve the orchestra's performance and increase the number of world premieres. A key figure in the history of the royal theater, he is considered in greater detail in the chapter below.

The main problem confronting Platen was the theater's financial state. Its steady deterioration was to have considerable repercussions on artistic developments as well as his relationship with the court. The theater was run on the principle that when funds ran out, the king paid. In 1875, the royal treasury (*Hofzahlamt*) granted a subsidy of nearly 450,000 marks, plus costs for the orchestra—almost as much as the proceeds from ticket sales. As expenditure was not controlled by a regular budget—unlike at the civic theaters of Prague or Leipzig—the theater continued to make a loss.[30] In 1879, the royal treasury was obliged to supply 150,000 marks to prevent the theater from going bankrupt. And in November that same year, the lavish sets for operas including Goldmark's *The Queen of Sheba* (*Die Königin von Saba*) left the theater a further 80,000 marks in debt. The deficit rose to such dimensions after Platen's death in 1889 that remittances were paid a year late. Even the wealthy Dresden court could no longer afford the royal theater in these circumstances. To make matters worse, its constant overexpenditure was causing the standard of artistry to fall. Since the theater could no longer pay soloists competitive fees, they often sought work in Berlin or Vienna instead. The low morale of poorly paid chorus members and junior musicians and the high ensemble turnover did nothing to improve the situation.

When thirty-year-old Count Nikolaus Seebach, son of the Saxon ambassador in Paris, was appointed new General Director of the royal theater and orchestra in 1894, King Albert's main hope was that he would reorder the theater's finances. At his installation, the Royal Minister reminded Seebach that "the contribution His Majesty is compelled to pay for the maintenance of His orchestra and theater must be kept within strict limits and only drawn upon if absolutely necessary."[31] Initially, King Albert personally supervised the theater's accounts.[32] Remaining firm on the issue, he pledged a regular subsidy of 480,000 marks, raised to 560,000 marks from 1903, barring any further payments. Seebach rose to the challenge, not overstepping his budget and even making a profit some years. Yet the secret of Seebach's success was not rigid economizing—he explicitly warned the king against this[33]—but increasing the number of performances at the Semper Opera. Spoken drama was transferred to a separate venue in the central *Neustadt* district of Dresden. Ticket sales now amounted to 50 percent and more of the total budget—a level which today's central European state theaters can only dream of.[34] Finally, Seebach put an end to the confusion of bonuses, special fees, and individual salary increases. The king was henceforth content to withdraw to a purely figurehead role, leaving Seebach and Schuch with more artistic latitude, which they took full advantage of in the new century.

In the name of economy, Seebach even restricted the royal family's privileges. In 1907 he ruled that the king could only give away tickets if he made up the loss, and the number of complimentary seats reserved for the court was significantly reduced.[35] An invoice from that year charging King Friedrich August the sum of 5,736 marks for revenue shortfall due to a charity performance shows how stringently Seebach pursued his economic policy.[36] If the king wanted to invite people to the royal theater, he had to pay like any other customer. In short, the royal family was now a paying guest in its own theater. In March 1908, Seebach finally gained legal autonomy from the king. Friedrich August invested him with the authority to "represent Me in all matters concerning the general direction of My orchestra and My theater, especially to conclude or annul contracts in My name, and to represent Myself in and out of court within his sphere of activity."[37]

A fundamental change had occurred in Dresden. Control of the royal theater had begun to elude the court with Platen's appointment as director shortly before the accession of Albert I. Professional and opinionated dramaturges, conductors, and theater directors had then begun to pursue their ideas with confidence—even more so than before the 1848 revolution—and displaced the ruling dynasty and its court officials.

The emancipation of the royal theater under Seebach coincided with its greatest artistic heyday since the days of Weber and Wagner. Opera fans from all over the German Empire and neighboring Austria came to Dresden to hear stars like Therese Malten, Marie Wittich, and Karel Burian sing and to witness the newly ennobled conductor Ernst von Schuch in action. The ensemble stabilized, providing Schuch with familiar singers on whom he could rely for his many new productions. The most spectacular successes in the new century were the world premieres of four operas by Richard Strauss, which might have sunk in a storm of controversy had it not been for Seebach's clever diplomacy. *Salome* in particular scandalized the public at its premiere, but the devoutly Catholic royal family did not intervene either here or at the premiere of *Elektra* in 1909. The only objections from above were raised against *Der Rosenkavalier* (*The Knight of the Rose*), and these came not from the Wettins but from Seebach himself. Count Seebach, scion of an ancient Saxon line, protested against the obvious caricature of the nobility embodied by the character Ochs von Lerchenau. Strauss, in turn, complained about Seebach's "moralizing tone" in a letter to Schuch and refused to cut out the offending lines in the first act.[38]

At first glance, the new economic framework, greater autonomy, and changes in the repertoire established since the opening of the second Semper Theater may appear to signify a middle-class takeover of the royal theater. Indeed, Seebach's short inauguration speech, stating that he intended to serve the royal theater "with tireless effort, selfless fulfillment of my duties and consistent subordination of any personal interests,"[39] perfectly encapsulated the middle-class work ethic. The *Ochs von Lerchenau* incident, however, is a reminder of the importance of the aristocracy.[40] Schuch and the star soloists at the royal theater aspired to an aristocratic way of life, complete with titles.[41] Conversely, even at the turn of the century, members of the chorus and many orchestra musicians lived on such meager salaries that financially they fell below middle-class norms.

In view of this, the changes at the royal theater between 1815 and 1914 should not be attributed simply to a process of *embourgeoisement* (or *Verbürgerlichung*) but more accurately described as a gradual emancipation from royal influence. The royal theater's withdrawal from the court took place in several stages. In the run-up to the revolution of 1848, a new generation of artists sought freedom for art. Wagner, Devrient, and Gutzkow rebelled against Lüttichau—to them, the embodiment of royal control—and tried to gain independence for the royal theater and orchestra. Their endeavors were interrupted by the suppression of the revolution but resumed from the 1860s as the theater fell into the hands of an increasing number of professional agents. Von Platen's appointment as General Director of the royal orchestra and theater saw professional qualification prioritized for the first time. In a striking parallel, qualified experts were now also appointed to the highest positions at the royal opera in Vienna, as only they could fulfill its educational mission and ensure its success on an international level.[42] In the years that followed, kings and the court became less involved in the theater until almost complete autonomy was granted to the royal theater and orchestra under Count von Seebach. This development occurred by a process of modern differentiation,[43] prompted by the desire for artistic freedom and propelled by the dynamism of a professional theater on a quest to educate.

Notes

1. The personal files of Dresden theater directors were archived under this heading until the nineteenth century. See the section *Directeur des Plaisirs re. Anno 1763* (SHAD, loc. 15132).

2. On Friedrich August's singing talents see also Brescius, *Die königliche*, 10; Börner-Sandrini, *Erinnerungen*, 12.
3. See also *Tage-Buch 1843*, 24; Otto Schmid, *Richard Wagners*, 10.
4. On the *gouvernement* see also Gross, *Kurstaat*, 321–23. On theater in the Russian *gouvernement* see Nentwig, *Körners Beitrag*, 25–29.
5. Quoted in a letter from Vitzthum to the government, in Prölls, *Geschichte*, 382.
6. Other German *Mittelstaaten* like Bavaria and Baden also pursued a similar policy of investing heavily in the arts as a substitute for other political fields of activity, especially after the founding of the empire. See Langewiesche, *Nation*, 73–74.
7. On Dresden's significance as a city of culture, see Jäckel, *Aspekte*, 422.
8. Poles could count on considerably more support in Saxony than in Prussia. This is evident in newspaper reports on the Polish revolt in the Grand Duchy of Posen. See "Polens Verdächtigung." in *Dresdner Journal und Anzeiger*, published from 1851 under the shorter title *Dresdner Journal*), April 16, 1848, 1–2.
9. See Wagner, *Mein Leben*, 417 onward.
10. On the significance of the first Semper Opera, see Mallgrave, *Gottfried Semper*, 119–20.
11. On the architecture of various royal theaters, see Lange, *Vom Tribunal*.
12. See Schnoor, *Die Stunde*, 87. On the unique acoustic qualities of Semper's theater see Mungen, *Raum und Orchester*, 200.
13. On this debate see the files of the *Landtag* from the years 1839–40, *Beilagen zu den Protocollen der zweiten Kammer*, Dresden, 109–18; Files of the *Landtag*, 1839, *Dritte Abtheilung, die Protokolle der IIten Kammer enthaltend*, vol. 1, Dresden, 270–76. The constitutional crisis and parliamentary debates are also discussed in Mütterlein, *Gottfried Semper*, 78.
14. See also the figures in Prölls, *Beiträge zur Geschichte*, 216.
15. On this debate see *Mittheilungen über die Verhandlungen des ordentlichen Landtags im Königreich Sachsen während der Jahre 1869–1870. Zweite Kammer*, vol. 4, Dresden 1870, 2708–2710.
16. See the files on the *Landtag* from the years 1873–74. *Berichte der zweiten Kammer*, vol. 2, 97–106. See also the list of subsidy payments 1877–1895 in SHAD, MdKH, loc. 41, no. 25, 40; loc. 43, no. 19, 60; and loc. 44, no. 25, 63. On the amount of subsidies from the civil list, see Blaschke, *Hof und Hofgesellschaft*, 204.
17. On Saxon disapproval of Prussia, see Weichlein, *Sachsen zwischen Landesbewußtsein*. On Saxon domestic policy see also Retallack, *Sachsen in Deutschland*.
18. On Johann's activities in this period, see Kretzschmar, *König Johann*, 25.
19. On this performance, see *Tagebuch 1850*, 27
20. On Germany, see also Kocka, *Das lange 19. Jahrhundert*, 98–138.
21. On Friedrich August III, see Fellmann, *Sachsens letzter*; the citation here is from 23.
22. The emergence of a "music theater field" can be made out here, comprising the personnel of the royal theater and other royal cultural institutions. On the formation of a "literary field" in Paris, see Bourdieu, *The Field*, 145–214.
23. See Wagner, *SSD*, vol. 12, 151–90.
24. His application can be found in SHAD, loc. 15132, 103–104.
25. See "Wissenschaft und Kunst," *Dresdner Journal und Anzeiger*, May 17, 1849, 5–6.
26. Meyerbeer was also tremendously popular at the Vienna Royal Opera. *The Prophet* was performed 33 times in 1850 and 174 times by 1869. See Hanslick, *Musik*, 310; Jahn, *Metamorphosen*, 180.
27. On the context of the creation of *The Prophet*, its political content and reception, see Fulcher, *French Grand Opera*, 146–63; Gerhard, *Die Verstädterung*, 222–27. On the

opera's positive contemporary reception see *Dresdner Journal und Anzeiger*, Feb. 1, 1850, 6. In 1850 alone, operas by Meyerbeer were performed on 37 evenings. See Prölls, *Geschichte des Hoftheaters*, 602. Meyerbeer's opera *Nordstern* followed in 1855 and *Dinorah* in 1860.

28. Quoted in Bartnig, *Der Zopf*, 280.
29. See *Das Dresdner Hoftheater 1888*, 7.
30. See SHAD, MdHK, loc. 41, no. 13, 1–2.
31. A report on his installation in office can be found in "Kunst und Wissenschaft," *Dresdner Journal*, March 7, 1894, 1.
32. See SHAD, MdHK, loc. 44, no. 25, 156–57.
33. See SHAD, MdHK, loc. 44, no. 32, 127.
34. An overview of the budget from 1906 can be found in SHAD, MdHK, loc. 44, no. 40, 111. Annual budgets are listed in ibid., no. 38, 129–37; no. 45, 128–41; no. 46, 115–28.
35. See SHAD, MdHK, loc. 41, no. 16, 93 & 113.
36. See his correspondence with the ministry in SHAD, MdHK, loc. 44, no. 38, 138.
37. Authorization of March 20, 1908 in SHAD, MdHK, loc. 44, no. 6a, 70.
38. On the dispute between Seebach and Strauss, see Schuch, *Richard Strauss*, 108. On the different versions of *Der Rosenkavalier*, see also Schuh, *Hugo von Hofmannsthal*.
39. Quoted in *Dresdner Journal*, March 7, 1894.
40. This theory is condensed in Kocka, *Das lange 19. Jahrhundert*, 121–22.
41. On Schuch's taste for honors and titles, see SHAD, MfV, no. 14430, 96; Knaus, *Richard Strauss*, 98.
42. In Vienna, Director of the Royal Opera Franz Ritter von Jauner (1875–1880) achieved total executive freedom in personnel matters and effected the removal of hierarchies. See Hadamowsky, *Wien*, 436.
43. On the development of autonomous systems in society, see Luhmann, *Differentiation of Society*.

CHAPTER TWO

Constructing National Culture

Italian Opera versus German Opera

Carl Maria von Weber's appointment as Principal Conductor in Dresden heralded the emergence of a German branch of opera. His work as composer and conductor should not, however, be regarded as the fulfillment of nationalistic ambitions. To appreciate Weber's understanding of nation and the political content of his operas, a distinction must be made between his Romantic nationalism and the ethnic nationalism of the subsequent generation, born in the 1810s.

Like most cultured people of the age, Weber believed that music bore specific national characteristics. But while he subscribed to the theory of different national styles, he did not link these with any notions of hierarchy. Weber especially admired French opera, regarding it as the model on which to base German opera. His programs, first at Prague's Estates Theater and from 1817 in Dresden, were mostly made up of French operas which had been translated into German. But he had little alternative, since at this point there were not enough high quality German lyrical dramas (*Singspiele*) available to fill programs or theaters.

The first opera Weber performed in Dresden was a production of *Joseph* by Méhul (under the title *Jacob und seine Söhne*), which, with its gothic scenes and dramatic orchestration, was to have a considerable influence on his own *Freischütz* (*The Marksman* or *The Freeshooter*).[1] Later he produced translated works by Boieldieu, Cherubini, Grétry and Catel—all French composers of international renown in the early nineteenth century. Thus Weber realized the maxim he had formulated in his unfinished novel *Tonkünstlers Leben* ("A Musician's Life"), writing: "It goes without saying that I am speaking of *the* opera that the German and the Frenchman wants, a self-contained, complete art work, in which all the elements and influences of the relevant and employed arts blend into one, disappearing and thus, in a sense destroyed, forming a new world."[2] Although Weber favored German-language libretti for his own compositions, translated

French operas were as acceptable to him as German operas. He did not make it his task to establish a canon of "authentic" German works, or *Originalstücke* as they were called.

Weber was not, then. a specifically nationalist—still less nationalistic—artist, as was widely claimed in the second half of the century. The enthusiastic reception of his opera *Der Freischütz* in 1821 was not sparked by any nationalist intentions of the composer but by the expectations and interpretations of the middle class public. It was the "springtime of nations" (*Völkerfrühling*) and the first phase of mass mobilization for the German national movement. In this spirit of early nationalist fervor, the public was craving to see and hear a German "national opera." The wars against Napoleon had inspired a wealth of patriotic songs (some by Weber) but there had hitherto been no work placing this body of song in the respected and celebrated context of opera. In fact *Der Freischütz* is not unambiguously German in setting. The central scene of the action, the "Wolf's Gorge" (*Wolfsschlucht*) is situated in a thoroughly Czech part of western Bohemia. Having worked as principal conductor at Prague's Estates Theater, Weber was certainly aware of this, but he belonged to a generation with widely divergent views on where to locate the German nation. He apparently included the Kingdom of Bohemia in it.[3] Unlike later "national operas" *Der Freischütz*, contained no clear reference to the nation's history, no direct appeal to patriotic sentiments, and no battle scenes or comparable dramatic devices. The chief national element of Weber's opera—a *Singspiel* containing a large proportion of spoken dialogue—was the language.[4] Audiences delighted not only in the use of their native language but also in the emotiveness and spontaneity of the commoner protagonist Max, a personification of Romantic ideals. This and other nineteenth century operas were popular successes because they reflected the middle class world of the audience and addressed its hopes for political and social change on the stage.

After his premature death, Weber came to be erroneously regarded in Dresden and throughout Germany as the founder of German national opera. From a combination of popular reference points—*Der Freischütz* as the first supposed German national opera, the songs which Weber had composed during the Wars of Liberation, his work as director of the German opera in Dresden—he was posthumously stylized a national hero, an image which was reinforced by tales of his suffering at the hands of an unpatriotic court and Italian scheming at the royal theater.[5] The role of villain was conferred on the hook-nosed director of the Italian opera, Francesco Morlacchi. Many accounts told of the Italian opera director putting obstacles in Weber's path and begrudging him his success (similar narratives exist about the "evil" Salieri in Vienna, who supposedly opposed Mozart and German-language operas). However, recent research on the Dresden Opera in the nineteenth century has shown that the alleged rivalry between Weber and Morlacchi—between German and Italian opera—has been exaggerated. In fact, the two chief conductors cultivated a generally supportive relationship and disputes were rare.[6]

Without Weber, the genre of German opera entered a crisis.[7] The gothic romance of the kind portrayed in *Der Freischütz* became outmoded and the popularity of German operas, with their high proportion of spoken dialogue, began to fade in comparison to the melodious works of Rossini, Bellini and Donizetti.[8] Later, when "Rossini fever" and the fashion for Belcanto subsided, French grand opera arrived in Germany. *La Muette de Portici* was performed more than fifteen times in the year after its premiere. Richard Wagner was not entirely wrong when, in his essay "On the Nature of German Music" (*Über deutsches Musikwesen*), he categorically accused German composers of a "stupid lack of self-confidence."[9]

Richard Wagner in Dresden

Shortly after Wagner had written this paper in Paris, his opera *Rienzi*, which Giacomo Meyerbeer personally recommended to the King of Saxony, was premiered in Dresden. With its many borrowings from French grand opera, it was favorably received, and soon afterward Wagner was appointed Principal Conductor. A good year after taking up his post, Wagner staged the most successful performance of his entire tenure in Dresden. This, however, took place outside the theater. Despite the skepticism of Weber's widow and the resistance of Wagner's superior, Lüttichau, he had Carl Maria von Weber's remains transported back to Dresden from London. The ship entrusted with this task, strikingly decorated with black garlands, was met at the mooring by torch-bearers and an eighty-man brass and woodwind orchestra. They played two funeral marches, composed by Wagner of motifs from Weber's opera *Euryanthe*, as they accompanied the coffin to the Catholic cemetery in Dresden's *Friedrichstadt* district. A throng of black-clad ladies—singers of the royal theater—was waiting in the chapel "and, as the coffin was set down between them, silently, with tears in their eyes, [they] laid laurel leaves and everlasting wreaths upon the same." The body was laid in state for a day to allow the dramatic tension to rise before the climax of the burial. In a speech given at the still open grave, Wagner called out, "Never has a more German (*deutscherer*) musician lived than you!"[10]

In this first step toward establishing a pantheon of dead national heroes, Wagner took the role of defender of a German music tradition[11] which extended from Mozart and Beethoven to Weber and—he anticipated, with no false modesty—himself. In this capacity, he set about implementing changes which helped the German opera in Dresden reach new heights of popularity. By increasing the proportion of German works on the program and having the remaining Italian-sung operas translated and performed in German[12], Wagner achieved the "nationalization" not only of the language of opera but also of the repertoire.

His own works, however, met with a subdued response. The Dresden audience found *Der Fliegende Hollaender* (*The Flying Dutchman*) too lyrical at the cost of drama and it was dropped after only four performances.[13] *Tannhäuser*, with its subtitle evoking the legendary medieval minnesingers' meeting (*The Singers' Contest at the Wartburg*) seemed to hold more promise, suggesting parellels with the popular choral movement of the day. It also contained a number of patriotic songs, fulfilling a demand which Wagner had himself formulated in an essay.[14] It portrayed the Germans as a nation of singers and brought the myth of the musical nation to life on stage. This work had the potential, then, to supersede *Der Freischütz* as the epitome of national opera. King Friedrich August generously supported the performance, donating 8000 talers for the stage sets by Parisian designer Édouard Despléchin.

Much to the king's and Wagner's disappointment, however, the opera was not a resounding success. The Dresden public could not identify with the eponymous hero's philosophical dilemma—torn between a virtuous life and sensual temptation—and viewed his withdrawal from the world in the third act with skepticism. The conventional scenes in the second act, however, featuring alternating solos, choral and orchestral parts, were warmly received.[15] Contemporary audiences were accustomed to the emotional, romantic arias of grand opera and expected thrilling ensemble scenes performed against the background of social or national strife.[16] They were not prepared for Wagner's psychographic plot and music reflecting the sound of the German language. Consequently, *Tannhäuser* was dropped after a further five performances.

Wagner wasted no time in writing and composing his next opera, *Lohengrin*, while also writing the first draft for *Meistersinger von Nürnberg (Mastersingers of Nuremberg)*. Today *Lohengrin* is known as a Romantic opera with a fantastical love story. But this opera also contains a political element which is rarely appreciated today. When the action begins, King Heinrich is struggling to keep the German Empire together. He is supported by Lohengrin, acclaimed by the people as Heinrich's potential successor. Audiences certainly read this as an allusion to the contemporary liberal demand for the democratic legitimization of the monarchy. Similarly, they might have seen the figure of Heinrich—historically, the first ruler of Saxony to also become German king, thus uniting a regional Saxon identity with a national German one—as a model for Friedrich August II. The hope that he would lead the individual states of the German Confederation toward unification was widespread among liberals at the time. *Lohengrin* portrays an imperial German nation[17], with men of various German tribes swearing allegiance to Heinrich while "striking their weapons."[18] Although the focus then shifts to the tragic love affair between Lohengrin and Elsa, it remains within the context of a Saxon-German national opera, and Lohengrin prophesies a brilliant future for the German Empire before finally disappearing in his swan-boat. This work, then, even better fulfilled the criteria of a national opera. Yet the increasingly bitter conflicts between Wagner and director Lüttichau and the events leading up to and following the revolution prevented *Lohengrin*'s premiere in Saxony. It was not until eleven years later, in 1859, when the circumstances of its performance and reception were very different, that it was performed in Dresden for the first time.

This opera looked both ahead to Germany's future and back at the history of the nation in a dim and distant past. In the Romantic view of history held by Wagner, the *Lohengrin* myth was in some respect more authentic than positivist historical science as it stemmed from the heart of the people. Its claim to authenticity was reflected in the stage sets, which offered naturalistic views of the banks of the Scheldt and medieval Antwerps. In this way a medieval legend was blended with historical fact and presented as a tangible experience on the stage. Taking inspiration from an imagined national past, Wagner innovatively harnessed national subject matter for the opera. His "invention of tradition" was intensified by the very distinctive sound of his German language-orientated music (or *Sprachtonfall*).

Wagner applied his creative energy not only to the art form of opera but also to the institution of the opera. Although the royal theater had moved to the new site of the first Semper Theater in 1841, its internal organization remained the same. The royal family and Lüttichau, who was addressed as His Excellency, still held the reins of power. Wagner began directing his efforts toward freeing the orchestra from its many sacred duties at court to allow it to concentrate on the theater.[19] Although he argued plausibly that this would improve the orchestra's performance, Lüttichau flatly refused to even listen to Wagner's suggestions as, in his view, the principal conductor—one of the lowest ranks at court—had no place devising plans for one of the most distinguished royal institutions.[20]

Undeterred, in 1848 Wagner wrote a "proposal for the organization of a German national theater for the kingdom of Saxony."[21] In it, he argued once again for the separation of court and theater which, he insisted, should be the responsibility of the ministry of education and the arts. But Wagner did not confine his plans to Dresden. He envisioned an association of state-subsidized national theaters throughout Saxony which would have a monopoly on theater performances. Dresden was to lead the association, while the Leipzig Theater would be run as a subsidiary. In short, he was proposing the establishment of state control over theaters in Saxony—literally nationalizing them—to the detriment of independent theaters and especially the Leipzig Municipal Theater.[22]

Furthermore, Wagner proposed turning the royal orchestra into the German National Institute for Music, Dresden, no longer to perform works by Rossini, Bellini, Donizetti, Auber, or Adam, which Wagner regarded as the root of "effete, frivolous taste," but operas by "more contemporary and lesser known composers" who would join together in a Society of all Composers of the Fatherland.[23]

This society would negotiate the price of new operas with theater directors, resulting in a national cartel and a national repertoire, cleansed of all Italian and French competition. Wagner supported the nationalization of opera not only on patriotic grounds but also to protect his own interests. His ideas were later echoed by developments at Prague's Provisional Theater and National Theater.

Soon Wagner was being drawn ever more into the maelstrom of the revolution. At a meeting of the "fatherland society" on June 14, 1848, he made an inflammatory speech in favor of revolution while also extolling the monarchy as the best system for Saxony.[24] Lüttichau would have dismissed him immediately but Wagner wrote directly to the king appealing for clemency, which was granted. That summer, however, Wagner requested leave and traveled to Prague where his associate at the Estates Theater, Jan Bedřich Kittl, had set *Bianca und Guiseppe oder die Franzosen vor Nizza* to music. In an example of the close cooperation between Prague and Dresden, Wagner had supplied the libretto for this "revolution opera," which was performed at the Estates Theater from February 1848.[25] From Prague, Wagner traveled to Vienna where he tried to disseminate his ideas on national theater. But shortly after the Viennese newspaper *Wiener Abendzeitung* of July 20, 1848, mockingly asked: "Is there nothing to reorganize in Dresden?" Wagner returned, frustrated, to Saxony.[26] While his position there was already threatened by growing debts and Lüttichau's hostility, it was the revolution that brought his tenure to an abrupt end. Spurned on by the anarchist Bakunin and music director Röckel, Wagner took part in the May Uprising of 1849 but managed to flee just as the Prussian troops moved into Dresden to suppress the insurgency.

Legend has it that Spontini, former director of the Berlin Opera, on hearing of Wagner's involvement in the revolution, called out in dismay "What ingratitude!"[27] Indeed, King Friedrich August had generously supported Wagner in times of personal need and as an artist. In the king's eyes, Wagner was a traitor who deserved to be punished. King Johann, who succeeded Friedrich August after his death in 1854, continued to bear deep resentment toward the former revolutionary. And Count Friedrich Beust, the longstanding Prime Minister of Saxony, not only disapproved of Wagner's politics but also had an "unconcealed aversion to Wagnerian music," as he wrote in his memoirs.[28]

The ambitious young composer clashed with the haughty court officials, especially Lüttichau, to some extent due to personal differences. But conflicting interests within the organization of the royal theater and other court institutions caused additional tension. The Wettins relied on experts to run their theater effectively but demanded that they submit to the strict court hierarchy. The royal orchestra was expected to maintain the highest musical standards and be able to perform any given opera yet at the same time forced to devote much time to routine duties in the royal chapel. Wagner attempted to break these chains with his proposals for reforms. By calling for the royal theater and orchestra to be released from their courtly functions, and for music to be free to serve itself, he was anticipating later concepts of "art for art's sake."

Conflicting ideas of nation widened the gulf between the court and Wagner along with other artists and academics in the service of the royal family. Although Wagner certainly had a sense of allegiance to Saxony, he welcomed the prospect of a unified German nation. Turning the royal theater in Dresden into a "German national institute for music," and the royal orchestra into a nationalized music institution, was not, however, in the Wettins' or Lüttichau's interests. To them, these institutions were the proud achievements of their dynasty and state alone.

The progressive visions for the royal theater, moreover, encroached directly on the political sphere. Saxony, where there was a limited degree of public participation in politics thanks to the constitution of 1831, may have seemed liberal compared to Prussia or Austria. But had the Wettins actually handed over control of the royal theater to Wagner, Devrient and Gutzkow, and dismissed the court officials, it would have had repercussions for the power structure of the entire state. The Wettins were not ready for such far-reaching changes in cultural policy. Wagner's futile attacks on the status quo, which climaxed in his active involvement in the revolution, illustrate the fate of a generation of intellectuals who began their careers working for the state and royal institutions but later turned away from them. Nevertheless, Wagner left a lasting legacy in Dresden by "nationalizing" opera in terms of singing language, repertoire and especially by his "invention of tradition."

Singing for National Unity

With no one to fill the creative void he left, Wagner's exile put an end to this flowering of German opera. Other prominent composers in Saxony, such as Albert Lortzing and Otto Nicolai, had passed away, Heinrich Marschner had past his peak and Count Friedrich von Flotow wrote mainly comic operas. While the Beust government maintained a firm stance against Wagner, issuing a renewed warrant of apprehension in 1853, on a cultural level it was increasingly difficult to suppress him. In the mid-1850s *Lohengrin* was performed regularly in Breslau, Leipzig and other major cities with a strong civic identity. Prague's Estates Theater mounted the first Wagner cycle in 1856. News of the success of *Lohengrin* in neighboring cities reached the Dresden public, partly via the flourishing music press, and the Semper Opera could no longer ignore Wagner's work. *Lohengrin* was finally performed in Dresden in 1859. The progovernment newspaper *Dresdner Journal* marked the occasion by devoting an entire page to the piece and its composer. While the article criticized Wagner's personal conduct and especially his Zurich publications, it praised his music for its "truth of expression, inwardness of feeling and rich description in detail, the powerful atmosphere and romantic musical artistry with particular sensory appeal, surprising innovation and force of instrumental shading."[29]

Dresden's now positive reception of Wagner's work was aided by a new wave of German national sentiment. To retain their position in spite of this, the Wettins ensured they were involved in celebrations of German culture and unity. King Johann personally welcomed participants to the national choral association festival of 1865, presenting himself to the thousands as a "friend of the arts" and "supporter of German unity." One of the main speakers, Professor Fricke of Leipzig, took the opportunity to declare that "German song" held the essence of the German nation: "Blessed be you, the German people, thanks to your German song . . . O, protect, purify, gain command of this sacred gift. Celebrate all your high days as this day, in joyful, unshaken reverence. They are a part of your innermost, god-given being." All five days of the choral festival were permeated with religious symbolism. Fricke even concluded his address with a pious "Amen." The *Dresdner Journal* described a solemn procession, moments of reverent silence, choral fervor and songs as "gifts from God." The German middle class—the predominant social group in the choral association—had found a substitute religion in music. All that was missing was an exalted figurehead.

German unity was a central concern at the festival. Fricke declared: "And yet, friends, it is the crowning glory to our festival that with every song we play our part in helping to sing together the hearts of Germany toward a greater, much-longed-for unity."[30] The pan-German unity the professor spoke of was reflected in the composition of his audience. As well as many German choral society members from nearby Bohemia, there were a number of Hungarian and Tyrolean choir enthusiasts, and a special train service brought participants from Vienna. The strong Austrian presence would seem to contradict Dieter Langewiesche's view that Austrians played a negligible part in the German process of cultural nation building.[31] In Professor Fricke's words, by singing together, "all classes and levels of society without exception, yes, all those often so bitterly divided denominations take shelter under the consecrating, peace-making, unifying power of art."[32]

According to the *Dresdner Journal*, on the third day of the choral festival, "over 200,000 people" from Dresden and the surrounding area were joined by 20,000 guests from abroad.[33] Although these figures may have been exaggerated in the prevailing mood of euphoria, few other public events in Germany in the nineteenth century approached these dimensions. It was certainly the largest public gathering in Dresden before the First World War. The *Sängerbundfest*, as it was known, presented an outlet for political expression, especially the demand for German unity, through music. Furthermore, singing in unison with tens of thousands of others proved a deeply enthusing experience, moving many participants to spontaneously embrace their neighbor, openly weep, or break into other shows of emotion, with a contagious effect on those who had only come to watch.

After the opening procession, participants gathered in the festival hall where the second, official part of the program began, featuring songs by well-known composers. There were no works by Wagner on the festival program but demands to rehabilitate this best-known—and most controversial—German opera composer were increasingly being voiced in Dresden. Crown Prince Albert liked his music, and Wagner insisted in his various pleas for clemency that he had fallen under a corrupting influence during the revolution. The balance finally tipped in his favor when productions of *Tannhäuser* in Paris in 1861 were repeatedly disrupted by organized French hecklers, causing the opera to be dropped from the repertoire. When it was premiered in Dresden a short time later, audiences eager to defend their countryman demonstrated their support with deafening applause.[34] Wagner was finally pardoned by King Johann in 1862 and permitted to return to Dresden.

Figure 5. Realistic stage sets for *Tannhäuser* in 1866.

In the years that followed, the royal theater performed ever more Wagner operas. In January 1869, it was the second theater after Munich to produce *The Mastersingers of Nuremberg*. With its majestic music, call for national unity and portrayal of the Protestant middle class as the real bearers of German culture, this opera was rapturously received.³⁵ The singers, stage designers and conductor took several curtain calls as the applause persisted after the premiere. Even King Johann, robed and ready to leave after the final chord, stopped for a moment to applaud. *Mastersingers* was performed a further fourteen times in the eight months before the first Semper Theater was destroyed by fire. It was a triumphant return for Richard Wagner, and with him German opera. Subsequently, *Mastersingers* played to record audiences in Leipzig, Berlin and other major German cities.

Wagner took advantage of his popularity to strike an even more nationalist tone during the war of 1870–71, writing satirical verses against the French, a poem entitled "To the German Army outside Paris" (*An das deutsche Heer vor Paris*), and a bombastic Emperor's March. He hoped that his festival theater project in Bayreuth would be supported by the new state. But neither Bismarck nor the emperor offered much encouragement as culture was the responsibility of the individual states in the new German Empire. The newspaper *Norddeutsche Zeitung* commented in 1871 that Wagner should not think he owned a monopoly on the German spirit.³⁶

For many years, Wagner's radical views on art, too, provoked opposition, especially his Zurich letters, written after fleeing Dresden. In "Opera and Drama" and a number of other essays, he called for the total abandonment of contemporary opera conventions.³⁷ He condemned opera's fixation with arias, which to him had degenerated, like Rossini, into a "fragrant substratum for . . . the luxury class," and demanded an end to number operas; in his view, a pointless stringing together of popular hits. He also rejected multivocal ensemble scenes which, he felt, just created pleasant harmonies but made the text incomprehensible. Wagner bluntly claimed that in contemporary opera the means of expression (the music) had become the purpose, while the purpose of expression (the drama) had become the means.³⁸ He called for operas to be arranged around a well-devised dramatic plot. In his view, then, the story and the language of operas were of primary importance, and the music should transport the sound of the language.

Although the search for a "German spirit" and "German essence" preoccupied him all his life, Wagner's nationalist motivations have hitherto not received the attention they deserve.³⁹ Yet his activities in Dresden and his Zurich letters on art are evidence of his determination to promote the nation on a political and on a cultural level. The question is, then, why was he not regarded as the paragon of German music sooner, in the 1850s or 1860s?

The public and many critics in those years were taken by surprise by Wagner's music. Conventional listening habits did not prepare them for the strong orchestration, expressive musical landscaping and highly varied chromatics—for which Wagner's oeuvre was later admired—and they were perceived as more challenging than enjoyable. The extent of controversy surrounding Wagner cannot, however, be attributed only to aesthetic disagreements. His uncompromising personality also provoked resistance. Some of his contemporaries—Ludwig II of Bavaria is one famous example—were enthralled by him, while others, such as the Viennese music critic Eduard Hanslick, were so repelled that they refused to agree on any level.

As the public's various negative opinions on Wagner converged, anti-Wagnerism mounted. Criticims of his music were often confused with disapproval of his theories. One example of this is a skeptical review of *Lohengrin* in the *Dresdner Journal* of 1859, which opens with a lengthy critique of Wagner's errant writings, only mentioning in an aside that, in his Romantic phase, Wagner had not always worked according to his own later theories.[40] Wagner contributed to this confusion himself, disseminating theories that did not necessarily correspond with his musical work. He was, therefore, vulnerable to attack both as a writer and as a composer.

For this reason, it is not surprising that of all his works created after 1848, *The Mastersingers of Nuremberg* remained the best loved. As well as its nationalist and middle class content, its relatively conventional compositions found broad approval. *Mastersingers* contained several arias which quickly gained independent popularity as sheet music arranged for piano and vocal parts. Critics admired the many ensemble and mass scenes and choral parts; in other words, all the aspects that corresponded more with conventional contemporary opera than with Wagner's concept of "music drama." While *Mastersingers*, *Lohengrin* and *Tannhäuser* were also very popular, excerpts from *The Ring of the Nibelung*, which were performed in Dresden in 1875 and 1876 at a number of privately organized concerts, met with a considerably more subdued response.[41]

Germanic Opera

The war of 1870–71 and the founding of the German Empire were accompanied by a groundswell of German nationalism. After the heady mood of victory had subsided, however, Germans still questioned what made up their specific national identity. Bismarck offered the "blood and iron" on which his empire was built. But the liberal bourgeoisie did not identify with Saxony's reactionary government, and the German Empire had no positive founding legend to invoke besides military victory over France. The country's democratic spirit was undermined by the dominance of Bismarck, the Hohenzollerns and influential conservatives. Denominational differences made a religious identity for the nation and state unfeasible. And there was considerable antagonism between the middle class and the working class, especially in Saxony. Bismarck sought to overcome these inner divisions by a strategy of "negative integration."[42] This involved channeling hostility toward Catholics, Poles, the working class, western and particularly French civilization and Jews, at first on home ground and soon also abroad.

In the cultural sphere, Germanic myths and Norse sagas provided one common point of identification. Saxony, Dresden and the royal court especially delighted in the mythical Germanic past. The first opera to take up a Germanic-Norse theme, *Die Folkunger*, was staged at the Dresden royal court in 1874—a year before the Monument to Hermann was completed in the Teutoburg forest near Detmold and Felix Dahn's bestselling novel *Ein Kampf um Rom* ("A Battle for Rome") was published. But the success of *Die Folkunger* was far from certain. Composer Edmund Kretschmer was unknown outside Dresden and librettist Salomon Mosenthal had not had a success for two decades, since Otto Nicolai's popular opera *The Merry Wives of Windsor* in 1849. Nevertheless, *Die Folkunger* was enthusiastically received at the premiere and went on to become one of the most successful operas in imperial Dresden.

Alternating between a wild, lonely landscape, a royal castle and a bustling town square which lent itself well to mass scenes, the opera fulfilled all the requirements of an opulent grand opera. It was set in Sweden, which could be perceived as a further-flung site of ancient Germanic history. The plot focused on the conflict between Prince Magnus and his usurper Bengt, who is brought to justice in the wake of a national uprising. At the outset, the evil antagonist Bengt makes Magnus, the last of the Folkunger line, swear an oath that he will renounce his claim to the throne and live forthwith in isolation under a new name, never to reveal his true identity. Magnus duly retreats to the remote Swedish mountains leaving the throne to Bengt, whose position, however, is dependent on the support of the Danes. Meanwhile trouble is brewing among the people. Men rebelling against Bengst's tyranny elect—surprise, surprise—Magnus as their leader. Magnus is reluctant to lead the uprising because of his oath. But when Bengt prepares to marry Maria, the putative last descendant of the Folkungers, in Uppsala, Magnus and his followers march on the city. Still incognito, he is arrested as an impostor. In the castle, he is looking on a portrait of his mother when he hears the strains of a familiar nursery song being played and is moved to reveal his identity. He makes his escape by jumping off the castle balcony and, miraculously, survives unharmed. In the meantime, in Uppsala, there is open fighting between the Swedish people and the Danish troops. Maria and the last of Bengt's allies desert him and he is thrown into the sea. In a monumental mass scene, Magnus is declared king and all's well that ends well.[43]

Like the story, the music also obeyed grand opera conventions. The critic writing for the *Dresdner Journal* praised the ensemble movements, the rich orchestration and the skilful use of instruments, the lively dances and especially the coronation march, acknowledging them as the work of a "talented, technically accomplished, intellectually assiduous musician."[44] The only criticisms were aimed at the drawn-out plot, the tendency to "broad lingering" in the music and the lack of originality in the piece as a whole. Eduard Hanslick more acerbicly commented that it cooked up a pot pourri of Weber, Marschner, Meyerbeer and Wagner together with a "sing-along style and amateur male choir sentimentality."[45] But it was precisely the trivial, heavy-handed and unambiguous that the public loved most in the early days of the German Empire, and *Die Folkunger* continued to play to full houses even after the turn of the century.[46]

Music example 1. *Die Folkunger* by E. Kretschmer.

An important element of the work's appeal was the set and costume design. The performers' appearance corresponded exactly with the popular image of Norse warriors: stout-hearted and brave, ruggedly dressed, with swords at the ready. Nevertheless, some critics remained unimpressed and complained that the opera and main character, Magnus, were not heroic enough. The *Neue Zeitschrift für Musik* felt that Magnus vacillated too long between whether to keep his oath or act patriotically.[47] But Edmund Kretschmer, a now obscure composer, was able to follow up this success with *Heinrich der Löwe*, which premiered in Leipzig in 1877 before showing at the Saxon royal theater and several other German theaters.

At the height of this fashion for all things Germanic, Felix Dahn, the author of *Ein Kampf um Rom*, wrote the libretto for Berlin composer Heinrich Hofmann's heroic opera *Armin*. The action begins with the subjugation of the Germans by the Romans and goes on to focus on the differences between Fulvia and Thusnelda, Varus and Armin, and culminates in the battle against the Romans in the Teutoburg forest. The *Dresdner Journal*'s correspondent complained that the plot was not as tight as that of Kleist's *Die Hermannsschlacht* (*The Hermann Battle*) but felt this was more than compensated for by some rousing singing on the approaching liberation of Germany, the summer solstice festival in the third act and other impressive ensemble scenes. The journalist praised the music's "dramatic temperament, scenic life, dynamic progress," although the arias were so intense that they often ended in screams. As in *Die Folkunger*, the lavish production and painstaking "realization of time, place and nationhood" captivated audiences.[48]

The term "realization" is a key to understanding the significance of Germanic operas for contemporary German audiences. Critics blithely confused the time in which these operas were set with their own time. Formally speaking, *Armin* takes place around the year 9 A.D. but reviews frequently referred to the characters as "Germans." Modern Germans and ancient Germanic peoples were blended into one ethnically defined *Volk*. In both *Armin* and *Die Folkunger*, the lovingly detailed, naturalistic stage sets and costumes seduced audiences into feeling this was part of their own national history. They so enjoyed the heroic deeds of their Teutonic counterparts that they were prepared to overlook weaknesses in the libretto and the music.[49] As Rainer Kipper noted in his book on Germanic myth in the German Empire, the contemporary bourgeoisie had a taste for "historically mediated self-reflection."[50] On a dramatic level, greater artistic license could be taken with ancient Germanic plots and characters than with those from more recent history or the present.

The popular tradition of Germanic operas played a key role in aiding the reception of Wagner's difficult *The Ring of the Nibelung*. Records of the Dresden premiere of the cycle show that it was staged in a similar manner to other Germanic operas, with naturalistic stage sets, based on those of the original Bayreuth production. Whatever Wagner's intentions were, *The Ring* thus became a part of the Germanic cult that drew a line of historical continuity from the ancient Germanic peoples to modern Germans. This Germanic interpretation of *The Ring* predominated until 1945.

Political interpretations of *The Ring* were rare until World War I. Allusions to the demise of the bourgeoisie, the peril of unbridled power hunger and the dangers of capitalism, which George Bernard Shaw saw in the cycle as early as

1898 and which inform most of today's productions, were absent from the work's performance and reception.⁵¹ This was partly a consequence of Wagner's own newly apolitical course, having distanced himself from his revolutionary activities in 1849 and politics in general. The *Dresdner Journal*'s best known critic, Carl Banck, thus confined himself to discussing the emotional ties between the opera's main characters.⁵²

Since the political aspects of the *The Ring* were largely ignored, other aspects of the cycle took the foreground. The stage sets and technical effects, which Wagner had devoted much attention to in Bayreuth, fascinated both the public and critics alike. The dragon emerging from the mists in *Siegfried*, the forging of the sword and the blazing fire around the eternally sleeping Brünnhilde were truly sensational. The *Dresdner Nachrichten* enthused that "rainbows, thunder, lightning, the wonders of Nibelheim could not be more excellently conveyed."⁵³ Not only were technical trickery and the newly invented electric light put to great effect, but human and animal performers also created stunning imagery. During the "Ride of the Valkyries," Brünnhilde, performed by a rather corpulent Therese Malten, galloped across the stage on a live horse and even leapt over a burning bonfire, which lent an olfactory element of authenticity. The three spectacular *Ring* cycles of summer 1886, which took a record 46,524 marks⁵⁴, restored the royal theater in Dresden to its former high rank among theaters in Saxony. Once again, Dresden was the leading light ahead of Leipzig, where standards had begun to drop since the departure of the impresario Angelo Neumann.

With *Lohengrin*, *Tannhäuser* and *The Mastersingers of Nuremberg*, Wagner completed a historical tableau spanning ancient Germanic history, the High and Later Middle Ages and the early modern period. Audiences perceived these as portrayals of their perennial national German history and the characters in them as the actual forefathers of the nation. Wagnerian myths were popularly understood not as abstract tales or parables, as they are today, but as aspects of history which, thanks to dramatic illusions, could be seen, heard and even smelled.⁵⁵

The success of these Germanic operas demonstrates the enduring influence of the Romantic view of history, which Wagner shared, that historical myths were an integral part of national history. While Kleist's focus on the ancient Germanic struggle for freedom had promoted the notion of an essentially democratic German character, the Germanic cult in Bismarck's empire stressed the idea of ethnic continuity and especially exclusivity.

The overwhelming success of *The Ring* in Dresden finally cemented Wagner's reputation as a hero of the native opera scene. In 1887 the Dresden journal *Der Kunstwart* published a lengthy leading article on "Richard Wagner's national significance."⁵⁶ It declared the former principal conductor of the royal theater to be a "genius" and the embodiment of Germanness, and his music to be the "quintessential product of Germanic spirit."⁵⁷ The well known music critic Otto Schmid, however, observed a "dark side of the Wagner cult that is raging here."[58] He rightfully asked whether a balance was still being maintained in a season (1889–90) featuring six Mozart operas and fifty seven performances of Wagner operas. Contemporary composers also stood little chance of breaking Wagner's dominance. Although Ernst von Schuch tried to support artists from Saxony, performing operas by Karl Grammann, Felix Draeseke and other relative newcomers, apart from a few exceptions—most notably Kienzle's *Evangelimann* and Humperdinck's *Hänsel und Gretel*—new German operas failed to make an impact.

The popularity of Carl Maria von Weber's work, by contrast, experienced a new upswing. In 1886 the royal theater presented a five evening-long Weber cycle and in May 1894, it marked the 500th performance of *Der Freischütz* with a gala complete with requisite festival prologue, written by councilor and playwright Franz Koppel-Ellfeld. It began with the words "Oh, German forest!" and went on to stylize the composer as a hero of the Wars of Liberation against Napoleon: "You boldly awoke the ancient saga/Soaked in your fount of melodies/And in the fierily kindled songs of heroes/Sounded your knight's golden wonder-horn/How brightly the fresh hunting tunes ring out/Which praise the noble huntsman's work pure and free/And ha! How proudly the lyre then resounded/To the sword that the German warrior brandished . . . In times when the credo was to assail strangers/You gave us this work—and we were silent/Every leaf of the forest would speak/And call out aloud: Hail to the Liberator—Thee!"[59] This was, of course, bombastic nonsense. The forest of *Der Freischütz* was Bohemian, Weber lived in Prague at the time of the wars of liberation and the volunteers who fought against Napoleon would hardly have been familiar with Weber's work. Yet Koppel-Ellfeld, a Rhinelander of Jewish descent, was prepared to overlook such details as long as he could increase the fame of a "national composer" and be seen to champion tradition. The wave of nationalism at the royal theater ebbed somewhat when Koppel-Ellfeld was convicted of plagiarism and dismissed from royal service with a "mercy pension," providing the biggest scandal at the royal theater since Wagner's involvement in the revolution.

The near total nationalization of opera since the late 1860s is especially remarkable considering that Dresden had possessed an institutionalized Italian opera after the Congress of Vienna.[60] Even in the 1850s, Italian and French operas were performed far more frequently than German works. But the national movement of the 1860s, Wagner's success and the Germanic cult attending the founding of the empire all promoted the development of German opera.

Changes in performance practice had as far-reaching effects as changes in the repertoire. Imported works were generally performed in translation from the 1840s and German became established as an hegemonic opera language. In comparison to Berlin or Vienna, Dresden was relatively quick to nationalize the once so international world of opera. Performing operas in the audience's native language not only made the plot and its significance easier to understand but also invited greater personal identification with them. Yet this process of nationalization had reached its peak by the late 1880s, after which new innovations were introduced to the royal theater. One person was largely responsible for this: the principal conductor and later general director of music, Ernst von Schuch. He had a greater influence on the Dresden Opera than any other conductor before or after him, and therefore deserves his own act in this book.

Notes

1. See Warrack, *Französische Elemente*, 123. Conversely, on Weber's influence on French opera, see Fulcher, *French Grand Opera*, 73.
2. Quoted in Heinemann, John, *. . . ein in sich*, 8.
3. E. T. A. Hoffmann took a similar view, setting a number of his stories in Bohemia.
4. On the problematic nature of the "national opera" in Weber's oeuvre, see Dahlhaus, *Die Musik des 19. Jahrhunderts*, 59.
5. This view is given in Prölls, *Geschichte des Hoftheaters*, 394–97, as well as in countless newspaper articles and the journals of the royal theater.
6. See Mungen, *Morlacchi, Weber*, 93; Kremtz, *Das "Deutsche,"* 110.
7. See also the pamphlet *Das königl. Hoftheater zu Dresden, in künstlerischer und administrativer Hinsicht; beleuchtet von einem Kenner der Kunst und Freunde der Wahrheit*, Leipzig, 1838.
8. In the 1820s, the Dresden Opera had no less than six operas by Rossini on the repertoire and rehearsed three new works by him in 1827 alone. See *Tagebuch 1827*, 55. On the royal theater's repertoire between 1814 and 1832 see Fambach, *Das Repertorium des königlichen*, 185–316. In Leipzig's Municipal Theater, German operas, especially those by Marschner, retained some of their popularity.
9. Wagner, *Über deutsches Musikwesen*, in Wagner, *SSD*, vol. 1, 152.
10. This event is covered in detail in *Leipzige Zeitung*. "Nie hat ein deutscherer Musiker gelebt als Du!" cit. from Kröplin, *Wagner und Weber*, 339. See also Brescius, *Die königlich sächsische*, 37; Richard Wagner, *Bericht über die Heimbringung der sterblichen Überreste Karl Maria von Webers aus London nach Dresden*, in Wagner, *SSD*, vol. 2, 41–49.
11. Although Wagner gives no indication in his letters of the origin of his idea for Carl Maria von Weber's ceremonious burial in Dresden, it is likely that he was inspired by Napoleon's burial at Les Invalides in Paris in December 1840. Significantly, this was not a political or military leader, but a cultural agent being publicly honored in Dresden.
12. Under Wagner the number of imported operas premiered fell to about a third of the total number. For more statistics on the theater under Wagner, see also Prölls, *Geschichte des Hoftheaters*, 541, 644–46.
13. On contemporary reactions see Otto Schmid, *Richard Wagners*, 18.
14. On Wagner's call for a German national anthem see his essay *Über deutsches Musikwesen* in Wagner, *SSD*, vol. 1, 153.
15. On the public's reception see Otto Schmid, *Richard Wagners*, 22–23.
16. Crossing political with private drama was one of the innovations and conventions of the grand opera. See also Döhring, *Oper und Musikdrama*, 144–63; Fulcher, *French Grand Opera*, 36.
17. On this concept see Langewiesche, *Nation*, 55, 69–74.

18. Stage directions in Wagner, *Lohengrin, Klavierauszug*, 11.
19. See Wagner's reform proposal, *Die königliche Kapelle betreffend*, in *SSD*, vol. 12, 151–200.
20. Lüttichau waited a year before responding—negatively—to Wagner's first major reform proposal.
21. "Entwurf zur Organisation eines deutschen Nationaltheaters für das Königreich Sachsen." A later version, edited by Wagner, of this draft is contained in *SSD*, vol. 2, 233–73. See also John, *Richard Wagners Schrift*.
22. Ibid. 269–70.
23. "Verein sämtlicher Komponisten des Vaterlandes." See Wagner, *Entwurf zur Organisation eines deutschen National-Theaters für das Königreich Sachsen* (1849), in Wagner, *SSD*, vol. 2, 242.
24. See Gregor-Dellin, *Richard Wagner*, 238–41.
25. See also Tyrell, *Czech Opera*, 67. Subsequently, this opera was reportedly staged in several German cities, including Hamburg.
26. Quoted in Gregor-Dellin, *Richard Wagner*, 243.
27. See Kretzschmar, *König Johann*, 16–17.
28. See Beust, *Aus Drei-Viertel*, 77.
29. "Wissenschaft, Kunst und Literatur," *Dresdner Journal*, Aug. 9, 1859, 2–3.
30. "Das deutsche Sängerbundfest in Dresden," *Dresdner Journal*, July 25, 1865, 3–4.
31. See Langewiesche, *Nation*, 207.
32. See "Das deutsche Sängerbundfest in Dresden," *Dresdner Journal*, July 26, 1865, 2–3.
33. Ibid.
34. On this scandal in Paris see Fulcher, *French Grand Opera*, 191–93. On the public reception of *Tannhäuser* in Dresden see Gregor-Dellin, *Richard Wagner*, 469.
35. See reviews in *Dresdner Nachrichten*, Jan. 23, 1869, 2, and in *Dresdner Journal*, Jan. 23, 1869, 1–2. On the public reception of *Meistersinger* see also Liebscher, *Die erste Dresdner Aufführung*, 294–95. On the national content of this opera see Mayer, *Richard Wagner*, 140–42, and Grey, *Die Meistersinger*.
36. ". . . er habe den deutschen Geist für sich gepachtet." Citation from Gregor-Dellin, *Richard Wagner*, 640.
37. *Oper und Drama* is published in Wagner, *SSD*, vol. 3, 223–320; vol. 4, 1–229. A good summary can be found in Bermbach, *Der Wahn*, 167–80.
38. Wagner, *Oper und Drama*, *SSD*, vol. 3, 231.
39. An exception is the research by Finnish cultural historian Hannu Salmi. See Salmi, *Imagined Germany*. On Wagner's preoccupation with the *deutsche Geist* and *deutsches Wesen* see also Gregor-Dellin, *Richard Wagner*, 765–76.
40. "Wissenschaft, Kunst und Literatur," *Dresdner Journal*, Aug. 9, 1859, 2–3.
41. See Schmid, *Richard Wagners*, 37 onward. Significantly, King Albert attended these concerts, thus giving his seal of approval to Wagner's later work.
42. On this concept see Wehler, *Das Deutsche Kaiserreich*, 96–98. On problems of integration in the early days of the empire see Groh, Brandt, *Vaterlandslose Gesellen*, 20–26.
43. On this opera see Heinemann, *Alternative zu Wagner*, 297–98.
44. See the review in *Dresdner Journal*, March 24, 1874, 1–2.
45. Citation from Heinemann, *Alternative zu Wagner*, 299.
46. The reviews also remained very positive. See the article on its 93rd performance in "Kunst und Wissenschaft," *Dresdner Nachrichten*, April 27, 1905, 4.
47. See Heinemann, *Alternative zu Wagner*, 298.
48. See *Dresdner Journal*, Oct. 16, 1877, 1–2.

49. Quite a few more Germanic operas were perfomed in Dresden, such as *Thusnelda und der Triumphzug des Germanicus* by Karl Grammann, which have all been forgotten and are too numerous to discuss here. See on these operas a very recent book by Barbara Eichner, *History in Mighty Sounds*. Another significant event of the time was a guest performance by the Meininger Theater of *Die Hermannsschlacht* by Kleist at the royal theater. On this performance see *Dresdner Journal*, Sept. 22, 1877, 1–2.
50. Kipper, *Der Germanenmythos*, 355.
51. See Shaw, *Ein Wagner Brevier*. Various interpretations of *Der Ring* 1876–1914 are surveyed in Bermbach, *Des Sehens*, 3–10.
52. See *Dresdner Journal*, May 16, 1885, 1. On Banck's and contemporary music critics' relationship to Wagner, see Kirchmeyer, *Drei Jahrhunderte*, 77.
53. *Dresdner Nachrichten*, Aug. 18, 1886, 3. See reviews on the entire *Ring* in *Dresdner Nachrichten* of Aug. 19, 21, 23, 1886.
54. On the theater's takings see SHAD, MfV, no. 14430, 22. This source is one of the few to contain a precise record of daily takings.
55. On the view of myths in Wagner's work as part of history, see Wilberg, 149–80.
56. *Der Kunstwart* 1 (1887), 121–25.
57. Ibid., 122.
58. Quoted in Schmid-Dresden, *Bunte Blätter*, 84. On public demand for more Wagner operas on the program see also SHAD, MdKH, loc. 43, no. 11, 26–27.
59. Citation from *Tagebuch 1894*, 89.
60. The proportion of original German works on the opera repertoire amounted to 58% in Dresden in 1894; a level which among all the major opera theaters was only topped by Munich (69%) and Leipzig (62%). See *Opernstatistik für das Jahr 1894*, 6–30.

CHAPTER THREE

Europeanization and Musical Modernism

Dresden's "Master Conductor" Ernst von Schuch

Conductor Ernst von Schuch (1846–1914) was the first person to leave a lasting imprint on the Dresden opera after Richard Wagner. Unlike his predecessors, he did not compose his own works and so broke with a long tradition of composer-conductors at German royal theaters. In confining himself to interpreting music, Schuch preceded Toscanini (1867–1957), to whom he is occasionally likened.[1]

Schuch's work and especially his cooperation with Richard Strauss are not only of interest for the study of music history. His activities at the royal theater highlight the link between its growing independence and its artistic blossoming. Dresden rose once again to prominence as an international center of opera. During this period of artistic achievement, the royal opera appealed to ever more social strata, even including members of the working class. Simultaneously, it followed a trend toward depoliticization. Psychological dramas replaced social and political subject matter—now the inner feelings rather than the collective fates of the protagonists were explored on stage.

Schuch's career in Dresden began in 1872 when, aged only 26, he conducted Donizetti's *Don Pasquale* for the guest performance of a touring Italian opera troup. His performance so impressed General Director von Platen that he immediately offered him a permanent position. In his first years in Dresden, Schuch conducted mostly Italian operas, including five pieces by Verdi in 1876 alone and his *Messa di Requiem*. Although not as popular as *Aida*, this work carried significant weight in the conflict between Bismarck's government and the Catholic Church (the *Kulturkampf*), proving a strong counterargument against the contention that Catholic culture and music lacked depth. The Catholics in the empire felt empowered by Verdi and his *Requiem*, and it was especially warmly received in Cologne, Munich and by the Wettins in Dresden.[2]

Following his successes with Verdi, Schuch began to build a reputation as a significant conductor of Wagner's work. The Dresden premiere of *Tristan and Isolde*—a piece that was considered too avant-garde and not performable for many years—was a particular triumph. The applause persisted well after the final curtain, demanding several extra bows from Schuch, and the critic writing for the *Dresdner Journal* noted: "The performance was an artistically accomplished one. The credit goes above all to the principal conductor, Schuch, his untiring tenacity in rehearsing the work together with his insightful knowledge and completely appropriate perception of the same, his sensitively invigorating and confident direction." Even the Wagner-skeptic Otto Banck was deeply moved by the performance. He had witnessed, he wrote, "the freest unfolding of effusive sensation, wild emotion, and passion and sensuality, boundlessly intensified in joy and grief, breaking out as in fever or delirium." This otherwise stern moralist even tolerated the infidelity in the plot and praised the "frenzy of love" in the second act.[3]

The love story of Tristan and Isolde struck a chord with the middle class of the late nineteenth century. A degree of political stability had been achieved by the mid-1880s. The *Kulturkampf* was resolved and fear of the labor movement drew the government and the former liberal opposition politically closer. Most members of the middle class had long since accepted the political and social status quo. Public interest now turned away from the sociopolitical subject matter of grand opera and toward private drama and psychological issues. Schuch recognized this paradigm shift and boldly took on Wagner's most difficult work. Where the stage sets were concerned, however, he did not take any risks. These were commissioned from the Viennese studio of Brioschi, Burghart and Kautsky, which also provided the sets for the Dresden production of *The Ring* two years later.

Before opera direction came to be valued as an independent artistic discipline, it was normal for conductors, in Dresden and other German theaters, to oversee this and most other aspects of performances.[4] Works were not interpreted as such, as the Dresden performance of *The Ring of the Nibelung* illustrates. Productions aimed mainly for historical authenticity with respect to the sets and costumes and a faithful rendering of the score and text or, in the case of *The Ring*, of the Bayreuth original.[5] Consequently, successive productions often appeared identical for decades. Furthermore, up to the end of the century, the Dresden Opera was chiefly a "novelties theater," serving a public with an appetite for new sensations. If a well-known opera was reprised, it was mostly to show improved sets and costumes or even more amazing technical illusions rather than different aspects of the drama.

Stage sets were expected to be as true to life (*naturwahr*, as critics wrote approvingly) as possible, and faithfully portray the time and setting of the piece.

Naturalism in theater did not cause any fundamental changes in this respect, since it demanded the realistic portrayal of modern social miseries. Neither did its counterpart in opera—*verismo*—have any impact on visual design.[6] It was not until the emergence of modernism and art nouveau in the 1890s that a new approach to stage design evolved.[7] In this period, the first symbolist stage sets were created, in which settings and their content were interpreted and reflected in abstract designs.

These developments did not, however, impinge on Schuch's work. To him, the music was key and not the text or plot or the themes that could be derived from them. Similarly, dramatic interpretation and visual design were secondary to opera conducting in Vienna under Gustav Mahler and at most other central European theaters. By exalting music in the sense of "art for art's sake," the Dresden opera took up a nonpolitical position, in contrast to the period before the 1848 revolution or before the founding of the German Empire. Even the works themselves contributed to depoliticizing opera. Wagner's operas, especially, were overwhelming and absorbing sensory experiences. It was not possible to listen to this music and carry on a conversation at the same time. This was art that demanded one's entire attention.

Furthermore, Schuch's personal correspondence betrays his own disinterest in politics. He held his high position at the royal theater on account of his intensive rehearsing, convincing performance as musical director and incredible productivity, presenting a total of 51 world premieres and 117 premieres in his 42 years in Dresden.[8] He became known as an eminent conductor throughout Germany and abroad and was acclaimed by public, composers and singers alike. Comparing him to Toscanini, Karel Burian eulogized: "In accompanying the singer, Schuch is unique. You just have to be properly indisposed and not able to move. He positively carries you to safety over dangerous obstacles on his baton, he breathes for you, with his miracle instrument—the orchestra—he dynamically compensates for your weaknesses—as where else is such piano played as under Schuch."[9] Richard Strauss also praised the *pianissimi* and unusually dynamic orchestra in Dresden, which Schuch had gained complete mastery of over the years. It was thanks to the conductor's exceptional command of the orchestra that expressive modern works such as *Elektra* or *Salome* could be performed without overtaxing the singers. From the early 1890s, Schuch also established an ensemble of soloists to compete with the star-studded theaters of Vienna, Berlin, and Paris. While these cities could afford the most fashionable singers, the Dresden ensemble's teamwork achieved outstanding performances too, especially at premieres.

Theaters are susceptible to internal crises, but Schuch's charismatic leadership ensured that any imminent conflicts were nipped in the bud. Aesthetic disagreements within the theater were rarely voiced and intrigues within the ensemble were kept in check. Meanwhile, the court provided the financial support necessary to run a successful opera house and navigate times of transition or upheaval, such as when the first Semper Opera burnt down in 1869 and following Von Platen's death in 1889. In short, ideal conditions prevailed during Schuch's tenure for opera to flourish in Dresden. This is especially significant in comparison with Lemberg and Prague.

Toward a European Repertoire

In one central aspect, Schuch's work was implicitly political: as director of music he internationalized the repertoire, long ahead of other German theaters. While performing works from all over Europe went without saying to Schuch, who had begun his career with Italian opera, other factors compelled him even more to broaden the program's horizons. The intolerance of Wagner devotees, who timed the master's operas and sneered if they were played too fast, was a thorn in Schuch's side. Certainly, Schuch sometimes performed *Tannhäuser* and *Ring* cycle pieces twenty minutes faster than at Bayreuth.[10] Wagnerians expecting Germanic profundity were outraged by this vivacious tempo.[11] Schuch's relationship to Wagner's widow, Cosima, remained cool in consequence. In spite of the fact that some of his own singers, including Therese Malten and Heinrich Gudehus, performed at Bayreuth, Cosima invited Schuch only once to the festival, to hear *Parsifal*. He was nevertheless a regular visitor, despite the frequent jibes he faced there. An incident in 1902 moved him to write to Cosima Wagner to defend himself against "the grotesque slander" that he had allegedly strolled across the stage with a lit cigar.[12] He took his revenge on the Bayreuth folk by refusing to stage a single piece by Siegfried Wagner, although he otherwise actively supported young German composers at the royal theater. The Wagnerians, meanwhile, did not stop hounding Schuch, even marking his death by claiming that he had had no "links to the intellectual heavyweights in music."[13]

As far as the German music press was concerned, no Italian composer could be counted among the above. But Schuch did not heed such bigoted opinions. Having concentrated on Verdi early in his career, he became one of the first to perform *verismo* operas in the 1890s, and later directed Puccini's *Tosca*, *La Bohème*, and *Madame Butterfly*. The composer traveled especially from Italy to attend the German premiere of *Tosca* in Dresden, and was called before the curtain no less than ten times, to the chagrin of the Wagnerians. The *Dresdner Nachrichten* rightly identified this as the beginning of an empire-wide wave of "neo-Italianism."[14] No other prominent conductor in the German Empire did as much for Italian opera as Schuch.

He also introduced Czech, Polish, and Russian operas to Germany. In 1882, Schuch discovered Antonín Dvořák and mounted the first German performance of his opera *The Peasant Rogue* (*Šelma sedlák*). By doing so, he was taking something of a risk, as Dvořák was known only for his instrumental compositions. But the opera, a rustic romantic comedy, was positively received and its composer, who attended the premiere in Dresden, received several ovations.[15] It was an immediate success, not least thanks to Schuch's wife, Viennese-born Klementine Procházka, who sang the lead role of Regine (*Běluška* in the original). The only obstacles to its enduring popularity were the mediocre libretto and its weak translation with many wrongly placed stresses. For this reason, the opera remained in the repertoire for only one year, but it opened the public's eyes and ears to Czech music. Smetana's sensational popular success in spring 1892 at the International Music and Theater Exhibition in Vienna finally marked the breakthrough of Czech opera in Saxony. The Dresden-based periodical *Der Kunstwart* published a several-page article on "Czech music" extolling Smetana's operas in particular: "The Czech opera of the Prague National Theater achieved quite extraordinary successes recently with a series of guest performances at the Music and Theater Exhibition in Vienna. Each review outshines the next in terms of enthusiasm and praise. Incredulity and regret that, in our music-hungry time, works of such great artistic significance and unique appeal, as especially the operas of Friedrich Smetana, are only now becoming known by a wider public."[16]

In 1894, an acclamatory review by Eduard Hanslick of Smetana's *The Kiss* (*Hubička*) at the Vienna court theater appeared in the *Dresdner Journal*.[17] Thus endorsed by one of the best-respected German-speaking critics of the day, Smetana became a permanent fixture in repertoires across Saxony. *The Bartered Bride* was performed in Dresden's Residenz Theater in late 1894 and in 1899 at the Royal Opera. The Leipzig Municipal Theater staged even more pieces by Smetana. Meanwhile, the royal orchestra in Dresden performed Czech instrumental music. In 1891, Schuch conducted two symphonies and a number of overtures by Dvořák as well as Smetana's major instrumental works.[18] Outside Bohemia, only the Viennese court opera under Gustav Mahler staged close to the same number of Czech operas as Leipzig and Dresden.[19] The well-known Dresden critic Ludwig Hartmann displayed an even deeper interest in Czech music than Schuch. He translated many Czech (and Italian) libretti, making it possible for these operas to be performed at all in neighboring Germany. Hartmann was a regular visitor to the Prague National Theater,[20] where he attended performances of all the latest works, and a tireless promoter of Smetana, Dvořák, and the new generation of Czech composers. The directors and assistant conductor in Dresden also traveled regularly to Prague to attend premieres. In 1899, the National Theater sent the costume designs for the Viennese production of *The Bartered Bride* to Dresden to facilitate a faithful rendition of the "Bohemian national opera." Conversely, the director of the National Theater, František Adolf Šubert, traveled to Dresden in 1893 to see a new production of *The Mastersingers of Nuremberg* and staged a Czech version some months later in Prague.[21] In the late 1890s,

Dresden hosted successively more guest performances by Czech soloists and in 1900 the royal theater even persuaded Director of Ballet August Berger to leave the National Theater for Dresden. Berger launched a new trend in Dresden with adaptations of folk dances.[22]

Around the turn of the century, Schuch's attention turned to Polish opera for the first time. Rather than choosing a piece by the relatively well-known composer Moniuszko, he premiered the opera *Manru* by Jan Ignacy Paderewski. As in the case of the young Dvořák's work, the opera was a daring choice as its composer was known only as a concert pianist who had written a few instrumental pieces. Polish opera was, moreover, unfamiliar territory for the German public. *Manru* was about a doomed relationship between a Polish girl, Ulana, and her gypsy husband, Manru, who is torn between love for his wife and yearning for the open road. Despite bearing him a child, Ulana struggles to remain loyal to the eponymous hero in the face of her mother's insistent disapproval and the villagers' collective opposition. Thus the plot centers less round external factors than the inner conflicts fought by the two main protagonists, who cannot escape the character that their culture and society has imprinted upon them. The opera complied, then, with the fin-de-siècle taste for psychological drama and pessimistic view of human nature. The libretto[23] was written by Jewish author Alfred Nossig, who came from Lemberg and later rose to prominence as a writer, philosopher, and Zionist activist in Vienna and Zurich.

Once again, taking a chance on a hitherto unknown composer paid off. *Dresdner Nachrichten* acclaimed the "tremendous achievement" of the composer Paderewski, who was called on to the stage at the end of every act and fêted with "enthusiastic exuberance" when the curtain fell.[24] The audience particularly enjoyed the dual exotic appeal of the opera, which mixed the dances and music of the Gorals, Polish mountain dwellers, with those of the gypsies, and the dream scenes exploring Manru's inner conflict. The set painters, costume designers, and ballet master had just a few sketches of Zakopane on which to base their portrayal of the Tatra mountain setting, but it was enough to conjure up a colorful, unfamiliar world on the stage. Like the music, it constituted a fanciful interpretation rather than a realistic portrayal of Tatra culture. Although it was Paderewski's first opera, he was familiar with contemporary composition techniques and knew how to express different psychological and dramatic nuances in music, using modal harmonies, various easily interpreted "floating" chords, and a similar chromaticism and leitmotif technique to that of Wagner. Indeed, *Dresdner Nachrichten* criticized the number of stylistic borrowings, identifying influences as diverse as Wagner, Bizet, and the "Young Italians."[25] But with its strong song-like element and ear-catching rhythms, it delighted the public.

Following *Manru*'s success in Dresden, it was quickly exported to other theaters, first in Poland,[26] where the premiere caused quite a stir, and later to the Metropolitan Opera in New York as well as to Zurich and Cologne. Political antagonism since, however, caused *Manru* to sink into obscurity in Germany. In late 1901, Paderewski gave a concert in Posen (*Poznań*) and donated some of the proceeds to the children of Września, who were holding a school strike in protest against the Prussian ban on the use of Polish, even in elementary school religious instruction. In counterprotest, audiences in Cologne and other German cities booed performances of Paderewski's opera and it was dropped. This was reason enough for the composer to break all ties with Germany and especially with Berlin, where the press had published anti-Polish comments following a concert he gave in 1893. Even the support of the comparatively Slavophile Dresden public and the high regard which Paderewski and the "genius" Schuch—in the words of the composer—had for each other could not smooth over the rift.[27]

After the 1901 summer break, Schuch gave the stage to another internationally unknown composer, Karel Weiss of Prague. His opera, *The Polish Jew* (*Der polnische Jude*), also reflected the prevailing mood at the turn of the century. Like *Manru*, it contains several dream sequences and is composed of floating harmonies and long, lyrical passages. The plot uses the device of a dual timeframe, with the inner turmoil of a conscience-stricken Alsatian innkeeper who has killed a Polish Jew for his money juxtaposed against the account of his trial in court. The Jew, symbolizing eternal justice, haunts the innkeeper's dreams, tormenting his murderer until he is compelled to confess. It was another intense psychological drama, albeit with a political message, condemning greed, xenophobia, and anti-Semitism. Despite some criticism of the sets and details of the plot, the *Dresdner Nachrichten*'s reviewer praised the opera as "a work of noble, artistically considered structure; as an art work in the higher sense."[28] Schuch and Weiss received several ovations after the final curtain and the opera held its position in the repertoire until early 1902.

The popularity of Czech and Polish operas in Dresden was due not least to Schuch's sensitivity to the music of these countries. His treatment of Smetana's music, especially, earned him a reputation that endured beyond his lifetime. The music critic of the *Münchner Zeitung*, Alexander Berrsche, wrote in his obituary of Schuch: "But how the man could interpret the Bohemian! Smetana by other conductors means dash, swing, fine entertainment. Smetana by Schuch was a frenzy, a whirl, an orgy. When it was over, it was surprising to find that the auditorium was still in one piece and everyone was sitting quietly in their seats."[29] After the turn of the century, the Saxon public's passion for Smetana gradually faded and Dvořák's major work, the opera *Rusalka*, was strangely overlooked.[30] Nevertheless, Czech, Polish, and Russian composers had gained a firm foothold in the repertoire and in the minds of Dresden opera lovers.

Richard Strauss and Modernism in Dresden

The name of this Bavarian composer appears at a surprisingly early date in the repertoire of the royal theater: in 1884, Strauss's *Concert Overture in C minor* was performed as part of a symphony concert. Strauss was only twenty years old at the time and thanked Schuch exuberantly for the "endearing encouragement" which, he declared, he would not forget for the rest of his life.[31] After this early collaboration, Schuch did not forget Strauss, giving occasional performances of his orchestral works and even requesting the score of his first opera—a "Germanic" piece entitled *Guntram*—despite its failure in Weimar in 1894.[32]

Some years later, Dresden was to host the world premieres of most of Richard Strauss's operas. In Berlin, where Strauss was engaged as principal conductor from 1891, theater director Bolko von Hochberg prevented the performance of his second opera, *Fire Famine* (*Feuersnot*), on account of contractual disagreements as well as an earthy bed scene in the final act.[33] This marked the climactic triumph of the loner Kunrad, descendant of an ancient family of sorcerers, who is first lured by the mayor's attractive daughter Diemut, then publicly humiliated. Resorting to his gift of magic, Kunrad takes revenge on Diemut and the entire town by extinguishing all lights and fires. The only release from the "fire famine" is if Diemut gives herself to Kunrad in her room. She does so, spurred on by the townsfolk, who quickly sacrifice their moral principles in their desperation to be relieved of the darkness. The scene culminates in the choir singing "All warmth springs from the body/All light comes from love—From your virgin body/Alone the fire inflames us" (*Alle Wärme quillt vom Leibe/All Licht von Liebe stammt—Aus Deinem jung-fräulichen Leibe/Einzig das Feuer uns entflammt*). This passage sparked outraged protests in Berlin and Vienna. Instead of bringing a Wagnerian message of hope for salvation, the baroque South German composer was celebrating physicality. With this opera, Strauss repaid the petit bourgeois, conformist elements of Munich society, for making not only his own life so difficult but also Richard Wagner's in the 1860s.

In view of the troubles he had encountered in Berlin, Strauss offered his opera to Schuch, imploring him to leave it unabridged: "Please, do not moderate anything: to reduce the opera's biting sharpness would only achieve success 'under false pretences.' I can well do without that: rather a good sound failure and the knowledge that a few hearty indecencies and brain-and-blood-clearing impertinences have been flung in the face of that Philistine rabble."[34] Not only was it performed in its entirety, but Schuch and Seebach also managed to persuade King Albert to attend the premiere in 1901, raising Strauss's status in the eyes of the public.

The critic writing for the *Dresdner Nachrichten* reported "jubilant applause" and celebrated "the invention of an inspired artist."[35] Here was a major success for Richard Strauss some years before his generally acknowledged breakthrough as an opera composer with *Salome*. *Dresdner Nachrichten* admired the music's expressivity, whether conveying the blazing summer solstice fires, the sudden, alarming darkness falling, or the shimmering sound of the light reappearing. Like his earlier symphonic poems, the opera featured Strauss's hallmark expressionism, and made impressive use of an extended orchestra of over 100 musicians, performing skillfully placed dissonances and sudden changes in tempo and instrumentation. The *Dresdner Nachrichten* commended Strauss for having finally confronted Wagner, against whom all composers of his generation were measured. Indeed, Strauss's treatment of his idol was positively postmodern. While showing posthumous solidarity with Wagner—one scene actually protests "You are driving Wagner away" (*Da treibt ihr den Wagner aus dem Thor*)—and quoting *The Mastersingers of Nuremberg* in several places, it rose above the master by way of a collage technique which Strauss later perfected in *Der Rosenkavalier*. No other German opera composer of the late nineteenth century had so elegantly quoted and distanced himself from Wagner at the same time.

Most significantly for Strauss, the success of *Fire Famine* increased his confidence as an opera composer. While another failure after *Guntram* would have considerably undermined his self-belief, he now felt emboldened to forge ahead with *Salome*. Appreciating Schuch's role in this, he thanked his mentor warmly. This marked the beginning of the self-proclaimed "artistic alliance" (*Künstlergemeinschaft*) between Richard Strauss and Ernst von Schuch.[36]

Salome was based on the play of the same name by Oscar Wilde, which ends with the murder—for rejecting Salome's sexual advances—of the only person of any moral integrity. It can be seen to address a number of different issues—for example, society's moral decline and the abuse of power[37]—but for the fin-de-siècle public the most important aspect was the psychological drama. *Salome* offered insight into the darkest depths of human nature. The eponymous heroine's seductive veil dance conjures up a potent image of untrammeled desire which culminates in the spine-chilling finale when Salome kisses the severed head of the prophet Jochanaan. This story, with its themes of love, loneliness, sensuality, violence, and death, corresponded exactly with Carl Schorske's definition of the fin-de-siècle zeitgeist as characterized by a skeptical view of the world and human nature and a vague premonition of the end of society as it was. But it would be wrong to reduce *Salome* to a mere product of its time. Technically, the opera broke new ground. The plot did not follow a conventional progression and the characters did not go through any inner process of development. The action took place at one intense point in time, detached from any kind of temporal continuity or psychological logic. The music broke rules of harmony and was fragmentary, situative, and sometimes violent.

The first protests were voiced during rehearsals. As a "decent woman," Marie Wittich, prima donna of the Dresden Opera and wife of a respectable Saxon mayor, objected to the role of Salome.[38] She even complained about it to Cosima Wagner, with whom she had a longstanding working relationship. Rumors of a coming sensation began to emanate from Bayreuth and circulate the city, intensifying the "feverish excitement"[39] which gripped the royal theater and the whole German opera scene. Although the drama was not new, but borrowed from Oscar Wilde's play, the opera caused a scandal. The press spoke unanimously of "perversion" and the conservative *Dresdner Journal* was especially severe in its criticism of Strauss's choice of subject matter.[40]

More interesting than these predictable criticisms were the press's attempts to retrieve the composer's honor and maintain the construct of "German music." Both Dresden newspapers blamed Oscar Wilde for the unacceptable aspects of the piece while portraying Strauss as an inspired musician. In this way, the "perversion" was externalized and the music embraced as brilliant and German. While the critics downplayed Strauss's provocative intentions—he had, after all, consciously chosen to base an opera on this play—they highlighted his "portraiture of the horrific," "blazing instrumental color," "brilliant treatment of moods," and his "masterful art" in general.[41] Indeed, the cold desire expressed by Salome's clarinet motif, the foreboding sound of the bass ensemble indicating the prophet Jochanaan's execution, and the dissonant C sharp major/D minor chord conveying Salome's subsequent emotional turmoil are still considered seminal today.[42] A shocked silence greeted the final curtain at the premiere. When the applause finally broke out, it lasted more than a quarter of an hour.[43]

The Dresden public supported Strauss, the *agent provocateur*, partly out of a sense of local honor. The *Dresdner Nachrichten* insisted that the royal opera had not seen such a sensation since Wagner's later works and declared it "a masterful achievement by a premier theater, which can not be surpassed by any theater in the world."[44] Saxony's cultural mission was revived once again, this time in a global context. Dresden's pride in hosting the most spectacular world premieres was also palpable at the premiere of *Elektra*. Professional critics, meanwhile, displayed an almost lascivious fascination with Strauss's subject matter. Despite claiming to disapprove of the sexual energy in *Salome* and its offending of all moral standards, they were clearly engrossed by its portrayal of the dark side of human nature.

The same combination of pointed disgust and pleasurable interest in psychological depths fostered the fashion for psychoanalysis. In the same year that *Salome* premiered, Sigmund Freud published his "Three Treatises on Sexual Theory" in which he identified the libido as the most significant motivating factor in human behavior. Hugo von Hofmannsthal incorporated this idea into his libretto for *Elektra*. Both Freud's publications and *Salome* were huge popular successes in fin-de-siècle Dresden. The opera was performed 24 times in 1906 alone.[45]

Music example 2. The dance of the seven veils in *Salome*.

The resounding success of *Salome* in Dresden stood out in stark contrast to how it fared in Vienna and Berlin. The censors prevented the opera from being performed in Vienna until 1918, and in Berlin the Hohenzollern rulers insisted on an incongruous addition to the finale in which the morning star announces the arrival of the Three Wise Men, thus attaching a Christian message of salvation to the story. Cosima and Siegfried Wagner issued an icy wind of disapproval from Bayreuth.[46] The opera was only unhesitatingly adopted in German cities with a strong civic identity such as Breslau, Cologne, Nuremberg, and Leipzig.[47] Strauss had not only Schuch's directing to thank for the opera's success in Dresden and elsewhere, but also his tenacity in the face of internal critics and the censors. In this instance, King Friedrich August's lack of interest in the theater was an advantage. He did not attend the premiere—in itself a gesture of disassociation—but raised no objections to it either. General Director Seebach's campaign for autonomy for the royal theater was bearing fruit.

Having achieved a second collaborative success, the alliance between Strauss and Schuch grew even closer. Strauss began signing his letters to Schuch, "Your loyal, very own composer" (*Ihr getreuer Leibcomponist*) and Schuch responded with "Your own true conductor" (*Ihr Leibdirigent*).[48] Both from the South of the German-speaking lands, they shared a similar temperament, sense of humor, and dialect, and spent many evenings joking and playing cards. Their correspondence provides a satirical survey of the contemporary opera scene. Schuch was sympathetic toward Strauss's jibes about the German *haute bourgeoisie* and court society and took the role of servant to Strauss's creativity, subtly influencing the composer by his estimations of the singers' abilities and limits.

A short time before the world premiere of *Salome*, Strauss came upon the material for his next opera, which he was also to offer to Schuch. It was Hugo von Hofmansthal's play *Elektra*, based on the tragedy by Sophocles, which was

Figure 6. Caricature of Richard Strauss's orchestration of *Elektra*.

premiered in Max Reinhardt's *Neues Theater* in Berlin. Hofmansthal and Strauss went on to coproduce the Dresden-premiered operas *Der Rosenkavalier* and *The Woman without a Shadow* (*Die Frau ohne Schatten*), cementing a creative axis between Berlin, Dresden, and Vienna. Like *Salome*, *Elektra* is a one-act opera exploring the destructive force of the human psyche. The plot revolves around the motif of revenge, which the eponymous heroine takes on her father Agamemnon's murderers. Again, it shows a society in demise. Only one figure, altruistic Orestes, provides a flicker of hope in an otherwise gloomy view of human nature. Based on a classical drama, it undermined one of the cornerstones of bourgeois society: ancient Greece had been extolled throughout the nineteenth century as the ideal on which to base contemporary society and culture, not least by Wagner and Nietzsche in their writings on ancient music drama. In terms of composition, *Elektra* outdid *Salome* in expressiveness, psychological precision, and force. For many years it was considered the ultimate opera house experience owing to the sheer size of the orchestra.

The words used by contemporary opera-goers and even professional critics to describe their reactions are strikingly emphatic: they were enraptured, overcome, exhausted, shocked, and shaken. An unprecedented number of people went to see and hear these two tragic works by Strauss. In the first year after its premiere, *Salome* drew roughly 50,000 visitors to the Dresden royal theater. Even taking into account the fact that some might have attended several times, and many came from out of town, this figure certainly included a considerable percentage of Dresden's adult population of roughly 300,000.

Despite the challenging nature of these performances, emotionally and intellectually, the royal opera began to interest ever broader sections of society, including members of the labor movement, who could afford the cheaper standing room tickets.[49] In the 1890s, Dresden's working-class press began publishing in-depth theater reviews, at first of mostly naturalist pieces in smaller theaters. In 1900, the *Sächsische Arbeiterzeitung* ("Saxon Workers' Newspaper") introduced an "Art—Science—Living" section to the front page on alternate days, featuring extensive coverage of opera productions at the royal theater including news of reprises and guest performances. The placement, number, and quality of these articles suggest that the newspaper's main critic, "Dr. S," who never missed an opportunity to allude to his visits to the Bayreuth festival, was not the only music lover—or opera-goer—in the newspaper's circles or among the readership. Remarkably, the *Sächsische Arbeiterzeitung* stopped covering working men's choir events and drama evenings hosted by the society for adult education.[50] After the turn of the century, a look at the week ahead at the royal theater replaced working class events in its program highlights for Dresden.

This newspaper, published by the later Saxon Prime Minister Georg Gradnauer, adhered to the national stereotypes in music assumed by the middle class, according to which Richard Wagner was the touchstone of opera,[51] Meyerbeer the negative model, and French "formalism" was opposed by a "German style" that "worked with the forces of an internal, spiritual art."[52] The royal theater promoted the embourgeoisement of the working class by agreeing to stage a "people's performance" (*Volksvorstellung*) once a month starting in 1902, for which the cheapest tickets cost a mere 20 pfennigs. In addition, in 1910, the royal theater pledged to supply the city council with cut-price tickets for companies and trade unions.[53] The *Sächsische Arbeiterzeitung* suggested that cheaper tickets for *The Ring of the Nibelung* be provided in this way.[54] Although the Semper Opera was not opening its doors wide to all—the Czech National Theater went much further in this respect—it was nevertheless making a notable political gesture.

The broader social significance and popularity of opera was reflected in the level of public interest in the world premiere of *The Knight of the Rose* (*Der Rosenkavalier*). The commotion surrounding this fourth and last Strauss premiere in Dresden under Schuch's direction eclipsed all others.[55] Weeks before the event in January 1911, the Dresden newspapers were reporting even the most minor details of the coming performance. The rehearsals provided material for in-depth reportage, hotels were booked-up well in advance, and the town was teeming with autograph hunters, ticket seekers, artists, singers, writers, and stage designers trying to make contact with the theater directors arriving from all over the world.

Der Rosenkavalier was less avant-garde than *Salome* or *Elektra*, causing some music critics to accuse Strauss of abandoning the path of modernism and progress.[56] As Michael Walter has set out, however, analyzing Strauss from a postmodern perspective, a different picture emerges. Many sections of *Der Rosenkavalier* are collages of existing sonic images and musical styles, which Strauss sampled and adapted, thereby creating something new.[57] Strauss's intention was to compose an opera in the style of Mozart, using waltzes to recreate the lightness of baroque-era Vienna. Whether the mood at the court of the arch-Catholic Queen Maria Theresa was really so cheerful and light is questionable, but Strauss and his librettist Hugo von Hofmannsthal managed to conjure up a convincing image of a friendly and joyful, mythical old Vienna. The stage design and direction were of a quality and level of innovation seldom seen in Dresden.[58] Richard Strauss commissioned the designs from controversial Viennese stage designer, Alfred Roller, whose recreation of rococo Vienna remained definitive for over sixty years and was copied in opera houses all over the world. At Strauss's request, Max Reinhardt from Berlin was appointed to apply his directing skills to reducing some of the opera's more drawn-out scenes. Since Reinhardt was, however, anathema in conservative circles, Seebach initially refused to let him on the stage and he was not credited in the program. The Dresden opera thus opened up late, but purposefully, to modern directing and stage design. It is to Schuch's credit that he tolerated—perhaps even fostered—these new tendencies despite the loss of influence it entailed for him.

Der Rosenkavalier went on to be performed more than 50 times at the Semper Opera within a year—an unbroken record to this day.[59] Only six weeks after the world premiere, the Czech premiere was staged under the name *Růžový Kavalír*. In 1911 alone, an estimated 100,000 people in Dresden went to see this apparently inoffensive opera about an oafish aristocratic suitor, a gracious lady, a youthful beau, and his pretty, middle-class sweetheart. *Der Rosenkavalier* was also a popular source of sheet music for piano and vocal parts. It is safe to say, then, that this most often performed of Strauss's works was familiar to much of Dresden's population.

Within the theater, however, the opera's plot and characters gave rise to tensions which marred its success. The lead male character is the ludicrously boorish Baron Ochs von Lerchenau, who tries to become engaged to the beautiful Sophie. Count Seebach, the General Director of the royal theater and orchestra, was not in the least amused by this portrayal of a member of the nobility and called for scenes to be cut. Strauss defended himself emphatically, insisting to Schuch that he encountered many such characters in real life. Although this was an indirect confirmation of Seebach's political misgivings, Schuch supported him. In the end only a few passages, alluding to aristocrats sexually harassing commoners, were shortened.[60] In this way, Schuch helped to save one of the major comic figures in German opera. The relationship between Seebach and Strauss, however, remained cool. The latter objected to the general director's supercilious tone while Seebach felt that Strauss was encroaching upon his authority at the royal opera.[61]

In contrast to Strauss's self-assurance, the Dresden middle class remained strikingly diffident. During Schuch's entire tenure, no protests of any note were recorded, although there were grounds enough. Neither Offenbach's operettas with their suggestive ballet scenes, nor the unflattering portrayal of the clergy in *Tosca,* nor the passionate excesses of *Salome* sparked any public complaints or boycott campaigns such as frequently flared up in Lemberg and Prague. A first, hesitant attempt by the public to influence the program was reported in 1877, when the chairman of the Albert Theater's shareholding association, Ernst Jordan, appealed to the royal theater's director to stage more dramas and operas. Von Platen replied that he would "only answer to and possibly have to account to His Majesty the King as my most gracious master," adding that by his mere response he was acting below his rank as general director. In Leipzig or Prague, this degree of arrogance toward the chairman of a civic association would have immediately triggered protests and press campaigns. But the Dresden appellant dutifully wrote to the king, who simply dismissed him as the director had done.[62] Jordan declined to take the matter further and left it at that. No major discussions surrounding the theater—as were common in Leipzig, Lemberg, and Prague—followed. If there were objections to such scandalous performances as *Salome,* the Dresden public and press bore them with restraint.

From the perspective of musical development, this lack of a critical public had its advantages. Although the royal theater depended on its middle-class audience financially from 1841,[63] it nevertheless enjoyed extensive artistic freedom. It was thanks to this latitude, combined with the artistic alliance cultivated by Schuch and Strauss, that Dresden came to host the most spectacular world premieres in the new century, and not the royal theater in Berlin where Strauss was principal conductor. In a precarious but productive way, the Dresden royal theater was "emancipated from the audience" as *Der Kunstwart* observed approvingly, and recommended for all German theaters, in 1891.[64]

In view of this, it is interesting to note the influence that the royal theater exerted on Saxony's civic theaters. The Leipzig Municipal Theater was initially run by a personally liable entrepreneur who was clearly far more dependent on the audience's favor than the director in Dresden. When the theater was placed under municipal control in 1910, directed by Max Martersteig, it was reorganized along the lines of Dresden's royal theater.[65] Now the competition in Leipzig was also a subsidized theater with an educational program to justify its enormous cost. As other insitutions followed suit, the achievements thus gained were moderated by an element of loss: the latitude that opera theaters had previously enjoyed was sacrificed to ensure the provision of highbrow culture. Was there an alternative? Would it have been possible to maintain the Enlightenment goal of serving all of society? These questions are answered by looking at the Prague National Theater, which was run as an institution for all members of the nation. Although the royal theater was officially dissolved after World War I when the monarchy was abolished in Germany, the old structures endured almost unchanged in the guise of a state theater. State officials took over the positions previously held by Lüttichau and his successors, and the Prime Minister presided over all instead of the king. The theater maintained its educational orientation as well as its dependence on state subsidies, which continued to grow in proportion to proceeds from ticket sales.

While continuity prevailed at the Semper Opera after 1918, what began as a royal theater had been through a profound transformation in the course of the long nineteenth century. By the end of this period, the Dresden opera was a royal theater only in name. The mechanisms of artistic autonomy which Richard Wagner had sought to establish ushered in a heyday of German opera under Ernst von Schuch and Richard Strauss, demonstrating that music history was made in the smaller cities of Central Europe as well as in the imperial capitals. The case study of Prague also provides convincing proof of this. Paradoxically, the many world premieres that took place in Dresden were to a certain extent made possible by the theater's detachment from the city and its mostly bourgeois public. It is, then, more accurate to speak of a process of emancipation from the court (*Enthofung*) than one of *embourgoisement*.

Another characteristic development at the Dresden Opera between 1815 and 1914 was the near total "nationalization" of what had been an international art form, in terms of repertoire, singing language and subject matter. This process of making opera national peaked, however, a decade before the turn of the century. Subsequently, priorities turned toward establishing a European repertoire, aided by lively international exchange.

Notes

1. See Schuch, *Richard Strauss*, 50–51. Unfortunately, very few audio recordings featuring Schuch as conductor exist to document his work.
2. After Cologne and Munich, the Saxon residence was the third city in the empire to present this work following its premiere in Vienna. On the public's reception of Verdi and especially his *Requiem*, see Kreuzer, *Verdi and German Culture*, 15–70.
3. Quoted in *Dresdner Journal*, May 24, 1884, 1–2.
4. See Langer, *Der Regisseur*, 9, 50.
5. On the ideal of authenticity, see Dahlhaus, *Textgeschichte und Rezeptionsgeschichte*, 109. On productions of *Der Ring* before the turn of the century, see Eckert, *Der Ring*, 36–41.
6. On Verismo see Dahlhaus, *Die Musik des 19. Jahrhunderts*, 295–302; on Verismo in Dresden, see Lederer, *Verismo*, 32–33.
7. On the definition and characteristics of modernism in music see Dahlhaus, *Die Musik des 19. Jahrhunderts*, 277–85.
8. For these statistics, see Kummer, *Dresden und seine Theaterwelt*.
9. Quoted in Schuch, *Richard Strauss*, 50–51. For Richard Strauss's similar assessment of Schuch, see Knaus, *Richard Strauss*, 47.
10. See *Dresdner Revue. Wochenschrift für Dresdner Leben und Kultur* 2, no. 20, May 15, 1914, 11. On Schuch's brisk conducting of Wagner see also Strauss's comments in Knauss, *Richard Strauss*, 9.
11. On Bayreuth's dictate on how to play Wagner in Germany, see Großmann-Vendrey, *Wagner*, 262.
12. On this incident, see Bartnig, *Ernst von Schuch*, 368–69.
13. See the obituary in *Dresdner Revue. Wochenschrift für Dresdner Leben und Kultur* 2, no. 20, May 15, 1914.
14. On the enthusiastic reception of *Cavalleria Rusticana* (then known by the German title *Sicilianische Liebesrache* or later *Bauernehre*) in Dresden, see Lederer, *Verismo*, 32–33; On the reception of *Tosca* see *Dresdner Nachrichten*, Oct. 23, 1902, 1; Bartnig, *Ernst von Schuch*, 364.
15. See the review in *Dresdner Journal*, Oct. 26, 1882, 1.
16. Quoted in *Der Kunstwart 5 (1891–92)*, 285. A similarly positive review was written in Vienna by Fleischer, *Die Bedeutung der Internationalen*, 65.
17. See *Dresdner Journal*, March 2, 1894, 2.
18. On the close contact between the Prague National Theater and the Leipzig Municipal Theater under Max Stägemann, see NA, Fond ND, Sign. D. 211, 73–87. Productions included *The Bartered Bride*, *The Kiss*, and *V Studni* by Blondek. On the Smetana concerts in Dresden, see Brescius, *Die königliche*, 102–104.

19. On Czech and Russian works in the repertoire of the Vienna royal opera, see Willnauer, *Gustav Mahler*, 48, 55.
20. See the correspondence between Hartmann and the Prague National Theater in NA, Fond ND, Sign. D 221, 28–31.
21. On the exchange between the royal theater and the National Theater, see their extensive correspondence in NA, Sign. D 211, 33–44.
22. He fell from grace in 1910, following accusations of abuse of underage dancers. See *Dresdner Rundschau*, Sept. 25, 1909, 4–5.
23. An English translation of the libretto was printed in *Polish Music Journal* 4, no. 2 (2001). See also the editorial by Maja Trochimczyk, *Rediscovering Paderewski*, http://www.usc.edu/dept/polish_music/PMJ/issue/4.2.01/trochimczyk4_2.html.
24. *Dresdner Nachrichten*, May 30, 1901, 4.
25. See *Dresdner Nachrichten*, May 31, 1901. A more informed assessment of the work can be found in Trochimczyk, *Rediscovering Paderewski*, http://www.usc.edu/dept/polish_music/PMJ/issue/4.2.01/trochimczyk4_2.html.
26. Its performance in Lemberg is discussed in detail in the following part.
27. On Paderewski's experiences in Berlin and his appreciation of Schuch, see *The Paderewski Memoirs*, 165–72, 124.
28. Quoted in a review in *Dresdner Nachrichten*, Sept. 9, 1901, 2.
29. Quoted in Schuch, *Richard Strauss*, 59.
30. This was partly due to its failure to premiere as planned at the Vienna royal theater. Although Mahler had intended to stage the piece, this was prevented by the Czech tenor Vílem Heš falling ill and Mahler's creative crisis as director of the royal opera. On the Mahler era in Vienna, see Willnauer, *Gustav Mahler*.
31. Quoted in Knaus, *Richard Strauss*, 23.
32. In terms of subject matter, *Guntram* continued the tradition of national, Germanic operas. On Schuch and Strauss's early contact, see Bartnig, *Ernst von Schuch*, 370.
33. Having finally been put on the program in Berlin, it was taken off a short time later after protests from the prudish Empress. See Walter, *Richard Strauss*, 174–75.
34. Quoted in a letter of Nov.17, 1901, in Knaus, *Richard Strauss*, 47.
35. *Dresdner Nachrichten*, Nov. 23, 1901, 1.
36. See the corresponding letters in Knaus, *Richard Strauss*, 51.
37. A comprehensive analysis with an overview of performance practices is contained in Piper's *Enzyklopädie des Musiktheater*, vol. 6, 82–89.
38. See Bartnig, *Ernst von Schuch*, 371. With her matronly figure, Marie Wittich was not the ideal person for the role, but there was no other soprano in Dresden with her vocal ability.
39. *Dresdner Journal*, Dec. 11, 1905, 1.
40. See the reviews in *Dresdner Nachrichten*, Dec. 10, 1905, 4; *Dresdner Nachrichten*, Dec. 11, 1905, 4 and *Dresdner Journal*, Dec. 11, 1905, 1. The workers' press was more restrained in judgement. See a review and sensitive assessment of the strengths and weaknesses of the opera in *SAZ*, Dec. 15, 1905, 1.
41. Citations from a review in *Dresdner Nachrichten*, Dec. 11, 1905, 4.
42. On the music and dramatic structure of the piece, see Puffett, *Richard Strauss*; for a short characterization, see the Strauss biography by Walter, *Richard Strauss*, 216–20.
43. See the first short review in *Dresdner Nachrichten*, Dec. 10, 1905, 4.
44. "Eine Meisterleistung eines allerersten Theaters, die von keiner Bühne der Welt überboten werden kann," Dresdner Nachrichten, Dec. 11, 1905, 4, last paragraph.
45. See the statistics in SHAD, MdKH, loc. 44, no. 38, 129–37, 111.

46. On censorship in Berlin see Walter, *Richard Strauss*, 177. In a letter of 1905, Cosima Wagner politely disassociated herself from the work. Later, however, an article in the periodical *Der Turm* quoted Siegfried Wagner as claiming that Strauss's doom-ridden works sullied German theater, and that *Elektra* was an insult to Sophocles and an abasement of all antiquity. See the correspondence between Cosima Wagner, Siegfried Wagner and Strauss in Trenner, *Cosima Wagner*, 257, 278–81.
47. Remarkably, *Salome* was never performed in Prague, and in New York, it was dropped after one performance following objections from the Metropolitan Opera's shareholders. On the dispute between the Met's director and the box owners, see Metropolitan Opera Archive (hereafter Met Archive), *Minute Books*, April 10, 1880—September 1892, 119–38.
48. See their correspondence of summer 1907 in Knaus, *Richard Strauss*, 110–12.
49. Ticket prices were fixed in 1877 at 50 pfennigs for the cheapest standing room and 5.50 for the most expensive balcony seat. For prices, see SHAD, MdKH, loc. 41, no. 13, 4 (in this file there are also price comparisons with the Munich royal theater. See MdKH, loc. 41, no. 13, 7a and no. 16, 1–2).
50. See *SAZ*, Nov. 25, 1874, 3.
51. See *SAZ*, Sept. 7, 1900, supplement, 1 and *SAZ*, Sept. 1, 1902, 1. After the turn of the century, so-called people's performances (*Volksvorstellungen*) were also given, at reduced prices. See SHAD, MdKH, loc. 44, no. 40, 158.
52. Quoted in an article in *SAZ*, Nov. 6, 1903, 1–2.
53. See SHAD, MdKH, loc. 44, no. 31, 115–16; SHAD and no. 43, 124–27.
54. See *SAZ*, Sept. 1, 1902, 1. Ten years earlier the periodical *Der Kunstwart* had called for reduced price tickets to be made available so that the theater could become a "reconciliatory force" between the unpropertied and the property owning classes. See *Der Kunstwart 5* (1891–92), 237–38.
55. For a comprehensive overview of contemporary press coverage, see the "Sammlung Otto Sohrmann," a special section of the archive of the Sächsische Staatsoper in Dresden.
56. After the First World War, criticism of Strauss grew stronger. See Walter, *Richard Strauss*, 318–19.
57. Michael Walter has demonstrated how Strauss musically referenced *Der Freischütz* and Beethoven's Fifth Symphony, among other things. See Walter, *Richard Strauss*, 267–72.
58. See the detailed director's sketches byAlfred Roller in Schuh, *Der Rosenkavalier*, 157–78. On the reception of *Der Rosenkavalier* see the many newspaper articles in the Sohrmann collection.
59. See the review in *Dresdner Nachrichten*, Dec. 15, 1911 (n.p., copied from the Sohrmann collection).
60. For the shortened passages see Schuch, *Der Rosenkavalier*, 218–20. The entire original version of the second act is reproduced on 196–218.
61. See Knaus, *Richard Strauss*, 157.
62. See the correspondence between the chairman of the stock association for the Albert Theater, Ernst Jordan, von Platen, and the King in SHAD, MdKH, loc. 44, no. 6a, 127–28.
63. On the proportion of ticket proceeds making up the budget, which was considerably larger than in Vienna or Berlin, see Walter, *Die Oper*, 90.
64. The relevant article first appeared in "Theater," *Die Freie Bühne*. See *Der Kunstwart 5* (1891–92), 210.
65. See Hennenberg, *300 Jahre*, 93–94.

Part Three

The Polish Theater in Lemberg

CHAPTER FOUR

Social Foundations

The Tradition and Rise of Aristocratic Theater in Central Europe

Aristocratic theaters, after royal theaters, were among the first institutions to stage opera in Central Europe. They were a prominent feature of the Habsburg Empire, Poland, Venice, and other countries with powerful aristocracies. In the rare instances when the term "aristocratic theater" is used in German or English language literature, it usually denotes theaters within mansions or castles.[1] Many of these existed in the Habsburg Empire, Prussia, and Russia. Similarly to the royal theaters of the eighteenth century, they were run as venues for private entertainment and attended by selected invited guests. Some of the wealthiest aristocratic families even maintained permanent orchestras for performing operas. Patronage by the nobility was vital, as the example of Joseph Haydn shows. It was thanks to his permanent position in the Esterházy residence that he was able to devote himself mostly to composing music. The central European nobility also took an active role in founding music societies and conservatories.[2] This involvement in music was partly motivated by political considerations: a lively music scene was a marker of prestige to the outside world and provided a counterbalance to the cultural hegemony of the royal courts. In the age of absolutism, when political and cultural centralism prevailed, this was of crucial importance.

In the light of Polish research and the history of Bohemia, this book broadens the definition of the term "aristocratic theater" to include public theaters founded and run by individual members of the nobility as well as theaters controlled by groups of aristocrats. Another factor by which theaters are defined here is their public. In Bohemia, where only 1 percent of the population belonged to the aristocracy, it was an insignificant force among audiences, while in Poland and Hungary, where the aristocracy constituted around 7.5 and 5 percent of the population respectively, it predominated in theater for many years.[3] It should be noted, however, that in these two countries, and especially in Galicia, nobility did not necessarily equal wealth, and many rural noblemen lacked the means to attend the theater. Lastly, the aristocratic theater can be defined by its repertoire. Besides questions of aesthetic orientation and day-to-day management, repertoire choices were the most hotly contended issues of the day in theater circles. Hence, one of the questions this case study of Lemberg asks is: how did contemporary observers view the aristocratic theater?

Several famous aristocratic theaters had existed in Central Europe long before the nineteenth century, such as Count Sporck's Theater in Prague. The first aristocratic theater to become a permanent institution, however, was the Count Nostitz National Theater (*Gräflich Nostitzsches Nationaltheater*), named after its founder, the royal governor of Bohemia. Similarly to Count Skarbek's theater in Lemberg, this establishment, later to become the Estates Theater, was privately run. When it opened in 1783, it was as expansive and impressively decorated as the best-known royal theaters in Europe.

But matching royalty in terms of architectural grandeur was not Count Nostitz's only concern. Naming his enterprise a "national theater," he signaled his progressive, patriotic aims, which he sought to achieve by staging lyrical and historical dramas. Like most of his rank, he objected to Viennese centralism under Emperor Josef II and intended his theater to directly compete with Vienna's Court and National Theater, investing huge sums to this end. Its renown spread—not least owing to the legendary world premiere of Mozart's *Don Giovanni*—far beyond the borders of Bohemia. From a political point of view, the second Mozart world premiere in Prague, *La Clemenza di Tito,* in 1791—was even more remarkable. The Bohemian estates commissioned this opera, portraying the rule of a just monarch, to mark the coronation of Josef's successor Leopold II as King of Bohemia and voice their expectations of the new sovereign. A hundred years later, the opera had apparently lost none of its explosive potential as the censors vetoed a centenary performance that was planned by the Czech National Theater.[4] Leopold, for his part, accepted the Bohemian crown and bowed to the political and cultural will of the Bohemian estates, which had been a driving force behind Mozart's penultimate opera.

The pursuit of political emancipation also shaped the history of the Lemberg Theater. Set up at the command of Emperor Josef II, the town's first theater was run by Galician governor Joseph Bulla (who actually hailed from Bohemia) from 1784. Sidestepping the long tradition of Polish drama, it initially staged mostly German pieces. This changed, however, when Wojciech Bogusławski, former director of the Warsaw National Theater, came to Lemberg in 1795 after being forced into exile in the wake of the Kościuszko Uprising. Taking up the post of director of the Polish ensemble, Bogusławski persuaded Josef Elsner, principal conductor of the German ensemble, to set Polish lyrical dramas to music. Bogusławski also translated several Italian operas and sang *buffo* bass in a number of performances. Not content with that, he even took over the faltering German ensemble (known as the "German theater") two years later. In this way, Bogusławski achieved in the cultural sphere what the Galician nobility aimed for in politics.[5] His return to Warsaw in 1799 caused a temporary lapse in Lemberg's Polish theater activities. But ten years later, when Austria was at its nadir, another nobleman—Jan Nepomucen Kamiński—founded a permanent Polish theater. Kamiński resumed Bogusławski's practice of translating imported operas, allowing the Polish theater to refer directly to the English or French originals without the diversion of German. Meanwhile, the Polish repertoire was also growing steadily. Since Austria, like Prussia, had justified Poland's partition by claiming that the Polish were uncultured and backward,[6] this independent cultural activity indirectly challenged Vienna's political hegemony.

Without the involvement of Czech aristocrats in culture and politics, the Prague Theater may not have overcome a crisis which struck in 1798. When the heirs of Count Nostitz were unable to provide the necessary funds and bankruptcy loomed, six prominent aristocratic families decided to buy the theater and run it as a corporate institution. Shareholders purchased "hereditary boxes" for 10,000 guilders each and the Bohemian estates—the highest political institution of the country—assumed legal responsibility for the theater.[7]

In 1821, the nobility in Lemberg showed a similar level of commitment to its theater. The Galician estates agreed on a subsidy to maintain the "beneficial influence which a well equipped national theater has on literature, the purity of the language, morals, the education of the young, and the diffusion of light to the more mature parts of the nation."[8] Polish creativity flourished again during this phase in which the dramas and comedies of Fredro and Korzeniowski were written. Nevertheless, the German ensemble continued to dominate the modestly sized theater, with capacity for around 600.

Being subsidized by the estates, the aristocratic theaters in Lemberg, Prague and, from 1838, Budapest were also subject to public control. The estates set up theater commissions to ensure that the playhouses were fulfilling their artistic task, that the finances were in order, and that an annual report was submitted. The theaters were leased to private manager-directors, who ran them at their own risk, without the security of a royal treasury to fall back on. Unlike the royal theaters in Vienna, Berlin, and Dresden, then, these theaters had to cater to their publics' tastes in order to secure their economic survival. Balancing fulfillment of their educational task and the public's desire for entertainment was no mean feat, and aristocratic theaters suffered frequent repertoire and financial crises. The bilingual arrangement at the theaters in Lemberg and Prague was an additional source of friction as Polish and Czech theater activists competed with German drama and opera departments for equal status and use of the stage.

In 1830, a group of mostly prominent noblemen set up a "private association of executives for the Polish Theater in Lemberg" (*Prywatne Towarzystwo Przedsiębiorców Teatru Polskiego we Lwowie*) in order to provide additional support for the Polish ensemble. Consisting of 60 almost exclusively aristocratic members, this society was reminiscent of the alliance of six Bohemian aristocratic families that took over the Estates Theater in 1798, the most significant difference being that the Galician corporation had ten times as many members but only a fraction of the means. The 3,800 guilders start capital was already expended by 1831 when a cholera epidemic prevented audiences from attending but personnel costs continued to accrue.[9]

Figure 7. Count Skarbek, founder of the Skarbek Theater.

It was then that Count Stanisław Skarbek (1780–1848) stepped in.[10] Owner of three towns and 37 villages, Skarbek was tremendously wealthy. While proud of his native Polish culture, he was also loyal to the Habsburgs. The emperor granted him the exclusive right, for the duration of fifty years, to build and run the only public theater in Lemberg. In return for this privilege he was required to guarantee provision of a Polish *and* German ensemble and productions for this entire period. A controversial figure among his fellow noblemen, Skarbek had made his fortune from property speculation, distilling and selling brandy, and trading the cattle, which he drove across the length and breadth of Austria. His business acumen was legendary; one anecdote describes how he responded to a price increase by the Viennese butchers' guild by buying a slaughterhouse and marketing his own beef. Begun in 1836, the Count's imposing new theater in Lemberg was completed in 1842. With a seating capacity of 1,800, it was the third largest theater in Central Europe after Munich and Dresden.[11] It gave Vienna cause to fear for her cultural supremacy and demands for a new theater in the capital to outshine the provinces were voiced.

Figure 8. The Skarbek Theater, built in 1842.

Similarly to the Estates Theater in Prague, the Skarbek Theater served as a focus of local pride as well as a symbol of prestige to the outside world. It was built in the style of Viennese Classicism, with an auditorium containing 69 visitors' boxes in three circles and the parterre.[12] As in Prague, Budapest, and Venice, then, the target audience was visibly the high nobility. The emperor's place was merely a generously sized box on one side, symbolically reducing him to a *primus inter pares*, in accord with the traditions of the Polish Commonwealth and the political aims of the Galician nobility. In court theaters, by contrast, the royal box always occupied a central position. The members of the audience who could not afford boxes, on the other hand, were marginalized in Lemberg too. Seating for the general public was only available in the last balcony and in the orchestra level. The predominance of boxes in the theater clearly reflected the distribution of power in Polish society in the prerevolution period.

Figure 9. Auditorium of the Skarbek Theater.

While no precise record of audience composition in Lemberg exists, there is much to suggest that the landowning nobility made up the majority until the later nineteenth century. The theater achieved best attendances at the time of the Carnival holiday and the annual land and property trade fair, *Kontrakty*, when many rural landowners came to Lemberg. Conversely, the theater struggled when the aristocrats stayed away. This was the case following the Galician Peasants' Uprising of 1846, which claimed the lives of over 1,000 landowners and stewards. The surviving noblemen were afraid to leave their estates for months after this bloody revolt.[13]

As in Dresden and Prague, many of the playwrights, composers, singers, and actors involved in the theater also came from aristocratic backgrounds. Since commercial activities were frowned upon, male aristocrats tended to choose between careers in the military, state administration, or estate management. Breaking into the arts was a way to escape convention. Although technically a theater director was just as much an entrepreneur as the manager of a department store, and a singer equally an employee, the glamour and prestige of involvement in the arts glossed over this. For aristocratic women, working in theater was a way to circumvent the need for marriage, which high dowry expectations and a lack of suitable candidates could render problematic. Moreover, aristocratic children traditionally received musical training. So, although the impoverished Galician low nobility (the *szlachta*), who often lived like peasants, was not especially qualified for a life in opera, members of propertied aristocratic families were. A scion of one of these was to become the leading Polish opera composer of the post-Moniuszko generation: Władysław Żeleński.

The first weeks after Skarbek opened his theater must have seemed like the apogee of his career. Performances were sold out well in advance despite distinctly higher ticket prices for the first nights.[14] Aristocrats from all over Galicia thronged to the capital, Lemberg, to attend the many supporting events as well as the evenings' performances. The Galician public was delighted both by the German ensemble, which launched the theater with Grillparzer's *Der Traum, ein Leben*, and the Polish ensemble performing *Śluby Panieńskie* by Aleksander Fredro. The new set designs garnered much admiration and it was agreed they could match any of the royal theaters'. On the opening night, stage designer Pohlmann, who was also responsible for the interior design of the theater, was singled out for applause after every act of Grillparzer's play. The local press fêted him as a "truly poetic designer" and declared his portrayal of a giant, convulsing snake to be "the most striking deception and greatest possible illusion."[15]

Records show that in the years that followed, audiences continued to favor light entertainment over heavy intellectual drama. One anonymous commentator made the following observation on the Lemberg public's taste: "You can be sure that if a play by Corneille, Voltaire, Schiller, or Iffland is showing, the number of audience members can be counted on one hand. If, however, there is a large notice announcing the *Syren of the Dniestr*, stay at home, or you will be crushed in the theater."[16] Indeed, in 1844 a farce about "the wicked women of the Seraglio" (*Die schlimmen Frauen im Serail*) was the sensation of the season, enticing audiences with the promise of "well-exercised ladies."[17]

Tailoring the repertoire to suit the public resulted in a predominance of farces and comedies. But rather than attacking the public's tastes, critics tended to accuse theater directors of too much compromise. Even Skarbek, despite his Enlightenment goals, received mostly bad press for his allegedly unpatriotic stance.[18] This was symptomatic of the inherently divergent perspectives held by Lemberg's different social strata. While the wealthy Galician (and Bohemian) nobility had a more cosmopolitan way of life, the local critics generally belonged to the intelligentsia, who could not afford to travel abroad and hence focused with more intensity on home.

One of the high nobility's most vocal critics at this time was Jan Dobrzański, publisher of the newspaper *Gazeta Narodowa*, who became known as an opponent of aristocratic theater in the 1860s. His protests that Count Skarbek was not serving the nation were justified in so far as Skarbek's primary motivation was indeed cultural emulation. Skarbek wanted to establish Lemberg as a *European* center for the arts and improve the standing of his Galician homeland. Creating a national repertoire and promoting Polish artists were not at the top of his agenda.

Skarbek and his theater colleagues regularly traveled across Europe to acquire new plays for their repertoire. In the decade before the revolution, Paris exerted a magnetic appeal far greater than that of Metternich-ruled Vienna. In Paris, Skarbek sought the material to keep his turnover of new productions high. He could not have achieved the 172 premieres staged in his seven years as director of the Polish theater relying only on native works.

German opera, on the other hand, was neglected during the Skarbek era. In 1844, the correspondent writing for the *Wiener Allgemeine Theaterzeitung* noted that "the preference for Italian music, despite the tireless efforts of a few individual Teutomaniacs, generally prevails."[19] One of the few exceptions to this rule was a performance of *Fidelio* in August 1843. According to the newspaper *Gazeta Lwowska,* "the entire hall seemed as if filled with electric sparks." The review went on to eulogize Beethoven, who was deemed a suitable substitute for Polish composers "when the native gods remain silent."[20] As well as Beethoven's hymnal music, the central theme of liberty captivated the hearts of the audience, reflecting, as it seemed, the contemporary political goals of the Polish elites. In *Fidelio,* an innocent prisoner is saved from execution by his wife, who offers herself in sacrifice, disguised as a man. Evil is personified by a scheming henchman of the regime, who ultimately faces his just deserts. Was not Mother Poland, embodied by her chivalric nobility, fighting reactionary powers? The public's response to this—and all patriotically tinged operas in the late nineteenth century—was particularly emotional.

Before the revolution of 1848, the Lemberg Theater's singers preferred performing Italian operas in order to shine in the well-known arias. Demonstrations of virtuosity often took precedence over faithfulness to the composers' intentions—something which Wagner railed against in Dresden—and soloists shortened or extended vocal parts to suit their tastes and abilities. In 1843, for example, the finale from Bellini's *La Straniera* (*The Stranger Woman*) was performed at the end of Donizetti's *Lucrezia Borgia* and a production of Rossini's *Barber of Seville* featured an aria from Bellini's *Bianca e Fernando*.[21] Repeating arias was common practice—in Polish the word *bisowanie* (from the term *bis* for twice) was coined—and opera involved far more improvisation than it did at the end of the century.

As in Dresden, opera gradually became more popular than spoken drama. Although this trend could be observed all over Europe, it was far from self-evident in

Lemberg, which had a long tradition of drama and celebrated native playwrights such as Aleksander Fredro. Drama provided, moreover, a vehicle for cultivating the mother tongue. Ultimately, however, music theater had more appeal, not least to Skarbek himself, and the Count frequently secured productions by personally paying for stage sets and costumes.

Yet all his commitment could not allay one of the theater's fundamental problems: the new premises of 1842 were simply too large for the town. Before the revolution, Lemberg did not even count 50,000 inhabitants. Excluding the children, laborers, and others who could not attend the theater, there was an estimated potential audience of roughly 5,000. In order to fill the 1,460 seats, each of them would have had to attend every third evening. That was too much to ask even of the most devoted opera lover, and too costly for teachers, journalists, and other members of the intelligentsia. As a result, not even premieres were consistently sold out. Spoken drama suffered especially from the lack of public interest and the actors' motivation waned. "Disheartened by playing to empty houses," Stanisław Pepłowski writes, "they performed their tasks as if doing labor service for a feudal lord."[22] The mood in the theater was so dejected, and attendance so low, that just one year after its launch a popular saying advised: "If you seek rest from struggle and feud, go to the theater—and find solitude."[23] Even opera's appeal was no longer reliable and Skarbek was compelled to inject more of his own money into his theater.[24]

Economic insecurity prevented Skarbek from realizing his original plan of setting up a charitable foundation to benefit from his patronage of the arts. The Count had presumed the theater would yield a profit, together with proceeds from leasing the in-house restaurant, confectioner's shop, and café. Skarbek had intended to channel these profits, as well as those from his estates, into setting up an orphanage for 600 children and a home for the elderly in the village of Drohowyże. He appointed the husband of his niece, Prince Karol Jabłonowski, executor and trustee of his foundation. However, both the foundation's statutes and Skarbek's last will failed to provide for the eventuality of the theater making a loss. Hence, there was nothing to prevent the endowment fund being used to make up the theater's deficit.

The "theater privilege" that the emperor had granted Skarbek ultimately proved a heavy burden. It demanded provision of a German theater until 1892, regardless of the diminishing public demand in Lemberg, and conceded considerable rights of intervention to the governor. The government and the police were authorized to approve the repertoire, casts, the director, and even the price of tickets. The town council was permitted to lease the theater to a third party if necessary. In this way, the Austrian authorities were able to gain control over the theater by a number of means.[25]

During Skarbek's term as director, these regulations were irrelevant. But he passed away in the revolution year, and Lemberg was one of the major trouble spots in the Habsburg Empire. There was armed insurrection in November 1848; the town was bombarded and fires raged for days. As in Dresden, the old theater was destroyed in the flames. The new theater, built from 1836 to 1842, faced vacant seats and increasing losses. After the troubles had died down, censorship was tightened, especially of Polish drama. In spring 1850, the governors dismissed Skarbek's replacement and trustee, Prince Karol Jabłonowski—a loyal supporter of the Habsburgs like his father-in-law before him—and assumed control of the theater.[26] The bureaucrats' management of the theater resulted in further high losses and frequent changes to the ensemble throughout the 1850s. Despite the disastrous state of affairs at the theater, the authorities believed that it could be used to Germanize society's elite, and the number of Polish-language performances was reduced from three to two per week.[27] Such neo-absolutist attempts to turn the clock back only served to strengthen public resistance to German culture. The German theater in Lemberg was increasingly regarded as a symbol of foreign rule and oppression.

The situation improved after Austria's political liberalization in 1860–61, when the Skarbek foundation regained its former independence and was able to appoint the director of the Polish and German ensembles. But the theater's social and political context had changed. Neo-absolutism had undermined the nobility's cultural and social hegemony, and a new social class, the intelligentsia, had evolved. Now a generation of lawyers, administrators, and professors working in Lemberg also wanted to have a say in the theater. When Jabłonowski appointed the actor and theater manager Adam Miłaszewski as the new theater director, the flourishing press, led by Jan Dobrzański's *Gazeta Narodowa*, ensured that a critical eye was kept on the theater's activities. As Miłaszewski's career reflects all the major developments in Polish theater history of the 1850s and 1860s, it deserves to be examined more closely here.

Miłaszewski first became known to the Lemberg public as an actor in 1849. He had a strong singing voice and sometimes performed cabaret songs and musical interludes. He left the Skarbek Theater in 1853 in order to direct the Polish Theater in Krakow, but resigned soon after, confounded by neo-absolutist chicanery. He went on to work in the capital of the Russian province of Volhynia, Żytomierz, and Kiev.[28] These places had also once belonged to Poland and, despite Russian rule, were still very much under the influence of the Polish nobility. The Polish elites' aspirations to share in Europe's cultural life and achievements, especially in theater, prompted them to invest considerable sums in constructing and equipping theaters and establishing orchestras in various cities.[29] Although Żytomierz had a population of only 40,000, a new theater was opened there in 1855, financed by public donations. Miłaszewski was appointed director and quite sucessfully satisfied the demands of the aristocratic audiences. In 1863, he was given a six-year contract in Lemberg on the strength of his achievements in Volhynia.[30]

Outwardly, Miłaszewski's first season seemed to herald a reversal of fortune for Lemberg's aristocratic theater, with improved sets and a greater number of premieres. But Miłaszewski lacked an objective for the theater. He was an entrepreneur without missionary zeal. In his first report to the Galician diet's theater committee in 1864, he set out his definition of a good theater as one which "is accountable to the public" and that respects the public's verdict. Ultimately, he obeyed the demands of the market and not any enlightened or nationalist ideals.[31]

His initially mixed program of light entertainment with some Polish dramas gradually came to be dominated by French comedies and operettas. Lemberg may have had little in common with Paris—it was not connected to the railroad until 1861 and its population did not exceed 100,000 until after 1870—but the French capital, symbolizing urbanity, progress, and liberal sexuality, exerted an undeniable allure on it. At this time, Paris was "the capital of Europe," as Walter Benjamin put it.[32] Miłaszewski was handsomely rewarded for his repertoire of light entertainment. The boxes, especially, were usually sold out and yielded an annual profit which went directly to Miłaszewski, as personally liable manager.[33] The German theater, meanwhile, was ruined. A succession of directors went bankrupt and the Poles of Galicia became the indisputable masters of the theater in their regional capital Lwów.

Theater Wars

Despite having successfully marginalized German theater, in 1865 Miłaszewski came under attack from the respected newspaper *Dziennik Literacki* for neglecting classical and Polish authors and replacing drama with operettas: "So, first short skirts, then even shorter, then none at all. A man's suit, a leotard; at least one 'Can Can.' Tastes are offended at a fatal speed and with deadly consistency, faster and more certainly than aesthetic improvements [are made]."[34] Backed by the conservative and powerful Jabłonowski, however, Miłaszewski could safely ignore this criticism. Two years later, the aristocratic theater was under fire again, this time from the defenders of patriotic interests. A critic writing for the journal *Nowiny* called for an Enlightenment theater to promote Poland's restoration: "For us, who are robbed of so many things, theater is in the broadest sense of the word an academy, a spiritual treasure trove, in which the jewels of the past are kept; a platform, a national pulpit—a temple."[35] The press called for the closure of the under-attended German theater in Lemberg, which was only kept alive by society events, rental payments from the Polish ensemble and above all subsidies from the Skarbek foundation. Devouring an astronomical 255,998 guilders between 1850 and 1864,[36] it was the main reason why the orphanage in Drohowyże could not be built, and made a mockery of Skarbek's theater "privilege."

In spring 1869, the Association of Friends of the National Theater (*Towarzystwo przyjaciół sceny narodowej*) was founded in Lemberg with the chief aims of dissolving the German ensemble and establishing a highbrow and national repertoire for the Polish ensemble.[37] In 1870, newspaper publisher Jan Dobrzański was able to gain a foothold in the association and set about pursuing his ultimate goals of breaking the conservative high nobility's cultural and political hegemony over theater and politics. The battle between Dobrzański and Miłaszewski—known in Lemberg as the "theater war" (*wojna teatralna*)—had begun, and was to last nearly 15 years.

The two adversaries fought each other with different weapons. Dobrzański used his newspaper, with the highest circulation in Galicia, as a mouthpiece for rallying the public to his cause. Miłaszewski, on the other hand, controlled the theater and had powerful allies. But Dobrzański held the ideological advantage, supporting an enlightenment concept of theater, like German or Czech intellectuals. He called for a repertoire focusing on classical dramas and comedies, and Polish authors to be given precedence to advance national awareness and Polish culture. Miłaszewski could only counter these principles with his record of economic success. The argument that the international operas and Parisian operettas he staged—by popular demand—had deflated the German competition cut no ice. Aware that operetta, especially, lacked the ideological validation sought in the prevailing mood of nationalism, Miłaszewski and his aristocratic backers could offer no resistance to Dobrzański's mounting attacks in *Gazeta Narodowa*. Moreover, as high-ranking noblemen, they would not stoop to justifying themselves to a petty aristocratic publisher or the intelligentsia.

The German theater eventually became a secondary, but decisive, theater of war. In 1870, its last independent director, a former actress of Vienna's Burg Theater, Anna Löwe, organized a gala performance to mark the Prussian victory over the French near Sedan. The auditorium was decorated with Prussian flags and *Wacht am Rhein* ("Guard over the Rhine") was sung.[38] Lemberg's Polish population responded with spontaneous shows of support for the French. These protests soon escalated into the town's first public demonstration against the German theater. As a consequence, Löwe was dismissed and a new director was sought for the German ensemble. Jabłonowski convinced Miłaszewski to stand. He agreed and assumed the post of director of the German ensemble. It seemed the zenith of his career.

However, Miłaszewski's dual role as director of both the Polish and German ensembles made him more vulnerable to opposition. Dobrzański stepped up his attacks in *Gazeta Narodowa*, portraying Miłaszewski as a pro-German traitor to the national cause, while also campaigning against the aristocracy's control of the theater and Jabłonowski's influence.[39] The mere toleration of a German theater bordered on treachery in the eyes of the nationalist intelligentsia. Criticisms began to be voiced by the theater committee, set up in 1871 by the Galician diet (the *Landtag*) to safeguard the appropriate use of state subsidies and ensure that standards were maintained. By 1872 Dobrzański's campaign had prevailed. The German ensemble was finally dissolved, leaving the Polish ensemble with a monopoly. Miłaszewski was forced to resign and Jabłonowski, who had supported him to the last, was politically tarnished. The Association of Friends of the National Theater—now a shareholding corporation—took over the running of the theater.[40]

Dobrzański, the newspaper publisher who had managed to become the de facto director of the Lemberg theater, was an intriguing figure. He came from a petty aristocratic family from the village Dobra on the left bank of the San.[41] His impoverished father had been forced to work in the service of a wealthy landowner. Although he had benefited from aristocratic patronage, enabling him to complete his education, he remained an advocate of the revolutionary ideals of 1848 and peppered his newspaper with anti-aristocratic allusions. He neither used his family coat of arms on his correspondence nor requested recognition of his nobility from the Austrian regime. Moreover, he remained a Greek Catholic in the Ruthenian tradition, which Miłaszewski mocked by using the Ukrainian version of his name, *Dobrianski*. The bitterness of their dispute was exacerbated by the lack of communication between the prosperous high nobility and the impecunious intelligentsia. The high aristocracy inhabited a world of magnificent residences while the intelligentsia, who often had *szlachta* roots,[42] moved in other, much more modest circles. Even at the theater the two classes did not mix as the Lemberg house, unlike many theaters, did not have a large foyer where social mingling could take place.

In spring 1873, it emerged that Dobrzański's was a Pyrrhic victory. The Association of Friends of the National Theater was set up on the basis that 250 shareholders each contributed 200 guilders to raise capital of 50,000 guilders. The relatively low price and broad range of dispersion of the shares reflected the corporation's democratic vision for the theater, analogous to the Young Czechs' ideas in Prague. This was explicitly set out in a statement by the corporation, declaring: "For the first time, the Lemberg Theater has ceased to be the venture of an individual person or society and become, in a sense, common property or the property of all theater-goers. The small shares make it easier for all classes to participate in the public ownership of the local theater."[43]

But the corporation was not able to sell the targeted number of shares and its registration had to be postponed. In summer 1872, Dobrzański won a major victory over his aristocratic adversaries by enticing the leading actors away from the Krakow Theater and its director, influential conservative politician Stanislav Koźmian.[44] But since the aristocracy was boycotting the Lemberg Theater, Dobrzański found himself struggling to pay the higher fees they demanded. The aristocracy-controlled Galician diet placed him under further pressure by threatening to stop the theater's subsidies.[45] To avoid impending bankruptcy, the theater's shareholders finally toppled Dobrzański in a *coup de théâtre*. His attempt to build the theater on a broad social foundation had failed.

A period of confusion and turmoil followed Dobrzański's ouster.[46] The Galician theater world, like Prague's, was small and close-knit. Disputes often took on a personal dimension and ended in public humiliation. In 1873, two counts tried their hands at running the Polish theater but, both failing, a successor was sought again in 1874. As none could be found within aristocratic circles, three ensemble members took over the theater. Lacking both capital and entrepreneurial skills, they too went bankrupt in spring 1875. By now the only appropriate candidate remaining was Dobrzański.

With his son Stanisław, a well-known actor and playwright, as Artistic Director, Dobrzański steered the theater out of its crisis. The chorus, orchestra and ensemble were extended so that lavish operas such as *Aida* and *Lohengrin* could be performed. An ensemble of soloists who could all sing in Polish was set up, breathing new life into Polish opera, and in early 1877, Moniuszko's *Straszny Dwór* (*The Haunted Castle*) was premiered. Significant premieres of more recent Polish operas and dramas were also staged, and the number of operettas was reduced. The years after 1875 saw the Polish Theater in Lemberg thrive. In a cultural sense, the town became Polish *Lwów* again.

But the Dobrzańskis' good fortune came to an abrupt end on the very evening that Emperor Franz Josef visited the theater. Dobrzański junior suffered a heart attack during the performance and died hours later. To make matters worse, the emperor took exception to the nationalist, emancipatory content of the program. The only Austrian element of the evening was the imperial anthem at the beginning. This was followed by scenes from *Straszny Dwór* and a number of national dances, then a four-verse song in which the Poles assured the emperor of their loyalty if he would only extend them his hand. The conditionality of the message was certainly not lost on the emperor. When this was followed by more national dances—traditional dances of the Huzul ethnic group, performed by the *koło huzulskie*—Franz Josef, not a keen theater-goer in any circumstances, had seen enough Polish patriotism. After just a little more than an hour, he left the theater.[47] Dobrzański's old opponents took this incident as an opportunity to renew their attacks on his directing. Miłaszewski soon reappeared on the scene and curried favor with the most powerful families in the land, sensing an opportunity to resume control of the theater.[48] Shaken by the death of his son and artistic director, Dobrzański decided not to stand for another term as director.

Miłaszewski's return marked one last reprise for the aristocratic theater in Lemberg, although he now demonstrated greater detachment from his supporters. The opening performance of the 1881 season featured a short piece by Kraszewski parodying the antagonism between the social factions and their conflicting demands. In it, the intelligentsia was represented by a vain, progress-obsessed, ultranationalist character while the nobility was personified by a bored and sybaritic baron.[49] But this initial ironic commentary–which seemed to come with a promise of mediation—was followed by an increasing number of operettas and farces and the complete neglect of Polish opera. In spite of the season tickets sold to a number of aristocratic families, Miłaszewski began making a loss. In fall 1882, a petition was started in protest against his direction and reliance on light entertainment. A total of 665 signatures were quickly collected.[50] Confronted with this "petition by the citizens of Lemberg," financial losses which he was personally obliged to cover, and the censure of the theater's executive committee, Miłaszewski decided to resign, announcing his departure for March 1883. The aristocratic theater in Lemberg had run its course, both artistically and financially.

Not only social but also cultural changes were the cause of this. An increasing number of small theaters, open air stages, and circus troupes regularly passed through Lemberg, offering light entertainment and an alternative to the Polish Theater. While the aristocracy had stagnated in numbers, the intelligentsia had grown, altering the profile of the Lemberg audience. The Jabłonowskis, Potockis, Badenis, and other prominent aristocratic families who had previously held sway over the theater spent more time in the imperial capital Vienna, where they attended more cosmopolitan venues.

Following Miłaszewski's resignation, the Executive Committee of the Galician diet, now in charge of appointing a theater director, was only too glad of aging ex-director Jan Dobrzański's offer to resume his former post. Dobrzański's second term as director, from 1883, saw a renewed emphasis on music theater and some spectacular world premieres.[51] *Konrad Wallenrod* by Władysław Żeleński was performed in February 1885 and followed a year later by *Jadwiga*, the first major opera by principal conductor Henryk Jarecki. The sets for this work alone cost over 10,000 guilders—half of the committee's annual subsidy for the opera. Dobrzański sold shares in his publishing house to finance these native grand operas and send out the signal that the Polish Theater did not intend to fall behind the recently opened Czech National Theater in Prague or Royal Opera in Budapest. But when Jan Dobrzański died in 1886, of heart failure like his son, a new era dawned for the theater, with its fate in the hands of the intelligentsia and the Galician diet.

A Middle-Class Finale

One of the distinguishing features of the Polish intelligentsia was that although its members were educated and therefore possessed cultural capital, in material terms they were not wealthy. In Lemberg, then, the educated classes which saw themselves as the natural guardians of the theater lacked the resources to run it. Following Dobrzański's death, no theater director in Lemberg was able to fill his shoes for longer than two or three years, each losing the battle to reconcile the ideal of Enlightenment theater with the need to accommodate public tastes.

The frequent disruptions at the theater damaged Lemberg's status as a city of culture in Poland and the Habsburg Empire. The theater in Krakow, where the nobility continued to predominate in cultural politics, soon superseded Lemberg as the leading venue for spoken drama in Galicia. Meanwhile, in Lemberg, none of the instruments, costumes, or stage sets were renewed or replaced, and if the theater invested in any new productions, it could not afford experienced singers to perform reprises. For this reason, operas often ran for only one season, which in turn meant that it was not worth investing in new stage sets. As a consequence, from 1866, opera was reduced to a short annual *stagione*, for which singers were engaged from Italy. These temporary soloists were, however, costly, and sometimes even failed to appear.

Eventually, the permanent crisis at the Lemberg Theater—and the imminent opening of a magnificent new municipal theater in Krakow[52]—roused the educated elite of the town to take action. In 1892, the Skarbek foundation's 50-year "theater privilege" expired and the question of an administrative successor arose. The Galician diet was reluctant to run the theater as a Polish National Theater, as some members proposed, in view of its high losses and frequent bankruptcies. After long negotiations, the city council announced it would run a new, municipal theater on the proviso that the Galician diet provided at least 400,000 guilders to cover the cost of construction plus an annual subsidy of 24,000 guilders.[53] A competition was held for the design of the building which, surprisingly, was not won by the distinguished Viennese architects Fellner & Helmer, who had already constructed dozens of playhouses in the Habsburg Empire. Their style was deemed too eclectic and international. The judges in Galicia preferred the entry by lesser known Polish architect Zygmunt Gorgolewski.[54] Construction began in 1896 in close proximity to the old theater, while an almost exact duplicate of the Fellner & Helmer design for Lemberg was built in Zurich.

The new building transformed the character of the city. In order to be able to construct it on the chosen site, the Pełtev River was diverted underground and canalized along the entire length of today's *Prospekt Svobody*, Lemberg's equivalent to Wenceslas Square in Prague. This connected the old town and the palatial quarter around the Ossolineum with the Galician parliament building and gave Lemberg a grand boulevard suited to a European metropolis. Furthermore, the *Teatr Polski* served as a symbol of the Poles' supposed cultural superiority over the Ukrainians,[55] who made up an annually growing proportion of the population in Lemberg, and later raised funds to build their own Ruthenian National Theater. But the theater came at a cost of 2.5 million crowns (the equivalent of 1.25 million guilders before the currency conversion in 1900), which was not only roughly 50 percent more than originally estimated but also two-and-a-half times the annual budget of Lemberg University, and nearly as much as the government's entire expenditure on high school education in Galicia in 1900.[56]

Figure 10. The new Lemberg Theater, opened in 1900.

An upturn for Lemberg's Polish theater appeared even before the new premises were opened in the shape of Ludwik Heller, its first long-serving nonaristocratic director. A former railroad employee, he had been introduced to the world of theater by his wife, a well-known opera singer. Heller was the first director since Dobrzański to have an understanding of the economics of theater. He immediately invested in new musical instruments and extended the chorus and orchestra so that even large-scale operas could be performed without the assistance of the military band. Preferring Czech and German to Italian and French works, Heller staged Smetana's *Bartered Bride* and *Dalibor* soon after taking up his post in 1896 and, in 1897, presented *Lohengrin* in Polish. World premieres of new pieces by Jarecki and Żeleński confirmed the renaissance of Polish opera. Once again, all the soloists in the ensemble could sing in Polish, enabling a hodgepodge of languages to be avoided.

Heller made maximum use of the orchestra, choruses, and soloists, playing not only in Lemberg but also touring to Krakow and the spa town Krynica in the summer and to Warsaw from mid-May to mid-September in 1898. The Warsaw public came in droves to this first Polish *stagione*, and Heller returned to Lemberg with a profit of 65,000 rubles.[57] Now the entrepreneurial director could also afford to produce less popular, modern dramas. Among the premieres in the period 1897–1899 were four plays by Gerhard Hauptmann, two by Ibsen and one by Tolstoy.

In view of his success, Heller assumed that the post of director of the new Lemberg Theater would be his. But the high nobility had already singled out Tadeusz Pawlikowski, charismatic director of the new municipal theater in Krakow. He came from a wealthy landowning family and had an elegant aristocratic air, in contrast to Heller's much less refined, petit bourgeois manner. Pawlikowski spoke fluent French, used an ebony cane and spoke with "noble distinction," as even the leftist newspaper *Kurjer Lwowski* noted admiringly.[58]

The contest between Heller and Pawlikowski—the third Lemberg "theater war"—in many ways resembled a modern election campaign. The two rivals' followers canvassed support in the press, with leaflets and handbills, and in the coffee houses. Pawlikowski seemed to have the greater advantage, being politically better connected and in a position to offer the town council a higher rent.[59] Indeed, shortly before the day of the vote, the councilors involved in the decision making gathered at a private reception held by Marshal Count Badeni.[60] Pawlikowski could moreover count on the support of a large part of the intelligentsia, impressed by his distinguished, cosmopolitan ways. Meanwhile, Heller rallied Lemberg's bourgeoisie and the National Democrats around him. After a long and heated debate, Pawlikowski won the town council's ballot by 55 votes to 33.[61]

The new director established a repertoire that is generally considered definitive for Polish theater. French ensembles were frequently invited to give guest performances, nourishing Lemberg's aspirations to be a European cultural metropolis. Improved directing prepared the actors and singers better for their performances and encouraged them to use the stage more effectively. Financially, however, Pawlikowski's tenure was a disaster. The theater had already accrued a huge loss of over 100,000 crowns at the end of his first season, and it continued to grow throughout the second season. By 1903 the deficit had doubled, and the town council agreed to write off a large portion of the rent owed. Despite this concession, the theater's finances still continued to deteriorate. In 1906, the press reported debts of 400,000 crowns. Even with his considerable private fortune, Pawlikowski could not meet such a substantial sum. Performance quality, especially of operas, began to suffer because of the theater's financial plight, and in April 1905, the Executive Committee threatened to hold back the opera subsidy.[62] Ludwik Heller must have observed all this with quiet satisfaction. He had stayed in Lemberg and turned his attentions to converting the old Skarbek Theater into premises for his newly founded Lemberg Philharmonic Orchestra. As in Prague, then, conflicts surrounding the theater gave rise to an independent orchestra and the pluralization of the music scene. Heller soon managed to secure guest appearances by such distinguished conductors as Gustav Mahler, Richard Strauss, and Ruggero Leoncavallo, performing with Lemberg's new orchestra.

In 1906, the theater director was due for reelection and a campaign was anticipated. But Pawlikowski, worn down by financial difficulties and increasing criticisms in the press, simply gave up. Heller was able to take over without a fight and promptly shifted the repertoire's focus back to music theater. Krakow theater critic Karol Estreicher remarked, "Heller has no lovers because he loves his wife, but he has a favorite, and that is opera or operetta. For this favorite he has abandoned young talents in comedy and drama."[63] Indeed, Heller, who lacked Pawlikowski's sense of mission with respect to modern theater, seemed to have no appreciation of spoken drama. But to avoid accusations that he relied too much on light entertainment, he nevertheless produced plays by modern authors almost as often as his predecessor had.[64]

This former railroad employee also staged Poland's first *Ring of the Nibelung* and *Rosenkavalier* in Lemberg. His love of music drama inspired him to produce *Mefistofeles* by Arrigo Boito, Italy's leading Wagnerian, Puccini's *Madame Butterfly*, and Tchaikovsky's *Eugene Onegin* and *Pique Dame* (*The Queen of Spades*). Like Dresden, then, Lemberg gained a European repertoire that rivaled the major theaters of Central Europe. When the curtain fell on Austrian Lemberg and its theater at the beginning of World War I, it marked the end of a truly middle-class finale.

Notes

1. See Staud, *Adelstheater in Ungarn*; Frenzel, *Brandenburg-Preussische Schloßtheater*, 158–64 and 170–84.
2. On the nobility's role in Prague, Lemberg, Vienna, and Germany see Bužga, *Deutsche Opern*, 270; Mazepa, *Towarzystwo;* Mikoletzky, *Bürgerliche Schillerrezeption*, 170; Reif, *Westfälischer Adel*, 411.
3. These figures are taken from Rostworowski, *Ilu było*, 8.
4. See NA, fond ND, sign. D. 50, *Minutes of the administrative board* (hereafter *Mab*) of Sept. 3, 1891.
5. See Mazepa, *Teatr Lwowski*, 77–78.
6. For more on Kamiński, see Lasocka, *Teatr Lwowski*, 55, 100. On Prussia's justification of Poland's partition, see Hackmann, *Ostpreußen*, 58. On Austria's attitude towards Galicia, see Wolff, *Inventing Galicia*.
7. On the Bohemian nobility's aims in the late eighteenth century, see Hroch, *Na prahu*, 18–22.
8. See the petition of 1821 in *Tsentralnyi derzhavnyi istorychnyi archiv Ukrayiny u Lvovi* (Central State Archive of the Ukraine in Lemberg) (hereafter TsDIAU), 165/5/8, 1–3.
9. See Barbara Lasocka, *Teatr Lwowski*, 77–79.
10. For more on Skarbek see *Polski Słownik Biograficzny*, vol. 38, 23–25; Lasocka, *Teatr Stanisława*.
11. Theaters in western Europe rarely seated more. The *Salle Le Peletier* in Paris, opened in 1821, seated 2,000 (see Gerhard, *Die Verstädterung*, 31); including standing room, Milan had capacity for up to 4,000. The figures vary, however, from source to source.

12. Lytiński presumes there were 62 boxes on three balconies and 14 parterre boxes. See Lytiński, *Gmach*, 55.
13. See Got, *Das österreichische Theater*, vol. 1, 405–406. On this uprising, see Grodziski, *W królestwie*, 179.
14. On the early days of the Skarbek Theater see Got, *Das österreichische Theater*, vol. 1, 353.
15. Quoted in Got, *Das österreichische Theater*, vol. 1, 356.
16. Quoted in Lasocka, *Teatr Lwowski*, 109.
17. See Got, *Das österreichische Theater*, vol. 1, 396.
18. See Lasocka, *Teatr Stanisława*, 170–71.
19. Quoted in Got, *Das österreichische Theater*, vol. 1, 392.
20. See the review in *Gazeta Lwowska*, no. 91, Aug. 5, 1843, 601–602. A detailed description of the performance can be found in Got, *Das österreichische Theater*, vol. 1, 442.
21. These and further details of theater life in Lemberg are described by Jerzy Got. See Got, *Das österreichischeTheater*, vol. 1, 363, 376.
22. Quoted in Pepłowski, *Teatr Polski*, 206.
23. Quoted in Got, *Das österreichische Theater*, vol. 1, 378.
24. Ibid., 407. By way of comparison, the monthly subsidy for the Kärntnertor Theater in Vienna amounted to 6,250 guilders in 1848. See Hadamowsky, *Wien*, 417.
25. The foundation's statutes and "theater privilege" are discussed in detail in Marszałek, *Przedsiębiorstwa*, 26–27.
26. See Got, *Das österreichische Theater*, vol. 2, 491–606.
27. See Got, *Das österreichische Theater*, vol. 2, 549. In Krakow, authorization for a Polish ensemble was finally given after lengthy negotiations.On the history of the Krakow Theater, see Got, *Teatr austriacki*, and specifically on the authorization of a Polish ensemble, 44.
28. More details on his career can be found in a report in TsDIAU, 165/5/12, 40–41.
29. Theater life in the southeasterly regions of old Poland is discussed in Komorowski, *Polskie Życie Teatralne*.
30. See TsDIAU, 165/5/12, 40. The Polish ensemble now played alternate Mondays, Fridays, and Sundays and in the weeks in between, Wednesdays and Fridays. See the relevant contract in TsDIAU, 165/5/12, 50–57.
31. See the theater report in TsDIAU, 146/4/3806, 7.
32. See Benjamin, *Gesammelte Schriften*, vol. V/1, 45.
33. The Polish Theater was making an average annual profit of 4,000 guilders at this time. See Marszałek, *Przedsiębiorstwa*, 30.
34. See "Teatr," *Dziennik Literacki* May 29, 1865, 350–51.
35. Nowiny, Dec. 20, 1867, 61. From a three-part essay on the Lemberg Theater of Dec. 20, 1867, Dec. 27, 1867, and Jan. 3, 1868.
36. On these losses and cross-subsidies, see Agnieszka Marszałek, *Lwowskie przedsiębiorstwa*, 30; also Got, *Das österreichische Theater*, vol. 2, 732, 530.
37. *Gazeta Narodowa*, June 10, 1869, 3, *Kronika*. On this society see also *Sprawozdanie z czynności wydziału towarzystwa przyjaciół sceny narodowej za rok 1869–70 t.j. od Maja 1869 do końca Maja 1870*.
38. See Got, *Das österreichische Theater*, vol. 2, 749–50.
39. For an example of criticism of the aristocracy and its cultural tastes, see "Kronika Lwowska," *Gazeta Narodowa*, March 17, 1872, 1.
40. The statutes for this corporation, as well as numerous other documents, are facsimiled in Marszałek, *Lwowskie Przedsiębiorstwa*, 237–43.
41. More information on the social structure of the village Dobra can be found in Ślusarek, *Drobna Szlachta*, 86, 99–101, 161. For a biography of Dobrzańskiego, see Poklewska, *Jan Dobrzański*; Lechicki, *Najpopularnejszyszy dziennikarz*.

42. The origin of the *inteligencja* has been the subject of much debate among Polish academics. The conflicting views are set out in Chałasiński, *Społeczna genealogia*; also Czepulis Rastnis, *Wzór osobowy*, 159–78. On the architecture of these residences and the many new constructions of the first half of the nineteenth century, see Zhuk, *The Architecture*, 115–16.
43. "Kronika," *Gazeta Narodowa*, March 15, 1872, 2.
44. On the history of the theater in Krakow, see Michalik, *Dzieje teatru*.
45. On this resolution, see TsDIAU, 165/5/14, 20, and for a report on the debate in the Galician diet, see *Sprawozdanie sejmowe XXII posiedzenie d. 6. grudnia 1872 r.* in *Gazeta Narodowa*, Dec. 8, 1872, 3.
46. This period is examined in depth in Marszałek, *Lwowskie Przedsiębiorstwa*, 39–122.
47. A detailed report is contained in Stanisław Pepłowski, *Teatr polski w Lwowie (1780–1881)*, 407–409. My thanks go to Daniel Unowsky for pointing out that the emperor on the whole took a skeptical view of theater.
48. See Marszałek, *Lwowskie Przedsiębiorstwa*, 157.
49. On the performance of this piece, see Pepłowski, *Teatr Polski we Lwowie (1881–1890)*, 5–16.
50. The forms with the names of petitioners can be found in TsDIAU 165/5/21, 34–54.
51. On the positive evaluation of the opera repertoire by the Theater Committee, see TsDIAU 165/5/23, 1–5.
52. On the financing and architecture of this theater, see Purchla, *Teatr i jego architekt*.
53. See *Dziennik Polski*, no. 100, April 4, 1891, 3, *Rada Miasta Lwowa*.
54. The construction and various technical and financial problems surrounding this project are described in detail in Grankin, Sobolevskij, *L'vivskij opernij teatr*. See also Szuliński, *Teatr Miejski*.
55. This is evidenced in the artwork adorning the theater's interior, portraying Polish culture as a central component of European civilization, and the Ukrainians, or Ruthenians, as quaint peasant folk. The iconography of the new theater is analyzed by Lane, *The Polish Theatre*, 157–60.
56. See Szuliński, *Teatr Miejski*, 28–53; Dybiec, *Finansowanie*, 203. The figures are taken from the state budget appropriation for 1900. The cost of construction is relativized, however, when one considers that between 1900 and the outbreak of the First World War state expenditure for education in Galicia increased six-fold.
57. Besides some popular operettas, the most successful piece of the Warsaw season was *Dalibor*, which was performed ten times. See the report in *EMTA*, Sept 19,1898, 475–76.
58. For more on Pawlikowski's career, see Michalik, *Legenda i prawda*. The author shows that Pawlikowski's own accounts of his life, work, and experience abroad were often embellished and exaggerated.
59. On the decade-long conflict between Heller, Pawlikowski and each side's supporters, see Krasiński, *Heller czy Pawlikowski*.
60. See Webersfeld, *Teatr miejski*, 45.
61. See the report in *Dziennik Polski*, April 11, 1900, 2.
62. See TsDIAU, 165/5/630, 27.
63. Quoted in a letter to Heller of Aug.27, 1906 in Bibliothek im Stefanika v L'vovie, *korespondencja Ludwika Hellera*, vol. 1, 251.
64. Nevertheless, criticism of Heller's lack of education, profiteering and artistic ineptitude persisted. See *Krytyka* 8 (1906), bk. 12, 471–77, *O teatrze lwowskim*.

CHAPTER FIVE

Provincial Opera

In Italy's Orbit

In the dramatic terms of opera, one might say that from the eighteenth century Lemberg languished under a curse of marginality. Throughout the many territorial changes in Central Europe, the town remained on the periphery. This was true in the Polish Commonwealth, the Habsburg Empire, restored Poland, and the Soviet Union and still holds true for present-day Ukraine. During the 146 years of Austrian rule, Galicia came to be a byword for remoteness and poverty. German-language literature frequently referred to the province as "semi-Asia,"[1] echoing the partition propaganda in which Prussia and Austria portrayed Poland as backward and uncultured to legitimize carving it up.

The extent to which partition obstructed cultural institutions can be gauged by contrasting cultural activity at either end of the long nineteenth century. In its early days, the Warsaw National Theater could match the leading German theaters of the age and Polish opera blossomed. But in the wake of each of the failed uprisings against the partition powers, in 1794, 1830–31, and 1863, the theater was temporarily closed, talented authors and composers were forced into exile, and censorship was tightened. Under these circumstances, it was impossible for Warsaw to maintain the same standards as in Vienna, Berlin, or Dresden.[2] The history of Polish theater is a history of the struggle to overcome the effects of partition and compete with the Western nation-states, at least on a cultural level. It was this goal that also motivated the construction of the second Lemberg Theater in 1842. Its founder, Count Skarbek, was not an anti-German, modern nationalist, but a Polish aristocrat who wanted to raise his homeland out of the doldrums of cultural provincialism to the heights of "European civilization."[3] Skarbek's new theater represented a quantum leap for Galicia. In architectural terms it was state-of-the-art, and equipped with the latest technology for creating stage effects. It was spacious enough to accommodate a large orchestra and a great number of spectators, so that ticket sales could balance the cost of investment in lavish productions. It was on this point, however, that the project foundered. As mentioned above, actors and singers often played to empty houses, their words and song dying away unheard. Lemberg's new theater placed the town on an equal footing with cultural centers such as Prague and Dresden. But, after a flying start, it landed back where it had come from: in a provincial backwater.

It first fell into decline—parallel to developments in the entire Habsburg Empire and in Saxony—in 1848. In the wake of the counterrevolution, the theater was seized by Austrian bureaucrats[4] who were both artistically and financially inept but intent on restricting the number of Polish-language performances. Modest attendances and ticket sales at the German theater meant that the budget only stretched to paying second-class directors and singers. While the Polish theater had a good reputation, its meager receipts were not able to compensate. The situation did not improve until the arrival of Miłaszewski as director. By ensuring that regular salaries were paid, he stabilized the ensemble, convincing the best performers to stay and attracting young talents.

Miłaszewski's dismissal in 1872, however, heralded a renewed period of conflict and decline which had a particularly negative impact on opera. When the actors' cooperative (*Społka artistów*) took over the theater in 1875, it reduced the opera season from twelve to four months as a cost-cutting measure.[5] This made it difficult for local singers, or orchestral musicians, to earn a living at the theater. Since they were forced to seek employment outside Galicia for most of the year, many moved abroad. In fact, it did not even make economic sense, as engaging soloists on short contracts involved greater administrative costs and higher fees. The temporary singers usually came from Italy and could not speak—or sing—Polish. Since conditions were no more favorable in Warsaw, this arrangement by the actors' cooperative threatened the very existence of Polish opera.

Dobrzański stepped in once more to straighten out the chaos left by his predecessors. He reinstated the full-length opera season and sent the ensemble on tour in the summer.[6] In October 1876, he staged the first sensation of his directorship: the premiere of *Aida*. The progovernment newspaper *Gazeta Lwowska* especially admired the sets which new stage designer Düll had created, following the example of the Viennese model: "This is the first time that we in Lemberg have seen an opera that was brilliantly and elegantly designed, with that outward splendor which is an almost indispensable requirement of a drama of this genre."[7] With its desert setting, ancient Egyptian costumes and pyramids, *Aida* was performed a record 35 times in one year. Statistically, over half the population of Lemberg must have seen this opera at least once. Even taking second and third viewings into account, this meant more than just the elites. At only 15 kreuzers for the cheapest tickets, *Aida* was affordable even for servants and apprentices.[8] The tremendous success of this opera heralded a long-lasting passion for Verdi in

Lemberg—from an earlier point than in the German Empire—which did not fade until the turn of the century.[9] With older works by Rossini, Bellini, and Donizetti still popular, the Galician capital remained a center of Italian opera.

Music example 3. *Straszny Dwór*.

A few months later, in mid-January 1877, Dobrzański celebrated an impressive triumph with *Straszny Dwór* by Stanisław Moniuszko, performed without the abridgements enforced in Warsaw. This opera portrayed the history of pre-partition Poland in such a glowing light that it seemed resurrected and brought to life in Lemberg. The main characters were two knights who sang of the might and excellence of the fatherland before seducing two pretty maidens, breaking their vows of celibacy. The predictable conclusion did nothing to dampen the audience's enthusiasm. The critic writing for the National Democratic newspaper *Dziennik Polski* particularly admired Moniuszko's hallmark national dances. But it was an aria about the castle clock that most touched the hearts of the nationally minded public. The stopped clock which is wondrously reactivated by the Polish heartbeat symbolized the metaphysical force of the Polish nation. The critic, moved to tears, concluded: "That is not any old clock, that is the genius of our fatherland, which, currently robbed of its physical powers, through the works of great poets, painters, and musicians calls out the warning to the whole world: Poland is not lost yet!"[10] The critic writing for *Gazeta Lwowska* claimed emphatically that "if *Straszny Dwór* were performed in the major theaters of the European capitals, in the Vienna or Paris Opera, it would be a great success."[11] This was only the second popular national opera for Poland after *Halka* but already Polish critics felt emboldened to compete with old established Europe.[12]

While *Straszny Dwór* was received with national fervor, the singers performing it actually came from very mixed backgrounds. Two of the four main roles were performed by Italian singers who had learned the Polish libretto. Adalgisa Gabbi sang the role of Hanna, one of the two maidens, and Fernando Tercuzzi sang Zbigniew, one of the knights. To *Gazeta Lwowska*, these two Italians were "the heroes of the evening."[13] Tercuzzi received countless ovations after the final curtain. Their performance of some arias from *Aida* in Polish later that season established them as firm favorites of the public. An American singer named Cathrin Smith, who used the Polish-Italianate stage name Katarzyna Marco, also sang in Polish. Thus Dobrzański succeeded in putting together an entirely Polish-speaking ensemble of soloists, which was crucial for staging other Polish operas.[14]

In April 1877, Dobrzański risked the first performance of a Wagner opera—*Lohengrin*—in Poland, even before London, Paris, and many other western European opera centers. As with *Aida*, it was the visual elements which most impressed the public. When Lohengrin appeared on stage with "silvery weapons," a murmur of astonishment went through the auditorium before thunderous applause broke out. His swan boat presented another feast for the eyes.[15] However, *Lohengrin* was performed in Italian, as it was in London a short time later. This rendered the plot, which was so important to Wagner, incomprehensible to most of the audience. At a musical level, too, *Lohengrin* met with a skeptical response. The critic writing for *Dziennik Polski*, Jan Lam, a descendant of German immigrants, found the music monotonous and complained of the loud brass section drowning the singing: "Well, pity our children if that is the music of the future—but who knows, maybe in future it will be a form of punishment. In any case, one act in the proximity of the bass tuba, a drum and two trombones, intensified by an enforced day of fasting, should count the same as a month of jail."¹⁶ *Lohengrin* was only performed a few more times before being taken out of the repertoire.

With these three major premieres of 1876–77, Dobrzański proved that Lemberg was not doomed to be a cultural backwater. Consequently, he managed to persuade the Galician diet to raise the theater's subsidy from 12,000 to 15,800 guilders and used the extra money to have the auditorium lavishly renovated in the summer break. News of the popularity of the Italian and American singers who performed in Polish reached Warsaw, and in summer 1878 the Warsaw Opera enticed Gabbi and Marco away from Lemberg with the promise of better payment. To the disappointment of the Lemberg public, they never returned, and Dobrzański's fortunes declined without them. The Italian singers hired for the next season could not be persuaded to learn the Polish language or stay in Lemberg. Apart from the obligatory production of *Halka* to open the season and the occasional guest performance, then, Polish opera was abandoned in 1879. Once again, performance practice in Lemberg was characterized by linguistic variety. Stanisław Pepłowski notes in his chronicle of the Lemberg Theater that performances often combined Italian, French, and Polish in one evening.¹⁷ During his second term as director, 1883–1886, Dobrzański reestablished a Polish ensemble of soloists. But after his death, the opera scene in Lemberg gravitated toward Italy again. As singers were hired per *stagione*, there was only limited time for rehearsing new operas. The few new productions which were staged rarely ran for longer than one season, making it difficult to recover the cost of new costumes and stage sets. As a result, the various directors in office between 1886 and 1896 tended to reprise old favorites of grand opera and Italian works. Polish and German operas were rarely performed, partly because the Italian singers engaged for the season—but also local singers who had received their training in Italy—were not familiar with them.

Polish Opera

Despite the goodwill of the local public and critics, Polish opera struggled with a number of logistical difficulties. The works produced then are nearly all forgotten today, even in Poland, although some were sensations when they were premiered. The first Polish composer to achieve a major success after the death of Moniuszko was Władysław Żeleński. The world premiere of his *Konrad Wallenrod* in 1886 was anticipated by the press for more than a week. Articles were published daily in *Gazeta Narodowa* revealing ever more details of the production. Critics traveled from Warsaw and Krakow to attend and numerous receptions, talks by the composer and other minor events were held in the run-up, ensuring a sustained level of excitement and interest in what promised to be a new national opera.

Music example 4. Dramatic scene from the fourth act of *Konrad Wallenrod*.

All educated Poles would have been familiar with the poem by Mickiewicz on which the opera was based. It described the turbulent life of the Lithuanian Prince Alf, who is abducted as a child by knights of the Teutonic Order. As a young man known as Konrad Wallenrod, he resolves to avenge himself on them from within their own ranks. The brave eponymous hero quickly rises to the highest rank of Teutonic Knights and is eventually elected Grandmaster. His scheme is confounded, however, by Aldona, the main female character, whom Wallenrod loves. Careless Aldona is taken prisoner by the Teutonic Knights and locked away in a tower (providing a wonderful setting for a number of arias sung by the two lovers). Wallenrod's devotion to the lady prisoner betrays him; he is exposed by his deputy and, charged with high treason, condemned to death. At the last moment he manages to escape with his beloved but is pursued by his enemies. Wallenrod turns and slays some of the knights before he and Aldona take a draft of deadly poison to avoid capture. The news of his death and his call for resistance quickly spread, ensuring that his endeavors have not been in vain.

This opera, with its interwoven political and personal narrative strands, can be classified as a typical grand opera, the aesthetic of which deeply impressed Żeleński as a youth.[18] Here at last was a specifically Polish, heroic, historical opera, earnest and tragic. It was not as provocative as Moniuszko's *Halka*, which contrasted a morally bankrupt aristocracy with the honest peasants it ruled. To the conservatives in Galicia, *Konrad Wallenrod* provided symbolic justification of their cooperation with the partition powers, suggesting that it was not only tolerable but legitimate as long as it served the higher goal of uniting the nation.

The music, too, was much acclaimed, and critics praised Żeleński for forsaking the obviously national ingredients of Moniuszko's style. On account of Żeleński's skilful combination of arias, duets, quartets, quintets, and mass scenes, the critic writing for *Gazeta Narodowa* applauded *Konrad Wallenrod* as "a work which inherently links the idea of the nation with a beautiful, one might say pan-European form."[19] In the fourth act, Wallenrod's escape from Marienburg castle is accompanied by a musical description of snow storms, and Aldona's plaintive cries from the tower contrast with the powerful strains of a female choir in a nearby church. The various mass scenes and set changes between Wallenrod's Lithuanian castle home, Marienburg castle and the snowy winter landscape provided ample visual appeal. The audience applauded jubilantly at the end of every act and showered the composer with bouquets after the final curtain.

No critic dared to spoil this major cultural landmark by expressing open criticism. But at five-and-a-half hours, including intervals, the opera was clearly too long. The poem by Mickiewicz—an elaborate 2000-line Romantic ballad—had been cautiously adapted for the stage by two Galician writers, who did their best to leave it intact but would have been better advised to edit more stringently. *Gazeta Narodowa* hinted at this by referring to the opera's "oratorio-like character." But this was brushed aside at the premiere. At a reception held in honor of the composer, the event was proclaimed a "national day of celebration." In turn, Żeleński confirmed that he regarded his work as a service to the nation. Thus a patriotic consensus was reached which fired the Polish public's enthusiasm for opera.[20] *Konrad Wallenrod* went on to be performed a further nine times and become the biggest success of the 1885–86 season. A year later, Dobrzański spared no expense to present the world premiere of Poland's next major opera—

Jadwiga—written by Lemberg's principal conductor Henryk Jarecki. However, the music and historicizing libretto of this opera were weaker than *Konrad Wallenrod*'s, and only five performances were given.[21]

In broad terms, the libretti were the Achilles' heel of Polish opera in the late nineteenth century. Not even Żeleński (1837–1921) managed to remedy this, avoiding topical subjects most of his life. The most distinguished Polish composer of his generation, as a child of eight he had lived through the *rabacja*—the Galician peasants' uprising of 1846—in which his father was killed and his mother critically injured. For more than half a decade Żeleński did not write or say a word about these events. He avoided political material in his work and, unlike Moniuszko, refused to address the widespread poverty in Galicia or the increasingly tense relations between the different nationalities. In the era of "organic work," the rise of the Polish national movement and the mobilization of the peasants might have been an obvious choice of subject matter for a convinced patriot like Żeleński. But using it would have meant confronting the traumatic events of 1846. Like many landowners in Galicia, Żeleński wanted to maintain the status quo. He did not have the same inclination as Moniuszko, who was married to a commoner, or Smetana, toward dealing with contemporary issues.

Żeleński addressed the subject of the nation and its history in dignified, heroic grand operas. Works in the vein of Smetana's *The Bartered Bride* or *The Two Widows*, which could be performed by a small and less costly ensemble, would have provided a more practical vehicle for popularizing Polish opera. But local critics did not entirely approve of comic operas.[22] The nation was a serious matter and not to be taken lightly—especially not on the stage.

At a technical level, the Lemberg Theater was out of its depth with a bombastic grand opera like *Konrad Wallenrod*. Żeleński had incorporated an intricate harp part in the overture, but neither the Lemberg Theater nor any theater orchestra in Galicia possessed a harp. The young Ignacy Paderewski had to imitate the sound of a harp on a grand piano. An independently wealthy nobleman, Żeleński obviously did not concern himself with the practicality of his works. In fact, the cost of staging such elaborate works could only be recovered if they were box-office hits, but the grand opera-inspired works of Żeleński and Jarecki were ultimately second best. There were plenty of French and Italian pieces already on the market to satisfy demand. The attempt to adapt this genre to the requirements of Polish national opera proved, then, to be a cultural transfer to the wrong place at the wrong time. From 1886, the shortfall in music theater was mostly made up by operettas, including *The Gypsy Baron* (*Der Zigeunerbaron*) by Johann Strauss, which was scheduled for every third evening in late fall of that year.[23] In addition, old favorites of belcanto opera and—as in Paris—grand opera were performed. Yet these old-fashioned productions only served to highlight the fact that the Lemberg Opera had begun to stagnate, both musically and visually.

At the International Music and Theater Exhibition in Vienna in 1892, it became clear how far the Lemberg opera had fallen behind developments in Dresden, Prague, Budapest, and Vienna. The six-month event was a world's fair for music and drama, where participating countries and nations showcased their instrument-making traditions and leading composers. Officially opened by Emperor Franz Josef, giving it the monarchy's seal of approval, the public flocked to see the many performances that constituted a kind of international theater competition. Among the illustrious theaters participating were the *Comédie Française* and the *Deutsche Theater* from Berlin.

The Music and Theater Exhibition presented a unique opportunity for the different peoples of the Habsburg Empire to show themselves to the public as cultural nations. The government allowed the Czechs and Poles to manage their own booths in the permanent exhibition. Thus they appeared almost as independent nations, conveying an impression of the empire as an oasis of multicultural tolerance. The German Empire, which had decided against stands for the individual federal states, seemed drearily uniform in comparison.

In Galicia, ambitious plans were forged for the exhibition in Vienna. The De Reszke brothers, who were stars in Paris, Milan, and the Metropolitan Opera in New York, and prima donna Marcella Sembrich were to lead a team of internationally famed Polish singers to represent the nation and to show Poland as a fount of talent. But snags in the details caused the organizers to stall. Should these international stars perform Polish operas they were not so familiar with or rather Italian and French operas they had mastered? Who was to cover the travel costs of the performers and the orchestra and the cost of the exhibition in Vienna? The private committee that had seen to collecting original scores, pictures, and old instruments for the permanent exhibition was not willing to pay the estimated 13,000 guilders required for the tour.[24] It was not conclusively decided to send the Polish theater from Lemberg to Vienna until July. A program was then hastily devised, featuring *Halka*, *Straszny Dwór* and one act of the lyrical drama *Krakowiacy I Górali*, to be repeated each evening apart from the last, when *Roméo et Juliette*, a twenty-five-year-old opera by Gounod, and excerpts from *La Traviata* and *The Huguenots* would make up the finale.[25]

In the event, Lemberg's four-day appearance in Vienna in September 1892 was a disaster. Marcella Sembrich, who was to sing the role of Halka, cancelled at the last minute and no suitable stand-in could be found. In consequence, the program was reduced to Moniuszko and a vocal revue performed by international singers of Polish descent. The orchestra gave its routine performance and the costumes were almost as old as the operas. The presentations elicited an outpouring of derision on Polish opera by the Viennese press. Commenting on *Halka*, *Wiener Tageblatt* wrote that Moniuszko's music was merely superficially national in character and "any talented German composer of the era around 1840 could have written most of the opera."[26] In contrast to the Czech National Theater, which had agreed promptly to participate and had six months to prepare, the Polish Theater was penalized for its hastily put-together, dated program as well as its old-fashioned stage sets.

The Lemberg public reacted to this loss of face by avoiding the theater. *Dziennik Polski* complained: "In truth, we no longer recognize our 'musical' Lemberg today. What happened to all those music lovers who, some decades ago—oh, not even so far back; just a few years ago, were able to fill the theater from top to bottom several dozen times over?"[27] The ban on operettas of 1894 did not help to improve attendance. Opera's lighter and more economical cousin, requiring only a small ensemble, was ideally suited to the Lemberg Theater. But it was either branded as foreign and Jewish, or, in the case of Viennese operetta—which had enjoyed great popularity in the 1880s—condemned as too German. Cutting operetta from the repertoire of the Lemberg Theater was, then, not only a strike against light entertainment but also a xenophobic act. Indeed, without operetta, the Polish theater lost contact to the Jewish public, who made up nearly a third of the town's population. In the past, deliberate attempts had been made to attract a Jewish audience, above all by Adam Miłaszewski. In summer 1871, when the heat threatened to keep the public away, Miłaszewski recast the drama *Der Pfarrer von Kirchfeld* by Ludwig Anzengruber in a Jewish setting and titled it *Der Oberrabbiner von Sadagora*. The program was even printed in Yiddish.[28] When the German ensemble, who gave this performance, was subsequently dissolved, the Polish ensemble could have tried to win the Jewish public for itself.

But Dobrzański was an avowed anti-Semite. His newspaper frequently portrayed Jews as a plague of exploitative, ungrateful immigrants and allies of Vienna and Moscow.[29] In fact, *Gazeta Narodowa*'s anti-Semitic rabble rousing did not stop with Dobrzański's passing. An article of 1890 headlined "Who in our town arouses anti-Semitism?" complained: "We have expressed regret that the Lemberg Jews still follow a cult of Germanness, that one encounters masses of Jews at every German production, . . . while at all national Polish productions, whether in the theater, at concerts or Polish readings, the Jews are extremely few."[30] If the reverse occurred, though, and a noticeably large number of Jews attended the Polish theater, they faced sneering remarks about their presence and corrupting influence on the repertoire. The anti-Semitic mood not only undermined the strong assimilation movement of the 1880s,[31] but it also had repercussions for the theater scene in Lemberg: in the 1890s an independent theater was opened specifically for the Jewish public, offering Yiddish performances.

The rural population also avoided the theater. A regional fair of 1894, entitled *Kościuszkowa* to mark the centenary of the Kościuszko Uprising, demonstrated this with startling clarity. Most of the thousands of visitors this exhibition attracted to Lemberg preferred the amusements of a traveling circus to the theater. A similar exposition in Prague in 1891, by contrast, attracted record numbers to the National Theater. This discrepancy cannot be explained by Galicia's often cited backwardness. The Lemberg elites—both the aristocracy and the intelligentsia—had made no effort to win the small-town and village populations for their theater.

Becoming a Wagnerian City

When Ludwik Heller took over the Polish theater with the help of an associate in 1896, it was close to collapse. The Warsaw arts periodical *Echo Muzyczne, Teatralne i Artystyczne* asked provocatively if the "ruin" that was Polish opera in Lemberg should not be demolished altogether rather than trying to revive it yet again.[32] Indeed, on an average opera evening, a substandard orchestra, sometimes assisted by a military band, would accompany second-class performers singing in various languages in front of decades-old stage sets.

In this situation, Heller audaciously took the offensive, staging five opera premieres in the first half of 1897 alone. The first in January was *Goplana*, by Żeleński, and a notable success. It marked the first time that this now sixty-year-old composer abandoned historical themes and the heroic national struggle to set a psychological drama to music. *Goplana* told the story of a woman who commits fratricide and is subsequently plagued by her conscience and failed attempts to find love. It was performed eight times in the first six months of the year.

In early February 1897, the second Lemberg premiere of *Lohengrin*—this time in Polish—was staged, followed by *Tannhäuser* a short time later. Both works were a magnet to audiences thanks to well-cast singers and the Polish libretto.[33] Now that the public was able to follow the action, Wagner was adopted by the Poles—as he was by the Czechs, Catalans and other "small" nations—as one of their own.

In summer 1897, Heller presented *The Bartered Bride,* his fifth premiere as director. *Gazeta Narodowa* had long called for this piece to be performed,[34] partly out of gratitude toward the Czech National Theater, which had previously staged the two Moniuszko operas *Halka* and *Straszny Dwór*. Throughout the 1880s and 1890s, the Polish theater in Lemberg and the Czech National Theater in Prague maintained extremely close contact, sending each other congratulatory telegrams and visiting delegations on various occasions and assisting each other on a number of pieces, guest performances, and stage sets. A group of Lemberg actors even attempted a mixed-language drama performance at the Bohemian Jubilee Exhibition in 1891.[35] In January 1898, Heller produced Smetana's great tragic work *Dalibor* in Lemberg. *Gazeta Narodowa* applauded Smetana in such glowing terms to make any Polish composer envious, and *Dalibor* went on to be performed a remarkable seven times in the first two months after its premiere.[36] Smetana's popularity and the new appreciation of Wagner were complementary.

The work of both composers demanded a new way of listening. Both *Lohengrin* and *Dalibor* were continuous compositions using devices such as recurrent motifs rather than the spoken passages of older operas to propel the action. Whoever liked *Dalibor* found it easier to access Wagner's complex opus.

Heller's next move was to rehabilitate operetta, staging no less than 188 performances in his first season. Operettas were good for business—takings were high while costs were low—and contrary to the persistent claims of the Lemberg arts pages, the operetta boom did not hinder the development of Polish opera. Heller followed up the premiere of Żeleński's *Goplana* with the world premiere of the lyrical ballad *Powrót Taty* by Henryk Jarecki, his first work to remain in the repertoire.[37] Żeleński went on to compose the opera *Janek,* which was performed at the opening of the new Lemberg Theater. This drama about the jealousies and rivalries of a band of thieves in the Tatra Mountains adhered to the aesthetic of *verismo* and was a remarkably contemporary choice of subject matter by Żeleński. But its central appeal was the local color conveyed by the dances and songs, modeled on those of the Gorals. *Janek* was kept in the repertoire for several years after the premiere and was also performed in Kiev and elsewhere in Ukraine and Poland.

The new theater's success culminated in its production of *Manru* by Jan Ignacy Paderewski, who is profiled above in the case study of Dresden. This opera contained not only the blood, romance, and passion of most *verismo* operas, but also a more complex psychological element, as the characters in *Manru* battle chiefly with their own cultural make-up.[38] Musically, too, Paderewski's opera was up-to-date and propelled the Lemberg Opera into the present day. As in Dresden, Wagner was now the standard by which all composers were measured, though from a standpoint which was peculiar to the region. While in Dresden Paderewski's eclecticism was regarded as impure, the Lemberg critics admired precisely his combination of Wagner-like chromaticism and leitmotifs with folkloric elements.[39] Eager to match Dresden's production of the opera, the new municipal theater had costumes and stage sets especially designed to portray the action as realistically as possible. Prague-born August Berger, ballet director in Dresden, was engaged to choreograph the dance scenes and the soloists' movements. The outcome was Goral and gypsy dances for Lemberg that were developed by a Czech based in Dresden—a colorful instance of how the era's supposedly authentic national imagery was created across borders. Pawlikowski enlarged the orchestra to 60 musicians and put them through extended rehearsals, sometimes lasting up to twelve hours. After the dress rehearsal had gone without hitch, Paderewski uttered the words that the arts-loving public in Lemberg had been longing to hear: "This is a truly European theater."[40]

Music example 5. Folkloristic dance in J. I. Paderewski's *Manru*.

Following this compliment from a man of international renown, the Polish premiere of *Manru* could only be a triumph. Paderewski was inundated with flowers and wreaths and the applause seemed unceasing, lasting even longer than it had in Dresden. Later, the opera's continued success in New York gave rise to hopes that the composer might become an ambassador for Polish opera and promote the genre internationally.[41] But Paderewski decided to concentrate on his career as a concert pianist. His memoirs do not offer any clear indication of his reasons but financial considerations probably played a role. For the Polish premiere of his opera in Lemberg, Paderewski received a one-off payment of 1,000 crowns plus guaranteed royalties of at least 1,500 crowns. Although 2,500 crowns was far more than the Lemberg Theater usually paid composers, it was only a fraction of what Paderewski would earn playing one concert in the US. At the final count, he would not have been able to maintain his large Galician estate, his villa in Switzerland and his *haute bourgeois* lifestyle by composing operas for Poland.

From 1901, Polish opera once again fell into decline. Any promising new works soon disappointed and Pawlikowski turned increasingly to spoken drama. After *Manru*, the only opera premieres of note were *The Valkyrie* and *Tosca* in 1903. Puccini's opera devoured 10,000 crowns, with 5,000 spent on sets and costumes and 3,000 on Milanese tenor Augusto Dianni who sang the lead role.[42] Despite this investment, a section of the audience greeted *Tosca* with the same hostility as it did Pawlikowski's avant-garde drama repertoire. The staunchly Catholic newspaper *Przegląd*, angered at the production's theatrical portrayal of a procession of priests and nuns and a bishop giving benediction, headlined its review "Sinfulness in the Municipal Theater." The newspaper's critic found the dance of the Roman masses in the churchyard a "second profanation," and concluded: "Both sinful examples show what an un-Catholic spirit prevails in our theater, that one has already become accustomed to, and that shows disrespect for all the religious and moral principles by which our public generally lead their lives."[43] Pawlikowski could initially ignore these protests, but they were prone to reigniting, having a potentially huge number of sympathizers among the population and a political lobby in parliament in the Peasant Party.[44]

The theater's dented reputation cast doubts among the leaders of the Ukrainian national movement—who were planning to build their own national theater in Lemberg—whether theater was a suitable site for patriotic education.[45] At the same time, rural members of parliament and pro-Peasant Party journalists raised objections to the theater's increasing subsidies, saying they would be better spent on village schools. Thus, under Pawlikowski, the theater became a focus of conflict between the rural and urban populations.

The disagreements over the repertoire reflected the conflicting views of nation and Europe within Galician society. Pawlikowski's supporters defended him in spite of his mismanagement because he had created a modern European repertoire, but his Catholic critics failed to see the value of this and condemned the cultural influences from the West.[46] In essence, the same sociocultural antagonism between an urban, Europe-oriented intelligentsia and a rural population acting as the moral guardians of the fatherland still exists in Poland today.

Ultimately, Pawlikowski proved a tragic figure. He established a sophisticated repertoire of a standard which most major theaters in Poland and Germany did not reach until the interwar period. He introduced a groundbreaking approach to directing in both spoken drama and opera, putting an end to performers standing at the edge of the stage, reeling off their arias, and encouraging them to move about the stage with dramatic reason. Significantly, he introduced the term *inscenyzacja* (opera/play production) on his theater programs. But these achievements were too subtle to be appreciated by more than a small section of the audience. Moreover, Pawlikowski's artistic abilities were undermined by his complete lack of business sense. It was the final straw when, in 1906, shortly before the director was due for re-election, his lover and favorite actress Konstancja Bednarzewska left him and went over to Ludwik Heller's camp,[47] breaking his heart.

Although Pawlikowski was of noble birth, his term as director cannot be regarded as the continuation of aristocratic patronage after Skarbek. The circumstances had changed since Skarbek's day, to Pawlikowski's distinct disadvantage. By 1900, the costs involved in running a professional theater far exceeded the resources of any individual aristocrat, unless he was an industrial magnate, such as the financer of *La Scala* and mentor of Toscanini, Visconti di Modrone.[48] After using up his fortune, Pawlikowski relied on the town of Lemberg to finance the theater. The age of traditional aristocratic patrons was over.

When Ludwik Heller resumed the post of director in 1906, he steered the theater back on to the course he had taken before the turn of the century. Once again, the priorities were putting together an all-Polish singing ensemble and staging spectacular premieres. The high point of his second term as director was the first Polish performance of all four parts of *The Ring of the Nibelung* in the 1910–11 season. This production of the complete cycle brought the Lemberg Theater up to a level with Paris, where the *Ring* cycle had been performed just a year earlier in the *Palais Garnier*. A leading protagonist of Galician Wagnerism was tenor Aleksander Bandrowski. He had built an international career singing Wagner roles before returning in 1907 to his Galician home, where he translated *The Ring* and wrote a book about Wagnerian myth. Another local Wagnerian named Marian Dienstl claimed Wagner was a Polish patriot on the grounds of his instrumental piece *Polonia* (1831), inspired by Saxon enthusiasm for Poland, and his purported plans to write an opera about Kościuszko.[49]

As in Prague and Vienna, however, there were also Wagner critics in Lemberg. Klemens Weitz was one, whose description of a performance of *The Valkyrie* for a satirical publication entitled *Lemberg Pearls* quipped:

> During the second act people could be seen fleeing as if from a burning house; slower ones could be heard snoring so loudly that they almost woke their neighbors who were dozing in their seats; others who had lost all hope of this ever coming to an end, and unable to leave the theater, could be seen searching in all their pockets for arsenic, strychnine or rat poison to put an end to the boredom by suicide ... The third circle resembled a row of sleepers, all were slumbering, even the doorman and the police guard ... When to everybody's surprise the third act actually ended, one could sense a great load being lifted from the Lemberg public, who thronged to the checkroom and left the theater at a gallop as if they suspected they might be ordered to return for a fourth act. Many could not fall asleep at home because they had already had a good sleep in the theater.[50]

Such parodies did not, however, curb the general enthusiasm for Wagner's work. Lemberg, which only twenty years earlier had oriented all aspects of its operatic practice—singers' training, performance practice, and repertoire—toward the Italian example, had now embraced Wagner. A German influence was clearly evident in the most significant Polish opera of the prewar decade, *Bolesław Śmiały* by Ludomir Różycki. This opera, with a libretto by Bandrowski, dealt with the murder, and murderer, of Saint Stanisław, focusing on the perpetrator's feelings of remorse, his escape and death. Musically, it was filled with leitmotifs and pushed the boundaries of conventional harmony, similarly to Strauss's one-act works. *Gazeta Lwowska* rejoiced in a three-part review that at last an authentic Polish music drama had been created, Polish opera had caught up with Western culture, and the twentieth century was set to bring a renaissance of Polish music theater.[51] Indeed, a number of composers associated with *Młoda Polska*, an informal group of Polish modernists, including Mieczysław Karlowicz and Karol Szymanowski, were garnering international attention, at least in the music world. *Młoda Polska* certainly displayed the same potential in the early twentieth century as the protagonists of the music scene in Prague.[52]

In the years preceding the First World War, more German operas were performed in Lemberg than French or Italian operas, including *Der Rosenkavalier*, which Heller had translated immediately after its premiere in Dresden. But Heller was not fixated on German opera and also looked to Russia in his second term. As well as two works by Tchaikovsky, he even staged *Boris Godunow*, although the "Polish act" it contained was a potential provocation to nationally minded Poles. Heller actively supported young Polish composers, producing 26 new Polish operas between 1906 and 1909 compared to only 17 foreign works premiered, and consistently had all imported works performed in Polish. Within his two terms as director, then, Heller withdrew Lemberg from the *stagione* system and Italy's cultural orbit. The Galician capital became a typically central European opera town, with a predilection for native opera performed by a permanent ensemble and a clear emphasis on music drama.

Theater as a School of Democracy

Any theater needs a degree of stability to be able to build a proficient ensemble and a sophisticated repertoire. It was precisely this, however, that was lacking in Lemberg. Yet Skarbek, Miłaszewski in his first term, Jan Dobrzański, and lastly Ludwik Heller managed to use the intermittent lulls in hostilities to lift the theater up to the level of the Royal Theater in Dresden and the National Theater in Prague. But the 1850s, the first half of the 1870s and the years between 1886 and 1896 were lost time for the theater, in which ensemble members and soloists came and went in quick succession and stage sets and instruments fell into disrepair. As a result, premieres were mediocre, revivals worse, and audience numbers—and receipts—steadily dwindled.

The "theater wars" between Miłaszewski and Dobrzański caused much havoc and Heller's rejection in favor of Pawlikowski as director of the newly built theater also proved a rash decision. A wiser solution would have been to combine the talents of the two, placing Heller in charge of administration and opera and employing Pawlikowski as artistic director specializing in spoken drama.

The dissolution of the German ensemble in 1872 entailed a loss not only for German but also for Polish culture. For while Polish theater now held a monopoly, there was no longer any call for solving disputes creatively. Moreover, the Polish ensemble was now cut off from artistic developments in the German-language sphere. Lemberg's long-lasting reliance on the *stagione* system, which was becoming out-dated even in Italy,[53] did nothing to improve the situation. The internationally rising cost of singers made it extremely difficult for Lemberg to engage professional singers for a whole season. But the cost of a three or four-month *stagione* in proportion to the receipts of the same period was far greater than for a permanent ensemble. In view of the constantly changing personnel, new pieces were usually performed for just one season. The seasonal arrangement forced the Lemberg Opera to restrict itself to a small international repertoire of works which the temporary soloists were familiar with. Both the number of premieres and attendance dropped as a result.

This situation placed Polish opera at an obvious disadvantage, some intermittent periods of fostering the native repertoire under Adam Miłaszewski, Jan Dobrzański, Ludwik Heller, and Pawlikowski (in the first years of his directorship) notwithstanding. Unfortunately, the two leading Galician opera composers of the late nineteenth century, Żeleński and Jarecki, failed to become architects of a genre with enduring appeal. Both relied on remote historical subjects which the public could not identify with as readily as with contemporary dramas such as Smetana's *The Bartered Bride*. Their music was, moreover, not as compelling as the international competition. Żeleński's compositions were conventional in structure, influenced by the contrapuntal school of the 1850s, and less expressive than the works of Wagner or Smetana. Jarecki, on the other hand, adhered to the characteristically Polish style of his teacher Moniuszko.[54] Although the national dances he habitually incorporated elicited outbursts of enthusiasm, they did not help to build up dramatic or musical tension. Moniuszko had at least applied this style to pieces with social and political relevance, such as *Halka*. Jarecki's approach, in contrast, was to set a series of loosely connected moments from Polish history to folkloric music. True, Jarecki and Żeleński also wrote long and tragic grand operas, but these demanded conditions which the theaters in Lemberg and Warsaw could not provide. As the Lemberg ensemble's guest performances in Warsaw, Krakow and Krynica show, the potential for a Polish *stagione* existed. But Heller had his hands full just in Lemberg.

Training singers in Italy was not without drawbacks, as they often failed to return or could only be persuaded to do so by the promise of high fees. It is no coincidence, then, that many of the most talented young native artists came from Jewish backgrounds, having grown up with the cantors and song of Jewish worship. In the neo-absolutist era, the Lemberg Jews became closely involved in the German theater. In 1853, for example, the Jewish community boys' choir took part in the spectacular premiere of Meyerbeer's *The Prophet*.[55] Later, a number of Galician Jews began their careers at the Polish Theater. Soprano Tereza Arklowa went on to international success, climaxing in appearances at *La Scala*. The tenor Władysław Florjański, born Kohman, went to Prague, where he contributed to the success of the Czech National Theater in the 1890s. Toward the end of the century, the influx of Jewish artists stopped for two main reasons: Vienna had become a training ground for aspiring artists from all over the Habsburg Empire. And the increasing anti-Semitism in Lemberg repelled Jewish artists as well as the Jewish public.

The Polish theater's repeated crises between 1872 and 1875 and 1886 and 1889 at least proved that Lemberg had a critical public which was not prepared to passively let others impose choices upon them. Unlike in Dresden, the Lemberg public participated in its theater, voicing opinions on the repertoire and the director. The petition against Miłaszewski in 1883 and the Heller versus Pawlikowski electioneering campaign are two impressive examples of democracy in action at a time when political democracy was in its infancy.

The battles fought over the theater led to a gradual transition of power from the conservative high nobility to a broader social basis. These "theater wars" formed a prelude to a more modern political system, based on participation, which was finally introduced in Galicia when the electoral law was reformed in 1913. The strong element of public participation in the opera may have contributed to the popular local image of Lemberg as a musical and "singing town," which continues to color recollections of the town's Polish era to this day.[56]

Although old, multicultural Lemberg and Polish Lwów were destroyed by the Holocaust and the ethnic cleansing of the 1940s,[57] the opera house survived. It became an important meeting place for the town's new, Ukrainian society. In 2000, to mark its centenary, the town had it lavishly restored. The amount this cost could equally have been invested in improving the old town's water supply or other infrastructure in need of urgent renewal. But just as in the nineteenth century, the appeal of a temple to the arts was too great to resist. Ukrainian L'viv continues to present itself to the world as a European town and a home of music.

Notes

1. See Klańska, *Galicja w oczach*. See also the recent book by Larry Wolff.
2. On Warsaw's music scene from the mid-nineteenth century, see Ritter, *Warschau und Wilna*, 89–137.
3. On Skarbek's political views, see Got, *Das österreichische Theater*, vol. 1, 352; and Pepłowski, *Teatr Polski*, 175; also Lasocka, *Teatr Stanisława*, 150–51.
4. See Got, *Das österreichische Theater*, vol. 2, 491–605.
5. See TsDIAU 165/5/16, 54 and Pepłowski, *Teatr Polski*, 363. On the parliamentary debate leading to this resolution, see Spraw. Sten., May 25, 1875, 711–12.
6. The opera season usually lasted from September until the end of May. On the duration of music theater seasons in Lemberg prior to 1914, see Wypych-Gawrońska, *Lwowski Teatr*, 58–59.

7. See *Gazeta Lwowska*, Oct. 30, 1876, 4. See also Pepłowski, *Teatr Polski*, 380.
8. In 1872 a manual laborer earned between 1.20 guilders (blacksmiths) and 1.80 guilders (bricklayers) and an apprentice roughly 80 kreuzers. At 15 kreuzers, the price of a standing-room ticket was equivalent to that of a kilogram of white bread. See Hoszowski, *Ceny*, 80, 144–45. 150.
9. The premiere of *Don Carlos* followed in the 1877–78 season. The operas *Ernani, Foscari, Ballo in Maschera, Rigoletto,* and *La Traviata* were already on the repertoire. See Wypych-Gawrońska, *Lwowski Teatr*, 94–95.
10. See the first review and the more detailed, three-column review in *Dziennik Polski*, Jan. 20, 1877, 2 and Jan 21, 1877, 1 (each under the heading "Kronika teatralna").
11. *Gazeta Lwowska*, Jan. 20, 1877, 4.
12. On Moniuszko's ideas on national opera, and specifically on *Halka*, see Golianek, *Twórczość operowa*.
13. Ibid. See also Pepłowski, *Teatr Polski*, 382.
14. Nearly all the Polish operas performed by the Polish theater are considered briefly in Wypych-Gawrońska, *Lwowski teatr*, 80–91. Only a few key productions are discussed here.
15. On Lemberg's reception of *Lohengrin*, see two extensive reviews in *Gazeta Lwowska*, April 23, 1877, 4; and April 24, 1877, 4.
16. Quoted in *Dziennik Polski*, April 29, 1877, 1. On this production, see the article by Marszałek, *O pierwsezej*, 143–44.
17. See Pepłowski, *Teatr Polski*, 410; also Wypych-Gawrońska, *Lwowski Teatr*, 140–41.
18. In 1853, Żeleński saw Meyerbeer's *Robert, der Teufel* (*Robert le diable*) in Vienna, which made a lasting impression on the sixteen-year-old. See the excerpt from his memoirs printed in *Wiadomości literackie* 14, no. 30, July 18, 1937, 2.
19. Quoted in *Gazeta Narodowa*, Feb. 28, 1885, 1.
20. On the accolades bestowed on Żeleński, see "Uczta na część Żeleńskiego,"*Gazeta Narodowa*, March 1, 1885.
21. See the review in *EMTA*, Jan. 11, 1886, 34–37. More information can be found in TsDIAU, 165/5/25, 42–45.
22. See *EMTA*, Jan. 11, 1886, 34, second column.
23. On the development of operetta, see Wypych-Gawrońska, *Lwowski Teatr*, 255–334.
24. See "Polski oddział na teatralno-muz. wystawy wiedeńskiej," *Gazeta Narodowa*, June 22, 1892; *Gazeta Narodowa*, June 23, 1892, 2.
25. The newspaper *Echo Muzyczne, Teatralne i Artistyczne* called for more Polish operas to be staged. See *EMTA*, July 16, 1892, 2.
26. Quoted in *EMTA*, Oct. 17, 1892, 446–49. A negative evaluation of Polish opera is also contained in Fleischer, *Die Bedeutung der Internationalen*, 65.
27. See *Dziennik Polski*, March 19, 1891, 3.
28. See Got, *Das österreichische Theater*, vol. 2, 760.
29. A particularly inflammatory article which repeats these stereotypes is printed in "Żydzi," *Gazeta Narodowa*, Oct. 25, 1873, 2.
30. See *Gazeta Narodowa*, March 20, 1890, 2.
31. See Mendelsohn, *Jewish Assimilation*, 99–106. An overview of Polish-Jewish relations in Lemberg is provided by Holzer, *Vom Orient*.
32. *EMTA*, March 19, 1894, 157–58, *Leopoliana*.
33. See TsDIAU, 165/5/625, 48.
34. See *Gazeta Narodowa*, March 15, 1893, 2. *The Bartered Bride*, however, came via Vienna as the Polish translation was based on the German version, not the Czech original. See Wypych-Gawrońska, *Lwowski Teatr*, 72.

35. See NA, Fond ND, sign. D 50, o. Bl. (*Protokoll des Verwaltungsauschusses vom 11.6.1891*) and the memoirs of Lemberg actor Roman Żelazowski in Żelazowski, *Pięcdziesiąt lat teatru*, 86–88.
36. See the relevant article in *Gazeta Narodowa*, "Dodatek do Gazety narodowej z dnia" Nov. 3, 1897, "Fejleton muzyczny." The critic mentions *Dalibor*'s premiere at the Vienna Court Theater under Mahler.
37. On the Theater Committee's positive evaluation of this opera, see TsDIAU 165/5/621, 1.
38. For more on *Manru*, see the previous part on Dresden; also Keym, *Zur Problematik*, 71–73.
39. See *Gazeta Narodowa*, June 9, 1901, 2.
40. See *EMTA*, June 2, 1901, 278. On the Polish premiere see also *Kurjer Teatralny* 1, no. 16, June 15, 1901, 266–67.
41. See *Gazeta Narodowa*, June 9, 1901, 2.
42. See TsDIAU, 165/5/628, 3.
43. "Świętokradztwo w tearze miejskim," *Przegląd*, March 7, 1903.
44. In spring 1901 a number of protests were held against plays performed at the theater, which were even discussed by the Galician diet. Government support for the theater and its repertoire was increasingly criticized. See the parliamentary debates of July 1907 and October 1903 in *Sprawozdanie stenograficzne z rozpraw galicyjskiego Sejmu krajowego, 15. posiedzenie, 1. sesyi VIII peryodu Sejmu galicyjskiego z dnia 11. lipca 1902*, 862–865; also *Sprawozdanie stenograficzne z rozpraw galicyjskiego Sejmu krajowego, 15. posiedzenie, 1. sesyi VIII peryodu Sejmu galicyjskiego z dnia 31. października 1903*, 1857–1861.
45. See Lane, *The Polish Opera*, 160–63.
46. See the parliamentary debate cited above.
47. See Solska, *Pamiętnik*, 65.
48. Visconti di Modrone's involvement in La Scala facilitated structural reforms and the theater's upswing under Toscanini. See Piazzoni, *Dal teatro die palchettisti*, 45–46.
49. On Poland's and especially Galicia's positive reception of Wagner after the turn of the century, see Skibińska, *Recepcja Twórczości*, 42–60.
50. Quoted in Weitz, *Lwowskie Perły*, 28–29.
51. *Gazeta Lwowska*, Feb. 13, 1909, 4; Feb. 16, 1909, 4; Feb. 17, 1909, 5.
52. Karlowicz died in 1909 in an avalanche in the Tatra Mountains. For more on *Młoda Polska* see Chomiński, Wilkowska-Chomińska, *Historia Muzyki Polskiej*, vol. 2, 76–91.
53. See Toelle, *Oper als Geschäft*; also Roselli, *Das Produktionssytem*, 124–60.
54. On the reasons for Polish opera's lack of popularity, see Dziadek, *Koncepcja opery*, 165–67.
55. The Jewish tenors Olski and Menkes are discussed in Pepłowski, *Teatr Polski*, 347; the production of *The Prophet* by the German theater in 1853 is considered in Got, *Das österreichische Theater*, vol. 2, 534.
56. See *EMTA*, Jan. 4, 1886, 26–27; also Weitz, *Lwowskie Perły*, 30–33; and the many memoirs published after the Second World War, discussed in Ther, *War vs. Peace*.
57. On Polish-Ukrainian relations in the Habsburg era, see Wandycz, *The Poles in the Habsburg Monarchy*, 88–89; also Ther, *War versus Peace*, 252–57. On the ethnic conflicts and cleansing in the twentieth century see Mick, *Kriegserfahrungen*.

Part Four

The Czech National Theater in Prague

CHAPTER SIX

Launching the National Theater Project

The Founders

The history of the National Theater in Prague is itself dramatic enough to serve as the plot of an opera. The first act would open with a group of dignitaries inspired by the idea of founding a national theater. But to do so they must overcome the weaknesses of the ascendant nation's cultural life, which they would sing of in the first ensemble scene: the neglect of the language, the meager repertoire, and the limitations of the public. Then a determined young lawyer, of such impressive stature that he would have to be a powerful bass baritone (František Ladislav Rieger), enters the stage and calls together a founding committee. The first hurdle is taken when the hostile imperial government consents to the project, aware that it cannot suppress all civil initiatives and assuming that culture is apolitical. The second act would show the theater project gaining momentum and, in spite of the inimical bureaucracy, becoming the hub of a national movement. A second mass scene would portray the ceremonious laying of the foundation stone as a moment of hope and pride. In the third act of this fictional opera, disputes between the various soloists and the opposing political factions (the so-called Old Czechs and Young Czechs) almost cause the project's collapse. The tragic nadir—but emotional climax for the audience—would be the disaster at the end of this act. Shortly before reaching completion, the theater—the labor of an entire generation—goes up in flames. Yet in the fourth act, which would musically link up with the first, the national theater would rise like a phoenix from the ashes. The joyous finale would show the theater's inauguration: curtain up on a newborn theater, curtain down on our fictional libretto.

Sometimes history writes the best libretti. After a lengthy founding phase between 1844 and 1883, Czech society actually did manage to construct a prestigious theater, build a rich repertoire and even create a new genre of music theater—Czech opera—within only two generations. The creation of the national theater discussed in this chapter is of interest not only for Czech history. It shows the dynamics that can be at work in a modern mass society and national movements. It demonstrates the social and aesthetic limitations of a nationalism which promised the (utopian) equality and participation of all the members of the nation as well as the cultural productivity of which German philosopher and founder of modern nationalism Johann Gottfried Herder had dreamed. Lastly, the National Theater was a site of great artistic creativity. When it was still only a vision, it inspired Smetana to write operas portraying the new departures in Czech society, it played a part in launching Dvořák's career, it hosted Fibich's original treatment of Wagner's legacy, and ultimately it became an important center of modernism in European music theater.

This rich chapter in Czech cultural history was ushered in by a group of 140 distinguished gentlemen, who joined forces in 1844 in order to found an independent Czech theater.[1] The group consisted mainly of Czech burghers and some prominent aristocrats who had been involved in the Estates Theater, where Czech dramas were occasionally performed, as well as the first Czech operas. But this did not satisfy the demands of the national activists who wanted to see the Czechs acknowledged as a legitimate and refined cultural nation in their own right. In 1845, the group petitioned the government for the construction of a Czech national theater on the following grounds: "Bitter shame fills us at the thought that we Czechs, who look back on our ancestors with pride and how they competed with their neighbors in all the noble arts, have fallen behind in this branch of art and in the circle of civilized nations are the only ones to still not have a theater. We no longer want to stand like barbarians alongside the last of the nations in the noble art of Thalia."[2] Hence the primary task of the national theater was to help promote the Czech language and foster native drama and opera.

Initially, however, the national theater was not a purely Czech project. For some years, notices promoting it were written in German as well as Czech and referred to a Bohemian (*böhmisch*) national theater. Significantly, in the Czech language no distinction is made between Czech and Bohemian.[3] The national movement aimed to incorporate all those whose mother tongue was Czech. Meanwhile, the Estates Theater also gained a last chance to be accepted as a Czech theater in the prerevolution period. Following a major structural reform in 1846, it was divided into two sections—Czech and German. Each section was assigned its own director. Thus Czech theater activists were placed in a similar position to the Polish nobility at the Skarbek Theater, where a native-language and a German ensemble also shared and alternately used the stage. In 1849, the two directors of the Estates Theater issued a new appeal to the nationally minded nobility to invest in hereditary boxes and make donations toward a Czech theater.[4] The Estates Theater had been financed in this way by a number of aristocratic families since 1798. But the Czech-oriented aristocracy lacked the means to support such an undertaking and so missed this chance to be in the vanguard of the national movement.

The failure of the revolution brought an end to this phase of German-Czech cooperation. In 1851, Karel Havlíček, a leading democratic Czech activist, wrote in the magazine *Slovan* under the heading "Our national theater": "actually the German theater in Prague is unnatural because the cluster of real Germans who live in Prague would never be able to sustain it were it not for the help of our pseudo-Germans. These pseudo-Germans will now, however, become annually less until the generation which was led out of Egypt dies out, and after the establishment of a completely Czech theater in Prague we will no doubt draw away a considerable number of patrons from the German theater."[5]

Despite having recently quashed the revolution, in 1850 the government authorized the founding of a Committee for the Establishment of a Czech National Theater in Prague (*Sbor pro zřízení českého Národního divadla v Praze*) in the belief that it would provide a safe outlet for general civil dissatisfaction. Yet the first public appeal for donations toward a national theater in 1851 betrayed its political volatility, since it clearly symbolized nothing less than a monument to the constitutional rights and equality of the Czechs.[6] The public's response was correspondingly enthusiastic and by 1852 enough funds had been raised to purchase a plot of land. Subsequently, the government tried to obstruct the project's progress by prohibiting public fundraising appeals. The committee reacted by dispatching 90,000 circulars and advertising notices, not only to destinations within Bohemia but also to Moravia, Galicia, Hungary, and Vienna.

From the mid-1850s, however, the flow of donations began to falter. By this time, the Czech-oriented members of the nobility had given generously, with Prince Jan Lobkowitz donating the highest sum of 6,000 guilders.[7] And lower middle-class supporters, especially, had exhausted their resources, having donated valuables such as clocks and jewelry as well as money. Furthermore, the scope of the Czech theater association's appeal was severely geographically limited. In the 1850s, 80 percent of the donations came from Prague and its immediate surroundings.

The October Diploma in 1860 and the subsequent liberalization of Austria allowed the committee to resume public fundraising and the project gained new momentum. In 1862, the so-called Provisional Theater was built, securing the regular performance of Czech drama until the national theater was completed. This era saw the inception of many other cultural institutions including the *Hlahol* choral society and *Umělecka beseda*. All were motivated by the desire to build an independent Czech cultural scene and break the hegemony of German culture, especially in Prague.

The Provisional Theater

The *Prozatímní divadlo*, which literally translates as "provisional theater," was indeed a temporary arrangement. With an only 900-seat capacity and a stage nine-and-a-half meters wide, it was modestly sized, and did not have a grand foyer.[8] The orchestra consisted of the members of a dance band, supplemented at first by musicians from the Estates Theater. A third of the singers were also under contract to the Estates Theater and they could only appear on their free evenings. Due to the shortage of Czech-language dramas, comedies, and operas, the number of performances was limited to three per week, and the theater soon accrued a large deficit. Impending bankruptcy could only be averted by the generous donations from some wealthy Prague burghers.[9] But Bohemia's Czech-aligned aristocrats determined to do their bit too. In 1861, Count Jan Harrach set up a handsomely endowed competition for comic operas and another for historical operas. The latter was won by Bedřich Smetana with his first opera *The Brandenburgers in Bohemia* (*Braniboři v Čechách*). Meanwhile, spoken drama at the theater also improved and in 1864 a Shakespeare festival was held. Performances were now given daily and the ensemble extended so that it was no longer dependent on the Estates Theater.

At this point, a crucial organizational reform took place. The personally liable impresario who had hitherto run the theater was replaced by a collective known as the National Theater Association (*Družstvo národního divadla*), consisting originally of 24 shareholder-members. On investing capital of between 500 and 1000 guilders each, they assumed liability for the theater's losses and became eligible to elect the director. Smetana eagerly accepted the position of Director of Opera, which at last secured him a steady income. Shortly after his appointment he performed his own *The Bartered Bride* to such acclaim that the Austrian Empress came to see it in October 1866.[10] Other, now all but forgotten composers, among them Karel Bendl, Blodek, Hřimalý, and Šebor, also supplied new operas and gradually a Czech repertoire accumulated.[11]

Surprisingly, it was the most gifted of all these composers, Bedřich Smetana, who encountered opposition to his major dramatic work, *Dalibor*. Some critics and members of the public objected to its allegedly Wagnerian style, with its strong orchestration, predominant use of brass, and storyline reminiscent of *Lohengrin*.[12] Since the very raison d'être of the Provisional Theater was to gain emancipation from German culture, this was a serious accusation indeed. It is true, Smetana was aesthetically oriented toward the New German School (*Neudeutsche Schule*) around Franz Liszt, with whom he maintained close contact throughout his life. But in essence, Bohemian debates on the merits and demerits of the Wagnerian style were attempts to resolve whether to write text-oriented, dramatic operas in the German style or basically adhere to the traditional Italian model and incorporate elements of Czech folk music. Some years later, after Smetana had cemented his popularity, this dispute abated.

Thanks to the fruits of the productive local music scene, over a fifth of the Provisional Theater's operas were soon of native provenance, roughly equivalent to the amount of Polish operas performed at the Lemberg Theater under Dobrzański. Imported works were usually translated into Czech. French operas were most often performed, making up a third of the repertoire.[13] With its good supply of French and Italian pieces and some popular Czech shows, the opera department of the Provisional Theater soon rivaled that of the Estates Theater.[14]

In broad terms, the Provisional Theater provided the right conditions for developing and experimenting with Czech opera. For the twenty years of its existence, the small stage was a positive advantage, automatically limiting the extravagance of productions and hence public expectations as well as the potential for financial losses. The native repertoire was able to grow without the pressure of having to fill a 1,800-seat theater like the Skarbek Theater in Lemberg.

This success sustained Czech plans to construct a national theater. A new appeal for donations in 1865 yielded 127,000 guilders within a year. An additional 70,000 guilders came from districts outside Prague and its immediate vicinity, indicating that the national theater initiative was now becoming a mass movement. Despite an interruption in the flow of donations when Prussia attacked Austria in 1866, by 1867, 150,000 guilders had been raised. With the cost of construction estimated at 427,000 guilders,[15] the new National Theater seemed within reach and the Committee prepared to officially begin construction work.

Mass Mobilization

The foundation stone ceremony over the weekend of May 16–17, 1868, was the largest mass event in Bohemian history in the long nineteenth century. According to the estimate by the Polish (and therefore perhaps impartial) newspaper *Gazeta Narodowa*, roughly 100,000 people lined the processional route and 200,000 more watched from specially constructed stands, balconies, and rooftops.[16] This number equaled the entire population of Prague and its suburbs. Crowds jostled at the stations as passengers poured out of well over 100 specially chartered trains with up to 70 carriages. All the hotels in town were fully booked and many visitors were spontaneously invited to stay in private accommodation.[17]

Bohemia was captivated by the prospect of a national theater weeks before construction began. The organizing committee responsible for the celebrations, in which left-wing liberals—later to become the Young Czechs—played a decisive role, resolved to lay not just one but nearly twenty symbolic foundation stones. Each was sourced from a site bearing significance for Czech myth or history and with its own local group of national activists. The largest stone weighed two tons and came from Mount Říp, just under 30 kilometers north of Prague where, according to legend, the ancient forefather Čech had founded the nation.[18] As the stone was being prepared for transport, 10,000 peasants took the opportunity to spontaneously demonstrate against new taxes introduced since Austria's defeat by Prussia. 100 horsemen then escorted the heavy load to Prague where 80,000 people had gathered to witness its arrival on May 12. Further stones arrived from the provinces almost daily, sustaining the mood of excitement in the Bohemian capital.

The celebrations reached a climax—like a nineteenth-century Czech Woodstock—on May 16, 1868. On this day, a grand parade of 60 groups representing different sections of Czech society was held. Craftsmen and laborers formed the largest groups, which were organized according to profession. The executive committee of the diet—Bohemia's highest political body—decided not to lead the procession but to walk among the others. The rural districts also sent delegations so that all regional administrative bodies were represented too. 2,600 choir singers and 1,500 gymnasts made up the second and third largest groups.[19] Each professional group had standard bearers wearing historical or traditional costumes. And all were escorted by a number of musical bands, making the parade an acoustically as well as visually impressive event.

The choreography of the parade was modeled on medieval coronation processions. But the fact that Prague had no king to lead the people in 1868 was a point of contention. The main speaker at the foundation stone ceremony, Karel Sladkovský, alluded to it several times[20] and called for the Austrian emperor to accept the crown of King Wenceslas. One year after Franz Joseph had agreed to be crowned King of Hungary following the Austro-Hungarian Compromise, thus recognizing Hungary as an equal nation-state, the Czech elites demanded an equivalent symbolic act to elevate the status of their nation. Contemporary operas reflected the political situation, in particular Bedřich Smetana's dramatic opera *Dalibor*, which was performed as part of the celebrations marking the laying of the National Theater's foundation stones.

The government in Vienna, however, stubbornly ignored Czech demands for equality on the political and operatic stage. The emperor and high-ranking representatives of the House of Habsburg were glaringly absent from the founding celebrations and so too was Prague's Cardinal. In his place, František Palacký, one of the leading agents of Czech cultural nationalism, "blessed" the theater in a quasi-religious ceremony. Journalists served to reinforce the popular perception of the National Theater as a hallowed site by referring to it as a "cathedral" and a "temple."[21]

A pan-Slavic congress was held in Prague to coincide with the second day of the founding celebrations. Among the congress guests were leading intellectuals and politicians from all Slavic countries. Many were overwhelmed by the celebrations and the beauty of Prague, and speaker after speaker at the ceremonial banquet assured the Czechs that they could rely on the solidarity of the Slavs and even of the "Slavonic nation."[22] While the speeches were not of any real political consequence, the sheer amount of congratulations and admiration served to boost the confidence of the Czech theater movement. Congratulatory telegrams, mostly from similarly emergent Slavic nations, filled the pages of Prague's newspapers for days. The mood of the pan-Slavic congress, and of the entire founding celebration, was deeply emotional. Speeches by the foreign guests were punctuated with tumultuous applause and interjections of "Bravo!" "Viva!" or "Splendid!" whenever reference was made to Slavic unity or the Czechs' brilliant prospects.[23] Unlike some Western Slavic languages, Serbian and Russian were not readily understood by the Czechs, but common ground was found nonetheless, especially late in the evening when plenty of drinks had been imbibed.

Rather than resting on their laurels—or idly nursing hangovers—after the grand celebrations, the theater activists harnessed the momentum thus gained and launched a coin collection (*Kreuzersammlung*) in 1869 which yielded 20,000 guilders. Vojtěch Hynais invested this in a magnificent stage curtain bearing the image of a widow with her children making a donation toward the *Národní divadlo*, which still hangs in the National Theater today. Large and numerous donations now also came from the more distant regions of Bohemia and Moravia.

For the Czech national movement, the celebrations of 1868 were just the first in a series of major events. The commemoration of Jan Hus, Palacký's seventieth birthday and the regional *Tábory* camps, named after those of the Hussites, were all occasions mobilizing hundreds of thousands of people. Yet the actual goal of equality with the Germans and Hungarians within the monarchy remained elusive. In October 1868, the government in Vienna clamped down, declaring a state of emergency in Bohemia and imposing severe fines and even prison sentences on prominent agents of the national movement. The mood among the national activists turned from festivity to embitterment.[24]

The younger generation in the national movement, among them Karel Sladkovský and the brothers Julius and Eduard Gregr, publishers of the newspaper *Národní listy*, took a more radical stance than their older associates including Palacký. A distinction began to be made between the Young Czechs and the Old Czechs around František Ladislav Rieger. But perhaps more than by age, they were divided by different upbringings. The Old Czechs grew up in the Biedermeier era, many beginning their careers in the service of the nobility, and identified with the Habsburg state, its aristocratic character and a cautious approach to reforms. The Young Czechs, by contrast, were mostly self-made men; lawyers, journalists, and successful businessmen. While the Old Czechs viewed the revolution of 1848 with skepticism, some Young Czechs had fought at its front line. The political constellation was essentially similar to that in Galicia, with conservative and moderate liberals confronting left-wing liberals and democrats. In

1873, a conflict broke out over how to respond to the government's repressive measures which culminated in an embittered election campaign a year later.

The political conflicts did not bypass the Provisional Theater. Fighting broke out in the auditorium at the premiere of Sardou's *Rabagas*. This satire on the social parvenus and flag-waving nationalists of Paris in the early years of the decade so enraged the Young Czechs among the audience, who took it as a personal affront, that they shouted down the performance and caused an affray.[25] A short time later, the Young Czechs set up a separate theater association with the aim of taking over the Provisional Theater. In 1876, the executive committee of the diet handed the theater over to the Young Czechs' association despite its limited capital stock. Within a year it was bankrupt—a scenario that was only too familiar to Lemberg.[26]

These constant disputes on the political and theatrical stage had drastic repercussions on the theater's fundraising campaign. In 1873, a stock market crash caused the value of the donation fund to sink to 67,000 guilders while the cost of construction was now estimated at 1.6 million guilders. In 1875, only 7,600 guilders were raised and in 1876, when the Young Czech theater association made a loss of 130,000 guilders, a mere 730 guilders. The national theater project faltered, but at crisis point, disaster was averted. Unlike in Lemberg in the period 1872–1875, where the aristocrats and the intelligentsia could not overcome their mutual antagonism, the Old Czechs stepped in to shore up the Young Czech theater association with extra funds. In April 1877, the Old Czech-dominated United Association (*Spojené družstvo*) was set up to cover losses, provide new capital and run the Provisional Theater.[27] Thus each of the political camps in Bohemia demonstrated their willingness to compromise and to cooperate for the benefit of the nation. They could not allow the Czech theater to go bankrupt or even temporarily close as long as Prague still had a German theater. Local composers, in part concerned for their royalties, also called for compromise. In October 1876, the Organization of Czech Dramatic Writers and Composers convinced the Young Czech theater association to negotiate with the Old Czechs and not let the Provisional Theater fall to a private impresario.[28]

With fresh optimism, the theater activists tried out new ways of rallying the people. In 1877, the Committee for the Establishment of a National Theater organized a lottery on the island of Žofin in aid of construction. Brass bands and choirs provided entertainment while visitors were invited to buy affordably-priced lottery tickets. Within a few months, 177,000 guilders had been raised. Meanwhile, the Theater Association advertised for new members. Nearly 2,000 wealthy burghers bought "shares" in the theater, filling its coffers with a further 100,000 guilders. Thus all levels of society were involved in different ways. In early 1881, after 30 years of fundraising, the goal of a national theater was on the verge of being realized.

Figure 11. A share certificate issued by the National Theater Association.

Destroyed and Rebuilt

The inauguration of the *Národní divadlo* in the same year was ill-starred from the outset. To stress its importance as a state occasion, František Ladislav Rieger, the driving force in the National Theater Association, invited high-ranking representatives of the monarchy to attend. With much effort, he managed to gain confirmation from Crown Prince Rudolf and his wife Stefanie of their attendance on May 25. But they canceled at the last minute due to Stefanie allegedly falling ill. The fact that they had attended the German-language Estates Theater just one evening previously exacerbated the Czechs' disappointment. Rieger's daughter, librettist Marie Červinkova-Riegrová, noted in her diary: "Prague is indignant. Stefanie is sick and they have announced that she will not be coming. In Prague all the preparations for her welcome were complete, they cost a lot of money, and many people who came from the country were of course disappointed."[29] Any visitors to Prague hoping for a repeat of 1868's festivities would also have been frustrated. Rieger had invited only 300 high-ranking figures in a deliberate bid to ensure a statelier event than thirteen years previously.[30] In this way, he hoped to avoid confrontation with the government and deprive the Young Czechs of a rallying opportunity. The public resented this elitist arrangement. Many had made donations to the National Theater and wanted to take part in its inauguration.[31]

Rieger was able to pacify these critics by promising a second opening ceremony on St. Wenceslas Day in September 1881, by which time the roof paneling and other final details were due to be complete.

But it never came to this. On August 12, 1881, welders working on the roof of the National Theater accidentally started a fire which soon set the whole building ablaze. Within a few hours the National Theater was gutted. *Národní listy*, the highest circulation Czech newspaper, printed a thick black border on the next day's issue surrounding the lines: "With tears in our eyes, with trembling hearts, we bring our countrymen this unexpected, terrible news! Our great, national theater, this toil and endeavor of two whole generations, this magnificent monument to our national rebirth—Oh, curse, if you have a Czech heart!—is no more, it is a ruin."[32] The emotional response was no mere journalistic device. In the streets, many people walked, tearful and distraught, to gaze on the site of the disaster. Rieger, who had initiated the project in 1845 and nurtured it for 36 years, sat at home and wept. Rumors began to circulate that envious Germans had started the fire.[33] But the actual cause—negligence—was ascertained and announced before any disturbances erupted.

The initial shock gave way to a mood of defiance. The very next morning, citizens began donating toward the rebuilding of the theater. Spontaneous collections were held in restaurants and inns and even on the streets. Within five days, 240,000 guilders had been collected. After two weeks the sum had risen to half a million and by the end of 1881 it totaled three quarters of a million.[34] The show of international solidarity was remarkable. The Lemberg town council made a spontaneous donation of 1,000 guilders; the municipal authorities in Krakow pledged 500 guilders and Poznań gave 1,400 marks, equivalent to 1,000 guilders. In Lemberg a charity bazaar was also held in aid of the National Theater.[35] 11 percent of donations came from districts outside the Bohemian Lands. Only Slovakia (then known as Upper Hungary) proved less openhanded.

After the fire, Czech relations with Poland intensified. *Divadelní listy* wrote in 1881 in response to the sympathy and donations from all three Partition regions: "The numerous voices from Galicia, the province of Posen, the kingdom, Polesia and Lithuania, indeed, from all sides where the sweet Polish language resounds, are precious evidence of the fact that the idea of our national fraternity is already in our blood and has permeated nearly all levels of Polish society."[36] Actually, this could not have been true of most Galician peasants, who could not read and had never set foot in a theater, but it was certainly true of the Polish intelligentsia. They regarded the *teatr narodowy w Pradze* as their own; as *swój*. In return, the Provisional Theater showed a number of Polish works, including Moniuszko's *Halka* in 1868.

All the many generous donations from abroad were outdone, however, by the contribution of the Habsburgs. Political discord notwithstanding, they appreciated the great symbolic value of a cultural institution like the National Theater. Franz Josef and the empress donated 20,000 guilders toward the reconstruction of the National Theater; heir apparent Rudolf and his wife Stefanie gave 5,000 guilders, and Archduke Ludwig Viktor, 1,000 guilders.

The Bohemian nobility also gave generously. A list of postfire benefactors records seven princes and 27 countesses and counts, and individual donations of up to 4,000 guilders.[37] Overall, however, the nobility played a lesser role than in the 1850s and 1860s. Some families had disassociated themselves from the theater initiative; others proved more cautious the second time around. The Young Czechs, who, like the Galician democrats around Dobrzański, opposed the aristocracy on principle, were partly to blame for this. *Národní listy*, for example, claimed that the "Czech and Moravian people" had done far more for the cohesion of the Bohemian Lands than the aristocracy,[38] implying that the aristocracy was not part of the Czech nation. For their part, the nobility did not identify with the new wave of Czech nationalism, which was language oriented and increasingly ethnically exclusive. Aristocrats benevolently subscribed to boxes in the Provisional Theater but preferred to patronize the Estates Theater, where they were among their own kind. Some Jewish families, who were more assimilated into Prague's majority society than the Jews in Lemberg, also made notable contributions.

As well as private donors, some institutions contributed to the rebuilding of the theater. The provincial diet donated a total of 208,000 guilders for the royal box, the chandelier in the auditorium, and improved fire precautions and sanitation. The city council and the Prague savings bank each donated 50,000 guilders, and the fire insurance policy yielded 275,000 guilders. In this way, then, a number of large and very many small contributions made up the total of 2.18 million guilders required for the construction and reconstruction of the National Theater.[39] Interestingly, these data destroy the myth that the Czech people carried the cost of their national theater alone.

On the outside, the rebuilt *Národní Divadlo* appeared almost exactly like its predecessor. A grand neorenaissance house, it called to mind Bohemia's last period of sovereignty, when Prague was the residence of the Habsburgs.[40] But inside, the design sparked a controversy. It struck a compromise between the old and the new world; between a classic box-theater and a civic theater. While there were nearly 40 boxes in three balconies directly adjoining the stage, the mid-section of the balconies facing the stage contained rows of seats where the audience could sit shoulder to shoulder. The orchestra level was similarly arranged, with comfortable armchairs near the stage.

Figure 12. The Czech National Theater in Prague.

Other opera houses and above all the Semper Theater had proven how seating arrangement influenced audience behavior and listening culture. In a theater with boxes, visitors could come and go as they pleased and behave in the boxes however they liked. An audience in open seating, however, was more obliged to conform to social norms. For many years, the European nobility regarded the action on stage as peripheral and gossiped, ate, or slept during performances. A certain Count Schönborn was notorious for his loud snoring during performances at the Provisional Theater. The burghers in Berlin, Paris, Vienna, and other major opera cities, by contrast, had urged audiences to focus on the stage as early as the prerevolutionary era. The arrangement of the seating, then, not only allowed for demonstrations of status but also signified which section of society dictated how to behave in the theater and listen to opera.

In the light of its political relevance, then, the seating arrangement in the National Theater was the subject of fierce debates after the fire. In fall 1881, almost 500 petitioners from Prague and the immediate vicinity wrote in an open letter published in *Divadelní listy*: "In the name of the Czech students, teachers, and the majority of the citizens, in the name of the Czech country dwellers and working people, we demand that the gallery is changed to be befitting to all and the orchestra level enlarged for standing even if it limits the amount of seating for the aristocracy and the wealthy."[41]

Once again, the broad mass of minor donors were claiming their share in the National Theater. And eventually the National Theater Association agreed to changes to the outdated auditorium.[42] The standing-room area was extended to accommodate 800 (as opposed to seating for 1073), which chiefly benefited the lower middle class. In addition, all the circles right up to the fourth were decorated in the same way, in symbolic recognition of the equality of all theater-goers, from the humblest to the wealthiest. The figurehead of the National Theater Association, Old Czech party leader and experienced political strategist František Ladislav Rieger, aligned himself with *Divadelní listy* when he declared in November 1881: "We can say that our National Theater, as it now stands, is the most democratic in the world. Nowhere else does the audience in the least expensive seats have such a good view of the stage."[43] While this was not strictly true, since the Semper Opera's expansive orchestra level, elliptical seating arrangement and set-back partitions between the boxes were probably more "democratic," nobody would quibble with Rieger's attempt to assert the importance of the National Theater. The Czech elites' belief in the democratic nature of their main theater transcended all party boundaries.

In spite of this, the *Národní divadlo*'s second inauguration was also reserved for an exclusively elite public. Unlike in 1881, however, the theater's directors were not prepared to make any concessions for the Habsburgs. When Crown Prince Rudolf and his wife once again wavered on the date, and not even Prince Jiří Lobkowitz was able to secure their confirmation, the opening ceremony took place without them.[44] Rieger, moreover, insisted on his choice of inaugural work. Lobkowitz was in favor of *Dimitrij* by Antonin Dvořák, a grand opera with no politically sensitive content. But the National Theater Association had chosen the opera *Libuše*, which Smetana had written especially for the occasion. It was set in the historical Czech past and extolled the glory and legend of the Bohemian crown. The opera ends with the legendary queen *Libuše* prophesying a magnificent future for the Czechs to majestic music. Crown Prince Rudolf would have understood this opera as a call to accept the crown of St. Wenceslas. Thus, to avoid offense when he attended on the seventh night, *Dimitrij* was performed instead.

The second premiere of *Libuše* on November 18, 1883 was in many respects a touching scene. The ailing Bedřich Smetana sat among the audience to watch the performance of his opera, although his deafness prevented him from hearing it. But the audience applauded his majestic soundscapes and recurring coronation motif all the more heartily. The opera's portrayal of the historical nation and its symbolic legends realized one of the Czech elites's highest political aims, at least on the stage of the National Theater. Opera became a substitute for politics and provided a source of strength for the nation to continue its struggle for equality.[45]

Not only that, the opening was a resounding financial success. The National Theater Association raised the cost of tickets to six times the usual price, making the most expensive box seats 50 guilders and the cheapest tickets for the orchestra level 5 guilders—the cost of feeding an average Prague family for a week. Tickets for the second and third performances cost on average two-and-a-half times more than usual.[46] These profits allowed the association to set aside a reserve fund for the future.

While the lower classes remained outside the theater, they celebrated in their own way. Despite the cold, several thousand people gathered in the streets of Prague's old town to mark the occasion. In the rural parts of the Czech Lands, those who had donated toward the National Theater placed a lit candle in their window as a symbol of Enlightenment.[47] *Národ sobě*—"the nation unto itself"— reads the legend over the stage of the National Theater. The Czech nation had created its own theater.

Notes

1. See *Dějiny českého divadla*, vol. 2, 311. On the social composition of the committee, see Rak, *Divadlo jako*, 50–51.
2. Quoted in Šubert, *Národní divadlo*, 17.
3. This book uses the term Czech National Theater although official documents generally refer to a Bohemian (*böhmisch*) National or State Theater. On the various appeals for donations, see the governorship's files in the National Archive, PM 1850–54, 2-23-4, č 49-50, and the archive of the National Museum.
4. See Bartoš, *Národní divadlo*, 78.
5. Quoted in Bartoš, *Národní divadlo*, 95.
6. The Czech and German-language formulations of this appeal can be found in NA (National Archive, formerly Central State Archive), PM 9, 858. The German version refers to a "Bohemian" (*böhmisch*) nation and national theater.
7. This shows that František Černy's theory that the nobility in Bohemia made "only a very insignificant" contribution to the construction of the National Theater is wrong (Černy, *Idea Národního*, 21).
8. On the architecture of the Provisional Theater, see Hilmera, *Česka Divadelní*, 25–26.
9. On the deficits of 1863 and 1864, see Kadlec, *Družstva*, 24.
10. The takings on this evening totaled a record 600 guilders (later to be broken). See Kadlec, *Družstva*, 22.

11. On the development of Czech drama after 1848, see the comprehensive anthology *Dějiny českého divadla/III.*
12. See Ottlová and Pospíšil, *K motivům*; also Locke, *Opera and Ideology*, 23–28.
13. Jan Havránek's statistics show that over 34 percent of the operas performed 1862–1883 were French, a quarter Italian, a good fifth Czech, and just under a sixth German. See Havránek, *Společenské*, 206.
14. On the opera repertoire from 1866, see J. Bartoš, *Prozatímní divadlo*, 219–74.
15. See the statistics in Kimball, *The Czech*, 123.
16. *Gazeta Narodowa*, May 19, 1868, 1.
17. On the population statistics see Hávranek, *Demografický vyvoj*, 73. On the preparation phase, see "Denní zprávy," *Národní listy*, May 16, 1868, 2.
18. For a complete overview, see Storck, *Kulturnation*, 223.
19. On this procession, see *Národní listy*, May 16, 1868, 4; May 18, 1868, 2.
20. Much of this speech is reproduced in Bartoš, *Národní divadlo*, 216–19.
21. See *Národní listy*, May 18, 1868, 3.
22. For a complete record of the speeches see *Národní listy*, May 19, 1868, 1–2; May 20, 1868, 1–2.
23. See also *Národní listy*.
24. On this and Vienna's failure to compromise with the Czechs see Křen, *Konfliktgemeinschaft*, 144–68.
25. See Šmaha, *Dělali jsme*, 109–10. *Rabagas* also caused feelings to run high in Lemberg, where democrats rejected the piece as a "disgraceful reaction against everything that is free and noble." See "Kronika," *Gazeta Narodowa*, March 7, 1873, 3.
26. See Kadlec, *Družstva*, 57–59; Bartoš, *Dějiny*, 60.
27. See Kadlec, *Družstva*, 87–92.
28. See Kadlec, *Družstva*, 80. On the political conflicts surrounding the National Theater see also Kváček, *Společenskopolitické zápasy*.
29. Quoted in Heidler, *Díl II*, no. 369, 145.
30. Entrance fees were also drastically raised. Tickets for the second, third, and fourth performances in the new theater cost twice as much as usual; at least 50 kreuzers for a regular seat and one guilder or more for an armchair in the orchestra level. See NA, Fond ND, Sign. D. 104/111, "minutes of the managing committee (spravný výbor)" (hereafter MMC) of May 14, 1881.
31. For criticism of the opening festivities, see *Divadelní listy*, April 25, 1881.
32. *Národní listy*, Aug. 13, 1881, 1.
33. See Marie Červinková-Riegrová's notes in Heidler, *Listáry, Díl II*, 154.
34. An exact breakdown of the donations from district councils, institutions, societies, and individuals is given in the appendix of Šubert, *Národní divadlo*. See also Pešek, *Sbírky*, 212.
35. On these donations see *Divadelní listy*, Sept. 10, 1881, 155–56. On currency conversions, see Schneider, *Währungen der Welt*, 95.
36. *Divadelní listy*, Sept. 10, 1881.
37. See the complete list of all donations in Šubert, *Národní divadlo*, appendix.
38. *Národní listy*, May 20, 1868, 1.
39. See Bartoš, *Národní divadlo*, 359.
40. On the historical references made by the various historicist architectural styles, see Marek, ed., *Bauen für die Nation*. By contrast, the new German theater was built in a neo-Baroque style, citing the era which Prague's Germans believed to be the monarchy's and Bohemia's historical prime. On the architecture of this playhouse, see Hilmera, *Česka divadelní*, 42–43.

41. *Divadelní listy*, 30, Sept. 17, 1881, 264.; See also Jiří Hilmera, *Česka Divadekní*, 28.
42. See "Opravy v Národním divadle," *České Noviny*, Aug. 23, 1881, 1.
43. Quoted in Kimball, *The Czech*, 144.
44. See the correspondence between Lobkowitz and Rieger in Heidler, *Listáŕy*, *Díl II*, 212–13.
45. Reports on the opening performance appeared in all the major Czech daily newspapers on Nov. 19 and 20, 1883.
46. A full list of prices is given in *Divadelní listy*, Dec. 7, 1883, 262.
47. See "Národ sobie," *Dziennik Polski*, Oct. 4, 1900, 3.

CHAPTER SEVEN

A Theater for all Classes

Theater Director František Adolf Šubert

The very grandeur of the National Theater posed a challenge to the people running it. It had capacity for nearly twice as many patrons as the Provisional Theater and was equipped with the latest stage technology. The public's expectations rose in consequence. Prague critics demanded performances which could measure up to those of the major European theaters and especially the Royal Theater in Vienna. New faces were called for to run the new theater. A "great assembly" of the National Theater Association, in which all shareholders were eligible to take part, was held in March 1883 to discuss potential candidates. Rather surprisingly, the writer František Adolf Šubert was elected director of the National Theater.[1]

Šubert was only 34 years old at the time and, as the sixth child of a saddler, from a humble background.[2] His career was an example of the opportunities offered by the Habsburg Empire's education system. Born in rural eastern Bohemia, Šubert attended high school in Königgrätz and university in Prague. At the time of his appointment he was known only among a small circle, mainly for his 1882 play *Probuzenci* ("The Re-awakeners"). He was elected thanks to support from Rieger and his affinity with the Old Czechs, who may have hoped to maintain their own influence by appointing a relatively inexperienced director. Endowed with only limited powers at first, Šubert required the approval of the National Theater Association's managing committee on important issues such as the engagement and dismissal of soloists. From the outset, then, the Prague theater director's position was far weaker than that of the director in Dresden or the impresario in Lemberg. The managing committee was also elected by the great assembly, which met twice a year and embodied the National Theater's grounding in Czech society. The committee and votes ensured that the theater's organization contained a strong democratic element—something which was totally absent in Dresden and only indirectly represented in Lemberg by the provincial diet and its theater commission.

Despite his meteoric career, Šubert did not forget his humble beginnings. His popular dramas depicted the life of simple folk and sympathized with the fate of the workers. Aesthetically, his main influence was Emile Zola.[3] He soon warmed to opera, which was initially alien to him, realizing that music theater was crucial for the financial well-being of his institution and hence for his own position. Although the general aims of the National Theater—strengthening Czech culture and the audience's national awareness—lay close to his heart, he was not a narrow-minded cultural nationalist. Immediately after his election he declared to the great assembly of the National Theater Association that he intended to "always combine ideal efforts toward artistic achievement at the theater with constant consideration for practical necessities."[4] In concrete terms this meant that, if need be, he would place box office considerations over those of a national and educational repertoire. Thus he set the course for a fundamental conflict during his tenure, which lasted 17 years, from 1883 to 1900.

Šubert was not involved in everyday politics but he understood the dynamics of the new mass society better than the Old Czechs' leadership. He saw the population's involvement in the National Theater project as an opportunity to broaden its public. For Šubert the theater was an instrument of *osvěta*, the education of the whole nation. He had experienced the mood of national awakening and the laying of the foundation stones as a youth and wanted to create a theater for all social strata. Toward the end of his tenure, his late-Enlightenment and egalitarian convictions transformed him from a conservative to a sympathizer of the Social Democrats.

Theater Trains and Workers' Performances

It soon emerged that Šubert had considerable organizational talent. While the National Theater Association was preoccupied with the grand opening, in fall 1883, Šubert set about publicizing specially arranged "theater trains" (*divadelní vlaky*); an offer he had devised to bring the rural population to the National Theater, often with an overnight stay included. Just ten days after the theater opened, on November 28, 1883, the first train arrived from Kolín, a town 50 kilometers east of Prague in the Bohemian heartland. So many people in Kolín had wanted to take the opportunity to see *The Bartered Bride* and the new National Theater that they could not all be accommodated in one weekend. After the initial group of 630, two further trains brought a total of 1,560 visitors from Kolín in January.[5] Hence about a sixth of the town's population of 13,000 traveled to the National Theater in the first three months of its existence.

Theater trains were soon offered across Bohemia. In ten months, 114 trains took passengers from all regions of the Czech Lands to Prague. In 1884, a contingent of 184 emigrants even arrived from the US via Hamburg.[6] Not only members of the middle class but also farmers and laborers who had donated to the

National Theater and wanted to see the final product—the "golden house" in Prague—took advantage of the theater trains. According to the records, they were very pleased and even moved by what they saw.

One account by a Polish commentator, then living in Bohemia, bears witness to this: "We arrived in the Golden City before the performance began and went as a body to the theater. There was something tremendously beautiful, uplifting, somehow allying, about this procession to Prague's shrine to art; a certain warmth prevailed, a special mood which simply cannot be put into words."[7] For many the trip to the National Theater was one of the best days of their life, not only on account of the performance but also the experience of community. The quasi-religious tone of the account above was characteristic of a widespread attitude. The National Theater's audience behaved as if in church. The people sat in reverent silence, devoting their attention to the action on the stage, which had in a sense replaced the altar. Only the saints were missing, but they were found in time. The recently deceased Smetana was the first to be enshrined in national memory.

Running theater trains made above all economic sense. In 1884 alone, the National Theater realized 80,000 guilders from visitors from the country. That was equivalent to a quarter of box office revenue. Thus guests from outside Prague yielded a greater profit than the primarily local, bourgeois subscription holders.[8] This income was vital in the early days of the National Theater and made it far more robust than the Polish Theater in Lemberg, which suffered frequent financial difficulties in the 1870s and 1880s, partly because it had no appeal beyond the Galician capital and its environs. Šubert's ingenious idea was soon imitated elsewhere in Bohemia. In 1888, the newly opened New German Theater installed a special train service to lure the German-speaking population from the border regions to Prague.[9] However, not only did the predominantly German-speaking towns such as Reichenberg have their own theaters but the inhabitants of the border regions could also travel to Dresden or Vienna with relative ease. Consequently, this train service did not prove as popular.

Emboldened, Šubert set about trying to reach the urban lower classes. In 1893, the National Theater introduced so-called "peoples' performances" (*představení pro lid*) in the afternoons.[10] These enabled craftsmen, junior clerks, young teachers, and maids to attend at little cost. Social tensions were rising, and Šubert feared the disintegration of the Czech nation into a mutually detached middle class and industrial under class. He viewed the Germans in Bohemia as a timely reminder that social elitism could weaken a community. They had dwindled to a minority in Prague two generations earlier, having alienated many of Bohemia's bilingual inhabitants. Moreover, the theater scene threatened to fragment if the industrial workers evolved their own subculture, as they did in Berlin and Vienna. The National Theater, to Šubert, was the place to preserve the unity of the nation and its cultural life.

In view of this, he began to promote the integration of workers both within the theater and without. Not content with convincing some labor associations to buy season tickets for the National Theater,[11] Šubert pushed through a proposal to open the theater exclusively to the Social Democratic laborforce on the eve of May 1, 1898, against opposition from the National Theater Association and the provincial diet. On this occasion, then, workers not only stood in the fourth circle but also occupied the best seats and boxes in the house. To open this politically controversial night's show, the orchestra played the dramatic overture *Husitská* by Antonín Dvořák, which was inspired by the history of the Hussites and lasted nearly quarter of an hour. It was followed by some poetry by Svatopluk Čech and a tableau vivant of laborers designed by the director-in-chief of the National Theater, Josef Šmaha. For the finale, the theater presented *Služebník svého Pána* by František Jeřábek, a naturalist tragedy and critique of capitalism written in 1870.

Extending the plan to open the theater to new sections of society also paid off financially. The workers, who filled the theater to capacity, left over 800 guilders in the cash box—distinctly more than an average evening's takings for spoken drama.[12] Politically, too, the occasion was a success. The enormous police presence in the street in front of the National Theater, ready to nip any disturbances in the bud, was not called upon. The simply but neatly dressed workers entered the theater, handed in their coats—as the Social Democratic newspaper *Právo lidu* had advised in the previous day's issue—and went silently to their seats. But the calm ended when the performance began. Every item on the program was followed by thunderous applause and there were repeated ovations calling for the curtain to be raised after Josef Šmaha's tableau vivant. František Jeřábek's play elicited strong personal reactions. During the scenes in which the dishonest and exploitative factory owner Dornenkron came into conflict with the ordinary Czech workers, the spectators grew so excited they could not stay in their seats. They animatedly followed every twist and turn of the plot, applauding in agreement or calling out objections. Finally, when the aristocratic factory owner with the German name and the Czech protagonist tragically perish, the audience was so stunned it remained seated for some time. *Právo lidu* ran an in-depth review the next day, describing the evening as a "great moral triumph for the proletarian cause."[13] And the workers had proven that they could be almost as disciplined an audience as the middle class. Yet while the working-class press praised Šubert for opening the theater up, the Young Czechs, who had dominated Bohemian politics since 1889, unleashed a storm of criticism. They called Šubert a traitor to the national cause for handing over the National Theater to internationalist Social Democrats but ignoring the Czech "national workers' political club." The following year, this conflict was avoided by giving two successive workers' performances.[14]

Ultimately, Šubert achieved his aim of broadening the theater's public by means of these special arrangements. While theater trains began to run less frequently toward the end of his tenure, more than ten percent of all performances were still "peoples' performances." In addition, the National Theater provided reduced price tickets on three to four afternoons a week and a special arrangement for schoolchildren and students once a month. In this way, sections of the population were integrated into the audience which would have been confined to the highest circle and standing room in the Royal Theaters in Vienna and Dresden and in Lemberg. As far as possible for the day, Šubert had created a "theater for all."

The Limits of Social Cohesion

All these achievements and even the overwhelming success of the National Theater at the International Music and Theater Exhibition in Vienna counted for little when it came to reelecting the theater's management in 1900. The provincial diet, under the sway of the Young Czechs, voted to entrust the National Theater to the Young Czech National Theater Association (*Společnost národního divadla*). They promptly launched a press campaign against Šubert and he was forced to give up his post.

Another major change introduced by the new management was an independent opera director. Karel Kovařovic, a conductor and composer of several popular operas and ballets, who had achieved some fame as director of the orchestra at the Bohemian ethnographic exhibition of 1895, was appointed.[15] In contrast to Šubert, he came from a financially secure, bourgeois Prague background. Irritated by the orchestra's supposed lack of dynamism and precision, the occasional imprecise entry, and intonation problems, Kovařovic made it his primary goal to iron out all the *Šlendrián*—the "sloppiness"—in the now independent opera department. He increased the number of rehearsals and scolded individual musicians in front of the entire orchestra. Singers or musicians who protested against his methods faced dismissal.

Kovařovic's arrogant, uncompromising approach soon precipitated a disaster. On February 9, 1901, during a performance of *Carmen,* Kovařovic became embroiled in an argument with one of the principal violinists, whom he accused of having played off key in rehearsal. The next day he dismissed the violinist for intentionally scratching the strings during the performance. That night—a performance of *Tannhäuser* was scheduled—the orchestra refused to play. Gustav Schmoranz, Šubert's successor as director of the National Theater, rushed to the scene to urge the musicians into action, since the audience was already waiting. But displaying neither tact nor sensitivity, he failed to defuse the situation. The members of the orchestra would not take their places until the deputy chief conductor stepped in.[16]

The next day, the orchestral musicians published a statement to the press listing the reasons for their strike. These included several attacks by Kovařovic on individual musicians, in which he hurled abuse and threatened them with dismissal. On one occasion he even accused the entire orchestra of playing like hurdy-gurdy men.[17] Yet it was not only humiliation at the hands of Kovařovic that caused the ensemble to strike, but also economic injustice. While the fees for soloists had more than doubled since 1883, the wages of chorus singers and musicians had barely risen. At a strike meeting, one member of the male chorus calculated that "90 percent of the staff subsists on 30-40 guilders" while the fees paid to Schmoranz, Kovařovic, and star tenor Karel Burian amounted to 68,000 guilders in one year.[18]

A day later, the strikers made it clear that they would not return to work until "the social differences in this 'golden house' are at least brought to a tolerable level."[19] The music journal *Dalibor* and a section of the daily press supported their demands. Solidarity also came from abroad. The Lemberg orchestra sent a telegram urging the strikers to "hold out" and colleagues at the New German Theater and in the Viennese musicians' association declared their support.[20] Meanwhile, the musicians and choir gave concerts to help fill the strike fund.

Like unscrupulous industrialists, the directors of the National Theater responded to the strike by dismissing the entire orchestra, followed by the male chorus and the stage technicians when they joined in support. The musicians were easily replaced, some well-known singers criticized the strike, and the pickets crumbled. Kovařovic rehearsed intensively with the new orchestra and on March 9, exactly a month after the dispute erupted, the opera department of the National Theater staged a complete performance of *The Marriage of Figaro*. Police patrolled outside the building and in the foyer. Plain-clothes policemen were deployed among the circles and in the standing room area in the orchestra level to ensure that order was maintained, and the gallery in the fourth circle was closed as a security measure.[21] The following night, the opera *Werther* by Massenet went off without disturbance. Kovařovic had won out. The new orchestra was no worse than the old one and more obedient.

The National Theater's public image, however, had been severely damaged. The working-class newspaper *Právo lidu* wrote with dismay: "The performance on Saturday, which took place under police protection, with the united cudgels securing the artistic and aesthetic values of the Czech bourgeoisie, did not do the theater administration credit. Nevertheless the truth must be told that the Czech bourgeoisie completely dominated the performance, even if only with the help of the police."[22] The sincerity of the theater's national mission was called into question by strikers and the left-wing press who accused the Young Czechs of using national arguments as a pretext for glossing over social divisions. The strike was called off, but a note of discord lingered. Schmoranz continued to vent his anger at the insubordination in the theater's annual report. The "minor theater staff" he declared, must have hoped for a "social revolution, by God" from the new theater directors.[23] This distinction between "important" people in the theater and merely "minor staff," which Šubert would never have made, was characteristic of the new generation of developed bourgeoisie, as Marx would have it. Meanwhile, one positive outcome of the strike was that an independent Czech Philharmonic Orchestra was founded, by musicians of the National Theater orchestra who were laid off in 1901.

The Czech population was rapidly transforming into a modern class society. Since the 1860s, the small Czech elite had been joined by the *haute bourgeoisie* and a large working class. The names and professions of the National Theater's season ticket holders reflect the patterns of social change. While the records for the Provisional Theater and the first years of the *Národní divadlo* show many artisans and small shop owners,[24] after 1900, there were mostly industrialists and property owners. Rather than signifying one social group's displacement by another, this was chiefly a sign of the social advancement of the founding generation. This new elite, like the nobility at the Estates Theater previously, treated their subscriptions like family heirlooms, making it increasingly difficult for newcomers to find vacancies.

By and large, the nobility withdrew from the theater. The Young Czechs, who were constantly agitating against the Bohemian nobility in *Národní listy*, were now in control. On the day that the strike began in February 1901, the lead article in the features section indirectly attributed it to a lack of aristocratic patronage at the National Theater.[25] The Schwarzenberg, Waldstein, and Thun families, who had generously supported the theater project in the 1850s and after the fire of 1881 and paid considerable sums for boxes, must have perceived this as gross ingratitude. They retreated to the Estates Theater and withdrew their names from the list of subscription holders.[26] The loss was not deeply felt by the National Theater. The doyens of the newly prosperous Czech middle class simply took their places.

Nevertheless, the National Theater could not avert an acute financial crisis in early 1902. Within the space of a few months, the theater's deficit had grown to over 120,000 crowns (60,000 guilders in old money), for which the members of the National Theater Society were liable. Angered at the losses and the delay in being informed, the entire committee resigned in May of that year. To make matters worse, the chairman of the society, Alois Wiesner, had become involved in an embezzlement scandal surrounding suspiciously high printing costs for tickets, the theater journal *Meziakti* and the National Theater's annual report.[27]

Yet the manner in which this situation was handled proved how efficiently the National Theater was run in comparison to Dresden's Royal Theater and the Lemberg Theater under Pawlikowski. Any corruption on a financial or administrative level was soon uncovered by the monitoring of the democratically organized association of sponsors. Once identified, the irregularities could be attended to. Wiesner was forced to resign and a commission was set up to devise economizing measures. The greatest financial challenge, meanwhile, lay in the steadily rising costs for fees, stage sets, and lighting. These expenses, which continued to grow exponentially after the turn of the century, made it difficult for the theater to provide seats at low prices. The amount of peoples' performances stagnated and the number of lower-class members of the regular audience declined.

Around the turn of the century, a series of additional playhouses—mostly for the working and lower classes—opened in Prague's suburbs.[28] In 1907, the defunct National Theater Association led by Šubert founded a prestigious theater in the Vinohrady district of Prague (*Divadlo na Vinohradech*) with its old capital stock. All these new venues vied with the National Theater, especially for the ordinary public. Moreover, the rural population no longer had to travel to Prague to attend the theater, since smaller towns such as Pilsen and Mlada Boleslav now also had theaters. Although the establishment of these local institutions was theoretically consistent with the aims of the early Czech theater activists, in practice it meant an end to the unity of all classes under one roof. The new theaters in Prague competed with the National Theater especially in the fields of operetta, comedy, and revues. The National Theater asserted its superiority—and justified its markedly higher subsidies since 1895—by offering distinctly sophisticated entertainment. But the highbrow repertoire did not have broad appeal and sometimes played to only half-full houses. The Enlightenment utopia of theater as a site of universal education had reached its limit.

And yet the aura of the "golden house" overlooking the Vltava River was remarkable. Even Czechs who never visited the theater knew it and identified with it. Although the extent of its social appeal was stagnating, Czech opera was gaining popularity. *The Bartered Bride*, for example, was performed nearly 500 times between 1883 and 1915 at the National Theater alone. Cautiously estimating that there was 80 percent attendance at each performance, at least three-quarters-of-a-million people must have seen this opera in this period. Other works such as *Dalibor*, *Lohengrin*, *Aida*, and *Faust* also played to six-figure audiences. This matched attendances at the New German Theater, where the most popular pieces, including *Manon, Lohengrin*, and *Mastersingers of Nuremberg*, attracted 200,000 to 300,000 patrons over the space of ten to fifteen years.[29] Music theater was, then, not only high culture but also popular culture. Opera was disseminated via other channels beyond the grand theater stage. Smetana's comic operas were performed in countless smaller theaters and open-air venues, and piano scores were published in editions of tens of thousands. The Czechs became an opera nation, as in love with the artform as the Italians.[30]

Notes

1. On Šubert's election, see NA, Fond ND, Sign. D. 97/12, Protocoll of the Great Assembly of the National Theater Association (herafter PVA) of March 12, 1883.
2. A family tree drawn by Šubert can be found in his book *Vývod Rodu Šubertův a Wobořilův ve východních Čechach s jejich nejbližším přibuzenstvem*.
3. In his writings, Šubert made frequent reference to Zola's 1881 publication *Le naturalisme au théatre*.
4. NA, Fond ND, Sign. D. 97/12, *MMC* of March 12, 1883.
5. See Šubert, *Dějiny*, CXXX and CXXXI. A more detailed account of the theater trains program can be found in Šubert, *Dějiny*, 76–77.
6. On the theater trains in the first year of the National Theater, see the theater's annual report, which can be found in the Archive of the National Theater (hereafter AND). Here: AND, Annual Report 1 (1884), 20 (Until 1900, the annual reports of the National Theater were drawn up by František Adolf Šubert, from 1900 by his successor as director Gustav Schmoranz. The numbering was included in the titles of the reports, which are therefore *První rok Národního divadla, Druhý rok Národního divadla* etc.).
7. *Dziennik Polski*, Oct. 4, 1900, *Národ sobie*.
8. See the annual balance sheet of 1884, which shows total income and expenditure of 450,000 guilders; Šubert, *Dějiny*, CXXXVII.
9. See *Národní listy*, April 19, 1888.
10. NA, Fond ND, Sign. D, 114/5, MMC of Nov. 4, 1893.
11. See NA, Fond ND, Sign. D. 50, MMC of Nov. 16, 1895.
12. See Šubert, *Dějiny*, CIX.
13. It is interesting to compare the reports in *Právo lidu*, May 1, 1898, 2, and the conservative newspaper *Hlas národa*, May 1, 1891, 3.
14. On the debate on workers' performances see *Hlas národa*, April 30, 1891, 2; also NA, Fond ND, Sign.D. 51, 527.
15. On Kovařovic's career and compositions, see Němeček, *Opera Národního*, 19–53.
16. See *Národní listy*, Feb. 11, 1901, 3. The conflict is closely considered in Němeček, *Opera Národního*, 59–80. Němeček is clearly writing in defence of Kovařovic. For a similar view, see also Kvapíl, *O čem vím*, 306–12. For a more critical view of Kovařovic, see Nejedlý, *Opera národního divadla od roku 1900*, 33–45.
17. See the orchestra's statement in the journal *Dalibor*, Feb. 16, 1901, 54–55.
18. *Právo lidu*, Feb 16, 1901, 3.
19. *Právo lidu*, Feb 17, 1901, 5.
20. *Právo lidu*, Feb. 17, 1901, 3; also Němeček, *Opera Národního*, 70.
21. *Právo lidu*, March 10, 1901, 3–4.
22. *Právo lidu*, March 11, 1901, 2.
23. AND, Annual Report 18 (1901), 18.
24. On social developments since the 1848 revolution, see Urban, *Die tschechische Gesellschaft*. On the social standing of subscription-holders, see the list of names of the same, printed annually in the theater diaries of the National Theater; *Divadelní Kalendář*, 1882–1914.
25. See *Národní listy*, Feb. 10, 1901, 1.
26. Prince Jiří Lobkowitz was the only aristocrat to keep his box after the turn of the century.
27. On the resulting losses, see NA, Fond ND, Společnost ND, Sign. 17, folder for 1902, no pagination, (my thanks go to the National Archive for making the unprocessed files available); and Němeček, *Opera Národního*, 137.

28. See the list of new theater buildings in, *Česka Divadelní*, 53.
29. See Tancsik, *Die Prager*, 58–60.
30. Any assertion of the popular appeal of opera should, of course, be founded on precise theoretical considerations. Among the groundbreaking studies of Italy in this field is, e.g., Leydi, *Verbreitung und Popularisierung*, 321–28.

CHAPTER EIGHT

The Opera Nation

Emancipation from German Culture

Looking back on the National Theater's first season, František Adolf Šubert proudly pointed out that not one German work had been performed. This anti-German sentiment, shared by many members of Czech society, was something of an *idée fixe*. A glance at the repertoires of the Provisional Theater and the National Theater in its first decade shows that most of the competition for Czech drama and opera did not come from Germany or Austria but from France and Italy.

This lasting antagonism toward German culture was rooted in a Czech sense of inferiority compounded by the arrogant German attitude that the Czechs were a nation without history or culture. Šubert wanted to prove to the Germans, and even more so to his fellow countrymen, that the National Theater could thrive without German-language dramas and operas. In 1882 he announced that no German works would be shown, even producing exclusively Czech operas for the first six weeks of the season. These included Smetana's *Libuše* and *The Bartered Bride,* two operas each by Antonín Dvořák and Karel Bendl and some other Czech works.

But the National Theater could not have fulfilled its educative duty to the Czech public without showing some foreign works. Šubert staged classic drama by Shakespeare, Corneille, Calderón and Schiller as well as operas by Mozart. It was contemporary works such as *Carmen, Faust,* and *Aida,* however, which were most popular. While these lavish productions increased the pressure on the German theater to compete, they were also a challenge to Czech opera. Smetana's *The Kiss* and *The Two Widows* flopped on the large stage of the National Theater as did new compositions by Bendl and Fibich. When members of the intelligentsia and music nationalists complained that native works were disadvantaged,

Šubert responded by warning that the Czech audience might be lost to the Estates Theater if deprived of the latest sensations and international repertoire pieces.

This reasoning led to the first production of a German opera in the second season: Wagner's *Lohengrin*. Demand to see the first Wagner work in Czech was so great that the premiere was sold out by ten o'clock in the morning. Unlike its performance in Lemberg in 1877, *Lohengrin*'s Prague premiere was a triumph. The critics praised the lavish sets by Viennese studio Kautsky and Brioschi, which were strikingly similar to the sets for *Libuše*.[1] The audience cheered the performers, including the theater's controversial principal tenor, Dalmatian Carlo Raverta, who had learned the part of Lohengrin in the Czech translation. Šubert, too, was much lauded for opening the National Theater to music drama and hence to "aesthetic progress." The various reviews of 1885 show that, for the most part, the Czech music scene had made its peace with Wagner.[2] Music theorist Otakar Hostinský, whose creative, positive reception of Wagner contradicted leading Viennese critic Eduard Hanslick, played a key role in this.

Contemporary Czech critics and musicologists seized upon the importance of narrative content in Wagner's work. Following the premiere of *Lohengrin*, the newspaper *Národní listy* wrote, in accord with Hostinský, that Wagner gave the libretto priority over the music. This was an adventurous interpretation of Wagner's Zurich essays, in which he actually described text and music as equally valid means of conveying drama.[3] Nevertheless, Hostinský's view shaped the further development of Czech opera, especially influencing Zdeněk Fibich, whose work is characterized by leitmotifs, continuous music, and an emphasis on drama. Hence the development of Czech opera took a different path from that of Polish opera in the 1880s and 1890s, which continued to take its cue from the set-number style of Italianate opera.

With its brilliant production of *Lohengrin*, the National Theater struck a blow against the Germans' claim to cultural supremacy in Bohemia. For decades, the Estates Theater had been known as one of the leading venues for Wagner operas and even been the site of Europe's first Wagner cycle in 1856. Now the National Theater's comparable success—in the first season alone there were 18 reprises of *Lohengrin*—challenged the very existence of the Estates Theater. Not all theater-goers shared the critics' view that Czechs should only attend the National Theater and Germans the German Theater. Many were quite prepared to try out the competition.[4] By 1884, the city's most famed institution was facing mounting losses. A year later, it was nearing bankruptcy. This did not bode well for the German-speaking population. Since the 1848 revolution, Prague had become a 90 percent Czech city in which the German and German-speaking Jewish communities had dwindled to small minorities, and whose theater had now also failed.

It did not, however, spell the end of the German competition, as it had in Lemberg in 1872 and Budapest in 1889. Prominent members of Prague's German-speaking population founded a theater association and embarked on a fundraising campaign following the Czech example.[5] Thanks to the generous donations of some wealthy German and Jewish members of the *haute bourgeoisie*, within the space of just a few years, the New German Theater was built according to a design by Viennese architects Helmer and Fellner. Opened in 1888, the new opera house provided the German speakers in Prague with a venue that could rival the National Theater in terms of opulence and technical equipment.

Even if *Lohengrin*'s positive reception in Prague signified a new Czech openness toward German culture, parochialism often prevailed in everyday life. The National Theater prided itself on the fact that, with the exception of some soloists, its ensemble was comprised exclusively of Czechs, or people who identified themselves as such. Nationality was not easy to define, especially among the generation that had begun their careers at the Provisional Theater. As in the case of Smetana, who conducted his private correspondence in German right up until the 1860s,[6] it was the individual's sense of allegiance that was decisive.

Twenty years later, a scandal surrounding Czech actress and singer Marie Pospišilová showed how intolerant Czech nationalism had become. One of the stars of the newly opened *Národní divadlo*, she was dismissed in late 1884 after falling out with Šubert. She subsequently toured Poland and returned to Prague six months later to give a performance—oh, the treachery of it!—at the Estates Theater. In fact, Pospišilová was acting in all pragmatism, since there was no other equivalent venue in Prague. But Šubert was furious, and the national press fumed that she should be banned from the National Theater.[7] The case was not yet closed as Pospišilová had friends in high places, including the governor, with whom she was having an affair. She now used her excellent political connections to rally support. In early 1886, a sizable group of subscription holders demanded her reinstatement in an open letter to Šubert. But this did not sway the director, who was determined to make an example of her. Nine years on, enough water seemed to have passed under the bridge and the executive committee of the National Theater Association proposed a guest performance by Pospišilová. On this occasion, however, the audience proved obstructive. Although the actress had pledged her earnings from the four evenings to Czech charities, "a storm of catcalls, whistles and boos resounded," that did not abate until the police had made numerous arrests.[8] Such a commotion in response to a perceived act of national disloyalty would have been unimaginable in Dresden, Lemberg, or Budapest, where the Habsburgs' compromise with the Poles and the Hungarians had reduced linguistic rivalry and eased tensions.

Tenor Carlo Raverta—the first Czech Lohengrin—also fell foul of national bigotry. The critics could not forgive him for failing to sing all of his parts in

Czech. Raised near the Adriatic Sea under the influence of Italian culture, Raverta was prone to getting carried away and bellowing out his solos—especially the well-known arias—in Italian, repeating them if the applause warranted it. A part of the audience loved this traditional *belcanto*, but the newspaper *Národní listy* and the music journal *Dalibor* demanded purely Czech performances. Finally, in 1886, the National Theater dropped Raverta, despite the protests of a group of over eighty subscription holders.[9] They did not know that an excellent replacement for Raverta was already waiting in the wings. Šubert had persuaded young tenor Władysław Florjański, an accomplished performer of lyrical as well as heroic roles, to leave Lemberg for Prague. A native Polish speaker, he was able to learn Czech with relative ease and Florjanský, as he was known in Czech, soon became a favorite of the Prague audience. The rakish and constantly impecunious tenor was especially adored by his female public, who helped to finance his glittering lifestyle by paying for private performances and signed photographs.

Fostering a star cult was part of Šubert's financial calculus. As many European stars of the stage were persuaded to appear in Prague as possible. Besides Emma Turolla, these included Maria Wilt from the Royal Opera in Vienna in 1884 and the indisputable queen of opera, Adelina Patti, in 1885.[10] The large fees demanded by such international personalities were easily recovered by higher ticket prices. After a time, *Narodní listy* reflected on the hyperbole surrounding these appearances with the ironic commentary: "The dearest to us was Miss Turolla, the fattest was Ms Wiltová . . . and the most expensive, Ms Adelina Patti."[11] Despite signs of public fatigue, the guest performances were continued because they helped to make money and to publicize the National Theater throughout Europe, which was essential for the Czechs to gain recognition as a cultural nation.

In 1885 Šubert extended his network to France and invited Camille Saint-Saëns to the theater. The founder of the *Société Nationale de Musique* had recently experienced the animosity of the Prussian public when a concert he gave in Berlin was booed, apparently in retaliation for Paris's rejection of *Tannhäuser* in 1861. It was, then, a strategic moment to invite Saint-Saëns to Prague. The composer's gala concert at the National Theater was a great success, and he was moved by the audience's cheers and unusually warm response. The Czech newspapers declared it appropriate compensation for the scandal in Berlin and contrasted their own civilized nation with the uncouth behavior of the Germans.[12] The old axiom that your enemy's foe is your friend had proved right again.

A few weeks after Saint-Saëns's appearance, Šubert traveled to Italy, where it was rumored that Guiseppe Verdi had composed a new opera at last. Although still a relative unknown among European theater directors two years into his tenure, Šubert managed to make contact with Verdi through Czech soprano Teresa Stolzová, who had performed the title role in the world premiere of *Aida* in Cairo and was the maestro's lover.[13] At a meeting she arranged in February 1886, Verdi asked

Šubert about the Bohemian and Austrian theater scenes and opera at Prague's National Theater and warmed sufficiently to Šubert to promise him first performance rights for *Otello* after the world premiere in Milan. In early 1887, the Vienna Court Opera and a number of German theaters began vying for the same rights. The Vienna Opera's offer of a large sum of money and a premiere in German on the emperor's saint's day was accepted and Šubert brushed aside by Verdi's publisher Ricordi. But thanks to Tereza Stolzová's mediation, Verdi renewed his promise to Šubert. *Otello* was hastily translated into Czech and given its first performance north of the Alps on January 7, 1888, in Prague. With this major coup, the National Theater finally gained recognition as an opera house of renown in Central Europe. Theater directors, conductors, and critics from Berlin, Dresden, Vienna, and many other cities attended the premiere in Prague which was well received on all sides. Verdi telegraphed his congratulations from Italy, expressing his "thanks and respect to all those who took part in the performance."[14]

Otello also marked the introduction of some important changes in performance practice at the National Theater, including a realistic style and more deliberate approach to stage direction. Director (and actor) Josef Šmaha urged the singers to move and act more expressively, forming a stark contrast to the opulently decorated but scantily directed productions in vogue at the major German royal theaters. Furthermore, Władysław Florjański gave a superb performance as Otello, which established him as the theater's star tenor. Henceforth, he sang all the leading roles of the opera repertoire. The Prague public received *Otello* with gratitude and appreciation, in contrast to audiences in Vienna, Berlin, or Dresden, who responded to the progressive style of Verdi's late work with surprising reserve. It was reprised 26 times in Prague in the season 1887–88. On account of this success, Šubert was granted extensive directorial rights, equivalent to those of Seebach in Dresden and Jahn in Vienna. Thanks to its many guest performances and spectacular premieres, the National Theater became known throughout Europe, increasing the fame not just of Czech opera. Whereas in the early nineteenth century, Prague was perceived as a German city, it was now a Czech city in the eyes of Italy and France.

Crisis and Triumph in Vienna

Promoting native authors and works was one of the most important goals of Czech theater ever since the Provisional Theater opened its doors. A considerable body of works was built up over the years, the authors of which became a force to be reckoned with. In 1874, the Association of Czech Dramatic Writers and Composers (*Jednota dramatických spisovatelů a skladatelů českých*) concluded a contract with the managers of the Provisional Theater which stipulated fixed rates for fees and royalties, many privileges, and greater protection of the works. Hence it gave native composers the distinct advantage over foreign artists. Shortly before the opening of the National Theater, when public interest in Czech operas was at a peak, authors' fees were significantly raised again.[15] Thus Czech composers formed a national cartel, influencing the price of their products and ensuring their place in the repertoire. Although composers were still unlikely to make a fortune, their prospects had markedly improved since the 1850s, when Smetana, for example, could not even afford his own piano. But in tandem with better conditions there was increased pressure to produce. The Czech public was hungry for new pieces that could compete with the European repertoire. And since the National Theater had shown only native operas in the first six weeks, the public expected its appetite to be satisfied.

By 1884, however, it was becoming clear that Czech opera's potential had been overestimated.[16] Only a few native pieces, such as Smetana's *Libuše* and *The Bartered Bride* and Dvořák's *Dimitrij*, were able to hold their own in the repertoire next to the lavish international operas of the day. As well as *Aida*, Goldmark's *Queen of Sheba* and Leo Delibes's *Lakme*, set in India, were presented on a breathtakingly elaborate scale. No expense was spared on sets by the influential Viennese studio of Brioschi, Burghart, and Kautsky or the equally renowned Quaglio workshop in Munich. Additional cultural transfers took place involving the costumes, which were frequently based on Viennese designs.

The most popular piece of the third season was not an opera but a ballet. Šubert had returned from his visit to Italy with performance rights to the ballet *Excelsior*, which had already been a great success there and in France. In Prague, it set a new record of 41 performances in the first season after its premiere in August 1885. The ballet yielded a total of 80,000 guilders—more than a quarter of the season's total ticket sales. In the years that followed, *Excelsior* was reprised over 130 times, even outnumbering performances of *The Bartered Bride*. What was the secret of its success? In part, it was petticoats and panties.[17] But it also gave an exciting impression of distant places and scientific development in the world, featuring scenes in a ruined Spanish city, the Sahara desert, China, a telegraph building, and the laboratory of genius inventors. The combination of pretty girls, exotic settings, and awe-inspiring innovation perfectly satisfied the tastes of the Prague public.

What did Czech opera have to offer in comparison? Since Smetana had hitherto proven to be highly popular, Šubert tried introducing his lesser-known works, *The Two Widows* (*Dvě vdovy*) and *The Secret* (*Tajemství*), but they flopped after a few performances. Critics blamed the director for not investing enough in the sets,[18] but in fact these pieces had the inherent weakness that they had been written for the smaller Provisional Theater. On the large stage of the National Theater they seemed somewhat forlorn. Even *The Brandenburgers in Bohemia* proved less appealing in 1885, because public interest in nationalist plots had waned.

But even more contemporary pieces such as *The Bride of Messina* (*Nevěsta messinská*) by Zdeněk Fibich failed to get established. Czech music theater in general was struggling to make an impact. While the theater activists' call to the Czechs to fulfil their patriotic duty by patronizing native operas had initially motivated the public, in the long term, it diminished the prestige of Czech opera. Failed premieres and restructured repertoires were the result. The number of opera nights featuring native pieces—a lasting preoccupation of the Czech public—fell from 90 in the season 1883–84 to only 33 in 1888–89.[19]

Šubert came under increasing attack from critics among the intelligentsia in consequence. The editor of the influential music journal *Dalibor*, Václav Vladivoj Zelený, accused him of neglecting native opera and investing only in light entertainment and opulent sets.[20] Zelený called for a canon of national operas to be recognized and operetta banished in favor of a strictly highbrow repertoire. No doubt this would just as soon have led to bankruptcy as it did in Lemberg, when operetta was banned in the early 1890s. Indeed, Šubert countered by drawing attention to the demands of the market as well as the low productivity of native composers. In defense, the latter promptly sent a memorandum to the National Theater Association, calling for greater consideration for Czech operas and composers. But the association sided with Šubert and favored an international repertoire, following the example of the Vienna Court Opera.[21] Šubert's argument was strengthened by his undeniable success with the public and the fact that he had personally removed operetta from the repertoire, as he pointed out. While he was prepared to make compromises with the entertainment-seeking public, then, he essentially shared the critics' belief in the need for a nationally oriented, educational theater. Ultimately, Zelený was dismissed as editor and Šubert was vindicated.

Hopes for Czech opera were raised again by the premiere of *Dalibor* in 1886, with Władysław Florjański in the lead role and Tereza Arklowa—another Jewish singer from Lemberg—as Milada. In this opera, the noble knight Dalibor comes into conflict with Bohemia's royal authorities and is sentenced to death for the murder of Milada's brother, a high-ranking nobleman. Despite the adverse circumstances, Milada falls in love with Dalibor and helps him to flee from prison. But the lovers face a tragic end, thwarted by the overwhelming might of the enemy powers. Thus Smetana's most popular dramatic work blended a romantic love story with a political conflict in the style of French grand opera. The plot was loosely based on historical incidents, lending it the aura of a "true" story, and alluded to various national myths, especially that of the Czechs as a musical nation. In the second scene of the second act, Dalibor dreams that his murdered friend Zdeněk visits him in the dungeon and plays a tune on the violin to which Dalibor sings an aria. When he awakes, his beloved Milada has not only brought him tools for him to engineer his escape but also a violin to musically accompany it. Dalibor fights *and* sings his way out of the dungeon, mirroring the political strategy of the Czechs in the Austrian empire. Dalibor's aria to his friend Zdeněk is among the most beautiful in Czech opera, and the scene seems to anticipate the focus on psychological themes to come at the turn of the century. Gustav Mahler was sufficiently impressed by this work, which is rarely performed outside the Czech Republic today, to perform it at the Vienna Royal Opera, in spite of the increasingly nationalist, anti-Czech mood in the imperial capital.[22]

Smetana's alleged Wagnerism, which was held against *Dalibor* in 1868, now turned to his advantage. In 1886, nobody criticized the parallels with *Lohengrin*. Both works were based on a medieval saga and told the story of a heroic knight and his tragic love for the female protagonist. Moreover, both were influenced by the political context of the time of writing, when the Czech and German national movements respectively were on the verge of gaining a mass following. Both composers were convinced national activists who deliberately used themes taken from national history and legend to proclaim the historicity of the nation. There are some direct parallels in the narrative: Dalibor's murder charge and appearance before the royal court mirror Telramund's charge against Elsa and Lohengrin's trial. In both operas, the trial scene is heralded by four trumpeters playing a specific motif and both scores feature extended wind passages and lavish instrumentation, posing comparable challenges to the musicians. Overall, however, it would be wrong to measure Smetana against Wagner. Smetana invented his very own musical language which was still perceived as fresh and modern even after his death, when his works began to be performed outside Bohemia.

Dalibor's success was followed up by Antonín Dvořák's acclaimed opera *Jakobín*. At about the same time, Zdeněk Fibich was beginning to establish himself as a composer. Fibich's major musical accomplishment was *Hippodamia*, a trilogy of melodramas about the ancient Greek line of the Pelopidae, using spoken text underscored by continuous music. The oratorio-like performance made huge demands of the actors and especially Josef Šmaha in the role of Oinomaos.[23] This three-part work, consisting of *The Courtship of Pelops* (*Námluvy Pelopovy*), *The Atonement of Tantalus* (*Smír Tantalův*) and *Hippodamia's Death* (*Smrt Hippodamie*), was inspired by a previous Bohemian innovation. Jiří (or Georg) Benda (1722–1795), a composer born in Staré Benátky and long-standing conductor of the royal orchestra in the German town Gotha, had introduced melodramas set to music with Storm and Stress-like emotionality in the late eighteenth century. His work *Ariadne on Naxos* (1775) was widely acclaimed and performed in Paris, Italy, Denmark, Sweden, and many other countries.[24]

Fibich's trilogy turned toward a universal subject matter at a time when most opera composers in central and eastern Europe—the German composers of the post-Wagner generation, the Polish composers discussed above, the "mighty handful" in Russia, and Ferenc Erkel in Hungary—were still drawing on national themes and mythology. With *Hippodamia*, Fibich showed that ancient subject matter was supremely suitable for setting to music. While interpreting ancient sources was essentially nothing new, in the late nineteenth century, it provided fresh impetus for music drama. The role of text-writer Jaroslav Vrchlický, who had also treated chiefly national subject matter as a young man but developed a more symbolist style later in life, should not be overlooked. His prose text broke conventions—prose did not gain broad acceptance in German opera until after the turn of the century—and stressed the intonation and rhythm of the spoken word, anticipating later developments in Czech opera such as the work of Leos Janáček.

Music example 6. Opening scene from the musical melodrama *Hippodamie*.

The significance of Fibich's major work can be gauged in comparison with Dresden, where a tetralogy on the Odyssey by August Bungert appeared almost a decade later but, meandering between Meyerbeer and Wagner, was musically obsolete. The *Hippodamia* trilogy would surely have been a better investment for Ernst von Schuch had it not been in Czech. The challenge of translating it prevented it from being widely exported abroad. Until the turn of the century, it was only performed in Croatia and Antwerp and not in a German translation until 1924, at the Vienna *Volksoper*. Although far from light entertainment, it was nonetheless positively received in Prague. From the premiere in February 1890 to the summer break, *The Courtship of Pelops* was reprised eight times. The second part of the trilogy, *The Atonement of Tantalus*, was first performed at the grand Bohemian exhibition of 1891, and the third part, *Hippodamia's Death*, late in the fall of that year.

The so-called Jubilee Exhibition was an auspicious event for the National Theater. While the public flocked to Prague from the surrounding areas to visit the exhibition center, housing a world's fair in Bohemian miniature, Šubert saw to it that as many of them as possible also visited the *Národní divadlo*, and made the ensemble perform on 87 afternoons in addition to the evening performances. During the five-month run of the exposition, 222 performances were given, 112 of which were of homegrown pieces.[25] The theater was rewarded with record takings, and native authors and composers benefited from the increased publicity. For the first time in many years, native works outnumbered the others on the program. Šubert deliberately focused on native works, presuming that the operatic newcomers from the country would respond better to them than to international innovations and elaborate sets. In the space of less than half a year, he performed all of Smetana's operas, to much greater acclaim than in 1884 and 1885, as well as reinstating other Czech composers in the repertoire. The ballet *Rákoš Rákoczy*, set in eastern Moravia, was the first piece by Brno's still unknown organ school principal, Leoš Janáček, to be shown at a major theater.

Like in 1868, Prague and the Czechs once again bathed in the glow of pan-Slavic unity. In late June, the Polish Theater from Krakow, directed by Stanisław Koźmian, gave a performance which *Národní listy* described as confirmation of the brilliant reputation of Polish stage drama.[26] A performance by the Ruthenian choir *Bojan* followed in late July, featuring some compositions by the Ukrainian national composer Lysenko, and in September, the Polish choral society *Lutnia* from Lemberg made an appearance. Delegations from Slovenia, Croatia, Serbia and Bulgaria each gave one evening's performance at the National Theater. Even the emperor complemented his visit to the exhibition with a night at the theater in late September. Guests from Slavic countries were ceremoniously greeted on arrival at the station and escorted with song through the town. In contrast to the foundation stone festivities of 1868, however, there was a striking absence of

Russians. But this was compensated for by an even larger Polish contingent, with whom an experiment in bilingual Polish-Czech performance was conducted.[27] The similarity between the two languages was closer then than today and, with a little effort, each side could understand the other. Communication was even easier through song, since the visiting Poles were familiar with Czech as well as Polish songs. Indeed, pan-Slavism was to a large extent rooted in the practice of men—women were rarely among the official delegations—singing together. This form of encounter created especially emotional bonds.[28]

The boom in attendance during the Jubilee Exhibition glossed over the financial crisis which had crept up on the National Theater since the New German Theater had opened. As well as the strong competition offered by the Germans under Angelo Neumann, drawing audience members away, rapidly rising expenditure had turned the high net profit of the first three years into a growing deficit since 1886. The fees for leading soloists rose inexorably over the 1880s. Florjański, for example, earned 8,000 guilders—far less than the top salaries at the New German Theater but still fifty percent more than the highest fee in 1883.[29] The increased number of orchestral musicians, ballet ensemble members, and technicians compounded the problem. Although the wages for the minor staff stagnated, the total expenditure for the ensemble rose from 240,000 guilders in 1884 to 300,000 guilders in 1894. More was also spent on sets to satisfy the higher expectations of the public. As a result, the theater's reserve melted to just half of its original level of 120,000 guilders between 1886 and 1888.[30]

Šubert tried to stem these losses by coming to an arrangement with the main competition in Prague. In 1888, the National Theater concluded a contract with the New German Theater imposing an upper limit of 6 percent on royalties for new operas and obliging both sides to secure performance rights of new pieces for both theaters. They also agreed to premiere all new German-language operas in the German theater and all new Italian and French works at the National Theater. In 1892 and 1894 a number of extra clauses were added to the contract, regulating minor details of the theaters' affairs, such as prohibiting the headhunting of each other's singers. The tone of the more than 400 letters between Šubert and Neumann was respectful and friendly.[31] But their cooperation was kept under wraps. Nationalistic sentiment prevailed in public and politics, and Šubert did not want to be seen to be conspiring with the enemy.

Despite these agreements, both theaters struggled with structural deficits in the late 1880s. Angelo Neumann, who was not only a great Wagner director but also an astute businessman, compensated to some extent by staging spectacular tours. Several guest performances of Wagner's *Ring* cycle in St. Petersburg and Moscow in spring 1889 yielded over 100,000 marks.[32] Meanwhile, the Jubilee Exhibition increased Šubert's receipts. But these isolated events did not provide lasting solutions to their financial problems. Consequently, in 1891, the two directors decided to appeal to the emperor to convert both establishments into royal theaters.

This request was nothing short of a sensation, the political significance of which has hitherto been overlooked. The National Theater Association was serving Emperor Franz Josef the Czechs' most prestigious national project on a plate. Rieger and his fellow party members proceeded with due discretion. Hardly a word about the offer was printed in the Prague newspapers and in Vienna nothing was leaked out of the direct communication channels to the court. Prime Minister Count Taaffe supported the application as a way of crowning his efforts toward a German-Czech compromise. But the emperor and his closest advisors failed to see the political opportunities that converting the National Theater into a royal theater might have held. Franz Josef turned the request down, not wishing to set a precedent for other national theaters.[33] Thus a unique opportunity to strengthen the monarchy was passed up. Count Taaffe later resigned and the Czech and German elites in Bohemia looked on as their political representatives once again became embroiled in mutual mistrust, invective, and boycotts.

Prominent experts on the Habsburg Empire, such as Robert Kann and Jan Křen, have attributed its decline to nationalism and mass politics.[34] This incident of a petition to change the National Theater into a royal theater points in a different direction. It indicates that a lack of foresight on the part of the emperor and Austrian neglect of cultural policy were responsible for the failure to reach compromise between the Germans and the Czechs.

In 1892, the Czech National Theater was once again at the top of the imperial agenda, albeit under quite different circumstances. Princess Pauline Metternich, granddaughter of the famous prerevolution prime minister Metternich,[35] organized the first International Music and Theater Exhibition. Designed to showcase different countries like a world's fair, the nationalities within the Austrian part of the empire were invited to present their own sections alongside the European nation-states. But more significant than the permanent exhibition, displaying instruments, old scores, portraits of, and artifacts belonging to well-known composers, were the performances by renowned European theater ensembles in the exhibition theater, in what resembled an international competition. When Princess Metternich, who had some sympathies for the Czech cause, invited Prague's National Theater to take part, many influential members of the National Theater Association feared it would end in ignominy.[36] But turning the invitation down would have meant passing up a unique opportunity for the Prague ensemble to prove its skill.

The Czechs arrived in Vienna as underdogs. The ensemble members traveled in second- and third-class train carriages in order to minimize the financial risk. They received expenses of a modest eight guilders per day. Despite the relative fame acquired with Verdi's *Otello*, nobody expected the National Theater to rival Berlin's *Deutsche Theater* or the *Comédie Française*. But Šubert had devised a clever program for the week-long appearance, consisting mainly of music theater, which was far more popular than spoken drama, and forgoing international operas.[37]

Figure 13. Original program of the Czech National Theater's guest performance in Vienna.

To open the National Theater's guest appearance, *The Bartered Bride* was performed, which was virtually unknown abroad. It was an immediate success. The entire Viennese press raved about the dynamic music, the realistic sets and the contemporary subject matter.[38] Indeed, *The Bartered Bride* was one of the few operas of the day which did not take audiences back in time with historical characters and scenery. As well as its contemporary relevance, its portrayal of rural life intrigued and delighted the urban public. On the second evening, Šubert presented Dvořák's grand opera-style *Dimitrij* and on the third evening, the first part of Fibich's trilogy *Hippodamia*. On the fourth night, the only non-Czech piece of the tour was performed, Tchaikovsky's *Eugene Onegin*, which had been a great success in Prague in 1888. Šubert's choices were a gamble: Fibich's work represented a new genre of music theater, *The Bartered Bride* was unusually realistic and *Eugene Onegin* was a lyrical opera which broke with contemporary dramatic conventions. Moreover, all these pieces were virtually unknown internationally. They were followed by *Dalibor* and a play by Šubert himself, the realist drama *Jan Výrava*. Šubert had planned to stage operas by two lesser known Czech composers as a finale,[39] but in view of the overwhelming enthusiasm for Smetana, he decided to simply repeat *The Bartered Bride* and *Dalibor*. Some Viennese critics placed these operas on a level with Wagner's major works and the National Theater was invited to extend its guest appearance.

Figure 14. Positivist costumes for *The Bartered Bride* in 1892.

This success finally marked the National Theater's international breakthrough and the Czechs' long-awaited recognition as a cultural nation. The demand for Smetana's major works abroad was tremendous and *The Bartered Bride* became a fixture on repertoires across Central Europe, at first in Vienna, then in Berlin, Frankfurt am Main, Dresden, Aachen, Leipzig, and eventually all the larger cities of the German Empire.[40] Even the less accessible *Dalibor* became established as a repertoire piece and Smetana's minor works such as *The Kiss* and *The Secret* were performed in many theaters. Vienna also benefited greatly from the Music and Theater Exhibition. Hosting such an acclaimed event invested the city with cultural authority in the German-speaking lands and confirmed its position as a European music capital.[41]

The National Theater's triumph in Vienna raised the status of Czech opera and boosted the self-confidence of the Czech elites. Smetana ascended into the pantheon of Czech national heroes and was revered as a Czech idol.[42] A bust of the composer was erected in the National Theater and plans for a Smetana Museum were forged. Šubert staged a cycle of all Smetana's operas, which was attended by numerous foreign guests. Since Czech opera had gained prestige abroad, it also appealed more to the Prague public. From 1893, Czech operas made up at least half of the National Theater's repertoire, comparable to the ratio of native works in Vienna and Hamburg since Wagner's breakthrough.[43]

At last the National Theater's financial situation improved. The number of subscription holders soared, yielding revenue in excess of 100,000 guilders for the first time.[44] Many prominent politicians and institutions now joined the National Theater Association. Count Jan Thun-Hohenstein, Prince Ferdinand Lobkowitz, Jan Lošťák, director of the national bank of Bohemia in Prague, and the regional committees of twelve Bohemian districts all purchased shares.[45]

Czech music was, however, to a large extent received on biased terms. Critics praised the purely national character of the music but failed to acknowledge its universal significance. What European critics most admired about Smetana's music was that it sounded "truly Bohemian." This appreciation was colored by a romantic sense of the exotic and, on a deeper level, criticism of western civilization. Smetana and the Czechs were perceived as fresh, unspoiled, and natural. To maintain this appeal, the opera houses that staged *The Bartered Bride* usually imported the designs and costumes directly from Prague or copied them from the models by Josef Šmaha. Dvořák's *Dimitrij*, by contrast, was less positively received even during the exhibition in Vienna because it lacked the distinctly national character that critics so admired.[46]

Nonetheless, Dvořák was consistently promoted as a Czech or Slavic composer on his concert tours.[47] In 1892, he was invited to the United States to advise the Americans on developing an independent music tradition. Here, Dvořák not only composed his famous *From the New World* symphony but also concluded that America should harness the musical potential of its former slaves and the English language to establish its own operatic tradition. He later formulated this theory in an essay on national music in the US.[48]

Although the purely national reception of Czech music theoretically concurred with the demands of Prague's cultural nationalists, it opened it to prejudice. German critics, especially, commonly took a disparaging view of Czech opera, bracketing it together with Polish and Russian opera. "Slavic opera," as they were collectively referred to, was *only* national, while German music and above all Wagner was considered to have universal value. This dichotomy between an eastern European national music culture and a German universal music culture is still upheld in the German-language and most of the English-language literature on opera today. Appreciation on a purely national level, however, does not do justice to Smetana's music and in the case of Dvořák is completely inapposite.

Comparison with Wagner shows that it was the political context of reception which determined music's national character rather than any supposed inherent national essence. Smetana's nationalism was articulated mainly in his choice of subject matter. Like Wagner, he avoided contemporary folk music and national "color"—a common stylistic devise in grand opera. But, conversely, a number of his compositions were absorbed into the nation's body of folk song. In view of this, *The Bartered Bride* must be seen as more than just a Bohemian country farce with quaint drinking songs and dances. Smetana's opera drew directly from real life, but remains an artistic invention.

Unfortunately for the National Theater, since its triumph in Vienna, there was sudden international demand for its singers. The bass Vilém Heš, who began his career singing arias in his father's tavern, and soprano Berta Foersterová-Lautererová left for Hamburg in 1893–94. Heš subsequently went on to the Vienna Court Opera.[49] These departures unsettled the ensemble and put an end to the homely atmosphere which had hitherto prevailed. Without its best singers, the National Theater was reluctant to embark on any further tours and turned down invitations from Frankfurt, Berlin's Lessing Theater, the Metropolitan Opera in New York, and the World's Fair in Chicago.[50] A guest performance in Vienna during the summer break, however, seemed a feasible option and a corresponding offer was made. But the directors of the Vienna Court Opera apparently felt it would lower the tone of their house.[51] Moreover, the authorities wanted to avoid enhancing the political status of the Czechs in the imperial capital. Here is another example of a missed opportunity in the history of the Habsburg Empire, caused by the Viennese court's resistance toward Czech ambitions.

Several requests came from Galicia for the National Theater to perform in Krakow or Lemberg but Šubert felt the travel costs would be too high and the theaters too small. An extended tour of Europe, such as Angelo Neumann frequently undertook, could have broadened Czech opera's public. The requisite body of work was available: from 1903, in addition to Smetana's works, entire cycles of Czech opera were staged in Prague, half-jokingly referred to as *český Bayreuth*.[52] But Šubert and his successors lacked the spirit of adventure—and financial incentive—to attempt such an enterprise. The National Theater was doing very well in Prague and its regular public would have objected to lengthy absences.

France formed an exception in Europe for remaining impervious to Czech opera. An initial guest appearance in Paris following the Viennese Theater and Music Exhibition was canceled for economic reasons.[53] Subsequently, a circle of lovers of Czech music tried to organize a production of *The Bartered Bride* during the Paris World's Fair. A venue was found, the *Théâtre de la Renaissance*, but it required 10,000 francs to host the production. In best National Theater tradition, a fundraising campaign was launched. After some weeks, however, the music journal *Dalibor* posed the justified question: "Why is it still necessary to pay for someone else to discover the musical beauty of our beloved opera?"[54] This performance, too, was abandoned and it was not until the interwar period that Smetana was "discovered" in France.[55]

The Model and Transfer of Czech Music

The success of the Czech National Theater had by far the greatest impact on Germany, the Habsburg Empire, and southeastern Europe. All the Austrian Slavs were concurrently engaged in cultural nation-building, led by the Polish and Ruthenian national movements in Galicia and their equivalents in Croatia and Slovenia. Poland, with its history of statehood and tradition of national theater, initially preceded the Czechs in this process. But, hampered by a number of obstacles discussed above, the Polish theaters in Warsaw and Lemberg eventually fell behind the Prague National Theater. The Czech triumph in Vienna and simultaneous disgrace of the Lemberg Theater made this clear to an international public. Many Galician intellectuals therefore looked with respect and increasingly with admiration toward Prague. Lemberg actor and director Adolf Walewski, who briefly held the post of director of the Polish Theater, wrote in a pamphlet entitled *Theater at Home and Abroad*: "If any theater puts the democratic idea, the concept of ordinary emotions, the unity of the nation, into practice in a noble manner, it is without doubt the Czechs' theater."[56] The Galician press routinely reported on events at the Prague National Theater. Although the Polish theater was run by impresarios until 1918 and never became a national theater, it nonetheless to some extent followed the Czech example. Director Heller, in particular, pursued a similar strategy to Šubert in Prague when he set up a Polish ensemble and tried to promote native composers. Of course, he also included Czech operas in his repertoire.

The Ruthenian elites were even more fascinated by Prague than the Galician Poles. Telegrams and delegations were sent as signs of Ukrainian sympathy for the National Theater cause, not to mention a donation of 100 guilders by the metropolitan of the Greek Catholic Church in 1868. Inspired by the foundation stone festivities, a group of Ruthenians launched an initiative to set up an own national theater in L'viv. The two Ukrainian delegates attending the opening of the *Národní divadlo* in 1883 declared: "The Ruthenian people will strive to adapt the fine example you have set to achieve a great goal."[57] The Ruthenian national theater, too, was to be financed by public donations and built on a broad social basis. But the conflicts between rival factions within the Ukrainian national movement—some tending to align with Russia (the Russophiles), others taking a more independent stance (the Ukrainophiles)—slowed the initiative's progress.[58] Nevertheless, by the eve of the First World War, the Ukrainian theater project in Galicia had reached about the same stage as the Czechs' in the 1870s. It had a fund of initial capital and a design for the building, combining classic Western theater elements with Ruthenian sacred architecture.

The relationship between the Ruthenians, or Ukrainians, and the Czechs was based on reciprocal appreciation of their cultures. In 1891, for example, the National Theater invited a Ukrainian choral society and a Ruthenian drama ensemble to take part in the Jubilee Exhibition. Evidence exists of a number of cultural transfers, going as far as the Russian part of the Ukraine. The work of the leading Ukrainian opera composer prior to World War I, Nikolai Lysenko (1842–1912), contains parallels with Smetana's music of a generation earlier. Lysenko, too, used comic material as well as themes from national myth and history. His instrumentation betrays a Wagnerian influence as well as incorporating folk rhythms. These cultural transfers were effected less by the study of scores or from work to work than by personal contact. Lysenko was a student in Leipzig just as Wagnerism was gaining ground and in Ukraine he saw many Czech musicians and conductors performing works from their home country.

There is also evidence of direct cultural transfers from Prague to Posen and the Prussian partition of Poland. One year after the foundation stones were laid in Prague, which received in-depth coverage in Polish newspapers, a commission was formed in Poznań with the aim of constructing a national theater. In 1871, this commission became a shareholding company which began fundraising with such success that construction was symbolically inaugurated (in the former garden of the Potocki estate) only two years later.[59] By 1875 the theater was already complete, thanks mainly to donations from rich aristocrats, and bore the same legend over the entrance as the National Theater in Prague was to later: *Narod sobie*—"the nation unto itself."

Some equally striking cultural transfers to the Germans in Bohemia can be observed. The German-speaking population in Prague was slow to develop initiatives in support of nationally defined cultural institutions since German culture was traditionally preeminent. Performances at the Estates Theater were already given chiefly in German, and the influential aristocrats among the audience did not sympathize with the modern trend toward linguistic nationalism. When the German theater went bankrupt in 1885 as a result of maladministration and competition from the National Theater, Prague's Germans took matters into their own hands and, following the Czech example, began fundraising for the construction of a German national theater.[60] Unlike the Czech theater's supporters, the German theater's sympathizers were almost exclusively urban, numbering far more upper-class Jewish Prague citizens than German speakers of Bohemia's border regions. This situation gave an early indication of the later rift between the "Sudeten' Germans and the German-speaking minority in Prague. The New German Theater thus remained essentially a theater for Prague and failed to become a German-Bohemian national theater. In view of its director, Angelo Neumann, and the composition of its public, it is perhaps best described as a German-Jewish theater and an example of the fruitfulness of this symbiosis.[61]

Southeastern Europe, including Bulgaria as well as Croatia and Slovenia, also looked on the Czech National Theater as a beacon. Following the demise of neo-absolutism, the Croatian elites pursued a similar political strategy in the Habsburg Monarchy to the Czech national movement, demanding cultural equality and autonomy for the historical territory of the kingdom of Croatia. In 1861, the provincial diet resolved to found a Croatian university, national museum, and national theater. When the foundation stones for the Czech National Theater were laid in 1868, prominent Croatian, Serbian, and Slovenian intellectuals were in attendance. Slavic solidarity was demonstrated by countless congratulatory telegrams from practically all Croatian and Slovenian towns.[62]

Prague's National Theater remained a role model for the Croatians not least because the founding of their own national theater was hampered by problems and delays. These were due less to the political resistance of Hungary, to which Croatia belonged, than to the limitations of the capital city Zagreb, with a population of less than 30,000 in 1880. Nevertheless, the Croatian National Theater (*Hrvatsko narodno kazalište*) was opened in 1895.[63] The neobaroque building was built by the Viennese architects Fellner & Helmer, who had also designed the remarkably similar New German Theater in Prague. At the inauguration, attended by Emperor Franz Josef, the historical opera *Nikola Šubić Zrijnski* by Ivan Zajc was performed, telling the story of the brave eponymous hero.[64] With its heroic plot and ample incorporation of folk music motifs and dances, this work followed the pattern of the majority of national operas.

The pomp of the inaugural ceremony could not disguise the shortfalls on Croatia's cultural scene.[65] Like the Provisional Theater in Prague, the Croatian National Theater did not have enough native-language pieces to make up a repertoire.[66] Good actors were scarce and experience of staging operas minimal. But the Czech National Theater reliably provided a helping hand. Croatian theater studies expert Slavko Batušić describes the transfer between the two nations thus: "Due to the similarity in our political, cultural, and social circumstances, European influences in general often came to us via the Czechs. Where theater was concerned, the *Národni divadlo*, this Czech equivalent to the Burg Theater, served us as a more acceptable model than the original itself."[67] Prague's assistance took a number of forms, from dispatching soloists, actors, and stage technicians to lending costumes. The national theater in Zagreb even requested help casting the chorus when it was short of three sopranos and altos for the opening. The costume designs for the first Croatian performance of *Lohengrin* did not come from Vienna or nearby Graz but from Prague. Josef Šmaha had a particular influence on the Croatian theater scene, giving several guest performances in Zagreb in which he demonstrated his innovatively realistic style. In 1898, he was made an honorary member of the ensemble. Conversely, members of the Zagreb ensemble traveled to Prague to see the latest operas or productions of particular interest and gain inspiration for their own performances.[68]

The Prague National Theater had even greater significance for what is now Slovenia. Šubert and his ensemble maintained close links with the Dramatic Association in Ljubljana (*Dramatično Družstvo v Ljubljani*), which organized performances and raised funds toward the construction of a Slovenian national theater. A new theater was opened in 1892, where performances were given in both German and Slovenian, although precedence was given to the latter. The architects of the building, the principal soloists, and many musicians were Czechs, and even the scores and costumes came from Prague.[69] The Prague National Theater lent the Slovenians the scores and some costume designs for *The Troubadour* and *Rigoletto, Lucia di Lammermoor, La Muette de Portici, The African Maid, Faust, Carmen, Halka,* and *The Flying Dutchman*.[70] Even Italian opera was communicated via Prague, despite Slovenia's geographical proximity to Venice and Trieste, because of the similarity between the Slovenian and Czech languages, making translations from Czech to Slovenian easier than from Italian. On the issue of devising a program for the inauguration, the Slovenian theater activists wrote admiringly to their colleagues in Prague: "We thought at first of a Czech opera . . . You have brought honor to all Slavs."[71] In the event, the theater opened with the comic opera *In the Well* (*V Studni*) by Blodek, a piece that does not make excessive demands of the singers and was therefore suited to an ensemble with limited strength and experience. It was followed a short time later by *The Bartered Bride* and other lighter works but by the end of the century the Slovenians, too, were taking on *Dalibor*. The repertoire in Slovenia in the late nineteenth century was strikingly apolitical. True, *Halka*—an opera criticizing feudal injustice—was especially well received, according to the press.[72] The program's overall emphasis on grand opera, however, indicates that the Slovenian theater intended to cultivate a standard European repertoire like the Czech theater it was modeled on.

The involvement of so many Czech singers and musicians in the theaters of other Slavic nations of the Habsburg Empire—and vice versa—also worked to the advantage of the National Theater in Prague. If there were no suitable Czech tenors available, Šubert enlisted Raverta from Dalmatia or Florjański from Lemberg. After the turn of the century, Croatian mezzo soprano Gabriela Horvátová was among the National Theater's leading soloists. Thus Prague's National Theater had access to singers who could learn Czech with relative ease and so supplement the ensemble. Without these imported artists, and especially Florjański, Czech opera might not have been in a position to rival the German competition in Prague or convince audiences at the Music and Theater Exhibition in Vienna.

The Czechs also played a key role for the most distant and southerly Slavic nation, the Bulgarians. In contrast to the Austro-Slavs, they had achieved independence in 1878. But the Bulgarian government still faced the challenges of developing national awareness and building an education system. Since there was no national elite to speak of, the young state looked abroad for leaders and especially to Prague. Here, the Bulgarian envoy was struck by an extraordinarily talented young man named Konstantin Jireček, son of the well-known author, who had qualified as Professor of History at the age of 25. The Bulgarian government appointed him General Secretary of the Ministry of Education in 1879, promoting him to Director two years later. Although Jireček stayed only a few years in Bulgaria, he left an enduring legacy, installing grammar school and higher education systems.

The construction of an emblematic theater, however, had to be postponed, since Bulgaria had no cities large enough to accommodate one. Sofia was a former Ottoman garrison with a population of only 100,000 at the turn of the century. Still, by 1906, plans for a Bulgarian national theater had progressed far enough for the government to look for a potential director. Again, a suitable candidate was found in Prague, where Josef Šmaha had been suffering a creative crisis since the Young Czech National Theater Association had taken over the theater. Not only had he fallen out of favor politically, but the realism he championed in theater in the 1890s was becoming outmoded. Šmaha gladly accepted the post in Bulgaria and moved to Sofia. Although he was not able to fulfill local hopes for an opera ensemble, he did establish a highbrow repertoire, a body of native works and a permanent theater ensemble.[73]

Thus the Czech model was transferred in two respects: first, on an institutional level, and second, on a musical level, since the Czechs led the way in creating an opera culture that was both a demonstration of status and in touch with the people.

Art Nouveau in Prague

Cracks began to appear in the carefully crafted edifice of Czech national culture in the 1890s. The Manuscript of the Queen's Court (*Rukopis Královédvorský*), said to prove the existence of a specifically Czech school of literature in the Middle Ages, was revealed to be a forgery. The discovery was hugely damaging for the construction of national history which historians, writers, and composers had been engaged in since the prerevolution period.[74] Meanwhile, the younger generation took the existence of the Czech nation and Czech culture as a given that did not need constant verification in a European context.

In 1895, a group of young authors who rejected prevailing theater conventions came up with a "Manifesto of Czech Modernity,"[75] calling for an end to sociopolitical and national subjects and greater focus on emotional and psychological issues. The modernists opposed the dominant view in theater that social reality should be portrayed on the stage and argued for conveying content in a symbolic way, forgoing the naturalism that had given rise to *verismo* in opera in the 1890s.[76] In practice this style resulted in works made up of a predictable sequence of love, betrayal, violence, and death—with correspondingly dramatic arias—rather than credible portrayals of real life.

In the search for new inspiration, influential authors turned to another ancient genre: fairytales. Julius Zeyer, who became a renowned symbolist beyond Bohemia, and Jaroslav Kvapil, who went on to become director of spoken drama at the National Theater, were the two leading Prague playwrights to publish works in this genre. Kvapil's *Princeska Pampeliška* and Zeyer's *Radúz a Mahulena* were both premiered in 1898 and, remarkably, both set to music, the former by Josef Bohuslav Förster, and Zeyer's Tatra tale by Josef Suk. The music in these works was not designed to create dramatic effect but to conjure up a lyrical mood and reflect the enchantment of the fairytale. *Radúz a Mahulena* caused quite a stir among the critics, who responded positively despite its length of over three hours.[77] The music by Suk, a pupil of Dvořák, was so popular that it was compressed into a half-hour suite to be performed independently. With nearly 50 reprises, *Princeska Pampeliška* was an even greater success.

A year later, Dvořák's *Čert a Káča* was the first production of a true fairytale opera by a contemporary Czech composer. This work, too, was warmly received and became the most often performed Czech opera in the year after its premiere. Kvapil went on to base his next project on another fairytale, the story of the mermaid Rusalka, inspired by a visit to Danish Bornholm and the story by Hans Christian Andersen. With Šubert's help, he contacted Antonín Dvořák, who had dealt with a similar theme in his symphonic poem *Vodník*, and showed him his draft of the libretto. Dvořák was immediately convinced and composed the music for *Rusalka* in only seven months. It was a cooperation between unlikely partners—Kvapil, a young playwright bent on breaking theater conventions, and Dvořák, a (supposed) traditionalist whose chief influence had been the neo-Romantic composer Johannes Brahms.[78]

The opera is an interesting illustration of the day's attitudes and preoccupations. The nymph Rusalka falls in love with a prince who appears at her lake. The witch Ježibaba agrees to help Rusalka win the prince—in exchange for her voice—by turning her into a human, but warns that if he is unfaithful, they will both be damned. The prince is fascinated by Rusalka and takes her to his castle but at the same time finds her strange and her silence alienating. At a ball, he flirts with a princess and Rusalka sees them embracing. Facing her doom, Rusalka lets the Water Sprite take her back to the lake, where Ježibaba tells her she can gain release if she kills the prince. She refuses to do this, but the prince seeks her out, sensing their fate. Full of remorse, he asks Rusalka to kiss him and dies in her arms.

This libretto is pervaded with fin-de-siècle pessimism and melancholy. Both main characters are trapped by circumstance; the nymph in nature, the prince in his social world. Death is the only escape and in it the two are united at the end. The prince's materialism and life at the court, symbolized by a conventional ballet interlude, are portrayed as superficial and shallow. Dvořák's music alternately reflects this glossy emptiness, the nymph's natural idyll and the allure of the dreamworld. When the action takes place in the real world, the music is hard and rhythmic, driven by traditional contrapuntal devices, but when Rusalka and the prince surrender to their desires, it becomes soft, full of *ritardandi*, resulting in an impressionist style. The aria *Měsíčku na nebi hlubokém* (*Song to the Moon*), in which Rusalka sings in silvery sparkling tones of the heavens and her sense of longing, is among the greatest European arias of the turn of the century. The contrast between the material world and the shadowy world of dreams, and the melancholy realization that the two main characters cannot overcome nature, binds the work into a dramatic whole.

Unfortunately the partnership between Dvořák and Kvapil was not to be continued. Aged sixty at the time of *Rusalka's* premiere in 1901, the composer passed away three years later. Zeyer and Dvořák's pupil Suk collaborated once again on the dramatized fairytale *Pod jabloní*. Kvapil worked with Otakar Ostrčil, who became director of the National Theater's opera department in the First Republic, on the piece *Sirotek*.[79] These works, accompanied by incidental music, were considerably more successful than most new Czech operas, of which only nine were shown at the National Theater between 1900 and 1906. Another extraordinarily popular piece was the ballet *Pohádka o Honzovi* with music by young composer Oskar Nedbal. The musicologist Brian Locke has attempted to classify the music of this era in terms of the opposite poles of traditional folk music and abstract modernism.[80] This dichotomy, however, no more reaches an incisive definition than classification according to certain schools.

Music example 7. Aria to the moon in *Rusalka*.

There is no broadly recognized equivalent in music history for the art nouveau genre (or *Jugendstil* in German) of art and architecture that so eminently shaped the face of Prague and Central Europe as a whole.[81] But similar themes of nature, symbols, fairytales, dreams, and ethereal beauty were dealt with in both the visual arts and in music. Dvořák's music for the opera *Rusalka* contained all the essential stylistic elements of art nouveau: lyricism, mysticism, color, and symmetry.[82] The term "impressionist" does not adequately describe the music of the era and can only be applied to a few western European operas, such as Debussy's *Pelleas et Mélisande*.[83] In the Habsburg Empire, the principles of art nouveau, by contrast, were evident in compositions by Mahler, Zemlinsky, Korngold, early period Schönberg and the Czech composers mentioned above as well as Mieczysław Karłowicz in Galicia. It seems appropriate, then, to apply this arthistorical term to music history. Doing so brings Prague's significance as a center of musical modernism, alongside Vienna, deservedly into focus.

Music example 8. *Pohádka o Honzovi*.

Although the National Theater continued to stage new pieces after 1900, a trend toward fostering tradition emerged in opera, and it became increasingly difficult for young composers to gain recognition. This and the rampant intolerance of contemporary nationalism are illustrated by an incident involving Karel Weis, composer of the opera *The Polish Jew*. Weis submitted his work to the National Theater in 1901 but received no response from Kovařovic.[84] The opera director's colleague delegated to assess it brusquely advised Weis to approach the German Theater instead. Why did the National Theater brush him off in this way? Weis was a Prague Jew who had based his opera on a German libretto. In turn-of-the-century Prague, he was therefore regarded as a *German* composer, although he had explicitly offered to translate the libretto into Czech. Angelo Neumann, to whom he subsequently submitted his work, knew him as a Czech composer[85] and hesitated to accept the piece as the National Theater held the first performance rights to Czech operas.

Shortly after the work was successfully premiered in the New German Theater, Schuch performed it in Dresden, where it was perceived as a Czech opera. Ludwig Hartmann, the critic writing for the newspaper *Dresdner Neueste Nachrichten*, however, peculiarly credited the composer as "Karol Weisz," using a partially Hungarian spelling.[86] The different responses to Weis's work in Prague and Dresden show how Prague's Jewish population fell between all national stools. In Prague, Weis was considered a German composer—contrary to his own attitude—while in Dresden he was regarded as Czech or something more exotic. The music critic Emanuel Chvála, a close friend of Kovařovic, told Weis on the success of his opera: "Now you are a German composer and you can only continue to act as such. There is no going back for us. You have burnt all your bridges."[87]

National rivalry was partly responsible for *Rusalka* not reaching audiences in Vienna, unlike the works of Smetana in previous years. Gustav Mahler, then director of the royal opera, had scheduled its Viennese premiere for August 1902. But the anti-Czech mood under Mayor Lueger was very strong. When Vilém Heš—due to sing the part of the Water Sprite—fell ill, the performance was dropped.[88] Meanwhile, at home Dvořák was accused by the critic Zdeněk Nejedlý of lacking in popular awareness and progressive spirit.[89] Ironically, Dvořák had written his later operatic works in the belief that they could achieve what his symphonies had not and reach all of society.

Around this time, Leoš Janáček approached the National Theater with the first version of his opera *Jenůfa*.[90] After close consideration, Kovařovic rejected the opera on account of "flaws" in the music.[91] He returned the score with notes criticizing insufficient leitmotifs, uneven and frequently homophonic instrumentation, especially an overemphasis on strings, and the absence of horns where they would be expected. Moreover, he objected to the frequent repetition of certain words and motifs which, in his view, failed to create suspense. Kovařovic, a late Romantic Smetana aficionado who had himself written some folkish operas, was not ready for Janáček's ethnographic approach.[92] Indeed, the subsequent preparations in Brno for the premiere of *Jenůfa* showed how unconventional and complex his music was. 50 rehearsals were needed for the orchestra to master the piece and its unusual rhythms. The opera was not performed in Prague until 1916, after much reworking.

According to Němeček, the National Theater rejected Janáček's first opera primarily because it feared incurring further losses. By the end of the 1903 season, a deficit of 30,000 crowns had accumulated, despite higher subsidies. For this reason, Schmoranz and Kovařovic felt compelled to stage more operettas and pursue a conservative program policy. Unlike a royal theater, the *Národní divadlo* could not rely on the resources of higher authorities. The theater's finances were supervised by the members of the theater association who could get quite unpleasant in defense of their investments. Comparison with the Šubert era, however, shows that the ability to take artistic risks was largely a question of conviction. Šubert had staged Fibich's *Hippodamia* trilogy, despite the National Theater's unpredictable financial circumstances, and even taken it to Vienna.

Nevertheless, it would be wrong to view the National Theater's development from 1900 as following a downward trajectory. The quality of the orchestra improved sufficiently under Kovařovic to venture a production of Wagner's *Tristan and Isolde*, considered one of the most sophisticated pieces of the international repertoire, in 1913. On January 1, 1914, the curious situation arose that *Parsifal* was premiered simultaneously in both the New German Theater and the National Theater in Prague. Other German operas were also translated into Czech and performed at an astonishing rate, including *Elektra* and *Der Rosenkavalier*, which was shown just one month after its world premiere in Dresden. Richard Strauss himself conducted performances of *Elektra* in the National Theater in 1910, to the chagrin of the New German Theater. The works of Italian composers, by contrast, were performed distinctly less after the fashion for *verismo* had waned. Although Verdi remained a permanent fixture on the repertoire, older Italian operas usually ran only one or two seasons after their first performance. The decrease in once so popular French opera was even more pronounced. But here, too, generalizations must be avoided, especially since the success of a work was dependent not only on the style of the music but also on the sets and singers. In broad terms, the foreign repertoire was shared between Italian, French, and German opera, indicating a remarkable rise in the popularity of German opera—in view of the fact that Prague also had the specialist New German Theater—and distinct parallels to Lemberg and Budapest.

Prague's response to *Der Rosenkavalier*, however, was not entirely positive, despite the record number of reprises. The premiere audience took exception to the scenes in which Ochs von Lerchenau and others behaved improperly to the female characters. Whistling at the open display of sexuality, the Prague audience, though much less religious, reacted similarly to the Catholic audience in Lemberg.[93] In Dresden, meanwhile, the director objected to the negative light

Der Rosenkavalier threw on the aristocracy. The fact that this opera picked up on contemporary issues on a number of levels certainly contributed to its outstanding success.

The drama section of the Czech National Theater maintained even closer contact to Germany than the opera section. Jaroslav Kvapíl, who was at first merely literary advisor but promoted to chief stage director in 1906 and to head of drama in 1911, maintained regular contact with Munich's *Künstlertheater* and Max Reinhardt in Berlin, whom he invited to Prague on several occasions. In 1906, the Moscow Art Theater, directed by Constantin Stanislavski, made its first guest appearance abroad in Prague.[94] The Art Theater was inspired by the authentic characters and portrayal of emotions in the plays of Anton Chekhov. Instead of the quick-fire dialogues, numerous entrances and exits and artificially streamlined plots of Parisian comedies, Chekhov devoted more time to moments of reflection, interrupted dialogue, and stream-of-consciousness expression. Here, the characters were multidimensional, sometimes broken; in other words, they mirrored the complexity of twentieth-century Freudian man and woman. Stage direction and set design underwent a thorough transformation. Kvapíl reduced and abstracted the sets in order to allow more space for the artists to make a personal impact. He instructed the actors to release their inner feelings to captivate the audience on an additional, subconscious level.

If one compares photographs of performances in Prague with those in the royal theaters in Berlin and Dresden at this time,[95] the difference is striking. While the historical stage sets in the German cities were cluttered and over-ornate, Prague could present its audience a thrillingly modern theater. Reduced stage sets and costumes opened up new scope for stage direction in opera. In Prague, new productions of nearly all the older works in the repertoire were created between 1900 and 1914, while at the royal operas in Dresden and Vienna, as well as at the Garnier Opera in Paris, existing productions were reused for decades. Having adopted stage direction as a significant element of stagecraft relatively early on—under Kvapíl and Kovařovic—the National Theater was able to continue drawing a mass audience to the operas of Smetana and Dvořák, and had less need to present new works. In this way, both modernism and the cultivation of tradition contributed to the development of a standard central European repertoire, which is considered more closely in the next chapter. Prague's National Theater etched itself on to the cultural map of Europe as a theater which had grown in significance since its founding phase. No longer simply a site of national art, as it was in the 1880s and 1890s, it was now also a center of modernism in opera.

Figure 15. Symbolist stage sets for *Libuše*.

Notes

1. See the review in *Národní listy*, Jan. 14, 1885, 3 (which alludes to many Germans having visited the Czech National Theater); see also the comments in Teuber, *Geschichte, Dritter Theil*, 779.
2. On Wagner's reception, see Hostinský; also Locke, *Opera and Ideology*, 23–28.
3. On the different interpretations of Wagner's work, see *Národní listy*, Jan. 14, 1885, 3; also Bernbach, *Der Wahn*, 191.
4. See *Národní listy*, June 3, 1885, 1. Teuber directly attributes the bankruptcy of the Estates Theater in 1885 to competition from the National Theater and especially its opera section. See Teuber, *Geschichte, Dritter Theil*, 789.
5. On the history of the New German Theater, see Ludvová, *Nationaltheater*, 44; also Tancsik, *Die Prager*, 31–33. For an English-language analysis see Cohen, *The Politics of Ethnic Survival*, 94, 115–16.
6. In 1860 Smetana apologized in a letter to a friend for his poor Czech and expressed the intention to use the language henceforth. See Teige, *Dopisy*, 38–39.
7. The mere arrangement of this guest performance made it to the front page of *Národny listy* (see the edition of June 3, 1885). On the internal debates in the National Theater Association, see NA, Fond ND, Sign. 97, 56–57, *PVS* of Jan. 15, 1885.
8. See the letter signed by 84 subscription holders which was also sent to the executive committee, in *Národní listy*, Aug. 29, 1886.
9. A very negative view of Raverta can be found in Nejedlý, *Dejiny*, vol. 1, 138–39. See also the petition in NA, Fond ND, Sign. 158, 55–56; also previous contracts with Raverta obliging him to sing in Czech, ibid., 14–54.

10. On Patti's voice and career, see Kesting, *Die großen Sänger*, vol. 1, 89–96.
11. *Národní listy*, June 22, 1885, 5.
12. On Saint-Saëns's visit to Prague and the preceding scandal, see *Dalibor*, Feb. 14, 1886, 55–56; and Feb. 21, 1886, 64–65.
13. Šubert's contact and negotiations with Verdi are described in detail in the former's memoirs. See Šubert, *Moje Vzpominky*, vol. 3, 21–40.
14. *Národní listy*, Jan. 9, 1888, 3.
15. One example is an agreement between the National Theater and composer Karel Bendl concerning his opera *Černohorci* in 1881. See NA, Fond ND, Sign. D. 104/109 and Sign. D 105/9. Bendl, who was chairman of the association of Czech composers, was originally offered 500 guilders for this work but eventually managed to negotiate 1000 guilders and considerably better royalties.
16. Similar phenomena also occurred in other fields of the arts. On literature and the visual arts, see Storck, *Kulturnation*, 146–49.
17. This was where *Národní listy* mockingly suggested *Excelsior's* appeal lay. See the edition of June 22, 1886, 2. For details of income, see Archive of the National Theater, AND, Annual Report 3 (1886), 34. On productions of Excelsior in Central Europe, see also Markian Prokopovych's new book on the Royal Budapest Opera.
18. See Němeček, *Opera Národního*, 5–10; also, more polemically, Nejedlý, *Opera Národního*, 150–67.
19. These statistics are taken from Šubert's annual reports in the 1880s.
20. This controversy is summarized, from Zelený's point of view, in Nejedlý, *Opera Národního*, 167–79. Šubert's response and view of the matter is recorded in the National Theater's annual reports. See AND, Annual Report 2 (1885), 12 and 34–39 and 3 (1886), 35–43.
21. This memorandum can be found in NA, Fond ND, Sign. 97, 55. See the reactions to it in NA, Fond ND, Sign. D 105/66, *MMC* of Feb. 12, 1883; NA, Fond ND, Sign. 97, 56–57, *PVS* of Feb. 15, 1885.
22. On the Viennese premiere, see Hadamowsky, *Die Wiener*, 88; also Willnauer, *Gustav Mahler*, 53.
23. For a critique of Fibich's *Hippodamia*, see Piper's *Enzyklopädie des Musiktheaters*, vol. 2, 200–205.
24. See Pilková, *Dramatická tvorba*.
25. See Nejedlý, *Opera Národního*, 218.
26. *Národní listy*, June 22, 1891, 2.
27. An account of this by actor Roman Żelazowski can be found in Idem, *Pięćdziesiąt lat teatru*, 86–88.
28. *Národní listy*, May 19, 1868, 1–2; May 20, 1868, 2; June 22, 1891, 1–2.
29. At the Estates Theater, the tenor was paid a salary of nearly 10,000 guilders, almost three times as much as the leading players of the Provisional Theater. See Teuber, *Geschichte, Dritter Theil*, 736.
30. The exact rate of fees and wages can be found in Šubert, *Dějiny*, CXLVIII–CLXVIII.
31. For the agreements of 1892 and 1894, see NA Fond ND, Sign. D 50, *MMC* of Feb. 11, 1892 and Sign. D 210, 177–80; also NA, Fond ND, Sign. 17, n.p. The entire correspondence between Šubert and Neumann can be found in NA, Fond ND, Sign. D 154 XVI, 106–13. On the position of the New German Theater regarding the various nationalities, see Cohen, *The Politics of Ethnic Survival*, 115–16.
32. See Ludvová, *National Theater*, 50; In Tancsik, 61, it is reported that a guest performance in Berlin's Lessing Theater in 1891 made a net profit of 60,000 marks.
33. See NA, Sign. D 50, *MMC*, Nov. 19, 1891; Dec. 28, 1891.

34. See Kann, *Das Nationalitätenproblem*, vol. 2, 199; Křen, *Konfliktgemeinschaft*, 223, 254–65.
35. On Pauline Metternich and her significance for the Austrian reception of Czech music, see Reittererová, *Vier Dutzend*, 82–84.
36. See Fond ND, Sign. D. 50, *PVA* of April 24, 1892; also *Národní listy*, April 25, 1892.
37. On the National Theater's appearance at the exhibition, see Šubert, *Moje Vzpomínky*, vol. 2, 43–59.
38. See Reittererová, *Vier Dutzend*, 227–92.
39. See the original plans for the tour in NA, Fond ND, Sign. D. 50, *MMC* of April 7, 1892; also *Národní listy*, May 10, 1892, 4.
40. In Vienna *The Bartered Bride* was first performed in German in 1893 at the *Theater an der Wien*. Its premiere in the royal theater followed in 1896 and further increased its fame. It was reprised 17 times in the first quarter after premiere. On the Viennese reception of Smetana and especially *The Bartered Bride*, see Reittererová, *Vier Dutzend*, 64–77, 225. On the Berlin production, in which conductor Adolf Čech and ballet director Augustín Berger were personally involved, see Šmaha, *Dělali jsme*, 151–52.
41. On Vienna's status as a center of music, see Nussbaumer, *Musikstadt Wien*.
42. See Reittererová, *Vier Dutzend*, 36–37. The Czech public consistently rejected proposals from Vienna, however, to have a bust erected in the Royal Opera commemorating him as the greatest *Austrian* composer; ibid, 35.
43. On the ratio of indigenous pieces to foreign works in the repertoire of all the major German opera theatres, see *Opernstatistik für das Jahr 1894*, 6–30.
44. See NA, Fond ND, Sign. D. 99/36, *PVA*, April 9, 1893. The situation was further improved by the diet raising the theater's annual subsidy to 100,000 guilders. See AND, Annual Report 2 (1885), 16, 34–39; Annual Report 3 (1886) and Annual Report 11 (1895), 4.
45. See Šubert, *Dějiny*, 369.
46. See the review in *Wiener Extrapost* which is reproduced in *Nejedlý*.
47. See Beckerman, *The Master's Little Joke*, 134–56.
48. In an interview with the *New York Herald* in May 1893, Dvořák said: "The future music of this country must be founded upon what are called the Negro melodies." Quoted in Horowitz, "Dvořák and the New World," 96.
49. See Šubert, *Dějiny*, 363–65.
50. See *Národní listy*, June 10, 1892, 5; NA, Fond ND, Sign. D. 50, MMC June 11, 1892; Šubert, *Dějiny*, 357–59.
51. This, at least, is the interpretation given in Šubert, *Dějiny*, 360.
52. On this cycle, see Němeček, *Opera Národního*, 116–17.
53. See Šubert, *Dějiny*, 359.
54. *Dalibor*, May 5, 1900, 171.
55. The first Paris performance was given to mark the 10th anniversary of the founding of Czechoslovakia in 1928. See Reittererová, *Vier Dutzend*, 84.
56. Walewski, *Teatr u nas*, 21.
57. Prominent intellectuals and the priest Stefan Kachala also traveled to Prague for the laying of the foundation stones. On Ruthenian attempts to found a national theater, see Lane, *The Polish Theatre*; also Got, *Das österreichische Theater*, vol. 2, 767–82. Citation from *Národní listy*, Nov. 20, 1883, 4.
58. For an overview of the development of the Ukrainian national movement in Galicia in the Habsburg period, see Rudnytsky, *The Ukrainians*.
59. Sivert, ed., *Teatr polski w latach*, 602–603.
60. See Ludvová, *Nationaltheater und Minderheitentheater*.

61. On the New German Theater see Cohen, *The Politics of Ethnic Survival*, 115–16.
62. The speeches given by Serbian, Croatian, and Slovenian dignitaries at the pan-Slavic congress are reproduced in *Národní listy*, May 19, 1868, 1–2; May 20, 1868, 1–2. This issue also contains most of the congratulatory telegrams.
63. See Batušić, *Hrvatsko narodno kazalište*, 185–87.
64. On this piece, see Katalinić, *Nikola Zrinyi*; also Everett, *Aspects of Musical-Dramatic Form*.
65. The opera department of the National Theater was actually closed 1902–1909 because it had become a financial liability. See Batušić, *Hrvatsko narodno*, 187–89.
66. See Gross, *Kultur und Gesellschaft*, 150.
67. Batušić, *Das Kroatische Nationaltheater*, 219.
68. The extent of their cooperation is evidenced by the correspondence between the Czech and Croatian National Theaters. See NA, Fond ND, Sign. D. 212, 153, 158, 161, 165, 194, 248; also NA, Fond ND, Sign. D. 50, MMC Aug. 6, 1891.
69. See the relevant article in *EMTA*, "Nowy Teatr w Lublanie."
70. See the correspondence between the Dramatic Association and the National Theater in NA, Fond ND, Sign. D. 212, 35–94.
71. Quoted in a letter to the National Theater of 9.8.1892 in NA, Fond ND, Sign. D. 212, 81.
72. NA, Fond D, Sign. D. 212, 81.
73. On Šmaha's experiences in Bulgaria, see his memoirs: Šmaha, *Jsme dělali*, 208–28.
74. This manuscript had inspired some of Dvořák's compositions, including *Lieder aus der Königinhofer Handschrift* (Opus 7, 1872), as well as a piece by Fibich.
75. See Vojáček, *Manifest*, 85–87.
76. On verismo, see Dahlhaus, *Die Musik des 19. Jahrhunderts*, 295–302.
77. See *Národní listy*, April 6, 1891, 2.
78. On the relationship between Dvořák and Brahms, see Beveridge, *Dvořák*, 56–58, 80–87. The Dvořák anthology by Beckerman calls the composer's classification as a traditionalist into question.
79. On these works and the opera repertoire between 1900 and 1906, see Němeček, *Opera Národního*, 109.
80. See Locke, *Opera and Ideology*.
81. Dahlhaus explicitly rejects the term *Jugendstil* in music history. See Dahlhaus, *Die Musik des 19. Jahrhunderts*, 279. A counter position is taken, however, by Gerlach in his monograph *Musik und Jugendstil*.
82. See Gerlach, *Musik und Jugendstil*, 4.
83. Massenet's two fairytale operas, *Cendrillon* and *Grisélidis*, which were first performed more or less contemporaneously with Dvořák's fairytale operas, in 1899 and 1901, might be considered comparable.
84. For the composer's view of this incident, see Weis, *Spravedlnost*, 4, 7, and his subsequent pamphlet in which he responds to the National Theater's criticism of his person and his first pamphlet: Weis, *Moje odpověd*, 8–9.
85. The National Theater had staged his first opera, *Viola*, in 1892, in Czech. On this and the dispute between Weis and the National Theater, see Němeček, 142–44.
86. This review is in parts reproduced and translated in Weis, *Spravedlnost*, 12–13. The rival newspaper, *Dresdner Nachrichten*, reported on Weis without tampering with his name. See *Dresdner Nachrichten*, Sept. 9, 1901, 2.
87. Quoted in Weis, *Spravedlnost*, 9. Jan Němeček, by contrast, blames Weis for the fact that the opera was not accepted by the National Theater (Němeček, *Opera Národního*, 143). His unfounded claim that, in writing music for a German libretto, Weis was "pri-

marily concerned with material gain and the effect of the work in foreign theaters," places his view in a questionable light. Should Weis have renounced all material concerns on account of his Jewish background? Němeček also criticizes the fact that Weis worked with a German libretto at all. This criticism is not only subliminally anti-Semitic but also false, in view of the amount of older Czech operas that were based on German texts.

88. *Rusalka* was, however, performed in Ljubljana and Zagreb before the outbreak of World War I.
89. Quoted in Zdeněk Nejedlý, "Česká moderní zpěvohra," in Smačny, *Dvořák*, 109.
90. The title refers to a naturalist play by Gabriela Preissová which was premiered in November 1890.
91. See Němeček, *Opera Národního*, 147–50.
92. Like Bartok and Szymanowski, Janáček criticized the traditional folk style. He had criticized Kovařovic's most successful opera *Poshlavci* for its superficial incorporation of national style elements and even dared to cast doubt on the work of the most exalted Czech composer, Smetana. Here, he was paying the penalty.
93. On the performance and reception of *Der Rosenkavalier* at the National Theater, see Němeček, *Opera národního*, vol. 1, 200–202.
94. See Černy and Kolárová, *Sto let*, 56.
95. A number of images are reproduced in a six-volume fifty-year anniversary publication on the National Theater. See *Dějiny národního divadla*, Praha 1933–1936.

Part Five

Comparison, Cultural Transfers, and Networks

CHAPTER NINE

Opera and Society

Music is inextricably linked with its social and spatial environment. The varying sizes and acoustics of opera theaters and concert halls clearly have a significant impact on the cultural practice of music. But there are also music spaces beyond the walls and boundaries of standing theaters or concert halls. This chapter about cultural spaces takes a topographic approach to address questions of when and why certain works, fashions, styles, and genres were diffused over considerable geographic and social distances.

Most literature on European cultural and opera history is written from a centrist viewpoint. Much more is known about musical life in London, Paris, or Vienna than in cities such as Budapest, Lemberg, or Kiev, although they too developed lively opera scenes. This occidental bias is justified to some extent by the fact that fashions, styles, and individual premieres in the traditional opera centers did indeed set standards for the entire continent. The process by which this occurred can be likened to a stone sending out concentric ripples when thrown into a lake. But the pluralization of opera in Europe meant that the lake was no longer an empty expanse. Impulses were refracted by new islands and shorelines and ultimately returned to the original source. Hence, a topographic approach, mapping music cultures, broadens and decentralizes the view of European history and allows equal consideration to be given to east and west as it is not bound to a static model of center and periphery. The examples of various emerging operatic cities show that formerly peripheral places could take on the function of centers, at least for the surrounding regions. Opera was, moreover, not just imported but adopted as a culture, sometimes with far-reaching effects on the old centers of music theater. This is illustrated by opera's nationalization (in the sense of endowing it with a national character), which began in the German lands and in Russia around the mid-nineteenth century and was taken up by various countries of Central Europe. Eventually the phenomenon even had a significant affect on the original brand of opera: the once universal genre of Italian opera was in certain ways reduced to one of many national traditions.

Considering cultural spaces and exploring cultural transfers, the conventional historical focus on individual case studies and a specific object—in this case, German, Polish, and Czech opera and their leading institutions—is shifted into a broader frame of reference. This concluding chapter aims to show how the world of opera in Central Europe and beyond was to a large extent shaped by reciprocal appreciation, cultural transfers, and networks.

The means of cultural exchange were revolutionized in the course of the nineteenth century. Innovations such as rail travel, steam ships, mass media, and the telephone gave rise to an exponential increase in cultural transfers on both an interpersonal and an intertextual level. The popularity of opera between 1815 and 1914 contributed significantly to increasing both the quantity and quality of cultural exchange. The number of permanent opera houses grew from only a few, mostly court establishments at the time of the French Revolution to a dense network of public theaters with their own opera ensembles by the First World War. Most large European towns, especially in Italy and the German and Austrian Empires, invested in a prestigious theater, whether they were rich or poor, industrialized, or still predominantly agricultural. There were waves of opera foundings—prior to the March Revolution of 1848, around 1870 and again around 1900—when the aristocracy and middle class were emboldened to seek autonomy and prestige and inspired by an ideal of European civilization. A list of the central European towns where new theaters were constructed in the nineteenth century would span the entire alphabet, from Augsburg, Basel, and Coburg in the west to Zagreb and Żytomierz in the east. The local elites in any town with a population of over 50,000 would aspire to have one. The demand for opera houses was so great that they were soon offered in a number of sizes and styles, like any consumer commodity. The Viennese architects Fellner & Helmer became the region's leading suppliers, overseeing the construction of 48 gilded and chandeliered theaters between the Rhine and the Dnieper in today's Ukraine from 1870 to 1913.

Aristocracy and Middle Class: A Comparison

Urban, regional, and national elites began to participate in what was once the domain of princes. In societies with an influential nobility, such as in Poland, Hungary, and late eighteenth-century Bohemia, it was often wealthy aristocrats who commissioned and financed new theaters. Elsewhere, middle-class citizens and, in the case of Ukraine or Estonia, even first- or second-generation descendants of peasants organized their construction.[1] This illustrates the relevance of cultural spaces for social history. Within them, sections of society were drawn to the opera which would hardly have set foot in an opera house in 1815 or indeed do so today.

Each strata of society supported opera and other music institutions at different points in time. While aristocrats were the cultural trailblazers of many countries in the first half of the nineteenth century, their influence dwindled later. Even in Poland, the landed nobility was superseded on and off stage by the intelligentsia. Hungarian aristocrats, meanwhile, maintained their influence longer thanks to the compromise with Austria, which conceded them a degree of participation in the affairs of the state and hence also in the National Theater.[2]

Comparing the cultural life of these different nations, a functional equivalence between the aristocracy and the middle class comes to light. The aristocracy were often the first to actively foster music. In regions or cities without a strong or socially diversified aristocracy, the middle class took the lead in theater and opera culture, and imitated aristocratic customs such as playing music at home and employing private music tutors for their children.[3] Conversely, aristocrats assumed habits which were previously considered bourgeois, such as sitting still during performances and concentrating on the stage. But this should not be interpreted as signifying the general acceptance of bourgeois values and conventions. The main models for the central European opera public were Paris and Vienna and how the audiences behaved there. The new approach to listening was, then, less a middle-class victory than the result of extensive cultural transfers.[4]

Comparison of Galicia and Bohemia shows that the aristocracy and the middle class pursued similar cultural ideals. Both believed that theater could fulfil an educational role and promote national awareness in the Enlightenment tradition. They disagreed, however, on the details of applying it. The aristocracy had no intention of reaching all of society through theater. They were merely concerned with "the diffusion of light to the more mature parts of the nation," as a petition of 1821 to the Galician Estates put it.[5] Theater-loving aristocrats did not believe or hope that class barriers would be raised in the theater. In his playhouse, Count Skarbek ensured that the crème de la crème of the audience occupied separate boxes away from the commoners in the orchestra level, as in Prague's Estates Theater. The ideal the aristocracy envisioned, then, was an oligarchy of equals rather than rapprochement with the common folk.

The middle class strove for a more universalist theater but was slow to develop a cultural policy to rival the aristocracy.[6] In Germany it was not until the decade preceding unification and the founding of the empire that cultural awareness and civic pride grew and Leipzig began to measure itself against the royal seat of Dresden. The city's spirit of cultural achievement was symbolized by the new, luxurious Leipzig Municipal Theater, built in 1868 by the celebrated Prussian architect Langhans the Younger. But here, as in Lemberg, the theater-going public was content to be among its peers and did not attempt to involve the suburban or provincial lower classes.

Over time, both the Bohemian and Galician aristocracies and the middle class in Saxony changed their priorities for theater. Before the 1848 Revolution, they regarded theater as an educational institution. This is illustrated by the repertoires and writings of Jan Nepomucen Kamiński and Karl Theodor Küstner, the two leading theater directors in Lemberg and Leipzig of the 1820s. Both put on a large proportion of classical dramas and avoided "lowbrow" genres. But such lofty aims were largely abandoned after the revolution, when the aristocracy and the (German) middle class were conceded limited political and full economic rights. With their social and political ambitions to a large extent achieved, their requirements of theater changed: they now sought lighter entertainment, and lost interest in classical and topical dramas. Hence, the often cited leitmotif of *embourgeoisement* in German historiography does not stand up to empirical examination. When civic Enlightenment theater was at its most productive in the eighteenth and early nineteenth century, it was not controlled by burghers. Later on, in the heyday of middle-class dominance in theater, municipal theaters cultivated a quite different repertoire from what Enlightenment-influenced authors and critics had envisioned.

Aristocratic theaters, meanwhile, went into a notable decline. The nobility in Bohemia and Galicia were progressively superseded both on stage and backstage. Even Lemberg's powerful aristocrats gradually lost their foothold in the Polish Theater from 1872. Theater director Miłaszewski's second tenure, especially, marked a low point in the theater's artistic and financial affairs. The nadir came for the Bohemian nobility when the Estates Theater went bankrupt in 1885. As a result, the New German Theater was built, financed chiefly by industrialists and Jewish patrons who were members of the executive theater association. The old Estates Theater was now merely a subsidiary of the new playhouse. Although its auditorium was still arranged like an aristocratic box-theater, its program was designed mainly to appeal to the diversion-seeking simple folk among the German-speaking population in Prague. This heralded a fundamental change in central European theater: architecture and seating no longer corresponded in the traditional way with the social composition of its audience, or only to a degree.

The demise of aristocratic theater in Lemberg and Prague occurred in two stages. Proving financially and artistically unfeasible in the long term, changes in organization became necessary. Subsequently, the nobility was outnumbered or even forced out by its middle-class associates. Not only that, it faced a growing contingent of middle-class men and women who had received a musical education and aspired to careers in opera. Although many actors, dramaturges and directors still hailed from the aristocracy at the end of the nineteenth century, they no longer dominated. And theaters were increasingly dependent on the approval of the growing middle-class element among the audience.

Nevertheless, the nobility's influence on the theater scene of Central Europe should not be underestimated. In an early phase, the nobility played a crucial part in emancipating opera from the royal courts and was responsible for the first public theaters in Bohemia and Galicia. By their sheer size, these monumental institutions set an entirely new cultural dynamic in motion. In addition to these highly visible activities, aristocrats also engaged in more discreet patronage of music societies, sponsored individual singers, and set up awards for composers.

The aristocracy was not, however, a homogenous group. The Galician nobility was as socially diverse as the *Bürgertum* in Saxony and opinions among it varied accordingly. Some Galician aristocrats objected to the Lemberg theater's emphasis on light entertainment—a label which had gained a derogatory overtone by the 1870s. Its severest critics were mostly members of the *szlachta*, the low nobility, such as Dobrzański, who held firm to the Enlightenment ideal of theater and accused the directors and their aristocratic backers of cultural neglect. Prague, Leipzig, and Dresden—where the term *bürgerlich* gained an equally negative connotation to *bourgeois* in French—witnessed similar disputes. The bourgeois claim to cultural universality was an issue of great contention in the late nineteenth century.

The national theaters of "small" nations,[7] by contrast, transcended the social boundaries confining aristocratic and civic theaters. With its special trains and many matinees, people's and workers' performances, the Czech National Theater did as much as possible to put the Enlightenment ideal of theater into practice. But the middle-class directors in Prague still faced similar dilemmas to those in Leipzig and other cities. Although the Czech theater was supported by a broad social movement, arguments over repertoire content caused deep rifts, with defenders of the exalted ideal of theater on one side and popular demand for light entertainment on the other. After 1900 the theater's powers of social inclusion began to fade perceptibly.

Disputes over the purpose of theater had deeper implications since they indirectly addressed issues of political hegemony. Whoever controlled the theater had a very prominent public institution of the city, region, or even country at his disposal. Consequently, men—there clearly was a gender bias—often fought for positions in theater administration as if they were standing for government, conducting canvassing campaigns. Although this disrupted the theaters' operations—see Prague's Provisional Theater in the mid-1870s and the Polish Theater in Lemberg on several occasions—it also kept them in the public eye. The events on and off the stage fascinated much of the public and were sometimes even affairs of state. There was less controversy, however, in Dresden, where the hegemony of the court remained unchallenged. While the Dresden newspapers rarely commented on the royal theater's directors or program, the press in Prague and Lemberg actively intervened in their theaters' affairs.

It was the press which ultimately upheld the ideal of educational theater. Editors and journalists were mostly members of the intelligentsia, or educated classes. Occupying the moral high ground, their argument that theater had an important humane task to fulfill was hegemonic. Light entertainment, by contrast, could be legitimized by no deeper reason than that it satisfied the demands of the market. Although Europe was in the first flush of liberal capitalism, the public was reluctant to accept its reasoning in the realm of culture. A gulf appeared between economic and cultural elites which would not adhere to the laws of the market. The theater directors in Prague and Lemberg tried to find a way to bridge it, supporting the Enlightenment purpose of theater while also respecting popular tastes by, for example, staging operettas. But the rift placed their theaters in a vulnerable position which was compounded by inherent social friction.

Since aristocratic and civic theaters grew increasingly similar in organization, audience, and repertoires, there is the fundamental question of whether opera theaters should be categorized according to concepts of social history. In fact, by the time middle class influence on society and culture was growing in the nineteenth century, *bürgerliches* theater in Germany was already in decline. The career of Leipzig-born Richard Wagner provides a paradigmatic example of this change in orientation. The continents's royal theaters, such as in Dresden, actually came closest to realizing middle-class ideals of enlightened theater. In a roundabout way, a highbrow repertoire was eventually adopted by all the theaters considered here. Rising costs made subsidies indispensable, but public funding was only approved if it secured an elevated repertoire.

Meanwhile, the diversifying theater scene in all the major European cities led to the creation of new cultural markets. Folk theaters, workers' theaters, restaurants, and variety theaters staged operettas, cabarets, and other forms of popular music theater. In these circumstances, narrowing the repertoire to educational and edifying pieces was a way for the large, prestigious theaters to signal that they were not competing with these venues. This finally put paid to the utopian idea that all classes of society could be united under theater's roof, even in Prague, where it endured the longest.

Thus the changes in the political system that took place in the German and Austrian Empires were mirrored in the arts—with far-reaching consequences. As Carl Schorske has shown, the middle class lost not only its political majority but also its authority to define aesthetic values. Modernism in music, literature, and art rejected the existing arts scene and deliberately broke with tradition. Modernist composers, nearly all from middle-class backgrounds, participated in this by defying musical conventions, breaking rules of harmony, and experimenting with rhythm.[8] Richard Strauss was the German opera composer of this period to push boundaries the furthest with *Salome* and *Elektra*. Of Czech modernist composers, Janáček stands out as the most innovative, and in Poland the members of the

Młoda Polska ("Young Poland") movement made a significant impact. The real cultural revolution, however, took place outside the opera houses. The operatic format, designed to fill large spaces with sound and enchant audiences for entire evenings, was not conducive to the kind of experiments in "intimate theater" that were being carried out in spoken drama. As a result modernist composers turned their backs on opera and the general consensus on aesthetic norms. Thus, the utopia of the synthesis of the arts, the *Gesamtkunstwerk*, became obsolete. This also holds true for the old liberal utopia of uniting all social classes under the roof of one cultural institution.

Opera's Popularity in Comparison

Today opera is commonly regarded as an elitist art form patronized by only a small, privileged section of society; as high culture. But it would be wrong to transpose this view on to the nineteenth century. The extent of opera's impact can be gauged by looking at the number of performances given of individual pieces. In 1894, *Der Freischütz* crossed the magic 500-performance mark in Dresden. *Halka* and *The Bartered Bride* matched this record in Warsaw and Prague a few years later. Multiplying the capacity of the theater by the number of performances, a total public of about one million can be estimated to have attended each of these operas. Such high attendances were, moreover, common in Europe. The best-loved French operas were reprised more than 1,000 times at the *Palais Garnier* and the *Opéra Comique* in Paris. Wagner's most popular works were shown almost as often. Even *Salome,* by Richard Strauss, whose music was perceived as difficult and provocative by many of his contemporaries, drew nearly 50,000 visitors to the opera in Dresden in the year after its premiere. The lighter-hearted *Rosenkavalier* was performed twice as many times in 1911. Well-known operas were not only put on stage at major theaters but also at seaside resorts, open-air venues, and countless smaller municipal theaters. In addition, sheet music of opera arias and piano scores were published in editions of tens of thousands. Folios containing the musical highlights of *Lohengrin* and *Dalibor*, best-of compilations of the work of individual composers and potpourris of favorite melodies were all in circulation. As the star cult surrounding opera's tenors shows, in the late nineteenth century, opera was not only high culture but also popular culture.

Yet opera theaters were sites of social distinction.[9] Patrons displayed their wealth and social status in their choice of seats or, failing that, in their orders at the buffet. Nevertheless, in the intervals, maids and other lower-class audience members could rub shoulders with society's upper echelons in the foyers. Unlike in London, for example, there were no separate foyers or staircases in Dresden, Prague, and Lemberg. The only exception was a private entrance for the king to the royal box in the Semper Opera. The institution of opera in Central Europe was therefore both exclusive and inclusive. The numerous reviews of opera performances in Dresden's working-class press in the early twentieth century attest to a fascination for opera beyond the aristocracy and the middle class. They can only have been written with an interested readership in mind.

Of the theaters considered here, Prague's National Theater reached the broadest public, on account of its peculiar social and political context as well as the personal influence of František Adolf Šubert. It was a theater for a nation without a state. As long as the Czechs failed to gain equality within the Habsburg Monarchy, and rivalry with the Germans in Bohemia continued, cultural nation-building remained a pertinent issue.

Comparable developments occurred in Western Europe in the arts of the Catalans, Norwegians, and Irish. Several national theaters were also founded on the fringes of the Russian Empire with the aim of mobilizing and educating emergent nations. In the Baltic States, the independent Latvian and Estonian theaters defended their nations against the cultural dominance of the Baltic Germans; in Lithuania, against the Poles. In the south of the empire, similar cultural bulwarks were constructed in Georgia and Azerbaijan. In all these examples, opera and theater can be seen as indicators of the existence of local social elites, eager to demonstrate their nations' cultural archievements and identification with European civilization.

In Germany, by contrast, the founding of the empire gave rise to a political dynamic that prevented popular movements from growing around specific cultural institutions or personalities. Similarly, in Hungary, the opera was separated from the National Theater, founded in 1838, and run as a royal theater from 1884. Here, opera became the prestigious reserve of the state and its elites. Meanwhile, among ordinary Hungarians, operetta, vaudeville and folk theater were hugely popular.

But even in Prague, theater reached the limits of its popularity. While the theater scene diversified, the Young Czech Liberals dominating the political scene remained largely insensitive to societal changes. As Czech society stratified, the National Theater's public became reduced to a stalwart core. This trend continued throughout the Czechoslovak Republic. It was not until after the Second World War that the vision of a theater for all strata—now called classes—was revived. A line of continuity can be drawn, then, from the rise of national awareness in the late nineteenth century to Communist cultural policy after 1948. The Lemberg Theater, by contrast, was at no point an all-embracing institution. Unlike the rural and small town populations in Bohemia, the Galicians had no special trains to take them to the theater. Only very few Galician peasants ever set foot in the theater and it remained alien to most.[10] Yet even in Galicia, theater attracted far broader sections of society in 1914 than in 1815.

The Czech National Theater is a prime example of a site of artistic productivity fostered by conditions of social mobilization. From 1860 to 1861, Czech artists—from a nascent society of only three million—produced an astounding amount of dramas, plays, operas, and other works. The bulk of today's Czech opera repertoire was created in the half-century between the opening of the Provisional Theater and the outbreak of the First World War. Members of the lower orders, sons and daughters of manual laborers and the petty bourgeoisie, played a considerable part in these social and artistic innovations. Antonín Dvořák and theater director Šubert were both of humble origins as were many of the great Czech singers. The distance they covered in terms of social mobility paralleled the geographical extent of the National Theater's fame.

As music theater's social and geographical relevance grew in the latter nineteenth century, a new generation of authors and composers emerged who contributed to both national and European music and opera repertoires with works under the paradigm of modernism. The cultures of other "small" nations underwent similarly dynamic developments. Norwegian drama and Catalan architecture are two examples. The Ukrainian and Baltic societies also blossomed around the turn of the century. Societies strove to demonstrate status and identity through a nationally defined opera culture right up to the Caucasus. In Sakhali Paliashvili and Uzeri Hadzhibeyli, Georgia, and Azerbaijan, each had a native composer to provide national operas.[11] Between 1815 and 1914, then, Europe's cultural topography changed not only quantitatively, in the number and dispersion of new opera theaters, but also qualitatively. But while the "small" nations contributed substantially to the cultural productivity of the traditional opera nations, the latter remained mostly ignorant of the works of the operatic newcomers.

Notes

1. On Estonia, see Rähesoo, *Estonian Theatre*, 23, 31.
2. On Budapest, see Prokopovych, *In the Public Eye*.
3. On the cultivation of music in middle class families, see Budde, *Musik in Bürgerhäusern*, 435–39.
4. On Paris, see Johnson, *Listening in Paris*, 228–36. The process by which this listening behavior was adopted across Europe is discussed in Müller, *Hörverhalten*.
5. See TsDIAU, 165/5/8, 1–3.
6. On the Leipzig Theater, see Ther, *Zivilgesellschaft und Kultur*, 199–202.
7. On the concept of "kleine Nationen," see Hroch, *Die Vorkämpfer*, 9–10.
8. The decline of binding musical and aesthetic norms is considered in Dahlhaus's reflections on the "emancipation of dissonance" in Dahlhaus, *Die Musik des 19. Jahrhunderts*, 319–32.
9. See Bourdieu, *Distinction: A Social Critique of the Judgement of Taste*.
10. See the memoirs of actor Roman Żelazowski, *Pięcdziesiąt lat*, 102.
11. On the development of Azerbaijani theater and the opera in Baku, see Altstadt, *The Azerbaijani Turks*, 70.

CHAPTER TEN

Nationalizing Opera

At the beginning of the nineteenth century, music theater was distinctly international in character, being almost synonymous with Italian opera in many countries. How did opera increasingly come to be perceived as an expression of the nation in various countries after 1848? How did national genres of opera develop? The three main elements indicating the nationalization of opera are the singing language, the dramatic and musical content of works, and their reception and the proportion of native pieces in the repertoire.

Changing Singing Languages

The existence of German, Polish, and Czech opera cannot be regarded as a given or the natural result of nation-building. New national opera genres flourished only where there was an ensemble that could sing in the native language. This was the case at different times in Dresden, Lemberg, and Prague.[1] In Dresden, King Friedrich August I established a German opera department as early as 1817 which, under the direction of Carl Maria von Weber, soon gained widespread renown. Initially, French operas were a strong component of the repertoire. But these were performed in translation, which gradually established German as a singing language to rival Italian. In 1831, the Italian opera department was finally closed down. Under the aegis of chief conductor Richard Wagner in the 1840s, all pieces were translated, no more performances were given in Italian, and Dresden became the first major royal theater to engage in nationalizing opera. After 1859 and the decline of neo-absolutism, no *stagioni* were held in Vienna either.

The nationalization of the singing language paralleled changes in the audience. By the time Dresden's Semper Opera was built in 1841, the Italian-speaking (or even singing) members of the court constituted only a small minority among the opera public. They were now outnumbered by the urban middle class, which was much less familiar with foreign languages and frequently held nationalist views. Consequently, the popularity of German-language performances increased. To ensure that audiences could understand the texts and follow the plot, greater emphasis was laid on declamation than today. Furthermore, nationalizing the singing language gave German operas the considerable advantage that they could be immediately assessed and rehearsed, whereas French or Italian works had to be translated first. This frequently detracted from the quality and, crucially, incurred greater costs. None of the opera theaters considered in this book remained unaffected by these market forces.

The history of Polish opera in many ways parallels the development of music theater in the German lands up to the end of the eighteenth century. Although there was no Polish Mozart, under Bogusławski and Elsner a native tradition of lyrical drama blossomed in Warsaw and Lemberg. Performances in Polish were common. This changed, however, in the period following the failed November Uprising of 1830–31. The suppression of Polish culture at the hands of Russia and Prussia stifled the development of Polish opera, which was then not strong enough to rival Italian opera. Native opera was further disadvantaged in Lemberg by the existence of a German and a Polish ensemble: since the German ensemble performed so many operas, the Polish Theater confined itself chiefly to spoken drama. Theater director Miłaszewski effected some changes after his arrival in the 1860s, staging more music theater with the Polish ensemble. But he tended to choose Parisian operettas over the Polish comedy dramas underscored with music.

Even the closure of the German Theater in Lemberg in 1872 did not herald a more productive phase for Polish opera. Ongoing social and political conflicts between the high nobility and the intelligentsia prevented a permanent, Polish-singing opera ensemble from becoming established. The reduction of year-round opera to one *stagione* in 1875 and again in 1886 compelled Polish singers in Lemberg to seek employment in Warsaw or elsewhere in central or Western Europe during the rest of the year. If they were talented and found success, they often stayed abroad. Singers who were prepared to work seasonally were usually employed from Italy. Thus the Polish Theater was reduced to a provincial theater in Italy's cultural orbit. Instead of contemporary pieces, mainly older French and Italian pieces were performed, blocking any fresh artistic input. It was not until 1896 that a permanent Polish ensemble specializing in music drama was established under Ludwik Heller. Polish opera finally enjoyed renewed success, with both Moniuszko's older standard works as well as more recent native works such as the *verismo*-inspired piece *Janek* by Żeleński and *Manru* by Paderewski.

The Czech National Theater indirectly profited from the instability of the Polish Theater. In 1886, the two most talented Lemberg soloists of the late nineteenth century, tenor Władysław Florjański and soprano Tereza Arklowa, went to Prague, where they rounded off the Czech-singing ensemble. Singing the lead roles in a new production of *Dalibor*, they contributed to popularizing Smetana's dramatic work. While Tereza Arklowa subsequently moved on to Budapest, Florjański stayed in

Prague and played a central role in the "triumph in Vienna" which marked the National Theater's international breakthrough. The careers of these artists show the effect of cultural transfers, involving both exchanges of works and of performers, and hence, intertextual and interpersonal cultural transfers

It would be an exaggeration, however, to attribute the upswing in Czech opera solely to these external influences. Smetana had already established an ensemble to rival the German-language Estates Theater in the predecessor Czech playhouse. Šubert, the first director of the National Theater, forged ahead with creating a Czech singing ensemble, sometimes by radical means. As the incident involving Marie Pospišilová shows, performers who had contacts with the German Theater were shunned by Czech society and the Czech ensemble. The National Theater's mission to reach all strata of society went hand in hand with a principle of ethnic exclusivity which was rigorously upheld by Šubert and his successor.

A comparison of developments in Lemberg and Prague leads to a jarring conclusion: Czech opera as an institution and as a genre was fostered by the Czechs' more radical and often xenophobic type of nationalism. Lemberg's more tolerant attitudes and sustained focus on Italian opera, by contrast, left Polish opera consigned to the realm of the provincial. It was not until Heller's arrival on the eve of World War I that Polish opera managed to "catch up." Nevertheless, from the broad perspective of the entire nineteenth and twentieth century, it would be wrong to interpret the Polish culture scene as backward, since the world's major theaters later also adopted the custom of singing in the original language. Although the Polish Theater in Lemberg was out of step with Central Europe in the late nineteenth century, from a contemporary perspective, it was ahead of its time.

National Operas in Europe: A Comparison

In musicology, "national opera" is an umbrella term denoting works created over the course of the nineteenth century which are regarded as representative of individual national opera traditions. Carl Dahlhaus has based his typology primarily on phenomena of reception. At the same time, he observes a number of important stylistic aspects of plot and compositional technique that these works have in common.[2] Curiously, Dahlhaus and English-language scholarship—with the exception of Hannu Salmi and a few others—fail to consider Richard Wagner in this context. Wagner has been omitted from research on national opera not on account of his works or personality but due to an inherently nationalist tradition of reception which emerged in the late nineteenth century in Germany and continues to have an impact on the English-speaking world today. In order to analyze this tradition, some works and the reception of central and eastern European opera composers of the nineteenth century will be compared below.

Music example 9. Scene from *Lohengrin* accenting *deutsch* (German).

    The German national movement's influence on Wagner is apparent in his early writings as well as in his choice of subject matter for operas. Following his appointment as chief conductor in Dresden, Wagner wrote *Tannhäuser*, his first attempt to deal with specifically national myths. The opera is set in the late Middle Ages at Wartburg Castle, a site of central importance for German legend, where the historical "singers' contest" referred to in the full title (*Tannhäuser und der Sängerkrieg auf Wartburg*) took place. It linked, then, the legendary medieval event with the nineteenth century's boom of choral festivals and supported the notion of the Germans' inherent musicality. But in spite of the opera's positivist elements and historical frame, it met with a lukewarm reception due to the psychological storyline which failed to touch a nerve with the public in 1845. *Tannhäuser* was dropped from the repertoire in Dresden after a few performances and no other theaters could be convinced of its merits before the 1848 revolution.

Despite this disappointment, Wagner continued to deal with national myths and history. He set his next opera, *Lohengrin*, in a key period of Saxon and German history, the reign of Heinrich I, the first Saxon prince to occupy the royal German throne. The opera opens with Heinrich making a rousing, symbolic appeal for national unity against the Hungarians who are threatening the empire. Many of Wagner's contemporaries would have recognized the allusion to autocratic Russia, which was hated by liberals like him but protected from direct attacks by the censors. The motif of armed struggle against foreign enemies was later taken up by nearly all central European and eastern European national operas, which also dealt with national unity, traitors to this noble cause (who were usually aristocrats), and the protagonist's heroic self-sacrifice for the greater good.

In political terms, Lohengrin is an interesting figure. Declared the king's future successor by the people, he has democratic legitimacy. He maintains the unity of the land by defending the just rule of the king against aristocratic intrigues. The action is regularly punctuated by monumental mass scenes with chorus singing—an element borrowed from grand opera[3]—in which the German nation is portrayed as a collective of regional groups. In the first act, the Saxons sing in a solemn C-major chord *"Wohlauf für deutschen Reiches Ehr"* ("Let us away! For the honor of the German empire!"), underlining their central role in the German unification process.[4] The other plotlines in *Lohengrin* are hence arranged around the framework of the political context. Lohengrin's departing prophecy of glory for the German Empire once again articulates the piece's national bias, which the music also manages to reflect, regularly accenting the word *deutsch* by a reduction of harmonic structure.[5] In short, both the subject and the music were ideal national opera material. But it was initially withheld from the public in the light of Wagner's involvement in and indictment following the revolution. *Lohengrin* was not performed until the social and political circumstances had changed.

Wagner's breakthrough as the foremost German opera composer finally came with *The Mastersingers of Nuremberg,* which portrays the Protestant middle class as the true proponents of German culture.[6] In the final scene, most often cited as evidence of Wagner's nationalism, the main hero Hans Sachs criticizes the German princes for their un-German ways and their preference of *welsch* culture (a pejorative term for Romance languages and cultures). *Mastersingers* was jubilantly received as a call for German unification by the premiere public in Munich in 1868, and again in Dresden a short time later. The nationalist middle class identified strongly with the hero Hans Sachs, who found his way into many households via piano music and other popular adaptations of the score.

Music example 10. Nationally encoded Marsh from *The Mastersingers of Nuremberg*.

On which terms can *The Mastersingers of Nuremberg* be defined as a national opera? Wagner opposed the use of folk songs and popular dance rhythms on principle. No local color of this kind can be found in *Mastersingers* or any of his other works. But he suffused his music with a specific character and created a unique sound by using historical instruments and composition techniques. The result is in fact summed up by the main hero Hans Sachs when he sings: *"Es klang so alt, und war doch so neu"* ("It sounded so old, and yet was so new").[7] As well as Hans Sachs's story, the sound of Wagner's music and eventually his entire oeuvre came to be perceived by the public as specifically German. *Mastersingers* can perhaps be regarded as the ultimate German national opera, especially in view of its reception on the fringes of and outside the German Empire. It was performed to inaugurate the New German Theater in Prague, for example, therefore providing the counterpart to Smetana's *Libuše* for the National Theater. It was enthusiastically received in Graz, Strasbourg, and other borderland towns in the context of nationalist demands and repertoire policy. Although nationalist aspects were less significant for the public in the heart of the German Empire, in Munich and Berlin, too, Wagner, *Lohengrin*, and *Mastersingers* were perceived as the embodiment of German opera culture.

How did other nations react to this new phenomenon of a national opera culture? The Czech elites encountered Wagner's work at the Estates Theater in Prague as early as the mid-1850s. Count Harrach, a supporter of the Czech national movement, was probably inspired by Wagner's success to set up a competition for the creation of a Czech national opera to inaugurate the Provisional Theater. The winning entry, Bedřich Smetana's *The Brandenburgers in Bohemia* (*Braniboři v Čechach*), focused even more intently than *Lohengrin* on a tale of defending the land against external enemies. The central plot strand of the "good" Czechs' battle against the "evil" Brandenburgers invited comparison with contemporary conflicts with the Habsburgs. The people's election of the beggar Jira to be king forms a key moment in the opera, premiered in 1866. In the following two acts, Jira goes on to rally the nation behind him and vanquish the intruders. As in *Lohengrin*, then, the election scene pleads the case for a democratically legitimized monarch. But rather than a mythical figure, Jira is a member of the underclass, which henceforth participates in society on equal terms and even takes a leading role in national politics. It is an irony of opera history that Smetana's democratically minded librettist, Karel Sabina, was a police spy.[8]

Musically, too, *The Brandenburgers in Bohemia* mirrored the age's mood of departure and Czech national awakening. This is articulated in the use of marching rhythms and choruses representing the nation on stage.[9] A musical contrast serves to heighten the drama: while the Brandenburgers are generally underscored by only a few instruments, King Jira appears to the sound of chorus-singing in the middle and lower registers and full orchestration. Thus the impression is created that the Brandenburgers acted in isolation while the mass of the people supported the national movement. Here, the romantic element was secondary to the political storyline but included as a requisite component of a work in the tradition of French grand opera. Jira's struggle to free three Czech girls abducted by the Brandenburgers ends predictably happily. Unlike his next two works (the *Bartered Bride* and *Dalibor*), this first of Smetana's national operas did not gain a central place in the repertoire, mainly owing to the libretto's weaknesses.

Music example 11. National mobilization in *The Brandenburgers in Bohemia*.

Today most productions of *The Bartered Bride* (*Prodaná nevěsta*) present the piece as a folkish *opera buffa*. But behind the villagers' dances and drinking songs lies some harsh social criticism. Sabina's libretto attacks the petty bourgeoisie for pursuing material wealth at the cost of the individual's well-being. But the opera's most innovative aspect was its contemporary setting, which broke away from the historical precedent set by Wagner and in French Grand Opéra. Smetana's realist perspective allowed the public to see the living nation portrayed on the stage, yet from a comfortable distance.[10] Urban audiences were clearly fascinated by the antics of the country folk which the opera so vividly described and *The Bartered Bride* went on to be a major international success.

Michail Glinka and Ferenc Erkel—who were to Russia and Hungary respectively what Smetana was to the Czechs—dealt with similar topics in their dramatic national operas. Erkel's *Hunyadi László* (first performed in 1844) portrays a bloody romantic intrigue which culminates in the murder of a queen of German origin and the execution of the Hungarian protagonist. This opera, too, addresses themes of national unity and the repulsion of foreign influences. In a subtext, the libretto criticizes some of the Hungarian nobility for cooperating with the Habsburgs in the prerevolution period. Musically, Erkel infused his work with a Magyar flavor by incorporating increased sevenths on the minor scale and *verbunkos*, a popular Hungarian dance.[11] He adopted a number-opera structure into which national dances and songs could be inserted. Croatian composer Ivan Zajc and, much later, Georgian composer Sakhali Paliashvili took similar approaches. It would fall beyond the ambit of this book, however, to analyze the work of these or the many other eastern and northern European composers acclaimed as the "fathers" of their country's opera traditions.

Music example 12. Construction of Polish national music in *A Life for the Czar*.

Glinka's *A Life for the Czar* (*Žyzn' za tsaria*) was the first work to be received as a national opera in Russia. It is set in the *smuta* era—a period of turmoil in the early seventeenth century when Russia was divided by dynastic conflicts and Moscow fell under Polish occupation for a time. It describes how the peasant hero Iwan Sussanin (the name by which the opera was known in the Stalin era) sacrifices his life in a subterfuge against the Polish army. On a political level, the opera can be interpreted in two different ways. On the one hand, it portrays peasants and the middle classes—who at the time of the opera's writing were mostly bondsmen—as equal members of the nation. But on the other hand, it seemed to endorse Russian autocracy to its liberal critics in Prague. Glinka underscored the actions of his Russian heroes with nationally coded sounds and illustrated the Polish act with Polish dances.[12] This contrast between the action and music of the two nations continued to elicit strong reactions many years after its premiere. A performance in Moscow in 1866 was interrupted by shouts from the auditorium of "Down, down with the Poles!"[13] Modest Mussorgsky developed this juxtaposition of national music styles further in *Boris Godunow* (first performed in 1874), where it served as a background to a more psychological drama.

While Moniuszko's opera *Halka* was received as an exemplary work of Polish music theater, it stands out from the pattern described above for focusing on an inner-social conflict. The peasant girl Halka is the tragic heroine who commits suicide after being seduced and abandoned by a nobleman. The opera contrasts Halka's sensitivity and integrity with the falseness and arrogance of the aristocrat Janusz. Along with Glinka and Smetana, Moniuszko disobeyed the classical requirement that tragic protagonists be of noble birth.[14] In classical drama, members of the lower orders were only deemed suitable for leading roles in comedies. The opera's harsh criticism of the aristocracy initially met with a skeptical response, but after the failed uprising of 1863, its implicit demand for equality for peasants and their integration into the Polish nation resonated with the public. The opera became a fixture in the Polish repertoire and was performed to open the season for many years.

Halka's reception as a national opera was promoted by a sense among Warsaw's music lovers that native music needed to catch up. The Polish nation required a homegrown piece to match Russia's emblematic national opera, *Żyzn za tsaria* by Glinka. The desire to keep up with neighboring lands or cities was indeed one of the salient factors contributing to the creation and reception of national operas. Moniuszko struggled to repeat his success with *Halka*, eventually opting for a comic subject—as Wagner and Smetana had done—for his opera *The Haunted Castle (Straszny Dwór)*. Similarly to Wagner's *Mastersingers*, the opera was set in the Renaissance period (when Poland had blossomed) and glorified the driving force of the national movement—in this case, the aristocracy. Superficially, the opera tells the tale of two knights' adventures wooing two noble sisters despite having taken oaths of chastity. This provided plenty of opportunity for singing of the chivalric and patriotic qualities of the nobility. In the third scene of the second act, the Marshal, father of the two brides, sings approvingly of the noble knight: "He must protect his homeland/ like the lioness her brood/ and where foes treacherously rage/ he would bravely give his blood."[15] The Russian censors in Warsaw saw to it that the foes in question were not explicitly named, but the public would have made the logical inference. Furthermore, foreign influences in Poland are criticized when the sisters turn down the advances of urbanite lawyer Damazy on account of his foreign dress. Although the theme of undesirable foreign influence can also be found in *Mastersingers*, in terms of composition there are few similarities between the two pieces. Moniuszko composed *The Haunted Castle* along the same lines as *Halka*, incorporating several folkloristic songs and dances in a number-opera framework. Nevertheless, Moniuszko's intention echoed Wagner's, as both were trying to create a specifically national sound—the latter by using archaic devices, and Moniuszko by integrating the contemporary popular music of his homeland.

Music example 13. Final scene from *Halka*.

Whether tragedies or comedies, these national operas have much in common. They all deal with the history of the composer's own nation, in marked contrast to French grand operas, which were usually set in foreign lands (Meyerbeer's *Les Huguenots* being a rare exception). As a rule, they sought to portray national histories from an affirmative perspective and bring them to life on the stage to be shared by the contemporary public. They conveyed nationalist values by treating issues such as national unity, treason, and self-sacrifice for the sake of the nation. Accounts of audiences' often emotional responses—weeping and cheering—attest to the truly moving impact of these operas on the public in the years immediately after their premieres.[16]

As well as nation-building themes, these operas also addressed social issues and conflicts. Two striking examples are the operas of Moniuszko and Glinka featuring comparatively negative portrayals of the aristocracy, despite the fact that the composers themselves were of aristocratic descent. These libretti identified a certain strata as the heart of the nation (the middle class in Germany and Bohemia; the nobility in Poland and Hungary) and called for the lower social strata to be integrated with them in the nation.

Comparison on a musical level, however, reveals greater diversity among these national operas. Erkel, Glinka, and Moniuszko incorporated stylistic elements of the (mostly urbanite) folk music of their countries, especially dances.[17] But no national coloring, in musical terms, can be found in Wagner's national operas. While the works of Smetana, Glinka, Moniuszko, and Zajc have been extensively researched by their compatriot musicologists, Wagner's use of folk songs and popular rhythms has been disregarded by German scholars. Perhaps this is due to an unwillingness to disturb the cult of genius surrounding the composer by associating his work with lowbrow music genres.[18]

In terms of compositional technique, Smetana falls between Moniuszko and Wagner. Like Moniuszko, he based his rhythms on the day's dances but, like Wagner, avoided contemporary folk music influences in his melodies and harmonies. Indeed, he prompted the converse reaction, influencing Czech musical tastes, and some of his songs and dances became popular hits in their own right. His proximity to Wagner is unsurprising considering the parallels in their biographies and the contact they shared with the New German School around Franz Liszt.

Comparison of these national operas brings two paths of development to light: an Italian path, by which composers (such as Moniuszko, Glinka, and Erkel as well as Zajc, who is not treated here) filled the traditional number-opera structure with folk melodies and dances; and a German path, using continuous music, a system of leitmotifs, and an emphasis on native-language text (as in the work of Wagner and Smetana, and *Taras Bulba* by Ukrainian composer Lysenko).

An essentialist interpretation of these works would be misplaced, since they were received as national operas largely independently of the music's affinity with the "folk music" of their countries. But they were nevertheless portrayed as typically German, Polish, or Czech, and so on by the contemporary press. The well-informed opera public arrived at the theater knowing what to expect. Audiences at the world premiere of *The Mastersingers of Nuremberg* in Munich or *Dalibor* in Prague in 1868 were prepared for a work of national character. Music publications nourished and exploited these expectations and marketed works by appealing to nationalist sentiments.

The "national style" which these operas represented should also be considered through the lens of nineteenth-century patterns of reception. Many musicological studies have explored the influence of folk music on the works of "national composers."[19] Several attempts were made in the twentieth century to uncover the popular roots of the work of composers such as Smetana in line with Communist ideology. However, even these studies generally concluded that the "folk music" of the composer's time served at most as a source of inspiration. In fact, ballroom music and other urban music forms were more significant influences.

In view of the parallels between these works and their reception by the public, it seems biased to omit Wagner from considerations of national opera. While Czech, Polish, Russian, and Hungarian opera is "only" national, Wagner's work is elevated, in a sense, above this category and implicitly endowed with an aura of universality. This view, propounded by German musicology and stemming from the nineteenth-century reception of his music, is still common in the English-language literature today. Its disregard of national influences on Wagner's music is unjustified, since Wagner was obsessed all his life with defining the term *deutsch* and infusing it with musical content.[20] During his time in Dresden, at least, German nationalism determined the parameters of his work, before he claimed access to more universal truths while in exile in Zurich. Certainly, Wagner should not be perceived merely as a national composer and his works only as national operas. The enduring appeal of *Lohengrin* and *Mastersingers* lies in the fact that they can be interpreted and enjoyed independently of their national themes. Without reducing these or other works to their national content, then, changes in their reception through history can be observed. Consequently, a view of operas not as timeless masterpieces but as products of their time, affected by changes in their interpretation, emerges.[21]

Paradoxically, the huge success of these national operas ultimately contributed to the genre's decline. The market for national opera became saturated. Although there was still scope for some innovation in the field—the opera *Dalibor* displaced *The Brandenburgers in Bohemia* in 1886, for example—later examples of the genre were at a clear disadvantage. While Mussorgsky was acclaimed in Russia for *Boris Gudonow* and Erkel in Hungary for *Bank Ban*, in Germany decades passed before any new opera was able to achieve the same level of popularity as *Lohengrin*, *Mastersingers*, or *Der Freischütz*. In Bohemia, Smetana's two major works, *The Bartered Bride* and *Dalibor*, continued to draw the highest attendances. Polish composer Władysław Żeleński's opera *Konrad Wallenrod* fulfilled all the criteria for a national opera but flopped in Warsaw and Lemberg, and Moniuszko remained the paragon of Polish opera. The diminished rate of success of national operas twenty or thirty years after their initial emergence shows that the public's acceptance of the genre remained confined to a few highly revered, symbolic works.

The next generation of composers in all the countries considered here used national material early in their careers, such as Richard Strauss with his debut opera, *Guntram*. But it was no longer a recipe for success. The emergence of musical modernism, evident in works such as Zdeněk Fibich's trilogy *Hippodamia* and Richard Strauss's *Salome*, finally marked a shift in focus away from national legends and folkloristic sounds. The composers of *Młoda Polska* and, in later life, Żeleński also worked with topics other than national myth and history.

Over the course of the twentieth century, the public's reception of national operas changed. Opera-goers increasingly sought universality rather than specifically national content or significance. *Lohengrin* has maintained its position in the repertoires of German and international theaters as a great Romantic opera with an enchanting, ill-fated love story. *The Bartered Bride* is still performed today as a realistic piece that has lost none of its vitality and relevance and is open to various interpretations.

National Composers

Wagner, Moniuszko, and Smetana achieved enduring fame in their mother countries, and partly also abroad, thanks to the popularity of their national operas. Their success was not, however, immediate. While they often encountered opposition in younger years, they were increasingly venerated toward the ends of their lives.

The incident at the Paris premiere of *Tannhäuser* in 1861 marked the beginning of Wagner's ascent to becoming a German figurehead. The German public was outraged at the disturbances caused by some of the Parisian audience, which not only wounded their national pride but also offended against established codes of behavior in the theater. The next performance of *Tannhäuser* at the Dresden Royal Theater was applauded with particular emphasis, in a demonstration of the Saxon audience's allegiance.[22] Subsequently, all of Wagner's Romantic operas became permanent fixtures on the Dresden repertoire in the 1860s. But even German opera lovers approached Wagner with a certain caution, not only on account of his controversial personality. Influential Dresden critics such as Carl Banck found his verse long-winded and his music unmelodious. In 1878, the Royal Ministry abandoned negotiations over a production of *The Ring of the Nibelung* in the Semper Opera due to doubts over whether the public, "although it loves all innovation," should be subjected to Wagner's "tedious, unpoetic texts."[23]

Most significantly, Wagner linked his national opera project with audacious artistic demands. Calling for the abolition of the number opera in his Zurich writings, to be entirely replaced by music drama with continuous orchestration, simply went too far for most opera lovers. Research has shown that national programs are most successful when they remain nebulous and allow space for individual preferences. Wagner's demands, however, were single minded and concrete.[24]

Yet soon after Dresden had rejected the *Ring* cycle, Wagner came to be seen in a more favorable light in Saxony and in Germany when the Municipal Theater in Leipzig under Angelo Neumann (who went on to become director of the New German Theater in Prague) proved that the cycle could be staged successfully. Here, the four operas from *The Rhinegold* to *The Twilight of the Gods* were each reprised twelve times in the first season alone. In January 1879, the Leipzig Municipal Theater was, moreover, the first to show the cycle on four consecutive nights. In 1882, shortly before his departure from Leipzig, Neumann also staged the highly acclaimed premiere of *Tristan and Isolde*.[25] The onus was now on the Dresden Royal Theater to retain its public, which could easily reach Leipzig by train. Since nothing is more popular than a success, in the 1880s, no major theater could afford to ignore Wagner's *Ring* cycle. Friedrich Nietzsche helped foster the cult surrounding Dresden's former chief conductor and further increase his fame. In Robert Prölls's 1878 history of the Dresden Royal Theater, Wagner is proudly described as a "genius" who "infinitely excels."[26]

Prague's reception of Smetana followed a similar pattern. During his lifetime, Smetana encountered disapproval from the public and critics who condemned his "Wagnerism" especially in *Dalibor*. But their arguments intentionally misconstrued the link between the two composers. While *Dalibor* contained similarities to Wagner's early operas, Smetana's critics objected to notions set out in Wagner's Zurich letters; in other words, aesthetic principles which Wagner formulated after composing *Lohengrin*. By openly sympathizing with the Young Czechs, Smetana fell afoul of their opponents in Bohemia. It was not until late in his career that he was wholeheartedly embraced as the leading Czech opera composer. Smetana's death in 1884 was mourned across Bohemia and has been commemorated regularly by the National Theater ever since. Posthumously, he achieved iconic status after the acclaimed revival of *Dalibor* in 1886 and the National Theater's triumph in Vienna in 1892.

Meanwhile, Smetana's similarity to Wagner enabled the German opera public to access his work and, by extension, Czech music theater in general. Dresden-based critic and translator Ludwig Hartmann, who once claimed to be "more excited about Czech music than any other German," was instrumental in this. Hartmann translated the libretti of Czech (and Italian) operas, reviewed countless concerts of Czech compositions and saw in the work of Smetana, Dvořák, and Fibich the "full naturalness of an art which is deeply rooted in its homeland."[27] Dresden music critic Otto Schmid gave Czech opera theoretical endorsement by claiming that Bohemia was one of the lands to produce a "German" type of music stemming from the Reformation. At the same time, he also acknowledged that its Czech branch had blossomed into an independent music tradition.[28] Schmid contrasted "German-style" abstract music-art with the Romantic tradition of emphasizing emotion and sensation. Hence he embraced Czech alongside German music in the context of a bias against French and Italian music.

By virtue of his national and international successes, Smetana became enshrined in Czech national memory and the first composer to indisputably represent the nation. His exalted, almost sanctified status worked to the detriment of Antonín Dvořák and his reception in Bohemia. Zdeněk Nejedlý and other critics associated with Young Czech and left-wing nationalist circles resented the high nobility's preference for Dvořák and disapproved of his contact with Brahms and the Old Czechs. Nejedlý condemned the lack of progressive spirit[29] he perceived in Dvořák's music, since it was not oriented toward Wagner and Smetana. In his later capacity as the first Czechoslovak Communist minister of education, he rejected the lyric opera *Rusalka* as it was not based on national material and did not conform to a national style. Thus the cult surrounding Smetana engendered a narrow-mindedness which not only worked against Dvořák but against the entire Czech music scene. Here, another parallel to developments in Germany is revealed, where late nineteenth-century composers struggled to overcome Wagner's legacy and find their own voice in opera.

Similarly, Moniuszko's exalted status in Poland made life difficult for the next generation of Polish composers. Taking Moniuszko's cue, Jarecki and Żeleński continued to incorporate folk melodies and dances in a set-number structure. But the lukewarm reception of their works showed that this was not enough to distract attentions from dull libretti. The modernist *Młoda Polska* group was the first to break away from this adherence to tradition.[30]

Nevertheless, some national operas retained their popularity even after the turn of the century. While this is no indicator of aesthetic value, it does provide evidence of the successful nationalization of opera. In Bohemia and Germany, where opera was most thoroughly nationalized, it was received by a wider radius of society than in countries where it retained its elitist status, such as Great Britain or the United States. Higher levels of social inclusivity, in turn, fostered cultural productivity. Countries where music theater remained the domain of small elites produced far fewer native opera composers than countries such as Italy, Germany, and Bohemia.

If an outstanding native opera composer could not be found, some nations identified with their fellow countrymen's instrumental music. Grieg became

Norway's figurehead national composer, similarly to Sibelius in Finland, Elgar in England—following in Handel's footsteps with his oratorios—and Bartók and Kodály in Hungary. These composers also found their places in the pantheons of their nations and were commemorated in street names and monuments.

Yet around the turn of the century, by the time a Smetana museum was opened in Prague, the notion of national style—the basic premise for the genre of national opera—was becoming outdated. Janáček, a Moravian, and the foremost Czech opera composer of the generation after Dvořák and Fibich, disassociated himself from the folkish, in his eyes superficially national music of the Smetana school. He pursued an ethnological approach, visiting remote areas of eastern Moravia in search of "genuine" folk music to inspire his compositions. These reflected the dichotomy between the city, the musical idiom of which was already contained in the canonized national style, and the country, where Janáček came from. Béla Bartok and Karol Szymanowski followed similar paths in Hungary and Poland, respectively, analyzing the music and culture of rural populations in a bid to overcome what they felt to be the inauthenticity of their predecessors and the limitations of a canonized national style. Although they were operating in the context of musical modernism, a hundred years ago, in terms of postmodern literary theory they were already engaged in deconstruction. This may serve as a slight reminder that the Gellnerian or Andersonian school of nationalism studies—despite all its merits—did not invent the wheel. At the Prague National Theater, meanwhile, director of opera Karel Kovařovic resisted change by defiantly staging a cycle of all the best-loved traditional Czech operas while rejecting Janáček's *Jenufa*. But in the long term, modernism could not be stopped. As ethnologically and regionally defined music came to the fore, the construct of a unifying and binding national style became obsolete. The idea of national music was deconstructed from within.

These developments in musical modernism shed light on the broader context in which opera and music history were evolving at the turn of the century. Modern nationalism was sustained by the promise of social equality, participation and a richer cultural life, as Herder had once envisaged. The Romantic-era, prerevolution proponents of nationalism had believed that European civilization would benefit from fostering national traditions and cultures. The Italian revolutionary Mazzini wrote in Paris of his hopes for the development of a "European music" combining the German and Italian schools.[31] Wagner expressed similar views as a young man. While cultural nationalism went on to engender great aesthetic productivity, spawning the careers of Wagner, Smetana, and Moniuszko, opera analyzed *as a source* shows that the aesthetic application of nationalism in music had been exhausted after about half a century and even came to obstruct innovation in opera. In this respect, music history mirrors the cultural history of Europe in general.

Richard Wagner, Nation Builder

Among all "national composers," Richard Wagner stands out, not only on account of his musical achievements—on which much has been written—but also because of his activities as a high-profile intellectual and writer.[32] He was adamantly opposed to positivist historiography, holding that myths and legends made up an equally salient element of history as concrete data and the biographies of political leaders. He believed, in a Romantic sense, that mythical traditions conveyed the "spirit of the people" (*Volksgeist*) and contributed to a more encompassing national history.[33] Juxtaposing the academic tradition of historiography with his concept of *Volksgeschichte*, he wrote: "The people is therefore in its poetry and artistry quite brilliant and truthful, while the learned history writer, who only adheres to the pragmatic surface of events . . . is pedantically untruthful because he is not able to understand the object of his own work with his heart and soul and therefore, without knowing it, is impelled toward arbitrary, subjective speculation."[34] Wagner, the historian, formulated this argument in an essay titled "The Wibelungen: World History as told in Saga" (*Die Wibelungen oder die Geschichte aus der Sage*) which later provided the inspiration for his *Ring* cycle. The "folk history" that he spoke of formed a national bond between the generations back to the earliest times. Part of the appeal of this Romantic view, blending documented history with legends, myths, and oral traditions into a perennial whole, was its great dramatic potential. Operas based on already studied and known historical characters and events were limited to an extent by factual parameters, whereas myths and legends allowed far greater scope for creativity.

At first glance, *The Ring of the Nibelung* does not appear to refer to any historical events. But in view of Wagner's original essay on the Wibelungen, it is evidently based on a blend of history and myth. To Wagner, the legend of the Wibelung, which he regarded as the etymological precursor of the Nibelung,[35] was proof of the unbroken continuity of the German nation from early times. He saw the tale of the Nibelung as a metaphor for the history of medieval German dynasties from Charlemagne, the Ottonians, and Salians to the Welfs and the Hohenstaufen. In this sense, Wotan stands for Frederick Barbarossa and the twilight of the gods symbolizes the demise of the Staufer dynasty and subsequent disintegration of the Holy Roman Empire of the German Nation.[36] That would explain why Wagner staged *The Ring of the Nibelung* in Bayreuth as a truly historical, costume opera, whereas today it is mostly interpreted as an abstract reflection on the abuse of power and love.[37]

Over the course of his life, Wagner created an operatic panorama of German history. *The Ring of the Nibelung, Lohengrin, Tannhäuser*, and *Mastersingers* spanned the history of the Germans from their imagined origins to the Renaissance and offered an enduring vision of perennial German history based on ethnic continuity. The characters donning horned helmets and other Germanic paraphernalia in the world premiere of *The Ring of the Nibelung* captured the imagination of the Wilhelminan public and contributed directly to the rise of the Germanic cult. Wagner insisted, moreover, that the original costumes were copied for further performances, ensuring that the national character of the *Ring* cycle was preserved.

Wagner's influence on his contemporaries' view of German history cannot be overstated. Unlike the majority of university lecturers, he had a vast audience at his command. His operas not only reflected the spirit of the age but also to some extent defined it. *Mastersingers*, especially, with its criticism of French and Italian culture and anti-Semitic sentiment, served to broadly disseminate the Wagnerian standpoint. Wagner's Protestant, middle-class, anti-Jewish and anti-western posture anticipated imperial Germany's dominant national code. In acknowledgment of the trail he blazed, he was elevated to the rank of paragon of Germans, the nation's composer.

No other national composer of any country was as prolific as Wagner, whose writings filled 12 volumes of *Collected Prose and Poetical Works*, nor had such a profound impact on his compatriots as a consequence. Moniuszko, Smetana, Glinka, and Erkel all focused entirely on composing, not even writing their own libretti. But although they rarely expressed political opinions in public, they too based their work on libretti with political content and dealt with crucial points in the histories of their nations. Their works had a progressive character, in a social as well as a national sense, and broke new ground by featuring members of all strata—the middle class, petty bourgeoisie, and peasants—in pivotal roles, in stark contrast to the *opera seria* performed at the European courts in the eighteenth century. Many popular works, including Wagner's *Mastersingers* and Smetana's *The Bartered Bride,* managed almost entirely without royal and aristocratic characters. When the aristocracy did appear, it was mostly in a negative light, in several works by Wagner and Smetana as well as in Moniuszko's *Halka* and later in Strauss's *Rosenkavalier*. While negative characterizations of the aristocracy were not entirely new—one need only think of Mozart's *Don Giovanni* and the portrayal of the count in *Le Nozze di Figaro*—in the mid-nineteenth century they became a central theme of German, Czech, and Polish opera. This is especially surprising in the case of Glinka and Moniuszko, who were themselves aristocratic by birth. The nobility now inveighed against its own role in history, displaying the kind of social self-criticism that is usually associated with the middle class.

It would, however, be naïve to assume that it was purely the political convictions of these composers that compelled them to work so closely with the national movements of their countries. There were, of course, market demands to be satisfied. Both for the sake of their artistic pride and their financial security, Wagner and his counterparts aimed to write popular pieces. As Smetana wrote in a letter to Franz Liszt in 1858, "It takes a great deal of self-denial and courage to write works for the moths."[38]

Wagner was convinced that German opera composers were underpaid and placed at a disadvantage by the competition from imported works. In his 1849 article on founding a Saxon national theater, Wagner proposed a solution to both problems. It involved the near-nationalization of the repertoire so that it would contain mostly German operas plus the best foreign pieces. He had more or less achieved this in his capacity as chief conductor in Dresden. But now he also called for the formation of a "society of dramatic writers and composers" which would participate in devising the program and running the national theater. Furthermore, it would be responsible for arranging higher, fixed fees for composers and authors with the theater directors.[39] In short, Wagner proposed establishing a protected opera market, operated by a national cartel of artists who codetermined the value of their work. These reformist ideas were embellished with national arguments and clearly aimed at improving Wagner's position and that of other German composers. His contemporaries in music theater in Bohemia, Poland, Russia and other European countries soon followed suit with comparable proposals.

Even the project which was closest to Wagner's heart, the festival theater in Bayreuth, arose from a combination of personal ambition and applied nationalism. Wagner originally envisaged a national opera theater and tried to rally public support for it through the numerous Wagner Societies across the country and by giving concerts. But a national opera theater dedicated exclusively to works by Wagner did not have as broad appeal as he had hoped and fundraising proved difficult.[40] The inclusion of other popular German composers such as Carl Maria von Weber would probably have convinced more members of the public to donate.

Wagner hoped the founding of the empire would improve the chances for his festival theater in Bayreuth, but he was disappointed. The nation-state came replete with an imperial capital, an imperial army and many other national institutions against which cultural projects like Bayreuth paled into insignificance. The arts, moreover, were one sphere in which the German princely states retained their autonomy, hence there was no need for pan-national opera theater. The nation-state formation was counterproductive for opera and theater in other countries as well. In Italy the subsidies for the former princely theaters were cut, precipitating a crisis in opera which was only weathered by theaters in firmly middle-class towns such as Milan, Bologna, and Parma.[41]

On the whole, continental empires proved more conducive to running opera theaters and other emblematic forms of national culture than nation-states. The Austrian and Russian Empires invested considerable sums in theater. In parallel with the imperial governments' efforts to demonstrate wealth and secure political interests through public theaters, the nobility, middle class, and ascendant national movements also mobilized their financial and social resources to political ends. It was especially important to rival nationalities in multi-ethnic cities, such as Prague and Lemberg, to have their own theaters.

Interestingly, Czech opera culture and the Prague National Theater project developed along similar lines to Wagner's reform proposals for Saxony. Czech theater activists managed to rally a considerable part of the nation to the construction of a national theater. One of its central tasks was to promote the production of Czech arts. As soon as the Provisional Theater was opened, it was supplied with a growing number of native operas, like in Dresden under Wagner, and as a rule Czech was the singing language. In 1874 the association of Czech dramatic writers and composers concluded a very favorable contract with the Provisional Theater.[42] This guaranteed Czech composers royalties of ten percent of receipts plus an additional 100 guilders after a work's third and fifth performance. They were also conceded the right to protest cuts and vote on the casting of roles.[43] The usual rate for royalties in most countries at the time was between seven and eight percent and the Provisional Theater often paid foreign composers less. Czech composers therefore profited directly from the conditions established by this national institution and the cultural nationalism on which it was based.

Smetana, Dvořák and Fibich, for their part, gave the Czech national movement much in return. Thanks to them, the Czechs gained international recognition as an equal cultural nation. Furthermore, their works dealt with all the central icons of national mythology and so helped to disseminate a view of history stretching back to the distant past—as Wagner's oeuvre did—and portray the perennial character of the nation. This self-affirmation was particularly important to Czech society which did not have the benefit of a continuous history as a nation with its own state and whose language had been completely marginalized in the eighteenth century. The public rewarded these composers by patronizing their operas. In Prague, it was nothing less than a patriotic duty to attend the premiere of a Czech opera.

Nationalizing Repertoires

The emergence of national opera made a deep impact on the repertoires in Dresden, Prague, and Lemberg, providing a growing proportion of works from the prerevolution period onward. In Dresden, moreover, the Italian and French operas still remaining on the repertoire during Wagner's tenure as conductor (1842–1849) were performed in translation. In the aftermath of the revolution, the number of German operas in the repertoire was cut, only to rise again in the 1860s in parallel with the German unification movement. Wagner, especially, now gained a permanent place in the repertoire of the Royal Theater, despite the skepticism with which some of Dresden's music critics and royal family viewed him. The national opera era was at its zenith in the 1880s, when numerous "Germanic" operas besides those of Wagner were performed. German operas filled roughly three quarters of the repertoire during this period.⁴⁴ By the turn of the century, however, the proportion had shrunk again to about sixty percent, mainly on account of the work of director Ernst von Schuch, a lover of Italian opera and of the *verismo* style and proponent of Russian, Polish, and Czech works.⁴⁵ By the eve of the First World War, the Dresden repertoire could be divided into four categories. German opera, constituting over half of the repertoire, continued to predominate. This was mainly due to the popularity of Wagner, whose operas were staged every fifth night. Italian and French operas were performed almost as frequently and each roughly made up another fifth. The fourth category in the program consisted of Czech, Polish, and Russian operas.

Changes to the Prague repertoire developed in a similar way, albeit somewhat later. The Provisional Theater's repertoire contained roughly 25 percent Czech operas. This mirrored the situation at the Lemberg Theater under Jan Dobrzański, and his efforts to promote Polish opera. In the first months after the Czech National Theater's inauguration, exclusively native pieces were staged. But by the late 1880s, the proportion of Czech operas had shrunk again to thirty percent.⁴⁶ The Bohemian exhibition of 1891 and especially the National Theater's triumph in Vienna a year later launched a renewed upswing in Czech opera and it henceforth constituted about half of the repertoire.⁴⁷ The repertoires in Dresden and Prague were not nationalized in a linear process, then, but in intermittent surges punctuated by international sensations such as the premiere of *Aida* or the creative hiatus of a popular native composer.

Up until the First World War, the non-Czech half of the National Theater's repertoire was made up of Italian, French, German, and Russian operas. Changes in the popularity of these imported works can also be observed. While French opera achieved best attendances in the 1880s, it was subsequently superseded by German opera, despite the fact that an independent venue for German opera in Prague also existed. The proportion of Italian opera performed, on the other hand, remained relatively stable. Prague was quick to produce Polish and Russian operas on account of the Czechs' pan-Slavism and close links with Poland.⁴⁸ Nevertheless, Polish operas were only staged during Moniuszko's lifetime. Russian operas, by contrast, remained in the repertoire, not least thanks to Šubert's efforts to perform the works of Tchaikovsky, Glinka, Borodin, and Dargomyshsky.⁴⁹ It is certainly no coincidence that Tchaikovsky, who was greatly influenced by Western European music and considered an internationalist in Russia, was the most successful Russian composer abroad. The National Theater's production of *Eugene Onegin* in 1888 in Prague and later at the International Music and Theater Exhibition in Vienna were of key importance for the reception of Russian operas in Western Europe. Tchaikovsky's lyric operas were subsequently performed in Hamburg, Austria, and the rest of the German Empire before being imported by Paris, London, and the United States.

In Lemberg (as in Warsaw) the repertoire was nationalized later still and in a more fragmentary manner than in Prague and Dresden. Despite the fact that Moniuszko's *Halka* was performed to open each season, Polish opera gained only a temporary foothold in the theater under Jan Dobrzański. After his death, the Polish repertoire was reduced to a few token "classics" and some ill-starred premieres. Later, under Ludwik Heller, the proportion of native pieces rose again to about a quarter, though still distinctly less than in Prague or Dresden. Furthermore, no Polish operas received a lengthy run outside Poland. As in Hungary, then, the Polish national opera tradition fared worse than its equivalent in Prague.

Imported French and, especially, Italian operas made up the shortfall in popular Polish operas. But toward the end of the nineteenth century, Lemberg, like Prague before it, became a Wagner city. The second performance of *Lohengrin* in 1897 was an acclaimed success and was soon followed by *Tannhäuser*, *The Flying Dutchman*, and all the operas of the *Ring* cycle in succession. Lemberg's warm reception of Wagner was promoted by the city's enthusiasm for Smetana.[50] As both composers' works were translated, there was now cause to set up a Polish ensemble, which earned Polish opera the upswing that contemporary nationalists had longed for.

Lemberg's enthusiastic reception of Wagner follows a pattern repeated across Europe from Barcelona to Prague, Kiev, and Tallinn. The fascination of "small" nations for Wagner was based, among other things, on his perceived mastery in creating a specifically national opera culture. The mythic and legendary figures that inhabited his opera world appealed so strongly to the public in Bohemia, Catalonia, Ukraine, and the Baltic states because they were in the process of finding such figures to represent their own national histories. These nations, just beginning to assert their individual cultures, possessed no, or only a small, body of Polish, Czech, Ukrainian, Estonian, or Catalan opera. At this point, moreover, before German became established internationally as a singing language, Wagner's operas were always translated, enabling audiences to experience them in their mother languages. This process of appropriating Wagner's oeuvre was crucial to his reception by the "small" nations of Western and Eastern Europe. While Italian opera was frequently regarded as an alien and aristocratic art form in these countries, Wagner was perceived to be modern and nationally relevant.

Italian opera was indeed the main victim of the wave of nationalization in music theater across continental Europe. Although it survived very well as a genre, by the end of the nineteenth century hardly any permanent Italian ensembles remained outside Italy. The Italian opera department met the same fate in Vienna as it did in St. Petersburg and Dresden—displaced by the newly established national ensembles. In some cases, the Italian ensemble was dissolved for political reasons, such as following the new constitution in Dresden in 1831 and the demise of neo-absolutism in Vienna in 1859. In the long term, however, European and global market forces had an equally profound affect. The great increase in the number of opera theaters in Europe and on a global level enabled Italian singers to demand higher fees.[51] Meanwhile, operatic newcomer countries and cities set up their own conservatories and music schools, ensuring a sustainable supply of homegrown, nationally molded singers and musicians. The entire opera market diversified in the same way as opera genres had done previously. Placing these long-term changes within exact time brackets is difficult since the circumstances varied from country to country. But when London's Royal Italian Opera—one of the international bastions of Italian opera—dropped the "Italian" and became simply the Royal Opera, in 1889, it marked a symbolic turning point. While Italian opera had been hegemonic until the first quarter of the nineteenth century, it now was just another national opera genre among many.

National stereotypes influenced the German reception of Italian opera and other imported genres. According to popular theory, Italians were the best inventors of melodies[52] while the French excelled in sensational effects, the Germans were profound and intellectual, and the culture of the Czechs and other "Slavic" peoples was pristine and essentially national in character. Respected critics in Lemberg and Prague held similar views of Italian and French opera. Such national stereotypes also gained currency in Western Europe, albeit with differently placed preferences. A tendency toward national pigeon-holing arose, which varied from country to country and city to city but had a far-reaching effect on the international reception of opera. Today, individual opera genres continue to be categorized as Italian, French, German, or Slavic, masking the diversity within these groups. National distinctions especially predominate in popular publications such as opera guides. In this respect, the twenty-first century can be seen as building upon the foundations of the long nineteenth century—one more reason to address this period in history.

Beyond Nationalisms: London and New York

The trend toward defining opera nationally spread from country to country, but did it encompass all of Europe? One place formed an exception in Europe and is a reminder that the continent should not be conceived as a single, homogenous cultural space. This exception was London. Opera theaters and concert houses in the British capital imported what they regarded as the best of European music culture. A clear preference for Italian opera predominated until the end of the nineteenth century and Italian remained the conventional singing language for many years. Even the first Wagner productions in London were sung in Italian, following the model of Bologna, the first major opera city outside the German and Austrian Empires to stage acclaimed productions of Wagner's works. Operas were not translated into English.

London's continuing tendency toward internationalism in opera gave rise to a new trend in the late nineteenth century. It was in the British capital that it became customary to perform operas in the original language. This occurred partly under pressure from Wagner devotees who insisted on hearing *Lohengrin* the way they had on their visits to Bayreuth, Dresden, and other German opera cities. London's theaters, at the center of the prosperous British Empire, were in a position to import whatever pieces they wished and invite the best conductors, soloists, and chorus singers from all over Europe to perform at the Royal Opera. Equally open to instrumental music, the British capital was known as *the* place, alongside Paris and Vienna, for composers to make a career and a fortune. In the 1880s, Antonín Dvořák established his international reputation in London and earned as much with a few evenings' guest conducting as he did in a year at home.

The eclecticism of London's music scene stemmed from Britain's peculiar position as the foremost global empire and the imperial—as opposed to cultural—nationalism this engendered. In the late nineteenth century, London taste dictated fashions around the world and British capital dominated the markets. Unlike the economic and political latecomer nations on the continent, or defeated France, Britain did not deem it necessary to assert a distinctive identity through singing language or a body of nationally defined operas. Although the British reception of Handel and Elgar paralleled the musical nationalism of Germany and France to an extent, on the whole, a more cosmopolitan attitude to culture prevailed in the British Empire up until the First World War. This pattern had already emerged in the eighteenth century and first half of the nineteenth century, when London was temporarily home to a number of central European musicians, including Georg Friedrich Handel, Joseph Haydn, and Carl Maria von Weber, whose careers climaxed here.

In the late nineteenth century, however, New York came to rival London with its rapidly developing economy. The inauguration of the Metropolitan Opera in 1883—the same year that the Czech National Theater was opened in Prague—marked New York's arrival as a main contender on the international opera market. Like the Prague National Theater, the Met was funded by private donors, albeit on a basis more like that of the New German Theater in Prague. Led by William H. Vanderbilt, a company of shareholders was set up by a number of wealthy New York families—members of New York's trade and industry oligarchy, including the Roosevelts, Morgans and Astors, Iselins and Goelets—bringing together a total of 1.7 million dollars.[53] The theater was lavishly fitted with boxes, reflecting the dominance of its rich elite patrons. The circle occupied by the very wealthiest was known as the diamond horseshoe. The original Metropolitan Opera of 1883 had a total capacity of over 3150, including a large standing room area in the gallery. With such high capacity and wealthy box owners, the Met was one of the financially strongest opera houses in the world.

Although far from the "old continent," the Met confronted issues which were very relevant to opera in Central Europe. In the first year after its inauguration, it hired an Italian ensemble as had hitherto been customary in New York. All operas were sung in Italian, including French works and *Lohengrin*, as they were in London. But the first season under director Henry Abbey recorded a high loss, for which the box owners were liable. Partly as an economizing measure, in 1884, the Italian ensemble was replaced by a German opera company. Had Wagner still lived, he might have applauded this as a victory for German opera. But in fact Italian was abandoned as the singing language in favor of German for more pragmatic reasons. As relative newcomers, German singers demanded lower fees in the late nineteenth century than their Italian counterparts. Moreover, the German immigrant population in New York was larger than its Italian counterpart, and immigrants were among the target audiences of cultural ventures such as the Met. The public, however, was not entirely convinced by the change. Leading newspaper critics objected to Bizet's *Carmen* and works by Verdi being sung in German and questioned the legitimacy of the linguistic monopoly, which was only broken for guest performances. For this reason, in 1891, Italian was reinstated as the main singing language, precipitating complaints from Wagner devotees and a petition signed by over 2,000 protestors.[54]

In 1895, the Met found a way to appease both sides by hiring a second ensemble with a German conductor to produce Wagner in German. It subsequently became standard practice to perform all operas in their original language. Not all opera houses could afford to internationally diversify in this way but, the Met, like the Covent Garden Opera, was one that could. In the early twentieth century, it even employed three choruses—Italian, German, and French—and engaged the best singers from all over Europe.[55] The similarities between the operas in New York and London illustrate that, in terms of opera history, England had more in common with the United States than with continental Europe. For many years, London and New York even shared a director: between 1897 and 1903, both Covent Garden and the Metropolitan Opera were directed by Maurice Grau's Opera Company.[56] Grau made his name and his fortune as an impresario in New York, where he codirected the Met from 1891. Grau and the Met controlled the opera sector in most of the United States, providing extended opera seasons in Philadelphia and Boston and giving occasional guest performances in the Midwest. Thus, at the turn of the century, a cultural space spanning the Atlantic emerged. This space was formed by cultural transfers, networks, and the similar tastes of the opera publics.

The example of London's connection with New York shows that there is not just one European history or space of opera. It would be wrong to draw a generalized picture of opera's nationalization, since its impact was far greater on continental Europe. The Metropolitan Opera remained international in orientation, hiring the world's top singers and most famous conductors, such as Gustav Mahler and Arturo Toscanini. It was not difficult to lure these stars across the Atlantic. By the end of the nineteenth century, they could reach New York within a week by ocean liner and expect double or even four times the rate of payment they would receive in Vienna or Milan.[57] As a result, the European market for singers and conductors was extended across the Atlantic.

While transatlantic activities did not yet have a direct impact on singing practice in continental or Central Europe, the Met did produce international stars like Jean de Reszke, predecessor to the even more celebrated Caruso. Reszke, of Polish origin, could famously sing in every major European language and did much to promote an internationalist approach to performance. Language pluralism became an eminently marketable value after World War I, as the option of performing a couple of seasons in New York became increasingly lucrative. In these circumstances, the international star system began to dominate the opera scene and the standing theaters in continental Europe faced difficulties holding on to their best known soloists for entire seasons. The availability of long distance flights and improved traveling conditions further contributed to the internationalization of opera after 1945. Today singing in one national language is a specialty of a few opera theaters, such as the *Volksoper* in Vienna and the *Komische Oper* in Berlin. In view of this, the nationalization of opera should be regarded as a phase of opera history which peaked in the late nineteenth century but was deflected by London and New York and eventually lost momentum in the period after World War II.

Singing in the original language made it possible to stage the world premiere of a work from almost any country. In 1910, for example, the Met produced the first performance of Giacomo Puccini's *The Girl of the West* (*La fianculla del West*), which introduced themes of American history into the world of opera. In the same year, the Met premiered a revised version of the opera *King's Children* (*Königskinder*) by Engelbert Humperdinck. On the opening night, Humperdinck gave a speech in praise of operatic life in New York: "I was in this country five years ago, and I want to say that America seems to have made a great stride in operatic progress since that time. The great composers of Europe are now having the first performances of their operas given over here instead of in their own country. European composers are coming to think that New York is the center of operatic art, and not the European cities."[58]

This quotation reveals a change in mental mapping. In New York, Humperdinck—a great admirer of Wagner—did not speak of German, French, or Italian opera but of the composers of Europe and European cities. Many newspaper articles of the late nineteenth century distinguish between the two spaces in a similar way. Indeed, according to the founding statute of the Metropolitan Opera's shareholding company, its express intention was to imitate, or outshine, "the opera houses in Europe."[59] The New York press compared the local music scene to that in "Europe" and even labeled opera a "European" artform.[60] From an American perspective, such as Humperdinck was assuming, distinctions between the various national schools of opera were less relevant than they were in their European places of origin. Preferences among the American public naturally differed, but whether one favored Italian opera or Wagner was not a cause for polemics as it was for Central Europe's musical nationalists. From the distance of another continent, the contours of intra-European peculiarities blurred and Europe and the art of opera were regarded more as a unit than within Europe itself.

Interestingly, this discourse on European music in New York was paralleled by music journalism in Poland and Russia. Observers on the fringes of Europe also saw opera more as a unit than most French, Italian, or German music journalists and theorists would have liked. The Warsaw journal *Echo Muzyczne, Teatralne i Artystyczne,* for example, ran a column in the 1880s titled "From Europe,"[61] featuring news of premieres, singers, and guest performances all over the continent. Of course, cultural spaces appear less complex viewed from without than from within. Nevertheless, it is remarkable that until 1914 no serious attempt was made to assert an American genre of opera. Although music journalists occasionally promoted the idea, as in London, native composers could not rely on any special support. With a large body of successful operas already satisfying demand by the turn of the century, and without any clearly nationalist lobby, there was no persuasive argument for taking a chance on an unknown local composer rather than staging works that had been tried and tested in London, Paris, and Vienna.

In both New York and London, then, the international repertoire denied native-born composers the advantage of a protected market niche to develop in. As a result, opera here provided less area for identification by the public, or for reflecting national prestige, and was regarded more as a means of entertainment. But should this lack of national opera be perceived as a deficit, as some American theorists and music critics did at the turn of the century? From the traditional perspective on music history as a linear progression,[62] the development of a national school of music may indeed appear to be an important stage of development. But some of the twentieth century's most successful modern operas were written by composers from countries which did not experience it. A case in point is Benjamin Britten in the United Kingdom. Perhaps his success was promoted by the very lack of a traditional national canon of British opera. Or in more proverbial terms: latecomers can also be newcomers. It was easier to develop a new genre of opera and to achieve individual success as a composer if the music theater market was not already saturated by an existent body of work. This interpretation presupposes a philosophy of history based on a cyclical concept of time, which was alien to the nineteenth-century protagonists in music, whether they were composers, critics, or musicologists. In modern Europe the cultural elites of most countries strove to "catch up" and become one of the more "civilized" nations inspiring the creation of national opera, music, and high culture. The notion of progress, then, has an inherently transnational dimension, which will now be addressed in the final scene of this book.

Notes

1. This is considered closely in the three case studies above. See above for the relevant literature.
2. See Dahlhaus, *Musik im 19. Jahrhundert*, 181–90. A similar argument can be found in Konold, *Nationale Bewegungen*.
3. On the influence of grand opera see Oberzaucher-Schüller, *Meyerbeer—Wagner*. The opera's national orientation is discussed in Bernbach, *Wo Macht*, 220.
4. See Wagner, *Lohengrin, Klavierauszug*, 11–12 (first act, bar 24).
5. See *Lohengrin, Klavierauszug*, (first act, bars 24, 72, 96). Hans Mayer points out that in *Mastersingers* Wagner again used C major in passages dealing with Germanness. See Hans Mayer, *Richard Wagner*, 148.
6. As well as the wealth of German language literature on Wagner, valuable insight is provided by Grey, *Die Meistersinger*.
7. Richard Wagner, *Die Meistersinger, Klavierauszug*, 201.
8. See Reittererová and Reitterer, *Vier Dutzend*, 109–13.
9. On the earlier usage and political significance of choruses in Italian and French opera, see Philip Gossett, "Becoming a Citizen," 41–64; also Fulcher, *French Grand Opera*, 40–42. Smetana's dramatic and musical use of the chorus in *Braniboři v Čechach* is reminiscent of Italian opera, especially Bellini's *I Puritani*. The influence of transfers from Italian opera on Smetana's work has, however, been much less researched than his alleged Wagnerism, which was the subject of much public debate.
10. Spoken-word dramas dealing with similar subject matter also enjoyed high attendance in the 1870s and 1880s. See the list of each evening's takings in the appendix of Šubert, *Dějiny*.
11. On Erkel's operas and composition principles, see Véber, *Ungarische Elemente*.
12. On this opera and its composer Glinka, see Taruskin, *Defining Russia Musically*, 25–47. On the musical-dramatic function of dances and folk music in Russian, Czech, and Polish national operas see Tyrrell, *Russian, Czech, Polish*, 163–74.
13. Piotr Tchaikovsky recounted this in a letter of April 1866 to his brother. Quoted in Neef, *Handbuch der russischen und sowjetischen Oper*, 193.
14. On the revolutionary plot of *Halka* and this style dictate, see Dahlhaus, *Die Musik im 19. Jahrhundert*, 186.
15. Translation by Charlotte Kreutzmüller.
16. On public reception, see the individual case studies of Dresden, Prague, and Lemberg.
17. On the conception of national music and operas in Moniuszko, see Golianek, *Twórczość operowa*; with regard to *Halka*, especially 126–28.
18. We must take Wagner's word, then, that the composition of *The Flying Dutchman* was inspired by East Prussian sailors' songs and *Tannhäuser* by the song of goatherds in northern Bohemia. See Gregor-Dellin, *Richard Wagner*, 172. The influence of local music on Wagner is considered briefly by the nineteenth century Dresden music critic Otto Schmid in *Richard Wagner*, 20.

19. One example is the analysis of Dvořák's music by Beckerman, *The Master's Little Joke*, 143–44.
20. Finnish historian Hannu Salmi has published some pioneering work in this field. See Salmi, *Imagined Germany*; also Gregor-Dellin, *Richard Wagner*, 765–76.
21. Some recent proposals and publications in musicology point in this direction, for example Hinrichsen, *Musikwissenschaft*.
22. On this scandal in Paris, see Fulcher, *French Grand Opéra*, 191–93. On the reception of Tannhäuser in Dresden, see Martin Gregor-Dellin, *Richard Wagner. Sein Leben, sein Werk, sein Jahrhundert*, 469.
23. Quoted in SHAD, MdKH, loc. 41, no. 13, 20. On the negotiations between Wagner's representative and the Royal Theater, see also the minutes, 13–14.
24. On ambiguous ideology in nationalism, see Hobsbawm, *Nations and Nationalism*.
25. On the Leipzig performances of *The Ring of the Nibelung* and *Tristan and Isolde*, see Hennenberg, *300 Jahre*, 79–81.
26. Prölls, *Geschichte des Hoftheaters*, 594.
27. Quoted in a letter to Šubert in NA, Fond ND, Sign. 221, 31, and a newspaper review in NA, Fond ND, Sign. D. 221, 28.
28. See Gojowy, *Das Deutsche*, 44.
29. See Locke, *Opera and Ideology*, 39–43; also Smaczny, *Dvořák: The Operas*, 105–106.
30. On Młoda Polska, see Chominski, *Historia muzyki*, vol. 2, 76–91.
31. See his reflections on European music in Mazzini, *Filosofia*, 33–77.
32. On Wagner's view of history, see Salmi, *Imagined Germany*; also Wilberg, *Richard Wagners*; Bermbach, *Wo Macht ganz auf Verbrechen ruht* (especially the chapters on *Lohengrin* and *Mastersingers*).
33. On the usage of these terms, see Wagner, *Die Wibelungen*, in Wagner, *SSD*, vol. 2, 124.
34. Quoted in Wagner, *Die Wibelungen. Weltgeschichte aus der Sage*, in Wagner, *SSD*, vol. 2, 123. For a detailed consideration of Wagner's understanding of history, see also Wilberg, *Richard Wagners*, 17–21.
35. See Wagner, *Die Wibelungen*, in Wagner, *SSD*, vol. 2, 124–25.
36. Myth and history are paralleled in this way in the text cited above (see previous footnote) especially on 120–22, 130.
37. On political interpretations of *The Ring of the Nibelungen* since Chereau's legendary 1976 production in Bayreuth see Bermbach, Borchmeyer, *Einleitung*, IX–X.
38. Quoted in Teige, *Dopisy*, 18.
39. Wagner, *Entwurf zur Organisation eines deutschen National-Theaters*, 270.
40. On criticism of Wagner in this period and the difficult process of fundraising for Bayreuth, see Gregor-Dellin, *Richard Wagner*, 640–41.
41. See Roselli, *Das Produktionssystem*, 111–12.
42. See part 4 on Prague.
43. See the terms of the contract in Kadlec, *Družstva*, 54.
44. See *Tage-Buch 1887*, 42–59. Twice as many French operas were staged as Italian operas in this period, making up about a sixth and a twelfth of the repertoire, respectively.
45. See programs of 1895 and the season 1900–01 in SHAD, Loc. 44, no. 25, 6–10 and loc. 44, no. 30, 115–24. The number of German operas performed in Dresden was roughly average for a major German opera theater. While in Munich and Leipzig somewhat more were staged, in Hamburg and Vienna the number was somewhat less. See *Opernstatistik für das Jahr 1894*, 6–30.
46. On the changing proportion of Czech, French, Italian, and German opera on the program in Prague, see Havránek, *Společenské*, 207. For the years 1883–1892, Havránek arrives at the following figures: 31.5% Czech operas, 22.2% French, 20.9% Italian,

20.7% German, nearly 5% Russian and Polish. Statistics on the performance of Czech operas 1883–1889 can also be found in AND, Annual Report 6 (1890), 20.
47. The programs are documented in their entirety in the annual reports of the National Theater.
48. The Provisional Theater staged Moniuszko's *Halka*, in the presence of the composer, as early as 1868. In 1886 a second, less-acclaimed premiere was staged in the National Theater which, according to the music journal *Dalibor*, honored an obligation toward "the nation most closely related to us." *Dalibor 8*, no. 36, Sept. 28, 1886, 356.
49. Between 1883 and 1914, a considerably larger amount of Russian and Polish spoken-word dramas were staged. This tradition climaxed in a combined Czech-Polish performance in 1891 and an appearance by the Moscow Art Theater under Stanislavski in 1906.
50. See part two on Dresden.
51. See Toelle, *Der Duft*.
52. The attitude of the influential Dresden music critic Otto Schmid provides a good example. See his collected reviews in Schmid-Dresen, *Bunte Blätter*, especially the citations on 67.
53. On the construction and funding of the Met, see Irving Kolodin, *The Metropolitan Opera 1883–1966. A Candid History*, 4–6. The basic capital stock amounted to more than one-and-a-half times as much as the cost of construction of the second Dresden Semper theater and two-and-a-half times as much as that of the National Theater in Prague.
54. See Kolodin, *The Metropolitan*, 119–20. For examples of reviews of Wagner in Italian, see "Lohengrin at the Opera," *NYT*, Dec. 2, 1893, 4; "Lohengrin Excellently Sung," *NYT*, Jan. 2, 1894, 5. The latter review praises the more lyrical Italian singing.
55. See the Metropolitan Opera Archive (Met archive), *Paybook 1906–07*, 11. In its "prospectus" of the Grand Opera Season 1908–09, the Met boasted that it had hired 130 musicians for its orchestra, "a larger number of musicians than is employed in the most important opera houses in Europe." (The prospectus for each season can be accessed in the archive of the Met.)
56. On this period, see Kolodin, *The Metropolitan*, 159–98.
57. See Met archive, *Paybook 1908–09*, 116–18. Mahler received 25,000 Austrian crowns per month, almost as much as he was paid per year as director of the Vienna court opera. In total, in the season 1908–09, Mahler earned $18,962, the equivalent of approximately 94,000 crowns.
58. "Hail Humperdinck," *NYT*, Dec. 31, 1910, 4.
59. See Met archive, *Minute Books*, April 10, 1880–September 1892, 12.
60. For comparative references to Europe in the press, see "The Outlook for Opera," *NYT*, Feb. 7, 1893, 4; "The National Theater," *Harper's Weekly*, Dec. 30, 1905, in Met archive, *Pressbooks*, Roll 1; "Six Million Dollars Paid to Foreign Musicians," *NYT*, Nov. 10, 1907. (There is no pagination in the huge collection of articles in the *William James Henderson Scrapbooks* which are preserved in the archive of the Met). References to Europe as a whole can also be found in the annual prospectus of the Met. For example, see *Metropolitan Opera House. Grand Opera Prospectus, Season 1908–1909*; on the controversy surrounding *Salome*, see Met archive, *Minute Books*, April 10, 1880–September 1892, 119–38.
61. *EMTA*, vols. 9, 10, 18.
62. On this debate in Germany, see the valid criticism of Hans Heinrich Eggebrecht, one of the doyens of postwar musicology in West Germany, in Vladimir Karbusicki, *Wie deutsch ist das Abendland?*

CHAPTER ELEVEN

Cultural Exchanges and Europeanization

Divergence and Convergence

On the surface, national opera traditions seem to have developed over the course of the nineteenth century by a process of divergence. In addition to the once universal genre of Italian opera and its slightly younger French offshoot, by around 1900, there was German, Russian, Czech, Polish, Hungarian, and Ukrainian opera. And the list could go on, to include the national opera traditions which emerged later on the periphery of the Russian Empire and in some western European countries.

Coincident with this divergence, however, is an element of convergence. Although tradition was "invented"[1] at different times and in many different ways, the results were similar. As the examples of German, Polish, and Czech music theater have shown, discrete national opera traditions were created, which functioned as symbols of civilization to the outside world and as definers of identity to the native public. These traditions were based on "national" schools of music and a number of representative works with which each opera season could be opened.

As well as a large proportion of native operas, the standard central European repertoire included Italian and French and, in Prague and Lemberg, German imports. In Saxony, Czech, and Russian opera were welcome "newcomers." Prague's reception of Russian opera was especially enthusiastic and launched it further west. Despite the many differences between Dresden, Lemberg, and Prague, they had more in common with each other than with their Italian and French counterparts.

In Milan and Paris, repertoires were made up almost exclusively of Italian or French pieces, respectively. Until shortly before the turn of the century, the only international aspect of opera in these cities was the lively exchange between them. The *Palais Garnier* in Paris presented mostly grand operas, especially works by Meyerbeer.² But after France's defeat by Prussia in 1870–71, it too fell under the spell of purposeful nationalism. Leading French composers formed the *Société Nationale de Musique* with the aim of promoting French music and an organic music scene to rival Germany's.³ In the shadow of cultural protectionism and the conservativism it engendered, Paris slipped from its position as a leading opera center in Europe. Italy was, in broad terms, equally resistant to German opera, though with varying vehemence from town to town. While Bologna proved open to new influences, staging the first *Lohengrin* on Italian soil, in Milan's *La Scala* there was rioting in response to the opera in 1873.⁴ But within the space of a generation, public curiosity won out, even in Milan and Paris. *Lohengrin* was staged again in Milan in 1888—this time without disturbances—and in the *Palais Garnier* in 1891. The French production was a posthumous triumph for Wagner, launching 50 reprises in the first six months after its premiere and a further 100 in the ensuing years.⁵ More Wagner operas soon followed on the stages of Paris: *The Valkyrie* in 1893, *Tannhäuser* in 1895, *Tristan and Isolde* in 1894, and finally the complete *Ring* cycle in 1909.

Other German and central European composers were eclipsed by Wagner's tremendous fame. Not one Czech or Polish opera was staged in Paris before 1914, and Strauss was the only German opera composer to gain renown after Wagner. Russian opera found a somewhat more favorable response, partly thanks to the Franco-Russian alliance against Germany. The municipal *Théâtre du Chatelet* played a key role, taking on the first Russian operas in cooperation with the *Ballets Russes* on the eve of the First World War.⁶ Later, the first Parisian performance of *The Bartered Bride* was also politically motivated, given to mark the tenth anniversary of the founding of Czechoslovakia in 1928. Meanwhile, in Milan, Toscanini brought foreign influences into the repertoire, including Wagner and Strauss from 1898 and later also Russian operas.

It is a striking paradox that in those cities where musical nationalism thrived, repertoires were more broadly European. In Dresden, Prague, and Lemberg, Italian and French operas still filled at least 40 percent of the program around the turn of the century. In Dresden (which had much in common with Vienna), moreover, the remainder was not only made up of national works but also several Russian, Czech, and occasionally Polish works.

From the late 1880s, repertoires all over Europe became more international. Even Milan and Paris were no longer bastions of Italian and French opera. Curiously, national operas were crucial to the creation of international repertoires. Classifying works as foreign did not always imply disapproval, such as in Italy's and France's initial response to Wagner, but could also signify a form of recognition. By the 1890s, Europe was overcoming its phase of musical chauvinism.

A further important aspect of convergence was the increasing emphasis on "classics," that is, pieces widely considered to be of timeless value and historical significance.[7] In the early nineteenth century, while Mozart, Gluck, and Lully were acknowledged to have set standards in opera, their works still vied with new pieces for a place on performance schedules and, more often than not, lost the contest. But less innovation in opera in the latter half of the century made cultivating old repertoires a reliable alternative and simultaneously served to establish national traditions. Anniversaries provided a good opportunity to celebrate certain schools or composers, such as the one hundredth anniversary of the world premiere of *Don Giovanni*. Both the Czech National Theater and the New German Theater hosted Mozart cycles to mark this occasion and claim the composer as one of their own.[8] While Schuch followed suit in Dresden, it took somewhat longer for London and New York to embrace composers like Mozart and Gluck. In the US, it was mainly Toscanini who vigorously promoted the opera classics.

A European ideal of civilization was at the heart of this body of classic works. Opera houses in ascendant cities mounted classics partly because it signified their aspirations and was perceived as a sign of cultural maturity. Few opportunities, on the other hand, were given to younger composers to present their work. Richard Strauss managed to get a short cycle of his works staged in Dresden in 1909, but this remained an exception.[9] Such shows of respect were generally reserved for the very famous or, even better, deceased: Verdi in Italy, Wagner in Germany, and Smetana in Bohemia.

Gradually the balance tipped away from world premieres in favor of revivals of older pieces. While Dresden and Vienna were distinctly more focused on novelties for most of the nineteenth century, the public's enduring love of Wagner—and Verdi in Vienna—ensured that the ratio of old to new works was approximately equal from about 1890.[10] Similar trends emerged in Lemberg and Prague, where the number of first performances per season also dropped.[11]

At the turn of the century, the standard central European repertoire consisted of two or three grand operas—usually Meyerbeer's *The Prophet* and *The Huguenots*—a number of more recent French works such as *Faust* and *Carmen*, and some operas in the *verismo* style as well as some native national operas. Verdi and Wagner were absolutely obligatory. Every major opera theater had at least three or four operas by these most venerated composers in the repertoire.

Contemporary opera composers, meanwhile, found it increasingly difficult to break through to audiences. Conservative programming was, then, already causing problems in opera before the competition from moving pictures arose on the eve of World War I. The advent of cinema heralded a new segmentation in the entertainment sector. Cinemas eventually became the venue for sensational innovations, as opera theaters once had been, while opera assumed the mantle of sublime, high culture.

Mounting classics called for greater emphasis on production style and turned the public's attention to stage directing, which came to be acknowledged as an aspect of stage art in its own right.[12] Inspired by its drama section, the Czech National Theater was more willing to experiment with opera productions than the theaters in Dresden and Lemberg.

While performance language diversified, on a visual level, opera productions largely adhered to international norms. Dresden, Prague, Lemberg, and other central European opera theaters mostly used standardized views of mountain ranges, Mediterranean landscapes, medieval towns, castles, or royal banqueting halls, as required. Exotic backgrounds, such as for *Aida* and *The Queen of Sheba* (set in the Orient) or *Lakme* (set in India) also followed standard models and were sometimes directly prescribed by the music publishers. Even the sets of national operas were virtually interchangeable. The productions of *Libuše* and *Lohengrin* in Prague's National Theater in 1883 and 1885, respectively, featured late Gothic townscapes which were almost identical down to the smallest details, but only approximated the early and high medieval periods the operas were set in. Why were sets so alike? One reason is that so many of them were created by a few famous ateliers, the most famous being the Viennese studio of Brioschi, Burghart, and Kautsky, suppliers to the entire Habsburg Monarchy as well as several opera houses in the German Empire in the late nineteenth century.

Figure 16. European landscape by the studio Brioschi, Burghart, and Kautsky.

Local stage designers in Prague were commissioned to create the interior views of the royal chambers for the above-mentioned production of *Libuše*. They hung them with Balkan tapestries and clothed the main characters in what they imagined to resemble ancient Slavic robes. The result was a pan-Slavic potpourri of various ages and regions rather than an accurate representation of the architecture and clothing of the *Přemyslid* dynasty. But since no criticisms were recorded by the press, it appears that the public was either unaware of or unconcerned about the designs' inauthenticity. Above all, stage sets and costumes had to be opulent and rich in detail to please the nineteenth-century public.[13]

In the early 1900s, Alfred Roller and associates in Vienna introduced a less ornate style of stage design. Under Gustav Mahler's protective aegis, Roller developed abstract and symbolic designs for the royal opera.[14] In Prague, fairy tale operas inspired similarly abstract stage sets. Although the Royal Opera in Dresden was innately more conservative, at the request of Richard Strauss, it commissioned Roller to design the sets for the world premiere of *Der Rosenkavalier*. But most performances remained what were known as "conductor productions" (*Kapellmeister-Inszenierungen*) with Schuch in Dresden and Kovařovic in Prague taking general responsibility for the sets as well as the directing. Being eminently more interested in the music than in the visual presentation, despite some cautious changes in imagery, they continued to adhere to the exaggerated realism of earlier set designs.

The rise of the classics added greater relevance to the distinction between opera and operetta. First emerging in Paris in the 1850s, operetta's popularity rapidly spread throughout Europe. But its critics railed against the titillating plots and sexist dance interludes, unleashing a battle of polemics which continued for decades.[15] Only the Dresden press remained compliant and uncritical, turning a blind eye to the occasional "comic opera" or "musical farce" (*Gesangspossen*) as they were euphemistically tagged. In Prague, however, operetta was banned from the repertoire of the National Theater from 1883 to 1888, and the Polish Theater in Lemberg was also purged of operetta in 1894.

The Czech and Polish press not only condemned operetta as immoral and decadent but also as foreign and Jewish. The composers Offenbach, Lehár, and Kálmán (who actually had Jewish roots) and even the Jewish public became the targets of their invective. In Lemberg, especially, local Jews were blamed for the popularity of operetta as journalists claimed a particularly large attendance of Jews when Offenbach's and other light pieces were performed. Some commentators even attributed the alleged decline in taste and culture in general to Jewish influences. Eventually, however, the boycotts of operetta at the Polish Theater in Lemberg and the National Theater in Prague were lifted, not by the resident Jews, but in response to pressure from the middle-class public and to increase ticket sales.

Operetta also elicited xenophobic reactions in Berlin and, to an even greater extent, Vienna.[16] Resistance toward operetta in tandem with greater respect for opera thus became a common characteristic of Central Europe as a cultural region. Although operetta could not be abolished, it could serve to more clearly define opera's role as a sublime art which was not only entertaining but also edifying and educational. To contrast opera with operetta was to distinguish between highbrow and lowbrow music—categories which did not exist at the beginning of the nineteenth century. More than ever, attending the opera became a means of demonstrating one's social distinction.

In its heyday, however, operetta represented an important artistic and financial building block for opera. Many soloists launched their careers performing lighter pieces, thus training their voices and gaining valuable experience without the strain of tackling challenging opera parts. Furthermore, including operetta in the program made more effective use of the orchestra and chorus. This was a crucial consideration especially for smaller theaters, such as Lemberg's, in financing opera.

Operetta to some extent superseded spoken drama. Many patriotic plays, in particular, became irrelevant in the changed political context of the latter nineteenth century. Germany achieved unification in 1871, the Polish nobility in Galicia gained far-reaching rights of autonomy in 1867, and the Czechs continued their inexorable rise to becoming a modern, stratified society. As each country's elites found their political demands increasingly fulfilled, they sought diversion rather than vindication in the theater. The success of operetta also attests to the Europeanization of audiences. Although the situations portrayed in Jacques Offenbach's Parisian comedies and social satires barely resembled everyday life in Lemberg or Prague, the public attended them in droves, curious to experience the life of the metropolis that was otherwise so far away. After the show, the central European public could return to life at home, set apart from, but informed of the goings-on in the big city.

Opera programs reflect audiences' changing tastes. They show that around the turn of the century social and political topics fell out of fashion while pieces which explored emotional issues and psychological states became the vogue. The outstanding success of operas such as *Salome* by Richard Strauss is evidence of this.

Comparison of Dresden, Lemberg, Prague, and other opera cities such as Leipzig and Vienna reveals a convergence on several levels. At the start of the period explored here, repertoires were influenced by local trends and differed from region to region. Later, "Rossini fever" and the popularity of grand operas marked the development of a pan-European opera market. While the emergence of national opera initially led to divergence, after the 1890s, even operas in this genre were increasingly exchanged between countries. Finally, musical modernism affected opera in Dresden, Lemberg, and Prague nearly concurrently. Time not only seemed to pass ever faster, contemporary observers noted, but the clocks of different countries and cities increasingly ticked synchronously.

Around the turn of the century, the programs of most opera theaters in Central Europe were based on a standard repertoire consisting of some native operas, a varying proportion of imported genres and a number of classics. There was also a convergence of visual presentations of opera and performance practice. As more emphasis was laid on plot subtleties, the practice of repeating arias became inacceptable and stage directing more important. Audiences, too, grew more alike in their habits as the tendency spread to concentrate solely on the music.

Cultural Europeanization

What explanation can be found for this convergence among opera theaters, despite the fact that they were differently organized, catered for distinct publics, and operated in different urban, regional, and national contexts? In the mid-nineteenth century, years might pass before a piece became known across Europe. After the turn of the century, however, works could be translated and exported within a matter of months. *Der Rosenkavalier* by Richard Strauss is a prime example. The Czech premiere in Prague was staged less than six weeks after the world premiere in Dresden.[17] That same year, it was produced in Italian in Milan and in Hungarian in Budapest and the following season in Polish in Lemberg.

As well as scores and libretti, singers, conductors, and composers also circulated around Europe. In contrast to the eighteenth century, when the famous tours of the *castrati* visited Naples, Paris, London, St. Petersburg, and other capital cities, in the late nineteenth century, not only a handful of celebrities but countless performers traveled from theater to theater and to various parts of the continent. Thanks to improvements in rail travel and shipping, cities all over Europe and overseas could now be reached more safely and in immeasurably greater comfort. New means of communication allowed the opera market to extend rapidly beyond Europe. It became common for composers and conductors to accept short- or long-term temporary engagements, even on the other side of the Atlantic. Taking musical activities in the European colonies into account, opera around 1900 can be regarded as the first ever global music genre.[18]

A new quality of exchange arose as whole ensembles engaged in touring. It was a guest performance by an Italian ensemble under Bernhard Pollini which gave the Dresden public its first opportunity in many years to hear Italian opera sung in Italian in 1872. The Royal Opera hired Ernst Schuch as conductor, who went on to refute the stereotypical German view of Verdi's work as hurdy-gurdy music by giving the first performance of his *Messa da Requiem* in a Protestant German city.[19] The guest performances by Angelo Neumann's Traveling Richard Wagner Theater also had an enduring impact on the cultural history of Europe.[20]

In the 1880s, Neumann's theater introduced the *Ring* cycle to Bologna, Turin, Rome, St. Petersburg, and countless other central European cities. The time, effort and money invested to do this—a specially chartered train transported the stage sets and costumes of the first tour plus a cast of 134 in five carriages—was rewarded with receipts of up to 20,000 gold marks per evening. Equally, Smetana owed his discovery outside Bohemia to the National Theater's appearance in Vienna in 1892. Designs for costumes and stage sets and, of course, scores were circulated even more.

Theater directors, stage directors, and dramaturges were frequent visitors to theaters in other countries. Šubert, director of the Prague National Theater, regularly traveled to Italy to see the latest operas and ballets. Attending world premieres in Vienna was one of the obligatory duties of a central European theater director. Musical pilgrimages to Bayreuth also became customary. The nineteenth century protagonists of music theater traveled more extensively across Europe, including Russia and Ukraine, than is common today.

While box office triumphs, styles, and fashions emerged mainly from Paris, Vienna, and Milan until World War I, singers often moved along an east-west trajectory. For a time, Polish singers were engaged in prominent roles in several Western European theaters. Tenor Jan Reszke (who was usually credited in programs as Jean de Reszke) sang Lohengrin in Paris to great acclaim in 1893 and went on to become as popular in New York as Enrico Caruso after him. In 1902, Salomea Kruszelnicka (Krushel'nits'ka, born in Galicia in 1873) was a sensation as Elsa at Milan's *La Scala* and contributed to the success of Wagner operas under Toscanini.[21] Polish and Czech singers performed in theaters in Vienna and all over the German Empire. Some of these stars, such as Emmy Destinn (Ema Destinnová), who often concealed their origins behind international pseudonyms, returned to their native countries toward the end of their careers, where they exerted a cosmopolitan influence on the local music scene.

Specialist music journals were also instrumental in forging links between the various opera cities. Even before the 1848 revolution, the *Wiener Allgemeine Theaterzeitung* and the Leipzig *Allgemeine Musikalische Zeitung* each had a Europe-wide network of correspondents at their disposal. They published articles not only about Paris, Vienna, and the new metropolis Berlin, but also about such remote towns as Lemberg, creating a broadly European public which has hitherto been little researched.[22] These two newspapers were explicitly aimed not only at musicians, composers, and other musical experts but also at a wider readership. They document the range of interests of the contemporary music public and hence their mental map of operatic Central Europe.[23]

The specialist journals published in Dresden, Lemberg, and Prague provide insight into the changing processes of cultural exchange in the latter nineteenth century. While the music journal *Der Kunstwart*, for example, ran reports on several European cities, coverage of developments in Paris and Vienna made up about half the correspondence.[24] Surprisingly little space was devoted to Italy. While Bohemia, Poland, and Russia garnered no interest in the 1880s, in about 1890 the first news and reviews of Russian and Czech music began to appear. In 1895–96, the Bohemian capital was profiled in two articles on the "well-known musical city, Prague." One year later, an in-depth review of the entire winter season in Prague was published.[25] Czech and Russian opera had, then, become imprinted on the mental map of Saxony's and Germany's arts scene.

The Czechs' musical orbit is best illustrated by the Czech music journal *Dalibor*. This weekly magazine, launched in 1879, was named after Smetana's foremost dramatic work and Wagnerian in orientation. In contrast to *Der Kunstwart*, it ran correspondence from across Europe from its inception, not only covering Paris and Vienna but also all the major opera houses of the Russian Empire. *Dalibor*, too, reveals a striking shift in focus away from Paris and, within the German-speaking world, from Vienna to Berlin from the 1880s onward. By 1914, almost twice as many articles were published about Berlin than about the capital of the Austrian Empire.[26]

Polish publications, by contrast, reported in depth from the various Polish Partitions and focused on the national arts scene. The same tendency could be observed in Germany, suggesting that big nations are more inclined toward introspection than small nations. Nevertheless, the Lemberg arts and music journals, most of which survived only a few years, and the Warsaw magazine *Echo Muzyczne, Teatralne i Artystyczne* were supported by a considerable network of international correspondents and freelance contributors. They were more focused on musical life in Paris than *Der Kunstwart* or *Dalibor*. And their greater interest in Berlin than Vienna after 1900 was partly due to the fact that the composers of the *Młoda Polska* ("Young Poland") group had all studied in Berlin. Simultaneously, Polish publications demonstrated a growing interest in Czech composers and writers.

The value of press sources is moderated by the personal bias of correspondents and editors which must always be factored in. In view of this, they cannot provide conclusive evidence of the interests of readers or opera publics. Nevertheless, certain patterns emerge from them. The most striking of these is the Europeanization of correspondence, which was more pronounced in Prague and Lemberg than in Dresden. Even, or perhaps especially, a relatively remote town such as Lemberg wished to be informed about the international music scene. In all three cities considered here, the daily press, too, covered a far broader range than is usual today.

Paris's importance in the music and opera world diminished as Europe became increasingly multicentered and hence more pluralist in musical tastes and production choices. Reports on a steadily growing range of cities including

Vienna, Berlin, Leipzig, Milan, and St. Petersburg were now published. In view of this plurality, Christoph Charle's comparison of Paris and Berlin leaves much of Europe's cultural topography in the late nineteenth century aside.[27] New and internationally recognized opera cities emerged in this period. Through supply and demand in opera, a European market was formed which no longer centered round only one or two sources. It is therefore right to speak of a process of Europeanization (without any Euro-constructivism intended) in terms of structural convergence and discourses.

This market developed partly along exchange routes which were subsequently abandoned and forgotten during the Cold War. One important axis of exchange for works, styles, singers, and conductors ran from Hamburg via Leipzig and Dresden, Prague, and Vienna to Budapest. The conductors and composers Gustav Mahler and Arthur Nikisch and the impresarios Angelo Neumann and Bernhard Pollini were among those who moved along this axis. Many singers also worked in a succession of these cities. Czech soloists often began their careers in Prague before proceeding to Hamburg, Dresden, or Budapest and—ideally—arriving at Vienna's court theater. Although less is known about the singers at the Dresden Royal Theater, records show that in 1889 and 1902, at least a quarter of the soloists came from the Habsburg Monarchy.[28]

An arc of exchange also existed within the Austrian Empire, populated by many singers, musicians, and theater directors. It began in Ljubljana in Slovenia and stretched over Graz and Linz to Prague, Krakow, and Lemberg. In the nineteenth century, all these cities had German-language theaters run by private leaseholders. Franz Thomé was a typical impresario who made a career in theater along this arc. He directed the Skarbek Theater in Lemberg, the united theaters of Ljubljana, Trieste, and Klagenfurt, the municipal theater in Graz and, briefly, the Riga Theater before reviving Prague's Estates Theater. His career is remarkable, not least for the range of locations it covered. Another interesting example is Wilhelm Jahn, a native Moravian who went on to become one of the Vienna court opera's best-known directors of the nineteenth century. He first made his mark as an actor in Temesvar (Timişoara) and gained further theatrical experience in Amsterdam, at the Estates Theater in Prague and in Wiesbaden.[29] Jahn's successor, Gustav Mahler, launched his career—after a stint as an operetta conductor in a spa resort—in Ljubljana. He subsequently worked in Olmütz, Kassel, Prague, Leipzig, Budapest, and Hamburg before finally taking his post at the Vienna court opera.

Some career trajectories ran all the way to the lower Danube. In the early nineteenth century, there were German-language theaters in Budapest, Transylvania, and, for a time, even in Bessarabia. Their heyday was in the run-up to the revolution of 1848, when German drama signified innovation and new departures. One of Thomé's successors at the Estates Theater in Prague was Eduard Kreibig, whose family history reflects the breadth of this German-speaking theater landscape. Kreibig's father was the founder of the German Theater in Bucarest and had also opened a German-language theater in Iassy, commissioned by a Romanian Boyar.[30] Eduard gained stage experience as a young man in Kronstadt (*Brașov*), Hermannstadt (*Sibiu*) and Temesvar (*Timișoara*) before moving to Bohemia. These theaters in remote provinces provided the springboard for the careers of no few potential artists.

The German-language theater landscape described above soon disintegrated after the 1850s, when the various nationalities along the Danube had established independent linguistic standards and theater traditions and no longer relied on German. While German remained the language of culture for educated Jews in the region, it was vital to the majority populations in Bohemia, Galicia, Hungary, and Romania to assert their own languages. Under Metternich, German had become the language of oppression and many intellectuals in Lemberg, Budapest, Prague, and other multilingual cities avoided it as a consequence. The Austrian government's support of German-language theaters in the neo-absolutist era—as an instrument of Germanization—made it all the more intolerable. The German theater in Krakow closed in 1867, in Lemberg five years later and in Budapest in 1889.

Beyond the German-dominated cultural sphere, there were other axes of communication. One ran from Krakow to Lemberg and Kiev, linked by the strong influence of the Polish nobility. Numerous direct transfers from Polish to Ukrainian music culture can be traced along this route. The composer of what is today Ukraine's national anthem, Mikhaylo Verbitskii (1815–1870), wrote twelve songs based on the drama *Karpaccy górale* by Józef Korzeniowski. The protagonists of this drama are the Gorals, familiar figures from the operas *Halka* and *Manru*, known as *Verkhovyncy* in Ukrainian.[31] The overture from Moniuszko's *Halka* was performed at the inauguration of the Ukrainain Theater in the Ruthenian national house (*Narodnii Dim*). Some years later, the entire opera was mounted there. This is just one illustration of the affinity between Ukrainian and Polish culture, both of which drew on the same source: the landscapes, social conflicts, and political problems of Galicia. As the Ukrainian national movement gained ground, converse cultural transfers also took place. Operas by Artymowski and Lysenko, for example, which were first performed in Kiev, were later performed in Lemberg by the Ukrainian Theater Society.[32] Polish, Ukrainian, and Russian theaters also employed many musicians from Bohemia, indicating that further networks existed here.

Some arcs of exchange stretched right across the continent, beyond what is now the European Union's eastern border. Around the turn of the century, for example, Lemberg and Barcelona were linked by one of the Galician capital's leading conductors. Antoni Ribera had cofounded the local *Associació Wagneriana* in his hometown Barcelona[33] before leaving to work at the newly built theater in Lemberg. There, he conducted the first Polish production of *The Ring of the Nibelung*. After the First World War, he returned to Bareclona and joined the *Teatru del Liceu*, where he continued to focus on Wagner. The starting point of his very European career was a period in Leipzig, where he studied under Hugo Riemann in the 1890s. The Catalans also admired Czech music and theater and the exemplary role the Czechs played in cultural nation-building. Like the National Theater in Prague, Barcelona's *Palau de la Música Catalana*, opened in 1908, was financed by public donations.

Bilateral cultural transfers were not the only form of exchange within the diverse networks spanning Europe.[34] Crucially, over the course of the long nineteenth century, continuous and permanent contact between opera theaters was established, giving rise to the multilateral networks and cultural spaces described here. An analysis of these networks can shed light on the intensity of cultural interrelations and the reciprocity of appreciation and communication[35].

The central European network, encompassing Hamburg, Leipzig, Dresden, (and increasingly Berlin), Prague, Vienna, and Budapest, facilitated an extremely dynamic pace of cultural exchange. The Austrian arc and the lower Danube region lay to the south. Participating in one network did not rule out other reciprocal relations. Prague, for example, was involved in the Austrian, central European, and European networks. In contrast to nation-states and other territorially defined spatial units, such cultural spaces are not fixed constructs. They expand and contract geographically, with some links existing longer than others.

European societies in the late nineteenth century became familiarized with the whole continent through opera. This not only applies to the directors, singers, musicians, and composers who actually traveled across Europe, participating in cultural exchange of an interpersonal nature. The music-loving public also kept in touch with the latest developments in Paris, Vienna, and other cities via specialist magazines and the daily press. This constitutes a form of intertextual exchange. The producers and consumers of music could, then, gain impressions of Europe, its cultural values and centers, in a number of ways. In the late nineteenth century, even overseas cities were marked on this mental map, stretching concepts of European culture beyond a Eurocentric view. Cultural spaces could (and can) touch other parts of the world. The cultural Europeanization which took place in the nineteenth century went hand in hand with a process of globalization which is evidenced by the transfer of the institution and art of opera across the Atlantic.

This process of Europeanization took place on a structural and a discursive level. Opera culture spread across Europe in the course of the nineteenth century, becoming a common feature of European cities. A visitor to Barcelona, Zurich, Prague, or Kiev could be sure to find at least one prominent opera house in the city, with a repertoire of works which conformed to certain expectations and standards. One theater resembled the next, not only architecturally, but also in terms of repertoire. At the turn of the century, a music lover could travel right across the continent to the Balkan states and the Caucacus and find familiar cultural elements in the furthest flung corners of Europe. Specialist magazines and literature on opera conveyed the operatic Europe to societies throughout the continent. Singers, musicians, critics, and composers gained supranational experiences through their travels. While the extent to which the growth of the opera scene in Europe actually engendered a European consciousness cannot be gauged, it can be asserted that the music culture of European cities bridged the boundaries created by states, encroaching industrialization, and cultural peculiarities. As a consequence, opera was increasingly perceived as a mark of European civilization, especially on Europe's periphery and overseas.

Seen through the prism of opera, Europe takes on a different shape to the one familiar from political maps. It is subdivided into regions shaped by Italian opera and those which were home to repertoire theaters where music dramas were performed in the local language. Although the national differentiation of opera created new divisions, this "Europe of the opera" was cohesive in a way which is barely imaginable in today's "unified" Europe. The agents and institutions of music communicated and interacted over long and short distances. Music networks can provide a basis for a mapping of European history that is independent of the territoriality of states. Borders charting territorial entities such as empires, nations, and regions are replaced by lines of communication. Like on a satellite image taken at night, state borders are barely visible. Instead, one sees the lights of the urban centers and the infrastructure linking them.

Despite the undeniable rivalry, opera theaters communicated values and aesthetic ideas which were more unifying than divisive, even via works which were initially sources of controversy, such as Wagner's operas. Europe's different nations came to know and appreciate each other in the opera with its specific traditions—no matter that they were invented. At the opera, audiences could experience diversity. To idealize this history of cultural exchange and networks would nevertheless be wrong. Cultural convergence was not welcomed by all. And musical nationalism could in some respects be interpreted as a defensive reaction to opera's internationalism. It is this duality of communication and conflict that shaped the history of Central Europe, to which the focus will return after these excursions into European cultural history.

Central Europe as a Space of Opera

At first glance, it may seem that operatic stimulus flowed mostly from West to East. It is true that for many years Paris and Vienna set the trends in opera, influencing details of performance even after the turn of the century. But it would be wrong to assume that the relationship between center and periphery was one-sided, as Franco Moretti has suggested in his atlas of the European novel.[36]

Nationalized opera originated in the former periphery and had an enduring impact on the old opera centers. Italian opera, especially, could no longer maintain its universal status, becoming just one national genre among many. This opened the door to Wagner's (some felt, sinister) success and, by extension, that of German opera. Over time, more national traditions emerged—of Czech, Russian and the initially hampered Polish tradition of opera—which deliberately broke away from German music culture or adapted it in a specific way.[37] Between 1815 and 1914, Europe's cultural topography was, then, not only shaped by the traditional centers in Italy and France but also by what might be labeled the periphery, although the static nature of this term does not do justice to the interrelations between the old and new opera countries.

Poland had an old tradition of high culture. But several obstacles hindered the development of Polish opera: partition by Prussia, Austria and Russia and the oppression of the Polish population after 1830 and again after 1863 as well as institutional difficulties in Posen and Lemberg. This is a negative example of the relevance of the state to music cultures. Czech opera, by contrast, profited from Prague's unambiguous status as the capital of Bohemia and the central role of the National Theater. Czech theater activists could concentrate almost all their efforts on one site.

The Czechs came to be regarded as paragons of cultural nation-building by the Austro-Slavs, Southern Slavs and Ukrainians. They had propelled a previously negligible opera culture to a position of importance. Czech opera's rise to preeminence implicitly disproves the paradigms of progress still prevalent in the study of history and musicology. It shows that, if the bulk of the population could be mobilized, "newcomers" such as the Czechs could adapt international cultural forms and outshine traditional cultural nations like the Poles. "Small" nations could even be innovators, especially with respect to modernism, as a comparison of the National Theater and the Semper Opera in the 1890s shows. While German opera remained fixated on national mythology—another of Wagner's legacies that proved so difficult to overcome—Prague's composers and authors began experimenting with universal fairy tale material and lyric opera. The influence of art nouveau notwithstanding, one should not overstate the National Theater's importance as a site of musical avant-gardism. Nor, indeed, is it helpful to revert to rigid time categories in music history or presume that any one place had a direct and steady influence on another. The crucial change that had occurred by the end of the nineteenth century was that Central Europe no longer had just one or two but several productive opera centers, which acknowledged and stimulated each other.

The network spanning Bohemia and Saxony, especially, facilitated an unsurpassed level of exchange. The Dresden Royal Theater's best known tenor, Karel Burian, and ballet director Augustin Berger came from Prague. Dresden music critic Ludwig Hartmann was a regular visitor to Prague, where he attended premieres, and Richard Batka, a leading correspondent for *Der Kunstwart*, came from Bohemia. The Royal Theater also maintained close links with Poland. Despite the deep political conflicts, even imperial Berlin became an important point of reference for Polish composers.

In addition to program similarities, it is this intensity of communication which legitimizes defining Central Europe as a cultural space. It should, however, not be envisaged as a closed container. All the opera theaters within this cultural space continued to look to Paris, receiving little attention in return. But the operas in Prague and Dresden, especially, profited enormously from the diverse influences arriving from Vienna, Italy, France, and Eastern Europe. Cultural transfers with these two cities were a pivotal factor in the emergence of modernism in art, not only in the operatic sphere but also in literature and painting, spearheaded by Kafka and the group of painters known as *Die Brücke*, respectively.

Prague itself was, moreover, a site of intense intercultural communication. The Czech and German theaters influenced and inspired each other despite their rivalry. In Lemberg, by contrast, the curtailing of cultural activity—by closing the German theater and marginalizing the Jewish population—also had a negative effect on local music theater. But around the turn of the century, Lemberg was in a similar position to Prague in the 1860s, as the rising Ukrainian national movement aspired to build its own national theater. Superficially, Dresden lacked this multinational aspect, although the city traditionally maintained close contact with Bohemia, Austria, France, and Poland.

Any idealization of Central Europe as a cultural space or rose-tinted nostalgia for its cultural heyday would, however, be misplaced. The mobilization of populations in support of public cultural institutions was accompanied by processes of ethnic division and exclusion. In Prague, this led to bitter frontlines being drawn between German and Czech culture. In Lemberg, the Polish intelligentsia and especially the press prevented the Jewish population from participating in the Polish Theater. Modern mass societies defined their rising numbers—and mobilized them for their cultural projects—by identifying those who did not belong. Even in the sphere of opera, where the universal language of music prevails, ethnic and social exclusivity played an increasingly important role.

In the course of cultural nation-building, the urban societies in Dresden, Prague and Lemberg became nationalized along with opera. To an extent, national cultures and opera traditions provided a defense against the outside world and supposed internal enemies. Anti-Semitism was especially virulent in Lemberg but also existed in Dresden and Prague. Modernity and cosmopolitanism—in fact, the very source of operatic life—came under attack. Some Galician intellectuals went even further than Richard Wagner in this respect. In 1893, actor-director Adolf Walewski, who ran the Polish Theater in Lemberg for some months in 1900, responded to the success of operetta and Parisian comedies by writing: "Away! We shout with all our might, away with the gangrene of the West that only shows us festering Paris . . . Begone! Begone! Begone from the Polish courtyard, our public should call, our mothers and youth. Away with the French dross, muck, and filth!"[38]

In the view of Walewski and many Czech and German music journalists, the antidote to these decadent influences from the West was to produce national dramas and operas with the aura of the authentic. An obsession developed with *Originalstücke*, as native pieces were termed in German, or *původní produkce* in Czech. Naming them such, commentators were implicitly contrasting their superiority with the inauthenticity and inferiority of imported or foreign pieces. But they also explicitly claimed that native music was earnest and profound and contained metaphysical qualities while foreign or Western music—that is, French and Italian—was merely melodious or sensationalist. The music press in Bohemia and Galicia disseminated such opinions, once expressed by Wagner, resulting in an increasing imbalance in the supply of operas in the late nineteenth century in Germany, Bohemia, Poland, and Hungary. Since native composers dealt mostly with earnest and heroic subject matter in the 1880s and 1890s, rarely creating comic operas, the public was offered predominantly *largo* music, stately and solemn. But if native music was coolly received, it was blamed on outsiders—the Italians, French, or Jews—who, to add insult to injury, wrote those hated operettas. An elitist attitude to culture endured throughout the interwar and postwar period in Central Europe and beyond. After World War I, musicals imported from the US replaced operettas as the subject of polemics and research, such as in Adorno's elitist sociology of music.

Cultural nationalism eventually became an aesthetic impediment to native composers. The honeymoon period ended, in which it gave rise to public institutions and opera was communicated to new strata of society, and national music traditions began to rigidify, as the Prague National Theater's rejection of Janáček illustrates.

National opera traditions were built in strict opposition to light entertainment and above all to operetta. Society's increasing tendency to differentiate between art music and popular music reflected how entrenched its individual strata had become. Attempts to communicate opera to broader sections of society were partly successful, especially in Prague. But even here, opera eventually became associated with the bourgeoisie. The utopia of a society liberated from class differences in the theater or concert hall was ultimately abandoned. Opera became high culture in all respects.

Notes

1. On this concept, see the introduction in Hobsbawm and Ranger, eds., *The Invention of Tradition*.
2. On the repertoire at the *Garnier* opera, see Wolff, *L'opéra*, 26–216. In the *Opéra Comique*, too, the core repertoire was made up of a few French pieces. See Wolff, *Un demi-siècle*, 15–82.
3. See Duchesneau, *L'avant-garde*, 15–17; also Döhring, *Oper und Musikdrama*, 282. The history of the *Société* is considered in detail in Strasser, *Ars Gallica*.
4. On anti-Wagnerism in Italy and the failed production of *Lohengrin* in Milan, see Jung, *Die Rezeption*, 438–44, 69–73.
5. See Wolff, *L'opéra*, 134–35.
6. See Zur Nieden, *Vom Grand Spectacle*.
7. On this concept, see *Ästhetische Grundbegriffe*, vol. 3, 289–304; here, with special reference to music, 292–93.
8. This was preceded by the Mozart renaissance at the Vienna court opera under Mahler. See Willnauer, *Gustav Mahler*, 47. In 1886, works by Mozart were performed on 23 nights at the Prague National Theater, (see AND, Annual Report 4 (1887): 3–11), much more than the European average.
9. On the Richard Strauss Week (*Richard-Strauss-Woche*), January 25–28, 1909, held to mark the world premiere of *Elektra*, see SHAD, MdKH, loc. 44, no. 40, 158.
10. In 1843, for example, there were six first performances and only one new production of a familiar piece. In 1895, by contrast, five works were reprised and five were new. See the relevant journals for 1843 and 1895. On the ratio of new pieces to reprises in the entire German-speaking world, see Langer, *Der Regisseur*, 51–52.
11. Reprises of familiar pieces distinctly outnumbered first performances in the National Theater in Prague.
12. On the changing concept of stage directing around the turn of the century, see Langer, *Der Regisseur*, 9, 50.
13. On the sets for Libuše, see Srba, *Jevištní výprava*.
14. On Roller's significance and style, see Willnauer, *Gustav Mahler*, 107–21.
15. On the history of operetta, see Klotz, *Operette*; Adorno, *Einführung*, 37–39.
16. On the anti-Semitic undertones in the discourse on operetta in Vienna, see Csáky, *Ideologie der Operette*, 219–20.
17. See *Dalibor 32*, no. 16–17, Jan. 27, 1911.
18. See Toelle, *Der Duft*.
19. On the reception of Verdi's *Requiem* in Dresden and other German cities, see Kreuzer, *Verdi and the Germans*, 39–85.
20. See Ludvová, *Hudební divadlo*, 365–70.
21. See Kesting, *Die großen Sänger*, vol. 1, 160–64; vol. 2, 705–707. This reference work makes a number of errors, however, concerning central and eastern European singers.
22. On the European readership of various publications see especially Kaelble, *Europäer über Europa*.
23. See Schenk, *Mental Maps*.
24. See *Der Kunstwart* 1 and 2 (1886–87). This journal bore the subtitle *Rundschau über alle Gebiete des Schönen* ("Magazine for All Fields of the Aesthetic"). From 1894, it was printed in Munich with no obvious effect on the authorship or choice of articles.
25. "Altberühmten Musikstadt Prag." Quoted in *Der Kunstwart* 9 (1895–96): 280–81. See also the overview of the season in no. 10 (1896–97): 74–75.
26. See *Dalibor*, 8, 22, 23, 32.

27. Charle postulates a "hegemony of Paris" in the sphere of literature and theater. On his comparisons between Paris and Berlin, see Charle, *Paris fin de siècle*, 16, 21–48.
28. This can be ascertained from Kohut, *Das Dresdner Hoftheater*, 219–372 and Wildberg, *Das Dresdner Hoftheater*, 142–209.
29. For an overview of Jahn's career, see *Jubiläumsausstellung*, 74–75.
30. On Kreibig's life, see Teuber, *Geschichte, Dritter Theil*, 701.
31. See Zakhaykevych, *Karpaccy górale*, 10.
32. On Ukrainian theater in Lemberg, see Got, *Das österreichische Theater*, vol. 2, 767–82; also Pepłowski, *Teatr Ruski*; Lane, *The Polish Opera*, 157–64.
33. See Marfany, *La cultura*, 361–62.
34. On the original concept of transfer history, see Espagne, *Les transferts culturels*, especially 35–37.
35. Transfer history has also come to consider regional units of research. See Espagne, Middell, *Von der Elbe*; also Espagne, *Le creuset allemand*.
36. See Moretti, *Atlas*, 206–17.
37. Mussorgsky, for example, wrote about German music: "In Germany we find the best and most convincing example of musical slavery, worship of conservatory wisdom and routine—music, beer, stinking cigars. If one were to force me (not in jest) to sing songs by Mendelssohn I would turn from a respectable person to a peasant oaf, lacking any social propriety." Quoted in de la Motte-Haber, *Nationalstil*, 47.
38. Walewski, *Teatr u nas*, 32–33. Such tirades against French culture were not rare. See, for example, the description of Paris's "leprous society" in "Teatr Lwowski," *Gazeta Narodowa*, Feb. 13, 1889, 2. This article goes on to demand the censorship of operetta.

Bibliography and Sources

Archival materials

Dresden

Sächsisches Hauptstaatsarchiv Dresden (SHAD)
(Saxonian State Archive Dresden)
Ministerium für Volksbildung
    Nr. 14318
    Nr. 14419
    Nr. 14429
    Nr. 14430
    Nr. 14446
    Nr. 14467–14480
    Nr. 14483
    Nr. 14930
Hof- und Haushaltungssachen, II.3.1.05
    Loc. 31.952–53
Ministerium des Königlichen Hauses III, 3,1 (MdKH)
    Loc. 9
    Loc. 10
    Loc. 20
    Loc. 35
    Loc. 40–45
    Loc. 15132
Archiv der Sächsischen Staatsoper Dresden (Archive of the Saxonian State Opera)
    Pressearchiv
    Sammlung Sohrmann

Lemberg (L'viv)

Tsentralnyi derzhavnyi istorychnyi arkhiv Ukrayiny u Lvovi (TsDIAU)
(Central Historical State Archive of the Ukraine in L'viv)
Statthalterei und Landesausschuss
146/4/3810–3811
146/7/4003
146/7/4471
165/5/13–30
165/5/613–635
835/1/962
Sprawozdanie Sejmu Krajowego
(Protocols of the regional diet)
Alegata do sprawozdań stenograficznych Sejmu Krajowego Królewstwa Galicyi i Lodomeryi z Wielkim Księstwem Krakowskiem, 1878–1880.
Stenograficzne Sprawozdania Sejmu Krajowego Królewstwa Galicyi i Lodomeryi z Wielkim Księstwem Krakowskiem: 1875, 1884–1887, 1890, 1892, 1901–03.
Derzhavnyi arkhiv L'vivs'koyi oblasti (DALO)
(State Archive of the Region of L'viv)
Magistrat Miasta Lwowa
3/1/3753
3/1/4415–17
3/1/4474–75
3/1/4864
3/1/4883
3/1/5477
Biblioteka Jagiellońska w Krakowie
(Jagiellonian Library Krakow)
Rękopis Nr. 6521 IV, Korespondencja Józefa Ignacy Kraszewskiego, seria III, Listy z lat 1863–1887.
Bibliotek im. Stefanika v L'vovie
(Stefanik-Library in L'viv)
Korespondencja Ludwika Hellera, Dyrektora teatru miejskiego we Lwowie

Prague

Národní archiv
(National archive)
Fond Národního Divadla
Sign. D. 50–51

Sign. D. 97–99
Sign. D. 102–105
Sign. D. 109–114
Sign. D. 122–124
Sign. D. 157–159
Sign. D. 212
Sign. D. 221
Společnost Národniho Divadla, Sign. 16–17
Prezidium Místodržitelství (PM)
    1850–1854, Sign. 2/23/4
    1860–1870, Sign. 8/6/2/87
    1881–1890, Sign. 8/6/15/2
    1891–1900, Sign. 8/6/15/13
    1901–1910, Sign. 8/6/15/11
Archiv Národního Divadla
(Archive of the National Theater)
Annual reports of the National Theater (1884–1914)
listed in the catalog under the names of F.A. Šubert (1883–1900) and G. Schmoranz (1900–1914)

Other archival collections

Metropolitan Opera Archive (Met archive):
    Paybook 1906-09
    Minute Books, April 10, 1880–September 1892
    Pressbooks, Roll 1
    William James Henderson Scrapbooks
    Grand Opera Prospectus, Season 1908–1909

Contemporary print media

Dalibor. Časopis pro všechny obory umění hudebního, 1881–1914.
Der Kunstwart. Rundschau über alle Gebiete des Schönen, Dresden 1887–1894 (since 1894: Der Kunstwart. Halbmonatsschau über Dichtung, Theater, Musik, bildende und angewandte Künste, München).
Dresdner Journal, 1848–1914 (1848–1851 published as Dresdner Journal und Anzeiger).
Dresdner Nachrichten, 1856–1914.
Dresdner Revue. Wochenschrift für Dresdner Leben und Kultur, 1913–1914.
Dresdner Volkszeitung, 1874–1914.
Divadelní Kalendář, Praha 1882–1914.

Divadelní Listy, Organ "Matice Divadelní" v Praze, 1880–1914.
Gazeta Narodowa, 1867–1914.
Dziennik Literacki, 1866.
Dziennik Polski, 1872–1914.
Echo Muzyczne, Teatralne i Artystyczne, 1880–1914.
Gazeta Lwowska, 1842–1914.
Hlas Národa, 1881–1914.
Krytyka. Miesięcznik poświęcone sprawom społecznym, nauce i sztuce, 1898–1914.
Kurjer Lwowski, 1893–1914.
Kurjer teatralny lwowski, 1870–71.
Národní Listy, 1862–1914.
Nasza Sztuka. Dwutygodnik poświęcony sztuce plastycznej, teatrowi i muzyce, 1893.
Nowiny, 1867.
Pravo Lidu, 1898–1902.
Przegląd, 1903.
Ruch Literacki. Tygodnik poświecony literaturze, sztukom pięknym, naukom i rzeczom społecznym, 1876.
Scena i Sztuka, 1907–08.
Tydzień. Dodatek literacki Kurjera lwowskiego, 1893–1914.
Wiadomości Artystyczne. Dwutygodnik poświęcony muzyce, teatrowi, literaturze i sztuce, 1900.

Encyclopedias

100 oper. Istoriia sozdaniia, siuzhet, muzyka. Leningrad: Muzyka, 1964.
Barck, Karlheinz, et al. *Ästhetische Grundbegriffe.* 6 vols. Stuttgart: Metzler, 2000–2005.
Brunner, Otto, et al. *Geschichtliche Grundbegriffe: Historisches Lexikon zur politisch-sozialen Sprache in Deutschland.* Stuttgart: Klett-Cotta, 1972–1997.
Dąbrowski, Stanisław, et al. *Slownik biograficzny teatru polskiego 1765–1965.* Warszawa: PWN, 1973.
Hostomská, Anna. *Opera. Průvodce operní tvorbou.* 10th ed. Praha: Albatros, 1999.
Kański, Józef. *Przewodnik Operowy.* Kraków: Polskie Wydawnictwo Muzyczne, 1985.
Kesting, Jürgen. *Die großen Sänger.* 3 vols. Düsseldorf: Claassen Verlag, 1986.
Ludvová, Jitka, ed. *Česka divedelní encyklopedie. Hudební divadlo v českých zemích. Osobnosti 19. století.* Praha: Divadelní Ústav, 2006.

Procházka, Vladimír. *Národní divadlo a jeho přechůdci. Slovnik umělců divadel vlastenského, stavovského, prozatímního a národního*. Praha: Academia, 1988.

Riemann, Hugo. *Musik-Lexikon, Zehnte Auflage*. Ed. bearbeitet von Alfred Einstein. Berlin: Max Hesse, 1922.

Seeger, Horst. *Opernlexikon*. Berlin: Henschel, 1978.

Pipers Enzyklopädie des Musiktheaters: Oper, Operette, Musical, Ballett, ed. Carl Dahlhaus and Forschungsinstitut für Musiktheater der Universität Bayreuth unter Leitung von Sieghart Döhring. München: Piper, 1986–1997.

Polski Słownik Biograficzny. Krakow: PAN and PAU, from 1935.

Bibliography

Adolph, Paul. *Vom Hoftheater zum Staatstheater. Zwei Jahrzehnte persönlicher Erinnerung an Sachsens Hoftheater, Königshaus, Staatstheater und anderes*. Dresden: C. Heinrich, 1932.

Adorno, Theodor. *Einführung in die Musiksoziologie. Zwölf theoretische Vorlesungen*. 3rd ed. Frankfurt a.M.: Suhrkamp Verlag, 1983.

Adorno, Theodor. *Versuch über Wagner*. Frankfurt a.M.: Suhrkamp Verlag, 1952.

Altstadt, Audrey L. *The Azerbaijani Turks. Power and Identity under Russian Rule*. Stanford: Hoover Institution Press, 1992.

Anderson, Benedikt. *Imagined Communities: Reflections on the Origin and Spread of Nationalism*. 2nd ed. London: Verso, 1990.

Antonicek, Theophil. "Biedermeierzeit und Vormärz." In *Musikgeschichte Österreichs*. Vol. 2. Ed. Rudolf Flotzinger and Gernot Gruber. Graz: Styria, 1979.

Applegate, Celia. "The Internationalism of Nationalism. Adolf Bernhard Marx and German Music in the Mid-Nineteenth Century." *Journal of Modern European History* 5 (2007): 139–59.

Applegate, Celia and Pamela Potter. "Germans as the 'People of Music': Genealogy of an Identity." In *Music and German National Identity*, ed. Celia Applegate and Pamela Potter, 1–35. Chicago: University Of Chicago Press, 2002.

Applegate, Celia, and Pamela Potter, eds. *Music and German National Identity* Chicago: University of Chicago Press, 2002.

Barbier, Patrick. *La vie quotidienne a l'Opéra au temps de Rossini et de Balzac. Paris 1800–1850*. Paris: Hachette, 1987.

Bartnig, Hella. "Der Zopf hängt ihnen hier noch gewaltig! Das Dresdner Hoftheater nach 1849 bis zum Engagement Ernst von Schuchs." In *Die Dresdner Oper im 19. Jahrhundert*, ed. Michael Heinemann and Hans John, 271–86. Laaber: Laaber Verlag, 1995.

Bartnig, Hella. "Ernst von Schuch und die Dresdner Hofoper" In Heinemann and John, *Die Dresdner Oper im 19. Jahrhundert*, 361–76.

Bartoš, Jan. *Národní divadlo a jeho budovatelé*. Praha: Sbor zřízení druhého Narodního divadla, 1933.

Bartoš, Josef. *Prozatímní divadlo a jeho opera*. Praha: Sbor zřízení druhého Narodního divadla, 1938.

Barwiński, Eugeniusz. *Heller czy Pawlikowski, Głos w sprawie oddania nowego teatru lwówskiego*. Lwów, 1900.

Batušić, Nikola. *Hrvatsko narodno kazalište u Zagrebu. 1840–1860–1992*. Zagreb: Skolska kniga, 1992.

Batušić, Slavko. "Das kroatische Nationaltheater in Zagreb und seine historischen Beziehungen zum tschechischen und polnischen Theaterleben bis 1914." *Maske und Kothurn* 12 (1966): 210–19.

Bauerkämper, Arnd. *Die Praxis der Zivilgesellschaft. Akteure, Handeln und Strukturen im internationalen Vergleich*. Frankfurt a.M.: Campus Verlag, 2003.

Beckerman, Michael. "The Master's Little Joke: Antonín Dvořák and the Mask of the Nation." In *Dvořák and his World*, ed. Michael Beckerman, 134–56. Princeton: Princeton University Press, 1993.

Benoni, Bohumil. *Moje vzpomínky a dojmy*. 2 Vols. Praha: Kočí, 1917.

"Beratung des Berichts der zweiten Deputation, den Bau eines Schauspielhauses in der Residenz betreffend." In Landtags-Akten vom Jahr 1839, Dritte Abteilung, die Protokolle der zweiten Kammer enthaltend, Erster Band, Dresden, n.d. 270–76.

"Beratung des Berichts der zweiten Deputation (Abteilung A) über das königlichen Dekret, den Neubau eines königlichen Hoftheaters in Dresden betreffend." In Mitteilungen über die Verhandlungen des ordentlichen Landtags im Königreiche Sachsen während der Jahre 1869–1870. Zweite Kammer. Vierter Band, 2665–2736. Dresden 1870.

"Bericht der zweiten Deputation (Abt. B) über die Pos. 2 des außerordentlichen Ausgabe-Budgets und das damit in Verbindung stehende königliche Dekret Nr. 34, den Mehrbedarf von 375.000 Thalern zum Neubau des Königlichen Hoftheaters betreffend." In Landtags-Akten von den Jahren 1873/74. Berichte der zweiten Kammer, Zweiter Band, 97–106.

"Bericht der zweiten Deputation der zweiten Kammer über das allerhöchste Dekret vom 10. November 1839, den Bau eines Schauspielhauses in der Residenz betreffend." In Landtags-Acten von den Jahren 1839/40, Beilagen zu den Protokollen der zweiten Kammer, Erste Sammlung, 109–18. Dresden no year.

Bermbach, Udo. *Der Wahn des Gesamtkunstwerks. Richard Wagners politisch-ästhetische Utopie*. Frankfurt a.M.: Fischer Taschenbuch Verlag, 1994.

Bermbach, Udo. "Des Sehens ewige Lust. Einige Stationen der Ring-Deutungen seit 1876." In *"Alles ist nach seiner Art." Figuren in Richard Wagners "Der*

Ring des Nibelungen," ed. Udo Bermbach, 1–26. Stuttgart: Metzler Verlag, 2001.

Bermbach, Udo. *Wo Macht ganz auf Verbrechen ruht. Politik und Gesellschaft in der Oper.* Hamburg: Europäischer Verlag, 1997.

Bermbach, Udo, and Dieter Borchmeyer. "Einleitung." In *Richard Wagner— "Der Ring des Nibelungen." Ansichten des Mythos*, ed. Udo Bermbach, ix–xii. Stuttgart: Metzler Verlag, 1995.

Bermbach, Udo, and Wulf Konold, eds. *Der schöne Abglanz. Stationen der Operngeschichte.* Hamburg: Reimer Verlag, 1992.

Beust, Friedrich Ferdinand Graf von. *Aus drei Viertel Jahrhunderten. Erinnerungen und Aufzeichnungen in zwei Bänden, Vol.1: 1809–1866.* Stuttgart: J. G. Cotta, 1887.

Beveridge, David. "Dvořák and Brahms: A Chronicle, an Interpretation." In *Dvořák and his World*, ed. Michael Beckerman, 56–91. Princeton: Princeton University Press, 1993.

Bianconi, Lorenzo, and Giorgio Pestelli, eds. *Geschichte der italienischen Oper. Systematischer Teil. Band 4. Die Produktion: Struktur und Arbeitsbereiche.* Laaber: Laaber Verlag, 1990.

Bianconi, Lorenzo, and Giorgio Pestelli, eds. *Geschichte der italienischen Oper. Systematischer Teil. Band 6. Theorien und Techniken, Bilder und Mythen.* Laaber: Laaber Verlag, 1992.

Blaschke, Karlheinz. "Hof und Hofgesellschaft im Königreich Sachsen während des 19. Jahrhunderts." In *Hof und Hofgesellschaft in den deutschen Staaten im 19. und beginnenden 20. Jahrhundert,* ed. Karl Möckl, 177–206. Boppard: Boldt Verlag, 1990.

Blau, Eva, and Monika Platzer, eds. *Shaping the Great City. Modern Architecture in Central Europe, 1890–1937.* München: Prestel, 1999.

Blaukopf, Kurt. *Musik im Wandel der Gesellschaft. Grundzüge der Musiksoziologie.* München: Piper Verlag, 1982.

Bogusławski, Woyciech. *Dzieje Teatru Narodowego na trzy części podzielone oraz wiadomość o życiu sławnych artistów. Wydanie fotooffsetowe z oposłowiem S. W. Balickiego.* Warszawa: Wydawnictwo Artystyczne i Filmowe, 1965.

Bolzano, Bernard. *O poměru obou národností v Čechach (1816).* In *Jan Novotný, Obrození národa. Svědectví a dokumenty.* Praha: Melantrich, 1979.

Börner-Sandrini, Marie. *Erinnerungen einer alten Dresdnerin.* Dresden: Warnatz & Lehmann, 1876.

Bourdieu, Pierre. *Distinction: A Social Critique of the Judgement of Taste.* Trans. Richard Nice. Cambridge: Harvard University Press, 1984.

Bourdieu, Pierre. *The Field of Cultural Production: Essays on Art and Literature.* Cambridge: Polity Press, 1993.

Braun, Christoph. *Max Webers "Musiksoziologie."* Laaber: Laaber Verlag, 1992.

Breig, Werner. "Richard Wagner als Dresdner Hofkapellmeister—Biographische Details aus neuerschlossenen Briefen." In *Der Klang der Sächsischen Staatskapelle Dresden. Kontinuität und Wandelbarkeit eines Phänomens*, ed. Hans-Günter Ottenberg and Eberhard Steindorf, 119–54. Hildesheim: Olms, 2001.

Brescius, Hans von. *Die königlich sächsische musikalische Kapelle von Reissiger bis Schuch (1826–1898). Festschrift zur 350jährigen Feier des Kapelljubiläums*. Dresden: Meinhold, 1898.

Budde, Gunilla-Friederike. "Musik in Bürgerhäusern." In *Le concert et son public. Mutations de la vie musicale en Europe de 1780 à 1914 (France, Allemagne, Angleterre)*, ed. Hans Erich Bödeker et al., 427–58. Paris: Fondation MSH, 2002.

Bužga, Jaroslav. "Deutsche Opern in Webers Prager Repertoire 1813–1816." In *Carl Maria von Weber und der Gedanke der Nationaloper. Wissenschaftliche Konferenz im Rahmen der Dresdner Musikfestspiele 1986*, ed. Günter Stephan and Hans John, 270–76. Dresden: Agenda, 1987.

Castells, Manuel. "Materials for an Exploratory Theory of the Network Society." *British Journal of Sociology* 51, no. 1 (2000): 5–24. http://dx.doi.org/10.1080/000713100358408.

Čech, Adolf. *Z mých divadelních pamětí*. Praha: Maje, 1903.

Cepnik, Henryk. *Dokąd Dążymy?! W sprawie teatru lwowskiego. Głos bezstronny pod rozwagę, krytyków i nie-krytyków*. Lwów: Nakładem autora, 1909.

Cepnik, Henryk. *Dwa lata w Teatrze miejskim we Lwowie (1900–02)*. Lwów: Nakładem autora, 1902.

Cepnik, Henryk. *Teatr polski w Wiedniu. Rzecz o występach Dramatu lwowskiego na scenie "Bürgertheater" w Wiedniu w dniach od 1. do 8. maja 1910 roku*. Lwów: Księg. Jana Maniszewskiego, 1910.

Černý, František. "Idea Národního Divadla." In *Divadlo v české kultuře 19. století*, ed. Felix Šejna, 17–25. Praha: Narodní galerie v Praze, 1985.

Černy. František et al., eds. *Dějiny českého divadla/II. Národní obrození*. Praha: Academia, 1969.

Černy, František, and Ljuba Klosová, eds. *Dějiny českého divadla/III. Činohra 1848–1918*. Praha: Academia, 1977.

Chałasiński, Józef. *Społeczna genealogia inteligencji polskiej*. Warszawa: Czytelnik, 1946.

Charle, Christophe. *Paris fin de siècle. Culture et politique*. Paris: Edition du Seuil, 1998.

Chomiński, Józef M., and Krystyna Wilkowska-Chomińska. *Historia Muzyki Polskiej*. 2 Vols. Kraków: Wydawnictwo Muzyczne, 1996.

Chvatík, Květoslav, ed. *Die Prager Moderne. Erzählungen, Gedichte, Manifeste*. Frankfurt a.M.: Suhrkamp Verlag, 1991.

Chybiński, Adolf. *W czasach Straussa i Tetmajera*. Kraków: Wspomnienia, 1959.

Cohen, Gary. *The Politics of Ethnic Survival. Germans in Prague 1861–1914.* 2nd. ed. Princeton: Princeton University Press, 2006.

Conrad, Christoph, and Martina Kessel. "Blickwechsel: Moderne, Kultur, Geschichte." In *Kultur & Geschichte. Neue Einblicke in eine alte Beziehung,* ed. Christoph Conrad and Martina Kessel, 9–42. Stuttgart: Reclam, 1998.

Csáky, Moritz. "Gedächtnis, Erinnerung und die Konstruktion von Identität. Das Beispiel Zentraleuropas." In *Nation und Nationalismus in Europa. Kulturelle Konstruktion von Identitäten,* ed. Catherine Bosshart-Pfluger et al., 25–50. Frauenfeld: Huber, 2002.

Csáky, Moritz. "Gesamtregion und Musik. Akkulturation in Mitteleuropa am Beispiel von Musik." In *Mitteleuropa—Idee, Wissenschaft und Kultur im 19. und 20. Jahrhundert,* ed. Richard G. Plaschka et al., 113–30. Wien: VÖAW, 1997.

Csáky, Moritz. *Ideologie der Operette und Wiener Moderne. Ein kulturhistorischer Essay.* 2nd ed. Wien: BöhlauVerlag, 1998.

Cudnowski, Henryk. *Niedyskrecje teatralne.* Wrocław: Ossolineum, 1960.

Czaplicka, John, ed. *Lviv. A City in the Crosscurrents of Culture.* Cambridge: Ukrainian Research Institute of Harvard University, 2000.

Czepulis-Rastenis, Ryszard. "Wzór obywatela ziemskiego w publicystyce Królestwa Polskiego." In *Tradycje szlacheckie w kulturze polskiej,* ed. Zofia Stefanowska, 55–78. Warszawa: Państwowe Wydawnictwo Naukowe, 1976.

Czepulis-Rastenis, Ryszard. "Wzór osobowy inteligenta polskiego w świetle wspomnień pośmiertnych (1863–1872)." In *Inteligencja polska pod zaborami. Studia.* Vol. 1. Ed. Ryszard Czepulis-Rastenis, 159–78. Warszawa: Państwowe Wydawnictwo Naukowe, 1978.

Czepulis-Rastenis, Ryszard, ed. *Inteligencja polska pod zaborami. Studia.* 6 Vols. Warszawa: Państwowe Wydawnictwo Naukowe, 1978–1991.

Dąbrowski, Stanisław, and Ryszard Górski, eds. *Wspomnienia aktorów (1800–1925).* 2 Vols. Warszawa: Państwowy Instytut Wydawniczy, 1963.

Dahlhaus, Carl. *Die Musik des 18. Jahrhunderts.* Laaber: Laaber Verlag, 1985.

Dahlhaus, Carl. *Die Musik des 19. Jahrhunderts.* 2nd. ed. Laaber: Laaber Verlag, 1989.

Dahlhaus, Carl. "Hegel und die Musik seiner Zeit." In *Kunsterfahrung und Kulturpolitik im Berlin Hegels,* ed. Otto Pöggeler and Annemarie Gethmann-Siefert, 333–50. Bonn: Bouvier, 1983.

Dahlhaus, Carl. *Musikalischer Realismus. Zur Musikgeschichte des 19. Jahrhunderts.* München: Piper Verlag, 1982.

Dahlhaus, Carl. "Textgeschichte und Rezeptionsgeschichte." In *Rezeptionsästhetik und Rezeptionsgeschichte in der Musikwissenschaft,* ed. Hermann Danuser and Friedhelm Krummacher, 105–14. Laaber: Laaber Verlag, 1991.

Dahlhaus, Carl. *Wagners Konzeption des musikalischen Dramas.* München: Deutscher Taschenbuch-Verlag, 1990.

Daniel, Ute. *Hoftheater. Zur Geschichte des Theaters und der Höfe im 18. und 19. Jahrhundert.* Stuttgart: Klett-Cotta, 1995.

Daniel, Ute. *Kompendium Kulturgeschichte. Theorien, Praxis, Schlüsselwörter.* Frankfurt a.M.: Suhrkamp, 2001.

Danuser, Hermann. "Zur Interdependenz von Interpretation und Rezeption in der Musik." In *Rezeptionsästhetik und Rezeptionsgeschichte in der Musikwissenschaft,* ed. Hermann Danuser and Friedhelm Krummacher, 165–78. Laaber: Laaber Verlag, 1991.

Danuser, Hermann, and Friedhelm Krummacher, eds. *Rezeptionsästhetik und Rezeptionsgeschichte in der Musikwissenschaft.* Laaber: Laaber Verlag, 1991.

Danuser, Hermann, and Herfried Münkler, eds. *Deutsche Meister—böse Geister? Nationale Selbstfindung in der Musik.* Schliengen: Ed. Argus, 2001.

Dějiny Národního Divadla. 6 Vols. Praha: Sbor pro zřízení druhého Národního divadla, 1933–1936.

Devrient, Eduard. "Das Nationaltheater des neuen Deutschland. Eine Reformschrift, Leipzig 1848." In *Geschichte der deutschen Schauspielkunst,* ed. Rolf Kabel and Christoph Trilse. Vol. 2. 393–424. München: Henschel, 1967.

Devrient, Eduard. *Geschichte der deutschen Schauspielkunst.* Ed. Rolf Kabel and Christoph Trilse. Vol. 2. München: Henschel, 1967.

Deyl, Rudolf. *O čem vím já.* Praha: Melantrich, 1971.

Dienes, Gerhard Michael, ed. *"Fellner & Helmer." Die Architekten der Illusion. Theaterbau und Bühnenbild in Europa anläßlich des Jubiläums "100 Jahre Grazer Oper."* Graz: Stadtmuseum, 1999.

Dienstl, Marian. *Ryszard Wagner a Polska.* Lwów: Altenberg, 1907.

Dobrzański, Stanisław. *Kilka słów o teatrze.* Lwów: Księgarnia Seyfartha i Czajkowskiego, 1874.

Döhring, Sieghart and Sabine Henze-Döhring. *Oper und Musikdrama im 19. Jahrhundert.* Laaber: Laaber Verlag, 1997.

Duchesneau, Michel. *L'avant-garde musicale Paris de 1871–1939.* Paris: Mardaga, 1997.

Dybiec, Julian. *Finansowanie nauki i oświaty w Galicji 1860–1918.* Kraków: Nakład Uniwersytet Jagielloński, 1979.

Dziadek, Magdalena. "Koncepcja opery narodowej w ujęciu kompozytorów i krytyków muzycznych przełomu XIX i XX wieku." In *Opera Polska w XVIII i XIX wieku,* Maciej Jabłoński et alia, 157–93. Poznań: Wydawnictwo Poznańskiego Towarzystwa Przyjaciół Nauk, 2000.

Eckert, Nora. *Der Ring des Nibelungen und seine Inszenierungen von 1876 bis 2001.* Hamburg: Europäische Verlagsanstalt, 2001.

Eggebrecht, Hans Heinrich. *Musik im Abendland. Prozesse und Stationen vom Mittelalter bis zur Gegenwart.* München: Piper Verlag, 1991.

Ehrenberg, Kazimierz P. *List* p. *Kazimierza Ehrenberga redaktora jako odpowiedź dla radcy miasta Lwowa w sprawie teatralnej*. Lwów, 1900.

Eichner, Barbara. *History in Mighty Sounds: Musical Constructions of German National Identity, 1848–1914*. Woodbridge: Boydell & Brewer, 2012.

Elias, Norbert. *Die höfische Gesellschaft. Untersuchungen zur Soziologie des Königtums und der höfischen Aristokratie*. Darmstadt: Luchterhand, 1969.

Elsner, Józef. *Sumariusz moich utworów muzycznych z objaśnieniami o czynnościach i działaniach moich jako artysty muzycznego, opracowała Alina Nowak-Romanowicz*. Kraków: Wydawnictwo Muzyczne, 1957.

Espagne, Michel. *Le creuset allemand. Histoire interculturelle de la Saxe (XVIIIe-XIXe siècle)*. Paris: PUF, 2000.

Espagne, Michel. *Les transferts culturels franco-allemands*. Paris: PUF, 1999.

Espagne, Michel, and Matthias Middell, eds. *Von der Elbe bis an die Seine: Kulturtransfer zwischen Sachsen und Frankreich im 18. und 19. Jahrhundert*. Leipzig: Leipziger Universitätsverlag, 1993.

Espagne, Michel, and Michael Werner, eds. *Transferts. Les relations interculturelles dans l'éspace Franco-Allemand (XVIIIe–XIXe siècle)*. Paris: Ed. Recherche sur les Civilisations, 1988.

Everett, William. "Aspects of Musical-Dramatic Form in Ivan Zajc's Nikola Subic Zrinjski (1876)." In *Zagreb i glazba/Zagreb and Music 1094–1994, Proceedings of the International Musicological Symposium "Zagreb and Croatian Lands as a Bridge between Central-European and Mediterranean Musical Cultures."* Ed. Stanislav Tuksar, 277–90. Zagreb: Croatian Musicological Society, 1998.

Fambach, Oscar. *Das Repertorium des königlichen Theaters und der italienischen Oper zu Dresden 1814–1832*. Bonn: Bouvier, 1985.

Fambach, Oscar. *Das Repertorium des Stadttheaters zu Leipzig 1817–1828*. Bonn: Bouvier, 1980.

Fellmann, Walter. *Sachsens letzter König Friedrich August III*. Berlin: Koehler und Amelang, 1992.

Fischer, Jens Malte. *Oper—das mögliche Kunstwerk. Beiträge zur Operngeschichte des 19. und 20. Jahrhundert*. Anif: Müller Speiser, 1991.

Fleischer, Oskar. *Die Bedeutung der Internationalen Musik- und Theater-Ausstellung in Wien für Kunst und Wissenschaft der Musik*. Wien: Internationale Verlags- und Kunstanstalt, 1894.

Frenzel, Herbert A. *Brandenburg-preussische Schloßtheater. Spielorte und Spielformen vom 17. bis zum 19. Jahrhundert*. Berlin: Selbstverlag der Gesellschaft für Theatergeschichte, 1959.

Friedlaender, Max. *Opernstatistik für das Jahr 1894. Verzeichnis der vom 1. Januar bis zum 31. Dezember 1894 in Deutschland und auf den deutschen Bühnen Oesterreichs, der Schweiz und Russlands aufgeführten Opern*. Leipzig, 1895.

Friesen, Richard Freiherr von. *Erinnerungen aus meinem Leben*. 3 Vols. Dresden: Wilhelm Baensch Verlagsbuchhandlung, 1880.

Fulcher, Jane F. *French Cultural Politics & Music: From the Dreyfus Affair to the First World War*. New York: Oxford University Press, 1999.

Fulcher, Jane F. *The Nation's Image: French Grand Opera as Politics and Politicized Art*. Cambridge: Cambridge University Press, 1987.

Fürstenau, Moritz. *Zur Geschichte der Musik und des Theaters am Hofe zu Dresden, Fotomechanischer Nachdruck der zweibändigen Originalausgabe Dresden 1861–1862 in einem Band mit Nachweisen, Berichtigungen und einem Verzeichnis der von Fürstenau verwendeten Literatur*. Leipzig, 1971.

Gall, Lothar. "Adel, Verein und städtisches Bürgertum." In *Adel und Bürgertum in Deutschland 1770–1848*, ed. Elisabeth Fehrenbach, 29–44. München: Oldenbourg, 1994.

Gall, Lothar. *Bürgertum in Deutschland*. Berlin: Siedler, 1989.

Geitel, Klaus. "Angelo Neumanns Wanderndes Richard Wagner Theater." *Theater und Zeit 12, Nr. 2.*, 21–27. Oktober, 1964.

Gellner, Ernest. *Nations and Nationalism*. Ithaca: Cornell University Press, 1983.

Gerhard, Anselm. *Die Verstädterung der Oper. Paris und das Musiktheater des 19. Jahrhunderts*. Stuttgart: Metzler Verlag, 1992.

Gerlach, Reinhard. *Musik und Jugendstil der Wiener Schule 1900–1908*. Laaber: Laaber Verlag, 1985.

Glasenapp, Carl-Friedrich. *Wagner-Encyklopädie. Haupterscheinungen der Kunst- und Kulturgeschichte im Lichte der Anschauung Richard Wagners. In Wörtlichen Ausführungen aus seinen Schriften dargestellt*. Leipzig 1891.

Głos mieszczańskiego grona radnych miasta Lwowa w sprawie teatru lwowskiego. Lwów: Nakładem własnym (z drukarni K. Wiesnera), 1898.

Głos szlachcica Polskiego (J. I. Kraszewski a zakon szlachecki). Lwów: Drukiem i nakładem drukarni ludowej, 1880.

Gojowy, Detlef. "Das Deutsche in der Musik, gesehen von Friedrich Nietzsche, Adalbert Gyrowetz und Otto Schmid-Dresden." In *Das Deutsche in der Musik. Kolloquium im Rahmen der 5. Dresdner Tage der zeitgenössischen Musik vom 1.-10. Oktober 1991*, ed. Marion Demuth, 42–45. Leipzig: UniMedia, 1997.

Golianek, Ryszard Daniel. "Twórczość operowa Stanisława Moniuszki a idea opery narodowej." In *Opera Polska w XVIII I XIX wieku*, ed. Maciej Jabłoński, 119–28. Poznań: Wydawnictwo Poznańskiego Towarzystwa Przyjaciół Nauk, 2000.

Gorzyński, Slawomir. *Nobilitacje w Galicji w latach 1772–1918*. 2nd ed. Warszawa: Wydawnictwo DiG, 1999.

Gossett, Philip. "Becoming a Citizen. The Chorus in Risorgimento Opera." *Cambridge Opera Journal* 2, no. 1 (1990): 41–64. http://dx.doi.org/10.1017/S0954586700003104.

Got, Jerzy. *Das österreichische Theater in Lemberg im 18. und 19. Jahrhundert. Aus dem Theaterleben der Vielvölkermonarchie.* 2 Vols. Wien: VÖAW, 1997.

Got, Jerzy. *Dzieje teatru w Krakowie. Teatr austriacki w Krakowie 1853–1865.* Vol. 3. Wrocław: Wydawnictwo Literackie, 1984.

Grankin, Pavlo. "Yevhen Sobolevskyi, L'vivs'kyi opernyi teatr: istoriya budovy i restauratsii." *Budujemo inakshe* 6 (2000): 42–45 and 1 (2001): 37–47.

Gregor-Dellin, Martin. *Richard Wagner. Sein Leben, sein Werk, sein Jahrhundert.* Berlin: Henschel Verlag, 1984.

Grey, Thomas S. "Die Meistersinger as National Opera (1868–1945)." In *Music and German National Identity*, ed. Celia Applegate and Pamela Potter, 78–104. Chicago: University of Chicago Press, 2002.

Grodziski, Stanisław. *W Królestwie Galicji i Lodomerii.* Kraków: Wydawnictwo Literackie, 1976.

Groh, Dieter, and Peter Brandt, eds. *"Vaterlandslose Gesellen." Sozialdemokratie und Nation 1860–1990.* München: Beck, 1992.

Gross, Mirjana. "Kultur und Gesellschaft in Kroatien von 1848 bis zum Anfang der achtziger Jahre des 19. Jahrhunderts." In *Bildungsgeschichte, Bevölkerungsgeschichte, Gesellschaftsgeschichte in den Böhmischen Ländern und Europa. Festschrift für Jan Havránek zum 60. Geburtstag*, ed. Hans Lemberg, 144–59. Wien: Verlag für Geschichte und Politik, 1988.

Groß, Reiner. "Kurstaat und Königreich an der Schwelle zum Kapitalismus." In *Geschichte Sachsens*, ed. Karl Czok, 297–331. Weimar: Böhlau Verlag, 1989.

Großmann-Vendrey, Susanne. "Wagner. Von der Rezeptionsgeschichte zur Rezeptionsästhetik." In *Rezeptionsästhetik und Rezeptionsgeschichte in der Musikwissenschaft*, ed. Hermann Danuser and Friedhelm Krummacher, 255–68. Laaber: Laaber Verlag, 1991.

Hackmann, Jörg. *Ostpreußen und Westpreußen in deutscher und polnischer Sicht. Landesgeschichte als beziehungsgeschichtliches Problem.* Wiesbaden: Harrassowitz, 1996.

Hadamowsky, Franz. *Die Wiener Hoftheater (Staatstheater). Ein Verzeichnis der aufgeführten und eingereichten Stücke mit Bestandsnachweisen und Aufführungsdaten, Teil 2, Die Wiener Hofoper (Staatsoper) 1811–1974.* Wien: Jugend und Volk, 1975.

Hadamowsky, Franz. *Wien. Theatergeschichte. Von den Anfängen bis zum Ende des Ersten Weltkrieges.* Wien/München: Oldenbourg, 1988.

Hanák, Peter. *The Garden and the Workshop, Essays.* Princeton: Princeton Univerity Press, 1998.

Hänsch, Wolfgang. *Die Semperoper. Geschichte und Wiederaufbau der Dresdner Semperoper.* Berlin: Verlag für Bauwesen, 1986.

Hanslick, Eduard. "Musik." In *Wien 1848–1888. Denkschrift zum 2. December 1888,* ed. Herausgegeben vom Gemeinerathe der Stadt Wien, 301–42. Wien: Konegen, 1888.

Haupt, Heinz-Gerhard, and Jürgen Kocka, eds. *Geschichte und Vergleich. Ansätze und Ergebnisse international vergleichender Geschichtsschreibung.* Frankfurt a.M.: Campus Verlag, 1996.

Havránek, Jan. "Demografický vývoj Prahy v druhé polovině 19. Století." *Pražský Sborník Historický* (1969–1970): 70–105.

Havránek, Jan. "Společenské předpoklady českeho divadla v Praze v 19. Století." In *Divadlo v české kultuře 19. století,* ed. Felix Šejna, 205–207. Praha: Národní galerie, 1985.

Hegel, Georg Wilhelm Friedrich. *Ästhetik. Mit einer Einführung von Georg Lukács.* Vol. 2. Frankfurt a.M.: Europäische Verlagsanstalt, 1965.

Heidler, Jan. *Příspěvky k listáří Dra. Frant. Lad. Riegra.* 2 Vols. Praha: České Akad, 1924–1926.

Heinemann, Michael. "Alternative zu Wagner? Edmund Kretschmars *Die Folkunger* in der zeitgenössischen Kritik." In *Die Dresdner Oper im 19. Jahrhundert,* ed. Michael Heinemann and Hans John, 295–302. Laaber: Laaber Verlag, 1995.

Heinemann, Michael, and Hans John. ". . . ein in sich abgeschlossenes Kunstwerk. Vorbemerkungen zu einer Geschichte der Dresdner Oper im 19. Jahrhundert." In *Die Dresdner Oper im 19. Jahrhundert,* ed. Michael Heinemann, and Hans John, 7–12. Laaber: Laaber Verlag, 1995.

Heinemann, Michael, and Hans John, eds. *Die Dresdner Oper im 19. Jahrhundert.* Laaber: Laaber Verlag, 1995.

Heinemann, Michael, and Hans-Joachim Hinrichsen. *Bach und die Nachwelt. Rezeption, Interpretation und Edition.* 4 vols. Laaber: Laaber Verlag, 1997–2000.

Heller, Ludwig. *Prześwietna Rado!* Lwów, 1903.

Hennenberg, Fritz. *300 Jahre Leipziger Oper, Geschichte und Gegenwart.* München: Langen Müller, 1993.

Hilmera, Jiří. *Česka Divadelní architektura.* Praha: Divadelní ústav, 1999.

Hinrichsen, Hans. "Joachim Musikwissenschaft. Musik—Interpretation—Wissenschaft." *Archiv für Musikwissenschaft* 57, no. 1 (2000): 78–90. http://dx.doi.org/10.2307/931068.

Hinrichsen, Hans Joachim. "Johann Nikolaus Forkel und die Anfänge der Bachforschung." In *Bach und die Nachwelt, Vol. 1: 1750–1850,* ed. Michael Heinemann and Hans-Joachim Hinrichsen, 193–254. Laaber: Laaber Verlag, 1997.

Hobsbawm, Eric. *Nations and Nationalism since 1780. Programme, Myth, Reality.* Cambridge: Verso, 1992.

Hobsbawm, Eric, and Terence Ranger, eds. *The Invention of Tradition.* Cambridge: Cambridge University Press, 1984.

Hoffmann, E. T. A., ed. *Schriften zur Musik. Aufsätze und Rezensionen. Nachlese.* 191–96. München: Winkler, 1963.
Holzer, Jerzy. "'Vom Orient die Fantasie, und in der Brust der Slawen Feuer...' Jüdisches Leben und Akkulturation im Lemberg des 19. und 20. Jahrhunderts." In *Lemberg—Lwów—L'viv. Eine Stadt im Schnittpunkt europäischer Kulturen*, ed. Peter Fäßler, 75–91. Köln: Böhlau, 1993.
Horowitz, Joseph. "Dvořák and the New World: A Concentrated Moment." In *Dvořák and his World*, ed. Michael Beckerman, 92–103. Princeton, New York: Princeton University Verlag, 1993.
Hoszowski, Stanisław. *Ceny we Lwowie w latach 1701–1914.* Lwów: Drukarnia L. Wiśniewskiego, 1934.
Hroch, Miroslav. *Die Vorkämpfer der nationalen Bewegung bei den kleinen Völkern Europas. Eine vergleichende Analyse zur gesellschaftlichen Schichtung der patriotischen Gruppen.* Prag: Univ. Karlova, 1968.
Hroch, Miroslav. *Na prahu národní existence. Touha a skutečnost.* Praha: Mladà Fronta, 1999.
Hunt, Lynn. "Introduction: History, Culture and Text." In *The New Cultural History*, ed. Lynn Hunt, 1–22. Berkeley: California University Press, 1989. http://dx.doi.org/10.1525/california/9780520064287.003.0001.
Jabłoński, Maciej et al., eds. *Opera Polska w XVIII i XIX wieku.* Poznań: Wydawnictwo Poznańskiego Towarzystwa Przyjaciół Nauk, 2000.
Jahn, Michael. *Die Wiener Hofoper von 1848 bis 1870. Personal—Aufführungen—Spielplan.* Tutzing: Hans Schneider, 2002.
Jahn, Michael. "Metamorphosen der Opern der Académie Royale (Impériale) de Musique im Teatro di Corte in Wien." Ph.D. diss., University of Vienna, 1992.
Jakubcová, Alena, Jitka Ludvová, and Václav Maidl, eds. *Deutschsprachiges Theater in Prag. Begegnungen der Sprachen und Kulturen.* Praha: Divadelni Ústav, 2001.
Jauß, Hans Robert. "Rückschau auf die Rezeptionstheorie. Ad usum Musicae Scientiae." In *Rezeptionsästhetik und Rezeptionsgeschichte in der Musikwissenschaft*, ed. Hermann Danuser and Friedhelm Krummacher, 13–36. Laaber: Laaber Verlag, 1991.
John, Hans. "Richard Wagners Schrift Entwurf zur Organisation eines deutschen National-Theaters für das Königreich Sachsen (1848)." In *Die Dresdner Oper im 19. Jahrhundert*, ed. Michael Heinemann and Hans John, 193–98. Laaber: Laaber Verlag, 1995.
Johnson, James H. *Listening in Paris. A Cultural History.* Berkeley: University of California Press, 1995.
Jung, Ute. *Die Rezeption der Kunst Richard Wagners in Italien.* Regensburg: Gustav Bosse Verlag, 1974.

Kadlec, Karel. *Družstva král. českého zemského a Národního divadla. Příspěvky k dějinám českého divadla.* Praha: Nákladem Družstva Národního divadla, 1896.
Kaelble, Hartmut. *Europäer über Europa. Die Entstehung des europäischen Selbstverständnisses im 19. und 20. Jahrhundert.* Frankfurt a.M.: Campus, 2001.
Kaelble, Hartmut, and Jürgen Schriewer, eds. *"Vergleich und Transfer." Komparatistik in den Sozial-, Geschichts- und Kulturwissenschaften.* Frankfurt a.M.: Campus, 2003.
Kamiński, Mieczysław. "Z moich wędrówek po świecie." In *Wspomnienia aktorów (1800–1925)*, ed. Stanisław Dąbrowski i Ryszard Górski, 305–23. Warszawa: Państwowy Instytut Wydawniczy, 1963.
Kann, Robert A. *Das Nationalitätenproblem der Habsburgermonarchie. Geschichte und Ideengehalt der nationalen Bestrebungen vom Vormärz bis zur Auflösung des Reiches im Jahre 1918.* 2 Vols. Graz: Böhlau Verlag, 1964.
Karbusicki, Vladimir. *Wie deutsch ist das Abendland? Geschichtliches Sendungsbewußtsein im Spiegel der Musik.* Hamburg: Von Bocker Verlag, 1995.
Katalinić, Vjera. "Nikola Zrinyi (1508–1566) as a National Hero in Nineteenth-Century Opera Between Vienna, Berlin, Budapest and Zagreb." In *Musica e Storia* 12 (2004): 611–31.
Keller, Katrin, and Josef Matzerath, eds. *Geschichte des Sächsischen Adels.* Köln: Böhlau, 1997.
Kertbeny, Karl. "Maria Zur Theatergeschichte von Budapest." In *Ungarische Revue* 1 (1881): 636–58; 2 (1882): 404–38.
Keym, Stefan. "Zur Problematik von Heimat, Nationalität und Sprache bei Ignacy Jan Paderewski und Feliks Nowowiejski." In *Mehrsprachigkeit und regionale Bindung in Musik und Literatur*, ed. Tomi Mäkelä and Tobias Robert Klein, 67–80. Frankfurt a.M.: Peter Lang, 2004.
Kimball, Stanley. *Czech Nationalism. A Study of the National Theatre Movement, 1845–1883.* Urbana: University of Illinois Press, 1964.
Kipper, Rainer. *Der Germanenmythos im Deutschen Kaiserreich. Formen und Funktionen historischer Selbstthematisierung.* Göttingen: Vandenhoeck & Ruprecht, 2002.
Kirchmeyer, Helmut. "Drei Jahrhunderte Beckmesserei. Kleiner Leitfaden zu einer Geschichte der deutschen Musikkritik. Mit einem Anhang, Wagner betreffend." In *Parsifal, Programmheft I*, ed. Wolfgang Wagner, 46–78. Bayreuth: Verlag der Bayreuther Festspiele, 1988.
Klotz, Volker. *Operette. Portrait und Handbuch einer unerhörten Kunst.* München: Piper Verlag, 1991.
Knaus, Gabriella Hanke. *Richard Strauss—Ernst von Schuch.* Berlin: Henschel, 1999.
Kocka, Jürgen. *Das lange 19. Jahrhundert. Arbeit, Nation und bürgerliche Gesellschaft.* Stuttgart: Klett-Cotta, 2001.

Kohut, Adolph, ed. *Das Dresdner Hoftheater in der Gegenwart. Mit Originalbeiträgen von den Mitgliedern des Dresdner Hoftheaters.* Dresden: E. Pierson's Verlag, 1888.

Kolodin, Irving. *The Metropolitan Opera 1883–1966.* New York: Knopf, 1967.

Komorowski, Jarosław. *Polskie Życie teatralne na Podolu i Wołhyniu do 1863 roku.* Wrocław: Zakład Narodowy Imienina Ossolinskich, 1985.

Komorowska, Małgorzata. "Polska Opera Narodowa." In *Opera Polska w XX wieku,* ed. Maciej Jabłoński, 9–24. Poznań: Wydawnictwo Poznanskiego Tow. Przyjaciół Nauk, 1999.

Konečná, Hana. *Soupis repertoáru Národního divadla v Praze 1881–1983.* 3 Vols. Praha: Národní Divadlo, 1983.

Konold, Wulf. "Nationale Bewegungen und Nationalopern im 19. Jahrhundert." In *Der schöne Abglanz. Stationen der Operngeschichte,* ed. Udo Bermbach and Wulf Konold, 111–28. Berlin: Reimer Verlag, 1992.

Krasiński, Edward. "Heller czy Pawlikowski? Polemiki i spory o teatr Lwowski Ludwika Hellera." In *Pamiętnik Teatralny* 1, no. 68 (1999): 71–133.

Krebs, Roland. *L'idée de "Théâtre national" dans l'Allemagne des Lumières.* Wiesbaden: Harrassowitz, 1985.

Křen, Jan. *Konfliktgemeinschaft. Tschechen und Deutsche 1780–1918.* München: Oldenbourg, 1996.

Kretzschmar, Hellmut. *Die Zeit König Johanns von Sachsen 1854–1873. Mit Briefen und Dokumenten.* Berlin: Akademie Verlag, 1960.

Kreuzer, Gundula. *Verdi and the Germans. From Unification to the Third Reich.* Cambridge: Cambridge University Press, 2010.

Kröplin, Eckhart. "Wagner und Weber. Der Vorgang einer Theatralisierung." In *Carl Maria von Weber und der Gedanke der Nationaloper. Wissenschaftliche Konferenz im Rahmen der Dresdner Musikfestspiele 1986,* ed. Günter Stephan and Hans John, 336–44. Dresden: Hochschule für Musik Carl Maria von Weber, 1987.

Kuchtówna, Lidia, ed. *Teatr Polski we Lwowie.* Warszawa: IS PAN, 1997.

Kummer, Friedrich. *Dresden und seine Theaterwelt.* Dresden: Verlag Heimatwerk Sachsen, 1938.

Kváček, Robert. "Společenskopolitické zápasy o národní divadlo v 70. letech 19. Století." In *Divadlo v české kultuře 19. století,* ed. Felix Šejna, 26–35. Praha: Národní galerie, 1985.

Kvapil, Jaroslav. *O čem vím. Sto kapitol o lidech a dějích z mého života.* 2 Vols. Praha 1946. Laaber: Laaber Verlag, 1990.

Lane, Hugo. "The Polish Opera and the Ukrainian Theater. Cultural Hegemony and National Culture." In *Lviv: A City in the Crosscurrents of Culture,* ed. John Czaplicka, 149–70. Cambridge: Harvard University Press, 2000.

Lange, Hans. *Vom Tribunal zum Tempel. Zur Architektur und Geschichte deutscher Hoftheater zwischen Vormärz und Restauration*. Marburg: Jonas-Verlag, 1985.

Langer, Arne. *Der Regisseur und die Aufzeichnungspraxis der Opernregie im 19. Jahrhundert*. Frankfurt a.M.: Peter Lang, 1997.

Langewiesche, Dieter. *Nation, Nationalismus, Nationalstaat in Deutschland und Europa*. München: Beck, 2000.

Lasocka, Barbara. *Teatr lwowski w latach 1800–1842*. Warszawa: Państwowy Instytut Wydawniczy, 1967.

Lasocka, Barbara. "Teatr Stanisława hrabiego Skarbka 1842–1848." *Pamiętnik Teatralny* 17 (1968): H. 2, 145–78.

Laube, Heinrich. *Schriften über das Theater*. Berlin: Henschel,, 1959.

Lechicki, Czesław. "Najpopularnejszyszy dziennikarz galicyjski XIX wieku (szkic biograficzny o Janie Dobrzańskim)." *Małopolskie Studia Historyczne* 4, no. 1 (1961): 3–11.

Lederer, Joseph-Horst. *Verismo auf der deutschsprachigen Bühne, 1891–1926. Eine Untersuchung seiner Rezeption durch die zeitgenössische musikalische Fachpresse*. Wien: Böhlau, 1992.

Leydi, Roberto. "Verbreitung und Popularisierung." In *Geschichte der italienischen Oper. Systematischer Teil. Vol 6. Theorien und Techniken, Bilder und Mythen*, ed. Lorenzo Bianconi, Giorgio Pestelli, 321–404. Laaber: Laaber Verlag, 1992.

Liebscher, Artur. "Die erste Dresdner Aufführung der Meistersinger im Jahre 1869 im Lichte der bisher unbekannten Tagebuchaufzeichnungen ihres musikalischen Leiters Julius Rietz." *Neues Archiv für sächsische Geschichte und Altertumskunde* 36 (1915): 278–99.

Lityński, Michał. *Gmach skarbkowski na tle architektury lwowskiej w pierwszej połowie XIX wieku*. Lwów: Nakładem Fundacji Skarbkowskiej, 1921.

Lityński, Michał. *Pamiątkowy opis Teatru Miejskiego we Lwowie*. Lwów: Z drukarni E. Winiarza, 1900.

Locke, Brian S. *Opera and Ideology in Prague. Polemics and Practice at the National Theatre 1900–1938*. Rochester: University of Rochester Press, 2006.

Lorenz, Chris. *Konstruktion der Vergangenheit. Eine Einführung in die Geschichtstheorie*. Köln: Böhlau, 1997.

Ludvová, Jitka. "Nationaltheater und Minderheitentheater. Ideen und Theaterpraxis." In *Deutschsprachiges Theater in Prag. Begegnungen der Sprachen und Kulturen*, ed. Alena Jakubcová, 43–55. Praha: Divadelní Ústav, 2001.

Luhmann, Niklas. "Differentiation of Society." *Canadian Sociological Review* 2, no. 1 (1977): 29–53. http://dx.doi.org/10.2307/3340510.

Macura, Vladimír. *Znamení zrodu. České národní obrození jako kulturní typ*. Praha: Pražska imaginace, 1992.

Mallgrave, Harry. *Francis Gottfried Semper: Architect of the Ninteenth Century.* New Haven: Yale University Press, 1996.

Mannstein, Heinrich Ferdinand. *Das königliche Hoftheater zu Dresden, in künstlerischer und administrativer Hinsicht; beleuchtet von einem Kenner der Kunst und Freunde der Wahrheit.* Leipzig, 1838.

Marcinek, Roman, and Krzysztof Ślusarek. *Materiały do genealogii szlachty galicyjskie, Część I: A-K.* Kraków: Towarzystwo Wydawnicze Historia Jagellonica, 1996.

Marek, Michaela, ed. *Bauen für die Nation. Selbstdarstellungsstrategien kleiner Völker zwischen nationaler Eigenart und politisch-sozialer Ambition.* München: Oldenbourg, 2001.

Maresz, Barbara. *Maria Szydlowska, Repertuar teatru polskiego we Lwowie 1886–1894.* Kraków: Towarzstwo Autorów i Wydawców Prac Naukowych Universitas, 1993.

Maresz, Barbara. *Występy gościnne w teatrze polskim. Z dziejów życia teatralnego Krakowa, Lwowa i Warszawy.* Kraków: Towarzystwo Autorów i Wydawców Prac Naukowych Universitas, 1997.

Marfany, Joan-Lluís. *La cultura del catalanisme: el nacionalisme catala en els seus inicis.* Barcelona: Empuries, 1995.

Marszałek, Agnieszka. *Lwowskie przedsiębiorstwa teatralne lat 1872–1886.* Kraków: Towarzystwo Naukowe Societas Vistulana, 1999.

Marszałek, Agnieszka. "O pierwszej operze Wagnera na polskiej scenie ("Lohengrin" we Lwowie, 21 IV 1877)." In *Dramat i teatr pozytywistyczny*, ed. Jan Błoński, 137–46. Wrocław: Wiedza o Kulturze, 1992.

Marszałek, Agnieszka. *Repertuar teatru polskiego we Lwowie 1875–1881.* Kraków: Towarzystwo Autorów i Wydawców Prac Naukowych Universitas, 1992.

Marszałek, Agnieszka. *Repertuar teatru polskiego we Lwowie 1881–1886.* Kraków: Towarzystwo Autorów i Wydawców Prac Naukowych Universitas, 1993.

Mayer, Hans. *Richard Wagner. Mitwelt und Nachwelt.* Stuttgart: Belser, 1978.

Mazepa, Leszek. "Towarzystwo św. Cecylii we Lwowie (1826–1829)." In *Musica Galiciana, Bd. 3. Kultura muzyczna Galicji w kontekście stosunków polsko-ukraińskich (od doby piastowsko-kziążęcej do roku 1945)*, ed. Leszek Mazepa, 105–26. Rzeszów: Wydawnictwo Wyższej Szkoły Pedagogicznej, 1999.

Mazepa, Tereza. "Teatr lwowski za dyrekcji Wojciecha Bogusławskiego w latach 1795–1799 (Zagadnienia repertuaru muzycznego)." In *Musica Galiciana, Bd. 3. Kultura muzyczna Galicji w kontekście stosunków polsko-ukraińskich (od doby piastowsko-kziążęcej do roku 1945)*, ed. Leszek Mazepa, 75–86. Rzeszów: Wydawnictwo Wyższej Szkoły Pedagogicznej, 1999.

Mazzini, Giuseppe. *Filosofia della Musica,* ed. Marcello De Angelis, 33–77. Firenze: Guaraldi, 1977.

Mendelsohn, Ezra. "Jewish Assimilation in L'viv. The Case of Wilhelm Feldman." In *Nationbuilding and the Politics of Nationalism: Essays on Austrian Galicia,* ed. Andrei S. Markovits and Frank E. Sysyn, 99–106. Cambridge: Harvard University Press, 1983.

Menninger, Margaret Eleanor. "Zivilgesellschaft jenseits der Bühne: Theater, Bildung und bürgerliches Mäzenatentum." In *Zivilgesellschaft als Geschichte,* ed. Ralph Jessen et al., 175–94. Wiesbaden: Verlag für Sozialwissenschaften, 2004. http://dx.doi.org/10.1007/978-3-322-80962-9_9.

Meyer, Stephen C. *Carl Maria Von Weber and the Search for a German Opera.* Bloomington: Indiana University Press, 2003.

Michalik, Jan. *Dzieje Teatru w Krakowie w latach 1865–1893. Przedsięborstwa teatralne.* Kraków: Wydawnictwo Literackie, 1997.

Michalik, Jan. "Legenda i prawda o młodości Tadeusza Pawlikowskiego." *Pamiętnik Teatralny* 24, no. 1 (1975): 45–80.

Michałowski, Kornel. "Pierwzy Wagner na ziemiach polskich." In *Księga in memoriam Karol Musioł 1929–1982,* ed. Lilianna M. Moll, 91–99. Katowice: AM, 1992.

Mick, Christoph. *Kriegserfahrungen in einer multiethnischen Stadt. Lemberg 1914–1947.* Wiesbaden: Harrassowitz, 2010.

Mikoletzky, Juliane. "Bürgerliche Schillerrezeption im Wandel: Österreichische Schillerfeiern 1859–1905." In *Bürgerliche Selbstdarstellung. Städtebau, Architektur, Denkmäler,* ed. Hanns Haas and Hannes Stekl, 165–84. Wien: Böhlau, 1995.

Mittmann, Jörg-Peter. "Musikerberuf und bürgerliches Bildungsideal." In *Bildungsbürgertum im 19. Jahrhundert. Vol. 2: Bildungsgüter und Bildungswissen,* ed. Reinhard Koselleck, 236–58. Stuttgart: Klett-Cotta, 1990.

Möckl, Karl, ed. *Hof und Hofgesellschaft in den deutschen Staaten im 19. und beginnenden 20. Jahrhundert.* Boppard: Boldt Verlag, 1990.

Moravánszky, Ákos. *Competing Visions. Aesthetic Invention and Social Imagination in Central European Architecture. 1867–1918.* Cambridge: MIT Press, 1998.

Moretti, Franco. *Atlas of the European Novel, 1800–1900.* London: Verso, 1999.

Möser, Albert. *Das Dresdner Hoftheater in den Jahren 1862 bis 1869.* Dresden: Lehmann, 1869.

Motte-Haber, Helga de la, ed. *Nationaler Stil und europäische Dimension in der Musik der Jahrhundertwende.* Darmstadt: Wissenschaftliche Buchgesellschaft, 1991.

Müller, Georg-Hermann. *Das Stadttheater zu Leipzig vom 1. Januar 1862 bis 1. September 1887. Nach amtlichen Quellen bearbeitet von Georg Hermann Müller*. Leipzig: Duncker & Humblot, 1887.

Müller, Michael G. "Der polnische Adel von 1750 bis 1863." In *Europäischer Adel 1750–1950*, ed. Hans-Ulrich Wehler, 217–42. Göttingen: Vandenhoeck & Ruprecht, 1990.

Müller, Sven Oliver. "Hörverhalten als europäischer Kulturtransfer. Zur Veränderung der Musikrezeption im 19. Jahrhundert." In *Wie europäisch ist die Oper? Die Geschichte des Musiktheaters als Zugang zu einer kulturellen Topographie Europas*, ed. Philipp Ther and Peter Stachel, 41–54. Wien: Böhlau, 2009.

Mungen, Anno. "Morlacchi, Weber und die Dresdner Oper." In *Die Dresdner Oper im 19. Jahrhundert*, ed. Michael Heinemann and Hans John. Laaber: Laaber Verlag, 85–106. 1995.

Mungen, Anno. "Raum und Orchester. Dokumente zu Gottfried Sempers und Richard Wagners Ideen eines klingenden Theaters." In *Die Dresdner Oper im 19. Jahrhundert*, ed. Michael Heinemann and Hans John, 199–212. Laaber: Laaber Verlag, 1995.

Mütterlein, Max. "Gottfried Semper und dessen Monumentalbauten am Dresdner Theaterplatz." *Neues Archiv für sächsische Geschichte und Altertumskunde* 34 (1913): 299–399.

Nejedlý, Zdeněk. *Česká moderní spěvohrá*. Prag: J. Otto, 1911.

Nejedlý, Zdeněk. *Dějiny opery Národního divadlu*. 2 Vols. Praha: Práce, 1949.

Nejedlý, Zdeněk. *Opera Národního divadla do roku 1900*. Praha: Sbor pro zřízení druhého Národního divadla, 1935.

Nejedlý, Zdeněk. *Opera Národního divadla od roku 1900 do převratu*. Praha: Sbor pro zřízení druhého Národního divadla, 1936.

Nejedlý, Zdeněk. *Zdenko Fibich. Zakladatel scénického melodramatu*. Praha: Královské Vinohrady, 1901.

Němeček, Jiří. *Opera Národního divadla v období Karla Kovařovice*. 2 Vols. Praha: Divadelní ústav, 1968.

Nietzsche, Friedrich. *Der Geburt der Tragödie aus dem Geiste der Musik*. Ditzingen: Reclam, 2002.

Nietzsche, Friedrich. "Richard Wagner in Bayreuth. Unzeitgemäße Betrachtungen, Viertes Stück (1876)." In *Richard Wagner in Bayreuth, Der Fall Wagner, Nietzsche contra Wagner*, 5–83. Stuttgart: Reclam, 1973.

Nossig, Alfred. *Internationale Musik- und Theaterausstellung Wien. Katalog der polnischen Abteilung*. Wien: Comitée für Betheiligung polnischer Kunst an der Internationalen Musik- und Theater-Ausstellung, 1892.

Nowakowski, Józef. "Sylwetki teatralne." In *Wspomnienia aktorów (1800–1925)*. Vol. 1. Ed. Stanisław Dąbrowski and Ryszard Górski, 387–427. Warszawa: Państwowy Instytut Wydawniczy, 1963.

Oberzaucher-Schüller, Gunhild, ed. *Meyerbeer—Wagner. Eine Begegnung.* Köln: Böhlau, 1998.

Osterhammel, Jürgen. *Geschichtswissenschaften jenseits des Nationalstaats. Studien zu Beziehungsgeschichte und Zivilisationsvergleich.* Göttingen: Vandenhoeck & Ruprecht, 2001.

Ottenberg, Hans-Günter, and Eberhard Steindorf, eds. *Der Klang der Sächsischen Staatskapelle Dresden. Kontinuität und Wandelbarkeit eines Phänomens.* Hildesheim: Olms, 2001.

Ottlová, Marta, and Milan Pospíšil. *Bedřich Smetana a jeho doba.* Praha: Nakladatelství Lidové noviny, 1997.

Paderewski, Ignace Jan, and Mary Lawton. *The Paderewski Memoirs.* New York: Scribner's, 1938.

Pajączkowski, Franciszek. *Teatr lwowski pod dyreckją Tadeuzsa Pawlikowskiego.* Kraków: Wydawnictwo Literackie, 1961.

Palamarchuk, Oksana. *Vasyl Pylypiuk, L'vivska opera.* L'viv: Svitlo, 2000.

Parker, Roger, ed. *The Oxford History of Opera.* Oxford: Oxford University Press, 1996.

Patureau, Frédérique. *Le palais Garnier dans la société parisienne 1875–1914.* Liège: Mardaga, 1991.

Paulmann, Johannes. "Internationaler Vergleich und interkultureller Transfer. Zwei Forschungsansätze zur europäischen Geschichte des 18. bis 20. Jahrhunderts." *Historische Zeitschrift* 267 (1998): 649–85.

Pauls, Birgit. *Guiseppe Verdi und das Risorgimento. Ein politischer Mythos im Prozeß der Nationenbildung.* Berlin: Akademie Verlag, 1996.

Pepłowski, Stanisław. *Teatr Polski we Lwowie (1780–1881).* Lwów: Gubrynowicz & Schmidt, 1889.

Pepłowski, Stanisław. *Teatr Polski we Lwowie (1881–1890).* Lwów: Gubrynowicz & Schmidt, 1891.

Pepłowski, Stanisław. *Teatr Ruski w Galicji.* Lwów: Nakł. Dziennika Polskiego, 1883.

Pere, Gabriel, ed. *El modernisme, 1890–1906.* Barcelona: Edicions 62, 1995.

Pešek, Jiří. "Sbírky na nové národní divadlo po požáru roku 1881." In *Divadlo v české kultuře 19. století,* ed. Felix Šejna, 210–12. Praha: Národní galerie, 1985.

Piazzoni, Irene. *Dal teatro dei palchettisti all'Ente autonomo: la Scala 1897–1920.* Firenze: Nuova Italia, 1995.

Pilková, Zděnka. *Dramatická tvorba Jiřího Bendy.* Praha: Strani nakladatelstvi krasne Literatury, 1960.

Piniński, Leon. *O operze nowoczesnej i znaczeniu Ryszarda Wagnera oraz o Parsifalu Wagnera.* Lwow: Wyd. osob, 1883.

Poklewska, Krystyna. "Jan Dobrzański (1820–1886). Szkic biograficzny." In *Prace polonistyczne, seria XVIII* (1962): 141–60.

Prokopovych, Markian. *In the Public Eye: The Budapest Opera House, the Audience and the Press, 1884–1918*. Wien: Böhlau, 2014.

Pröls, Robert. *Beiträge zur Geschichte des Hoftheaters zu Dresden in actenmäßiger Darstellung*. Erfurt: Fr. Bartlomäus, 1880.

Pröls, Robert. *Geschichte des Hoftheaters zu Dresden. Von seinen Anfängen bis zum Jahre 1862*. Dresden: W. Baensch, 1878.

Puffett, Derek, ed. *Richard Strauss: Salome*. Cambridge: Cambridge University Press, 1989.

Purchla, Jacek. *Teatr i jego architekt. W stulecie otwarcia gmachu Teatru im. Juliusza Słowackiego w Krakowie*. Kraków: Międzynarodowe Centrum Kultury, 1993.

Rähesoo, Jaak. *Estonian Theatre*. 2nd ed. Tallinn: Estonian Theatre Union, 2003.

Rak, Jiří. "Divadlo jako prostředek politické propagandy v první polovině 19. století." In *Divadlo v české kultuře 19. století*, ed. Felix Šejna, 44–52. Praha: Narodni galerie, 1985.

Raszewski, Zbigniew. *Krótka historia teatru polskiego*. Warszawa: Państwowy Instytut Wydawniczy, 1978.

Reif, Heinz. *Westfälischer Adel 1770–1860. Vom Herrschaftsstand zur regionalen Elite*. Göttingen: Vandenhoeck & Ruprecht, 1979.

Reittererová, Vlasta, and Hubert Reitterer. *Vier Dutzend rothe Strümpfe . . . Zur Rezeptionsgeschichte der Verkauften Braut von Bedřich Smetana in Wien am Ende des 19. Jahrhunderts*. Wien: Verlag der Österreichischen Akademie der Wissenschaft, 2004.

Ritter, Rüdiger. *Musik für die Nation. Der Komponist Stanislaw Moniuszko (1819–1872) in der polnischen Nationalbewegung des 19. Jahrhunderts*. Frankfurt a.M.: Peter Lang, 2005.

Roeder, Ernst, ed. *Das Dresdner Hoftheater der Gegenwart*. Dresden, Leipzig: Biographisch-kritische Skizzen der Mitglieder. Neue Folge, 1896.

Rosselli, John. "Das Produktionssystem von 1780–1880." In *Geschichte der italienischen Oper. Systematischer Teil. Bd. 4. Die Produktion: Struktur und Arbeitsbereiche*, ed. Lorenzo Bianconi and Giorgio Pestelli, 97–190.

Rostworowski, Emanuel. "Ilu było w Rzeczpospolitej obywateli szlachty." *Kwartalnik Historyczny* 95 (1988): 3–40.

Rudnytsky, Ivan. "The Ukrainians in Galicia Under Austrian Rule." In *Nationbuilding and the Politics of Nationalism: Essays on Austrian Galicia*, ed. Andrei Markovits and Frank Sysyn, 23–67. Cambridge: Harvard University Press, 1982.

Rudziński, Witold. *Moniuszko i jego muzyka*. 2nd. ed. Warszawa: Wydawnictwo szkolne i pedagogiczne, 1988.

Salmi, Hannu. *Imagined Germany. Richard Wagner's National Utopia*. Frankfurt a.M.: Peter Lang, 1999.

Salome. Musik-Drama in einem Aufzuge nach Oscar Wilde's gleichnamiger Dichtung. Musik von Richard Strauss Op. 54. Klavier-Auszug mit deutsch-englischem Text von Otto Singer. London: Fürstner Limited, 1910–1911.

Schenk, Benjamin. "Mental Maps. Die Konstruktion von geographischen Räumen in Europa seit der Aufklärung. Literaturbericht." *Geschichte und Gesellschaft (Vandenhoeck & Ruprecht)* 28 (2002): 493–514.

Schiller, Friedrich. *Was kann eine gute stehende Schaubühne eigentlich wirken? Eine Vorlesung, gehalten zu Mannheim in der öffentlichen Sitzung der kurpfälzischen deutschen Gesellschaft am 26sten des Junius 1784. von F. Schiller, Mitglied dieser Gesellschaft und herzogl. Weimarischen Rath,* in: Schillers Werke, Nationalausgabe, 20. Band, Philosophische Schriften. Weimar: Böhlaus Nachf, 1962. 87–100.

Schmid, Otto. *Richard Wagners Opern und Musikdramen in Dresden.* Dresden: Oscar Laube, 1919.

Schmid-Dresden, Otto. *Bunte Blätter.* Studien und Skizzen aus dem Reich der Töne. Berichte und Kritiken aus dem Dresdner Opernleben. Dresden: Schmidt, 1893.

Schneider, Frank. "Einiges über das Deutsche in der Musik oder Ankedoten aus der sächsischen Historie." In *Das Deutsche in der Musik. Kolloquium im Rahmen der 5. Dresdner Tage der zeitgenössischen Musik vom 1.-10. Oktober 1991,* ed. Marion Demuth, 8–17. Leipzig: UniMedia, 1997.

Schneider, Jürgen et al. *Währungen der Welt* Europäische und nordamerikanische Devisenkurse 1777–1914. Vol. 1. Stuttgart: Steiner Verlag, 1991.

Schnoor, Hans. *Die Stunde des Rosenkavalier. 300 Jahre Dresdner Oper.* München: Süddeutscher Verlag, 1968.

Schnoor, Hans. *Vierhundert Jahre deutsche Musik-Kultur. Zum Jubiläum der Staatskapelle und zur Geschichte der Dresdner Oper.* Dresden: Verlag Geschichte, 1948.

Schopenhauer,Arthur. *Sämtliche Werke.* 2 Vols. Stuttgart, Frankfurt a.M: Diogenes, 1960.

Schorske, Carl E. *Geist und Gesellschaft im fin de siècle.* Frankfurt a.M.: S. Wien: Fischer Verlag, 1982.

Schuch, Friedrich von. *Richard Strauss, Ernst von Schuch und Dresdens Oper.* 2nd ed. Leipzig: VEB Breitkopf & Härtel Musikverlag, 1953.

Schuh, Willi, ed. *Hugo von Hofmannsthal, Richard Strauss. Der Rosenkavalier. Fassungen, Filmszenarien, Briefe.* Frankfurt a.M.: S. Fischer Verlag, 1971.

Schweizer, Johanna. "Finanzierung und Organisation der Bayreuther Festspiele bis 1914." In *Wandel und Wechsel. Zur Inszenierungsgeschichte des Ring des Nibelungen bei den Bayreuther Festspielen. Abschlußbericht des Projekts: Wagner und kein Ende. Auf den Spuren des Bayreuther Jahrtausendrings,* ed.

Ulrich Bartels, 7–18. Hildesheim: Institut für Musik und Musikwissenschaften, 2000.

Seebach, Nikolaus. *Ehrengabe dramatischer Dichter und Komponisten. Sr. Exzellenz dem Grafen Nikolaus von Seebach zum zwanzigjährigen Intendanten-Jubiläum gewidmet.* Leipzig: Kurt Wolff Verlag, 1914.

Semper, Manfred, and Hans, ed. *Gottfried Semper, Kleine Schriften.* Berlin: W. Spemann, 1884.

Senelick, Laurence, ed. *National Theatre in Northern and Eastern Europe, 1746–1900.* Cambridge: Cambridge University Press, 1991.

Sieber, Maurycy. *Pogadanki o muzyce i towarzystwach muzycznych, in Mrówka.* Vol. 2 (1870): 60, 91.

Sivert, Tadeusz, ed. *Teatr polski od 1863 roku do schylku XIX wieku (Dzieje Teatru Polskiego, tom III).* Warszawa: Państwowe Wydawnictwo Naukowe, 1982.

Sivert, Tadeusz, and Maria O. Bieńka, eds. *Teatr polski w latach 1890–1918. Zabór austriacki i pruski (Dzieje Teatru Polskiego, tom IV).* Warszawa: Państwowe Wydawnictwo Naukowe, 1987.

Skibińska, Ewa. *Recepcja Twórczości Ryzsarda Wagnera w Polsce do 1914.* Kraków: Uniwersytet Jagielloński, Praca Magisterska, 1983.

Ślusarek, Krzysztof. *Drobna Szlachta w Galicji 1772–1848.* Kraków: Wydawnictwo Księgarni Akademickiej, 1994.

Smačny, Jan. "Dvořák: The Operas." In *Dvořák and his World*, ed. Michael Beckerman, 104–33. Princeton: Princeton University Press, 1993.

Solarska-Zachuta, Anna, Jan Michalik, and Stanisław Halabuda. "Teatr Lwowski w latach 1890–1918." In *Teatr polski w latach 1890–1918. Zabór austriacki i pruski, (Dzieje teatru polskiego, tom IV)*, ed. Tadeusz Sivert, 199–319. Warszawa: Państwowe Wydawnictwo Naukowe, 1987.

Solska, Irena. *Pamiętnik. Wstęp i opracowanie Lidia Kuchtówna.* Warszawa: Wydawnictwa Artystyczne i Filmowe, 1978.

Solski, Ludwik. *Wspomnienia. Na podstawie rozmów napisał Alfred Woycicki.* 2 Vols. Kraków: Wydawnictwo literackie, 1955–1956.

Spector, Scott D. *Prague Territories. National Conflict and Cultural Innovation in Franz Kafka's Fin de Siecle.* Berkeley: University of California Press, 2000.

Spohr, Mathias, ed. *Geschichte und Medien der gehobenen Unterhaltungsmusik.* Zürich: Chronos, 1999.

Sponheuer, Bernd. "Der 'Gott der Harmonien' und die 'Pfeife des Pan.' Über richtiges und falsches Hören in der Musikästhetik des 18. und 19. Jahrhunderts." In *Rezeptionsästhetik und Rezeptionsgeschichte in der Musikwissenschaft*, ed. Hermann Danuser and Friedhelm Krummacher, 179–92. Laaber: Laaber Press, 1991.

Sponheuer, Bernd. "Reconstructing Ideal Types of the 'German' in Music." In *Music and German National Identity*, ed. Celia Applegate and Pamela Potter, 36–58. Chicago: University of Chicago Press, 2002.

Sprawozdanie z czynności wydziału towarzystwa przyjaciół scney narodowej za rok 1869/70 t. j. od 26 Maja 1869 do końca Maja 1870. Lwów, 1870.

Srb, Adolf. *Upomínka na slavností otevření Národního divadla.* Praha: J. Otto, 1881.

Srba, Bořivoj. "Jevištní výprava představení smetanovy Libuše v národním divadle z let 1881 a 1883." In *Divadlo v české kultuře 19. století,* ed. Felix Šejna, 167–94. Praha: Národní galerie, 1985.

Staud, Géza. *Adelstheater in Ungarn (18. und 19. Jahrhundert). Theatergeschichte Österreichs.* Wien: Österreichische Akademie der Wissenschaften, 1977.

Stefanowska, Zofia, ed. *Tradycje szlacheckie w kulturze polskiej.* Warszawa: Państwowy Instytut Wydawniczy, 1976.

Stekl, Hannes. "Wiener Mäzene im 19. Jahrhundert." In *Bürgerkultur und Mäzenatentum im 19. Jahrhundert*, ed. Jürgen Kocka and Manuel Frey, 164–91. Berlin: Fannei & Walz, 1998.

Storck, Christopher P. *Kulturnation und Nationalkunst. Strategien und Mechanismen tschechischer Nationsbildung von 1860 bis 1914.* Köln: Verlag Wissenschaft und Politik, 2001.

Storey, John. "The Social Life of Opera." *European Journal of Cultural Studies* 6, no. 1 (2003): 5–36. http://dx.doi.org/10.1177/1367549403006001466.

Strasser, Michael C. *Ars Gallica. The Société Nationale de Musique and its Role in French Musical Life.* Urbana: UMI, 1998.

Šubert, František Adolf. *Das königlich böhmische Landes- und National-Theater in Prag.* Prag: Verlag des Nationaltheater-Consortiums, 1892.

Šubert, František Adolf. *Dějiny Národního divadla v Praze 1883–1900.* Praha: Unie, 1908–1910.

Šubert, František Adolf. *Moje vzpomínky.* 3 Vols. Praha: Unie, 1902.

Šubert, František Adolf. *Národní divadlo v Praze: dějiny jeho i stavba dokončena.* Praha: J. Otto, 1881.

Šubert, František Adolf. *Vývod rodu Šubertův a Wobořilův ve východních Čechach s jejich nejbližším příbuzenstvem.* Praha, 1891.

Sydow, Bronisław Edward, ed. *Korespondencja Fryderyka Chopina.* Vol. 1. Warszawa: Państwowy Instytut Wydawniczy, 1955.

Szuliński, Jan. *Teatr Miejski we Lwowie.* Warszawa: Neriton, 2002.

Szydłowska, Mariola. *Cenzura teatralna w Galicji w dobie autonomicznej.* Kraków: Towarzstwo Autorów i Wydawców Prac Naukowych Universitas, 1995.

Tage-Buch des Königlich Sächsischen Hof-Theaters. Dresden 1819–1917.

Tancsik, Pamela. *Die Prager Oper heißt Zemlinsky. Theatergeschichte des Neuen Deutschen Theaters Prag in der Ära Zemlinsky von 1911 bis 1927.* Wien: Böhlau, 2000.

Taruskin, Richard. *Defining Russia Musically: Historical and Hermeneutical Essays*. Princeton: Princeton University Press, 1997.
Teatr miejski we Lwowie. Ilustrowany przegląd teatralny, rok 1–4. 1911–1914.
Teige, Karel, ed. *Dopisy Smetanovy. Komentovaný výbor šedesáti čtyř mistrových dopisů*. Praha: Urbanek, 1896.
Tejřov, Xaver. *Rozkvět či upadek? Přispěvek k otázce zadání Národního divadla*. Praha: F. Šimáček, 1906.
Teuber, Oscar. *Geschichte des Prager Theaters. Von den Anfängen des Schauspielwesens bis auf die neueste Zeit. Zweiter Teil: Von der Brunian-Bergopzoom'schen Bühnereform bis zum Tode Liebich's, des größten Prager Bühnenleiters. (1771–1817)*. Prag: Haase, 1885.
Teuber, Oscar. *Geschichte des Prager Theaters. Von den Anfängen des Schauspielwesens bis auf die neueste Zeit. Dritter Teil. Vom Tode Liebich's, des größten Prager Bühnenleiters, bis auf unsere Tage (1817–1887)*. Prag: Haase, 1888.
Ther, Philipp. *In der Mitte der Gesellschaft. Operntheater in Zentraleuropa 1815–1914*. Wien: Oldenbourg/Böhlau, 2006 [Die Gesellschaft der Oper. Musikkulturen europäischer Metropolen im 19. und 20. Jahrhundert. Vol. 1].
Ther, Philipp. "Teatro e nation-building: Il fenomeno dei Teatri nazionali nell' Europa centro-orientale." *Contemporanea (Bologna, Italy)* 6, no. 2 (2003): 265–90.
Ther, Philipp. "War versus Peace. Interethnic Relations in Lviv during the First Half of the Twentieth Century." *Harvard Ukranian Studies* 24 (2000): 251–84.
Ther, Philipp. "Zivilgesellschaft und Kultur. Programmatik, Organisation und Akteure gesellschaftlich getragener Theater im 19. Jahrhundert." In *Die Praxis der Zivilgesellschaft. Akteure, Handeln und Strukturen im internationalen Vergleich*, ed. Arnd Bauerkämper, 189–212. Frankfurt a.M.: Campus, 2003.
Toelle, Jutta. *Bühne der Stadt. Mailand und das Teatro alla Scala zwischen Risorgimento und Fin de Siècle*. Wien: Böhlau/Oldenbourg, 2009. [Die Gesellschaft der Oper. Musikkulturen europäischer Metropolen im 19. und 20. Jahrhundert. Vol. 4]
Toelle, Jutta. "Der Duft der großen weiten Welt. Ideen zum weltweiten Siegeszug der italienischen Oper im 19. Jahrhundert." In *Oper im Wandel der Gesellschaft. Kulturtransfers und Netzwerke des Musiktheaters im modernen Europa*, ed. Sven Oliver Müller et al., 251–62. Wien: Oldenbourg/Böhlau, 2010.
Toelle, Jutta. *Oper als Geschäft. Impresari an italienischen Opernhäusern, 1860–1900*. Kassel: Bärenreiter, 2007.
Tokarz, Joanna. "Kultura muzyczna Galicji." In *Galicja i jej dziedzictwo, Vol. 4, Literatura—język—kultura*, 155–64. Rzeszów: Wydawnictwo Wyższej Szkoły Pedagogicznej, 1995.
Traubner, Richard. *Operetta. A Theatrical History*. City Garden: Gollanz, 1983.

Trenner, Franz, ed. *Cosima Wagner—Richard Strauss. Ein Briefwechsel.* Tutzing: H. Schneider, 1978.
Tretiak, Józef. *Powitanie (wygłoszone na scenie lwowskiej przez Teofilę Nowakowską 1 IV 1872 jako w dniu rozpoczęcia przedstawień przez akcyjne towarzystwo Sceny Polskiej we Lwowie).* Lwów, 1872.
Tyrrell, John. *Czech Opera.* Cambridge: Cambridge University Press, 1988.
Tyrrell, John. "Russian, Czech, Polish and Hungarian Opera to 1900." In *The Oxford History of Opera*, ed. Roger Parker, 157–86. Oxford: Oxford University Press, 1996.
Urban, Otto. *Die tschechische Gesellschaft 1848–1918.* 2 Vols. Wien: Böhlau Verlag, 1999.
Vodák, Jindřich. *Idea Národního Divadla. Otisk Přednášky, kterou proslovil ve slavnostním cyklu.* Praha: Jan Nešněra, 1933.
Vojáček, Milan. "Manifest České Moderny. Jeho vznik, ohlas a spory o pojetí České moderny, které vedly k jejímu rozpadu." *Časopis Národního muzea—řada historická* 169, nos. 1–2 (2000): 69–87.
Vondráček, Jan. *Dějiny českého divadla, II. díl. Doba předbřeznová 1824–1846.* Praha: Orbis, 1957.
W sprawie teatru lwowskiego (Uwagi nad sprawozdaniem posła Leona hr. Pinińskiego, jako referenta komisyi dla spraw szkolnych i artystycznych w ostatniej sesyi Sejmu krajowego o stanie obecnym sceny narodowej we Lwowie). Lwów, 1907.
Wagner, Richard. *Die Meistersinger von Nürnberg. Klavierauszug mit Text von Gustav F. Kogel (Edition Peters Nr. 3408).* Frankfurt a.M., n.d.
Wagner, Richard. *Lohengrin. Oper in drei Akten. Klavierauszug mit Text von Felix Mottl (Edition Peters Nr. 3401).* Frankfurt a.M., n.d.
Wagner, Richard. *Mein Leben.* München: List, 1963.
Wagner, Richard. *Sämtliche Schriften und Dichtungen.* 12 Vols. Leipzig: Breitkopf & Härtel, 1912–1914.
Walewski, Adolf. *Teatr u nas i u obcych.* Lwów: Druk. Dziennika Polskiego, 1892.
Walter, Michael. *Die Oper ist ein Irrenhaus. Sozialgeschichte der Oper im 19. Jahrhundert, Stuttgart.* Weimar: Metzlar Verlag, 1997.
Walter, Michael. *Richard Strauss und seine Zeit.* Laaber: Laaber Verlag, 2000.
Wandycz, Piotr. "The Poles in the Habsburg Monarchy." In *Nation-Building and the Politics of Nationalism: Essays on Austrian Galicia*, ed. Andrei S. Markovits and Frank E. Sysyn, 68–93. Cambridge: Harvard University Press, 1982.
Warrack, John H. "Französische Elemente in Webers Opern." In *Die Dresdner Oper im 19. Jahrhundert*, ed. Michael Heinemann and Hans John, 119–24. Laaber: Laaber Verlag, 1995.
Warzenica-Zalewska, Ewa. "Teatr Skarbkowski we Lwowie w latach 1864–1890." In *Teatr polski od 1863 roku do schylku XIX wieku (Dzieje teatru polskiego,*

tom III), ed. Tadeusz Sivert, 509–94. Warszawa: Państwowe Wydawnictwo Naukowe, 1982.

Wąsowska, Elżbieta. "Twórczość operowa Henryka Jareckiego." *Muzyka* 34, no. 4 (1989): 3–29.

Weber, Max. *Die rationalen und soziologischen Grundlagen der Musik*. München: Drei Masken Verlag, 1921.

Weber, William. "Mass Culture and the Reshaping of European Musical Taste, 1770–1870." *International Review of the Aesthetic and Sociology of Music* 8, no. 1 (1977): 5–36. http://dx.doi.org/10.2307/836535.

Weber, William. *Music and the Middle Class. The Social Structure of Concert Life in London, Paris and Vienna*. 2nd ed. London: Ashgate, 2004.

Webersfeld, Edward. *Teatr miejski we Lwowie za dyrekcji Ludwika Hellera 1906–1918*. Lwów, 1917.

Wehler, Hans Ulrich. *Das Deutsche Kaiserreich 1871–1914*. Göttingen: Vandenhoeck & Ruprecht, 1973.

Weichlein, Siegfried. "Sachsen zwischen Landesbewußtsein und Nationsbildung." In *Sachsen im Kaiserreich. Politik, Wirtschaft und Gesellschaft im Umbruch*, ed. Simone Lässig and Karl Heinrich Pohl, 241–70. Weimar: Böhlau, 1997.

Weis, Karel. *Moje odpověď správě Národního divadla na "Zasláno" v Národní politice ze dne 4. března 1906*. Praha, 1906.

Weis, Karel. *Spravedlnost či despotismus? Přispěvek k otázce zadání Národního divadla*. Praha: Naklad vl., 1906.

Weitz, Klemens. *Lwowskie Perły*. Brody: Klewe, 1909.

Weitz, Klemens. *Wesołe kroniki 1906–1908*. Brody: Klewe, 1909.

Werner, Michael, and Bénédicte Zimmermann. "Vergleich, Transfer, Verflechtung. Der Ansatz der Histoire croisée und die Herausforderung des Transnationalen." *Geschichte und Gesellschaft (Vandenhoeck & Ruprecht)* 28 (2002): 607–36.

Wikander, Matthew H. *Princes to Act. Royal Audience and Royal Performance, 1578–1792*. Baltimore: Johns Hopkins University Press, 1993.

Wilberg, Petra-Hildegard. *Richard Wagners mythische Welt. Versuche wider den Historismus*. Freiburg: Rombach, 1996.

Wildberg, Bodo, ed. *Das Dresdner Hoftheater in der Gegenwart. Biographien und Charakteristiken. Mit 112 Porträts*. Dresden/Leipzig: F. Pierson's Verlag, 1902.

Willnauer, Franz. *Gustav Mahler und die Wiener Oper*. 2nd ed. Wien: Löcker, 1993.

Wolff, Larry. *Inventing Galicia: History and Fantasy in Habsburg Political Culture*. Stanford: Stanford University Press, 2010.

Wolff, Stéphane. *L'opéra au Palais Garnier (1875–1962)*. Paris: l'Académie nationale de musique, 1962.

Wolff, Stéphane. *Un demi-siècle d'Opéra comique (1900–1950). Les oeuvres, les interprètes*. Paris: Edition André Bonne, 1953.

Wypych-Gawrońska, Anna. *Lwowski teatr operowy i operetkowy w latach 1872–1918*. Kraków: Towarzstwo Autorów i Wydawców Prac Naukowych Universitas, 1999.

Žákavec, František. *Chrám znovuzrození. O budovatelích a budově Národního divadla w Praze*. Praha: Štenc, 1918.

Zakhaykevych, Mariia. "Karpaccygórale J. Kozhen'ovs'koho v konteksti kompozytors'koi tvorchosti Mykoly Verbyts'koho, muzychno-teatralnoi ta pisennoi kultury Halychyny." In *Musica Galiciana. Kultura muzyczna Galicji w kontekście stosunków polsko-ukraińskich (od doby piastowsko-książęcej do roku 1945), Tom III*, ed. Leszek Mazepa, 9–18. Rzeszow: Wydawnictwo Wyższej Szkoły Pedagogicznej, 1999.

Zapolska, Gabriela. *I sfinks premówi . . . Wieczory teatralne wydane pośmiertne*. Lwów: Lector, 1923.

Żelazowski, Roman. *Pięćdziesiąt lat teatru polskiego. Moje Pamiętniki*. Lwów: Spółka Nakładowa Odrodzenie, 1921.

Żeleński, Władysław. "Mój pamiętnik." *Wiadomości literackie* 14, no. 30 (July 18, 1937): 2.

Zernack, Klaus. *Osteuropa. Eine Einführung in seine Geschichte*. München: Beck, 1977.

Zhuk, Ihor. "The Architecture of Lviv from the Thirteenth to the Twentieth Century." *Harvard Ukranian Studies* 24 (2000): 95–130.

Zimmermann, Reiner. "Die 'Hintermänner' der Freischütz-Partitur—Webers Organisation des deutschen Departements der Dresdner Hofoper." In *Der Klang der Sächsischen Staatskapelle Dresden. Kontinuität und Wandelbarkeit eines Phänomens*, ed. Hans-Günter Ottenberg and Eberhard Steindorf, 107–18. Hildesheim: Olms, 2001.

zur Nieden, Gesa. *Vom Grand Spectacle zur Great Season Das Pariser Théâtre du Châtelet als Raum musikalischer Produktion und Rezeption (1862–1914)*. Wien: Böhlau/Oldenbourg, 2010. [Die Gesellschaft der Oper. Musikkulturen europäischer Metropolen im 19. und 20. Jahrhundert. Vol. 6.]

Acknowledgments

The very last "Leitmotiv" of this book is gratitude. I would like to thank Charlotte Hughes-Kreutzmüller, who is as accurate as a translator needs to be, has elegantly conveyed the many special terms and compound words found in German and the Slavic languages that seem to be hardly translatable, and has shown wonderful sensitivity for opera and music. I am also greatly indebted to my colleagues who have made this book possible, first and foremost Gary Cohen, the series editor. My gratitude to him goes far beyond formalities; I have learned much from the many discussions we have had about opera and nationalism in Prague and the Habsburg Empire. I am also deeply grateful to Celia Applegate, Charles Maier, and Larry Wolff for their support and encouragement in critical moments. The transatlantic subchapter of this book was founded on work done during a sabbatical in New York in 2007. Thanks are due to John Micgiel, Mark Mazower, and Volker Berghahn for their invitation to come to Columbia University and to the staff of the Metropolitan Opera archive for providing access even when I came accompanied by a baby carriage and a small toddler. Many colleagues provided valuable feedback to early project presentations at the Center for European Studies at Harvard University and at the American Association for the Advancements of Slavic Studies (now the Association for Slavic and East European Studies) convention in 2004. Last, but not least, I would like to thank Charles Watkinson, the director of Purdue University Press, and his colleagues Rebecca Corbin and Dianna Gilroy for their support and assistance. I also would like to thank the reviewers of the manuscript for their helpful comments. Since this book is based on an earlier book published on the occasion of the Czech National Theater's one hundred twenty-fifth anniversary, *Narodní divadlo v kontextu evropských operních dějin (od založení do první světové války)* (Praha: Dokořán, 2008), I would also like to thank several Czech colleagues: Jitka Ludvová, Alena Jakubcová, the late Jiří Musil, and Miroslav Hroch for their comments, Jaroslav Kučera and Jiří Pešek for their support, and, of course, the staff in various archives. In Poland and Ukraine, Jacek Purchla, Agnieszka Marszałek, Maciej Janowski, Ostap Sereda, Markian Prokopovych, and Evgenya Lisovka have been wonderful hosts and discussants. In Vienna, I am grateful to Moritz Csáky for his longtime support. Most of the research for this project was carried out when I was working at the Center for Comparative History of Europe in Berlin. I still feel indebted to Jürgen Kocka for giving me so much academic and personal freedom in my formative years as a postdoctoral researcher and to my longtime mentor Klaus Zernack. I also profited much from my contact with musicologists, above all Jutta Toelle, and Hans Joachim Hinrichsen, Michael Walter, and Małgorzata Woźna-Stankiewicz. I am grateful to my German language publisher in Vienna, Böhlau Verlag, for allowing me to reuse and extend three major chapters of my earlier book, *In der Mitte der Gesellschaft. Operntheater in Zentraleuropa 1815–1914* (Vienna: Oldenbourg/ Böhlau, 2006) for inclusion in this new and hopefully improved version.

This book has also been influenced by the many discussions held in the course of two international research projects on the history of European opera and music cities. Heinz-Gerhard Haupt has been a great partner in leading these two projects. Michael Werner contributed important comments, and longtime staff members Sven Oliver Müller, Markian Prokopovych, Ostap Sereda, Vjera Katalinić, and the researchers around Gesa zur Nieden and Adam Mestyan broadened my research and my vision of opera. I am grateful to Böhlau Verlag in Vienna, particularly to Peter Rauch and Ursula Huber, for remaining committed to the series "Musical Metropoles in 19th and 20th Century Europe," and to the Volkswagen Foundation and the European University Institute for providing generous funding, including support for this English translation. The Alexander von Humboldt Foundation and the Körber Foundation provided grants for two sabbaticals which were pivotal for the research and early phases of writing. My wife Tina and my family supported me during this project which has accompanied and inspired me for more than a decade. The curtain on that work is now closing, but now a curtain is raised for English language readers. I am very grateful and happy that I can reach this wider audience.

Index

Persons

Albert I (King of Saxony), 38, 42
Arklowa, Tereza, 128, 165, 206
Auber, Daniel, 51

Banck, Carl, 61, 65, 218
Bandrowski, Aleksander, 125
Bartók, Béla, 221
Beethoven, Ludwig van, 23, 39, 49, 85, 96
Bellini, Vincenzo, 49, 51, 96, 113, 233
Benda, Jiří (also Georg), 166
Bendl, Karel, 136, 159, 188
Berger, Augustín (also August), 72, 122, 189, 250
Beust, Friedrich Ferdinand Count, 52, 53
Bismarck, Otto von, 56, 57, 61, 67
Bizet, Georges, 72, 230
Bogusławski, Wojciech, 14, 25, 90, 91, 206
Boito, Arrigo, 107
Brahms, Johannes, 181, 190, 220
Brendel, Franz, 16, 26
Bungert, August, 168
Burian, Karel, 22, 23, 27, 42, 69, 154, 250

Čech, Adolf, 189n49
Červinkova-Riegrová, Marie, 141
Cherubini, Luigi, 47

Dahn, Felix, 58, 60
Debussy, Claude, 183
Delibes, Leo, 164
Dobrzański, Jan, 96, 98, 100–103, 105, 108n41, 112-17, 120, 126–27, 137, 143, 226-27
Donizetti, Gaetano, 49, 51, 67, 96, 113
Dvořák, Antonin, 26, 70, 71, 72, 73, 134, 145, 152, 159, 164, 166, 172, 173, 174, 180, 181, 182, 184, 186, 189, 190, 191, 203, 220, 221, 225, 229, 234, 260, 261, 269, 279

Erkel, Ferenc, 166, 212, 213, 216, 217, 223, 233

Fellner & Helmer, 104, 177, 196, 264
Fibich, Zdeněk, 134, 159, 160, 165, 166, 167, 168, 172, 185, 218, 220, 221, 225
Florjański, Władysław (also Florjanský), 128, 162, 163, 165, 169, 179, 206
Forkel, Johann Nikolaus, 16, 26, 268
Förster, Josef Bohuslav, 180
Franz Joseph I (Emperor of Austria), 102, 119, 138, 143, 170, 177
Fredro, Aleksander, 91, 95, 97
Freud, Sigmund, 76
Friedrich August I (King of Saxony), 41, 205
Friedrich August II (King of Saxony), 31, 32, 33, 34, 35, 37, 38, 39, 40, 50
Friedrich August III (King of Saxony), 39, 44n21

Glinka, Michail, 212, 213, 214, 216, 223, 226, 233
Gluck, Christoph Willibald, 239
Goldmark, Karl, 41, 164
Gorgolewski, Zygmunt, 104
Gounod, Charles, 119
Gutzkow, Karl, 15, 39, 43, 53

Hanslick, Eduard, 44, 57, 58, 71, 160
Harrach, Jan Count, 136, 211
Hartmann, Ludwig, 71, 84, 184, 219, 251
Hauptmann, Gerhardt, 106
Hegel, Georg Wilhelm Friedrich, 3, 12, 13, 33
Heller, Ludwik, 105, 106, 107, 109, 121, 122, 124–28, 175, 206, 207, 227, 260, 268, 271
Heš, Vílem, 84n30, 174, 184
Hoffmann, E. T. A., 12, 26n53, 63n3
Hofmannsthal, Hugo von, 76, 80

Hostinský, Otakar, 160, 187
Humperdinck, Engelbert, 62, 231, 232

Jabłonowski, Karol Prince, 97, 98, 99, 100, 101
Jahn, Wilhelm, 163, 246, 254n29
Janáček, Leoš, 167, 168, 184, 185, 191n92, 200, 221, 252
Jarecki, Henryk, 103, 105, 118, 122, 127, 220
Johann I (King of Saxony), 32, 37, 52, 54, 55, 56

Kamiński, Jan Nepomucen, 91, 198
Karlowicz, Mieczysław, 126, 130n52
Kienzle, Ludwig, 62
Koppel-Ellfeld, Franz, 62
Korzeniowski, Józef, 91, 247
Kovařovic, Karel, 153, 154, 184, 185, 186, 191n92, 221, 241
Kraszewski, Józef Ignacy, 102, 266
Kreibig, Eduard, 246, 247, 254n30
Kretschmer, Edmund, 58, 59
Kruszelnicka, Salomea, 244
Küstner, Karl Theodor, 198
Kvapíl, Jaroslav, 186

Lassalle, Jean, 20, 26n57
Leoncavallo, Ruggiero, 106
Liszt, Franz, 136, 216, 224
Lobkowitz, Jiří Fürst (also Georg), 135, 145, 173
Lortzing, Albert, 53
Lüttichau, Wolf Baron von, 39, 40, 41, 43, 49, 51, 52, 53, 82
Lysenko, Nikolai, 168, 176, 216, 247

Mahler, Gustav, 69, 71, 84n30, 106, 166, 183, 184, 231, 235n57, 241, 246
Malten, Therese, 42, 61, 70
Marschner, Heinrich, 53, 59
Massenet, Jules, 154, 190n83
Mazzini, Giuseppe, 221
Méhul, Etienne-Nicolas, 47
Metternich, Clemens Prince, 96, 247
Metternich, Paulina, Princess, 170
Meyerbeer, Giacomo, 16, 40, 49, 59, 80, 128, 168, 216, 238, 239
Mickiewicz, Adam, 116, 117
Miłaszewski, Adam, 98, 99, 100, 101, 102, 103, 112, 120, 126, 127, 128, 198, 206

Moniuszko, Stanisław, 3, 18, 72, 95, 102, 113, 114, 115, 117, 118, 119, 121, 127, 142, 206, 214, 215, 216, 218, 220, 221, 223, 226, 227, 233, 235n48, 247
Morlacchi, Francesco, 48
Mozart, Wolfgang Amadeus, 6, 23n4, 39, 48, 49, 62, 80, 90, 159, 206, 223, 239

Neumann, Angelo, 61, 169, 174, 177, 184, 188n31, 219, 243, 244, 246
Nicolai, Otto, 53, 58
Nietzsche, Friedrich, 12, 79, 219

Offenbach, Jaques, 81, 241, 242
Ostrčil, Otakar, 181

Paderewski, Ignacy, 72, 73, 118, 122, 123, 206
Palacký, František, 138, 139
Patti, Adelina, 22, 26n60, 162
Pawlikowski, Tadeusz, 106, 107, 122, 123, 124, 125, 126, 127, 128, 155
Platen-Hallermund, Julius Baron von, 40
Pollini, Bernhard, 243, 246
Pospišilová, Marie, 161, 207
Puccini, Giacomo, 70, 107, 123, 231

Raverta, Carlo, 160, 161, 162, 179, 187n9
Reinhardt, Max, 79, 80, 186
Reszke, Jan, 119, 231, 244
Ribera, Antoni, 247
Rieger, František Ladislav, 133, 139, 141, 142, 145, 149, 170
Roller, Alfred, 80, 241
Rossini, Gioacchino, 3, 49, 51, 56, 63n8, 96, 113, 242
Różycki, Ludomir, 125

Saint-Saëns, Camille, 162
Schiller, Friedrich, 11, 13, 14, 15, 17, 95, 159
Schmid, Otto, 44, 61, 220
Schmoranz, Gustav, 153, 154, 185
Schopenhauer, Arthur, 12
Schröder-Devrient, Wilhelmine, 40
Schuch, Ernst von, 41, 42, 43, 62, 63, 67, 68, 69, 70, 71, 72, 73, 74, 75, 77, 78, 80, 81, 82, 168, 184, 226, 239, 241, 243
Seebach, Nikolaus, Count, 41, 42, 43, 74, 77, 80, 81, 163
Sembrich, Marcella, 119

Semper, Gottfried, 33, 34, 40
Skarbek, Stanisław, Count, 90, 92, 93, 94, 95, 96, 97, 98, 99, 104, 111, 124, 125, 126, 134, 137, 197, 246
Sladkovský, Karel, 138, 139
Šmaha, Josef, 19, 152, 163, 166, 173, 178, 179
Smetana, Bedřich, 3, 12, 18, 26, 71, 73, 83, 105, 118, 121, 127, 134, 136, 137, 138, 145, 146, 151, 156, 159, 161, 164, 165, 166, 168, 172–76, 184, 186, 187, 189, 191, 206, 207, 211, 212, 214, 216–20, 221, 223, 225, 227, 239, 244, 245
Spontini, Gasparo, 52
Stolzová, Tereza, 162, 163
Strauss, Richard, 39, 42, 43, 45, 67, 69, 74–82, 106, 118, 126, 185, 200, 201, 218, 223, 238, 239, 241, 242, 243
Šubert, František Adolf, 25, 26, 27, 71, 146, 147, 149, 150, 151, 152, 153, 155, 156, 159, 160–65, 168, 169, 171–75, 178, 179, 180, 185, 202, 203, 207, 226, 244
Suk, Josef, 180, 181
Szymanowski, Karol, 126, 221

Taaffe, Eduard Graf, 170
Tercuzzi, Fernando, 114
Thomé, Franz, 246
Tieck, Ludwig, 33
Toscanini, Arturo, 67, 69, 125, 231, 238, 239, 244
Turolla, Emma, 20, 21, 22, 162

Verbitskii, Mikhaylo, 247
Verdi, Giuseppe, 67, 68, 70, 112, 162, 163, 170, 185, 230, 239, 243
Vitzthum von Eckstädt, Carl Wilhelm Count, 33

Wackenroder, Wilhelm Heinrich, 12
Wagner, Cosima, 70, 76
Wagner, Richard, 3, 4, 13, 15, 16, 17, 18, 32, 33, 39, 40, 41, 42, 49–52, 54–57, 60–62, 63, 67, 68–71, 74–80, 96, 114, 121–122, 125, 127, 136, 160, 166, 168, 169, 172–74, 176, 185, 200, 201, 205, 207, 208–11, 214–26, 228, 229–32, 238, 243, 244, 248–252
Walewski, Adolf, 175, 251, 252
Weber, Carl Maria von, 16, 32, 33, 47, 49, 62, 205, 224, 229

Weber, Max, 3, 12
Weis, Karel, 73, 184, 191n87
Wilt, Maria, 162
Wittich, Marie, 42, 75

Zajc, Ivan, 177, 213, 216
Żeleński, Władysław, 95, 103, 105, 115, 117, 118, 121, 122, 127, 206, 218, 220
Zeyer, Julius, 180, 181
Zola, Emile, 50

Cities

Barcelona, 1, 227, 247, 248
Berlin, 6, 15, 16, 24, 31, 32, 34, 41, 52, 56, 60, 62, 69, 73, 74, 77, 79, 80, 82, 91, 111, 119, 144, 151, 162, 163, 171, 173, 174, 186, 211, 231, 242, 244, 245, 246, 248, 251
Bologna, 224, 228, 238, 244
Breslau, 53, 77
Brno (Brünn), 168, 184
Budapest, 15, 20, 22, 91, 93, 103, 119, 161, 185, 195, 206, 243, 246, 247, 248
Dresden, 31–85
Graz, 178, 211, 246
Hamburg, 150, 173, 174, 226, 246, 248
Hermannstadt, 247
Kiev (Kyiv), 98, 122, 195, 227, 247, 248
Krakow, 98, 101, 104–109, 115, 127, 142, 168, 174, 246, 247
Leipzig, 7, 18, 32, 34, 41, 51, 53, 54, 56, 60, 61, 71, 77, 81, 82, 173, 176, 197, 198, 199, 200, 219, 242, 244, 246, 248
Lemberg (Lwów, L′viv), 89–130
Ljubljana, 178, 246
London, 19, 49, 114, 195, 201, 227, 228, 229, 230, 231, 232, 239, 243
Milan, 6, 24, 107, 119, 163, 224, 231, 237, 238, 243, 244, 246
Moravia, 135, 139, 168, 221
Moscow, 120, 169, 186, 213, 214
Munich, 55, 65, 68, 74, 93, 164, 186, 209, 211, 217
Naples, 243
New York, 8, 22, 73, 119, 123, 174, 228, 229, 230, 231, 232, 239, 244
Odessa, 1
Paris, 3, 5, 13, 17, 41, 49, 55, 56, 69, 96, 99, 107, 114, 118, 119, 125, 140, 144, 162,

166, 175, 186, 195, 197, 201, 218, 221, 227, 229, 232, 237, 238, 241, 243, 244, 245, 246, 248, 249, 251, 252
Poznań (Posen), 73, 142, 176, 250
Prague, 133–191
Riga, 246
Sofia, 179
St. Petersburg, 6, 169, 227, 243, 244, 246
Tallinn, 227
Temesvar (Timişoara), 246, 247
Trieste, 178, 246
Venice, 89, 93, 178
Vienna, 163–175
Warsaw, 14, 18, 90, 91, 105, 111, 112, 113, 115, 121, 127, 175, 201, 206, 214, 218, 227, 232
Zagreb, 177, 178, 196
Zurich, 16, 53, 56, 72, 73, 104, 160, 217, 219, 248
Żytomierz, 98, 196

Operas

Aida, 2, 67, 102, 112, 114, 156, 159, 162, 164, 226, 240
African Maid, The (L'Africaine), 178
Armin, 60
Barber of Seville (Il Barbieri di Siviglia), 96
Bartered Bride, The (Prodaná nevěsta), 71, 83, 105, 118, 121, 127, 129, 136, 150, 156, 159, 164, 172, 173, 174, 175, 178, 201, 211, 212, 218, 223, 238
Bianca e Fernando, 96
Bohème, La, 70
Brandenburgers in Bohemia, The (Braniboři v Čechach), 136, 164, 211, 217
Bride of Messina, The (Nevěsta messinská), 165
Carmen, 153, 159, 178, 230, 239
Elektra, 42, 69, 76, 78, 79, 80, 185, 200
Eugene Onegin (Yevgeny Onyegin), 20, 107, 172, 226
Faust, 156, 159, 178, 239
Fire Famine (Feuersnot), 74, 75
Folkunger, Die, 58, 59, 60, 268
Freischütz, Der (The Freeshooter/The Marksman), 47, 48, 49, 50, 62, 201, 217
Girl of the West, The (La Fianculla del West), 231
Gypsy Baron, The (Der Zigeunerbaron), 118
Halka, 114, 115, 117, 119, 121, 127, 142, 178, 201, 214, 215, 223, 227, 247
Huguenots, The (Les Huguenots), 119, 216, 239
In the Well (V Studní), 178
Jadwiga, 103, 118
Jenufa, 184, 221
Joseph (Jacob und seine Söhne), 47
King's Children (Königskinder), 231
Kiss, The (Hubička), 71, 159, 173
Konrad Wallenrod, 103, 115, 116, 117, 118, 218
Life for the Czar, A (Zhyzn za tsaria), 213
Lucia di Lammermoor, 178
Lucrezia Borgia, 96
Madame Butterfly, 70, 107
Manru, 72, 73, 122, 123, 206, 247
Mastersingers of Nuremberg, The (Die Meistersinger von Nürnberg), 50, 55, 57, 61, 71, 75, 156, 209, 210, 217
Mefistofeles, 107
Muette de Portici, La (The Mute Girl of Portici), 49, 178
Nozze di Figaro, Le (The Marriage of Figaro), 223
Peasant Rogue,The (Šelma sedlák), 70
Pique Dame (The Queen of Spades), 107
Polish Jew, The (Der Polnische Jude), 73, 184
Prophet, The (Der Prophet), 40, 128, 239
Queen of Sheba, The (Die Königin von Saba), 41, 164, 240
Rhinegold, The (Das Rheingold), 219
Ring of the Nibelung, The (Der Ring der Nibelungen), 57, 60, 68, 80, 107, 125, 218, 222, 223, 247
Rigoletto, 178
Roméo et Juliette, 119
Rosenkavalier, Der (The Knight of the Rose), 42, 45, 75, 79, 80, 81, 107, 126, 185, 186, 191, 201, 223, 241, 243
Rusalka, 73, 180, 181, 182, 184, 220
Salome, 42, 69, 75, 76, 78, 79, 80, 81, 82, 200, 218, 242
Secret, The (Tajemství), 164, 173
Siegfried, 61
Straniera, La (The Stranger Woman), 96
Straszny Dwór (The Haunted Castle), 102, 113, 114, 119, 121, 214, 215

Tannhäuser und der Sängerkrieg auf Wartburg (*Tannhäuser and the Singers' Contest at Wartburg*), 50, 55, 57, 61, 70, 121, 153, 162, 208, 209, 218, 222, 227, 238
Tosca, 70, 81, 123, 124
Traviata, La (*The Fallen Woman*), 119
Troubadour, The (*Il Trovatore*), 178
Twilight of the Gods, The (*Götterdämmerung*), 219
Two Widows, The (*Dvě vdovy*), 118, 159, 164
Valkyrie, The (*Die Walküre*), 123, 125, 238
William Tell (*Guillaume Tell*), 3
Woman without a Shadow, The (*Die Frau ohne Schatten*), 79

www.ingramcontent.com/pod-product-compliance
Lightning Source LLC
Chambersburg PA
CBHW070018010526
44117CB00011B/1621